# Talons of the Eagle

## Latin America, the United States, and the World

PETER H. SMITH

*University of California, San Diego*

FOURTH EDITION

New York    Oxford

OXFORD UNIVERSITY PRESS

Oxford University Press is a department of the University of Oxford.
It furthers the University's objective of excellence in research, scholarship,
and education by publishing worldwide.

Oxford   New York
Auckland   Cape Town   Dar es Salaam   Hong Kong   Karachi
Kuala Lumpur   Madrid   Melbourne   Mexico City   Nairobi
New Delhi   Shanghai   Taipei   Toronto

With offices in
Argentina   Austria   Brazil   Chile   Czech Republic   France   Greece
Guatemala   Hungary   Italy   Japan   Poland   Portugal   Singapore
South Korea   Switzerland   Thailand   Turkey   Ukraine   Vietnam

For titles covered by Section 112 of the US Higher Education Opportunity
Act, please visit www.oup.com/us/he for the latest information about
pricing and alternate formats.

Published by Oxford University Press.
198 Madison Avenue, New York, NY 10016
www.oup.com

Oxford is a registered trademark of Oxford University Press.

**Library of Congress Cataloging-in-Publication Data**
Smith, Peter H.
Talons of the eagle: Latin America, the United States, and the world / Peter H. Smith.
—Fourth edition.
    pages   cm
Includes bibliographical references and index.
ISBN 978-0-19-985695-4 (paper: acid-free paper)   1. Latin America—Foreign
relations—United States.   2. United States—Foreign relations—Latin America.   I. Title.
F1418.S645 2012
327.98073—dc23                                                    2012035489

Printing Number: 9  8  7  6  5  4  3  2  1

Printed in the United States of America
on acid-free paper

*For My Students*

# BRIEF CONTENTS

# CONTENTS

# PREFACE

Welcome to this new edition of *Talons of the Eagle*. The book has undergone extensive revision, but it remains a personal statement. It reflects my belief that historical perspective is absolutely essential for the comprehension of contemporary international realities. During the 1990s there was much discussion, often naive and shortsighted, about the end of the Cold War and its presumably benevolent impact on U.S.–Latin American relations. Over the past few years, pundits have offered sage insight into long-term impacts of the terrorist attacks of September 11, 2001. In my opinion we can assess the novelty and significance of the current situation only by comparing it with previous epochs—not only with the Cold War itself but also with the era stretching from the American Revolution through World War II.

It reflects my commitment to interdisciplinary scholarship. The analysis attempts to blend insights from political science and international relations with the study of diplomatic, intellectual, cultural, and political history—of Latin America, the United States, and other parts of the world. There has been remarkably little communication among these apparently disparate fields. This volume seeks to draw connections.

It reflects my conviction that U.S. citizens—commentators, policymakers, investors, and others—must pay close attention to Latin American viewpoints. Too often the study of inter-American relations deteriorates into the study of U.S. foreign policy. One of my central arguments is that there has existed a coherent logic, at times infernal and perverse, in the conduct of U.S.–Latin American relations; an understanding of that logic requires an understanding of Latin American feelings, attitudes, and actions.

It expresses my appreciation for the task of intellectual synthesis, as distinct from original research. This book does not present an exhaustive chronology of U.S.–Latin American relations. My goal is to offer a framework for the comprehension of changing patterns of inter-American relations over a span of two centuries and to substantiate that analysis with solid factual evidence. The result is interpretive history (or, if one permits, historical political science). Of necessity, many topics and episodes receive cursory description. As a scholar, I am acutely aware that colleagues have published entire books on subjects that warrant only a paragraph or single sentence here. As a writer, I have sought to achieve the benefits of brevity without incurring costs of superficiality.

## NEW TO THIS EDITION

The book has been thoroughly rewritten and reorganized. A major conceptual innovation has been to reinterpret the post-9/11 period through the prism of two distinct "regimes" or "rules of the game"—one relating to geoeconomics (especially free trade), the other relating to geopolitics (specifically the war on terror). This has come about as the result of much deliberation.

At the suggestion of perspicacious readers, I have made other significant changes:

- Adding two new chapters (one on immigration, another on drug trafficking)
- Shortening most other chapters
- Bringing the narrative up to date (to 2012)
- Sharpening the distinction between "hard" and "soft" power.

To enhance readability, I have included numerous illustrations, cartoons, and "boxes" with enlightening commentary and illustrative anecdotes. I have kept citations to a minimum. I have avoided polysyllabic jargon. It is my fervent hope, in fact, that some readers will actually enjoy the book.

## ACKNOWLEDGMENTS

Years of reading, observation, and reflection on U.S.–Latin American relations have left a mountainous accumulation of intellectual debts. At this point I must begin by thanking John Challice, Jennifer Carpenter, and Maegan Sherlock—all of Oxford University Press—who persuaded, cajoled, and encouraged me to undertake this revision. For excellent research assistance (and sound editorial advice) I thank Kathryn Dove, a doctoral candidate in political science at the University of California, San Diego. Moreover I am grateful to colleagues who offered constructive suggestions for this new edition: Michael Allison, University of Scranton; Victoria A. Castillo, College of William and Mary; Pedro G. Dos Santos, University of Kansas; Mary Rose Kubal, St. Bonaventure University; Erick D. Langer, Georgetown University; Scott Morgenstern, University of Pittsburgh; Natasha Borges Sugiyama, University of Wisconsin–Milwaukee; Walt Vanderbush, Miami University; and Cristobal Zúñiga-Espinoza, SUNY–Stony Brook. I have benefited greatly from their wisdom and generosity.

Finally, I want to fulfill an obligation to my students—undergraduate and graduate, eager and inquisitive, from just about every part of the world—who have stimulated, provoked, challenged, and refined my thinking on U.S.–Latin American relations. For more than forty years it has been my privilege to work together with outstanding young men and women—at Dartmouth College, the University of Wisconsin–Madison, the Massachusetts Institute of Technology, the University of California, San Diego, and various institutions throughout Europe and Latin America. To all of them I dedicate this book.

P.H.S.
Fairfax and La Jolla, California
Summer 2012

# Introduction: Global Politics and U.S.–Latin American Relations

Relations between the United States and Latin America face great uncertainty. World events since 1989 have shattered long-held assumptions about international order. The ending of the Cold War—from the collapse of the Berlin Wall to the liberation of Eastern Europe to the implosion of the Soviet Union—led to epochal rearrangements in the distribution of power, terms of conflict, and patterns of alignment. Early optimism about the creation of a "new world order" gave way to widespread apprehension about ethnic strife, economic rivalry, and international conflict. And then, as though in fulfillment of nightmare scenarios, terrorist attacks against the United States on September 11, 2001, prompted fear, outrage, and, soon thereafter, large-scale military invasions of Afghanistan and Iraq. The world was in the grip of war again.

As the United States sought to defend its suddenly threatened security interests, nations of Latin America attempted to identify their own options and alternatives. All countries of the hemisphere confront perplexing questions: What is the effect of the war on terror on U.S.– Latin American relations? What are the governing principles of inter-American relations? What will happen in the years ahead?

Exploration of these questions necessarily requires rigorous comparison across historical epochs. We need to examine the Cold War in order to assess the long-term impact of its disappearance. By the same token, we can comprehend the meaning of the antiterrorist campaign only by comparing it with previous episodes. This exercise raises tantalizing issues: Does the current situation bear any resemblance to prior historical periods? Is it similar to the Cold War? Or is it wholly unique?

Speculation over the changing nature of U.S.–Latin American relations thus provokes complex questions of historical causality. Of logical necessity, it therefore requires an exploration of apparently remote and distant eras. One hesitates to invoke a shopworn cliché about the need to comprehend the present through the prism of the past. The fact is that it applies to this case.

Such concerns determine the structure of this analysis. To examine long-term trends and transitions, the volume offers an interpretive synthesis of U.S.–Latin

American relations from the late eighteenth century to the present, from the Monroe Doctrine through the Cold War to the North American Free Trade Agreement and the global war on terror. It is my contention that U.S.–Latin American relations have displayed recurring regularities. In other words, the dynamics of the hemispheric connection reveal an *underlying logic*. Inter-American relations have not been the product of whimsy, chance, or accident. Nor have they resulted from individual caprice, personal idiosyncrasy, or collective psychology. They have responded to the interaction of national and regional interests as interpreted within changing international contexts.

Accordingly, the goal of this book is to concentrate on the structural relationship between the United States and Latin America. Rather than focus exclusively on U.S. foreign policy or on Latin American developmental predicaments, I examine the linkages between the two. Three related questions will be central to this inquiry:

- What has been the stance of the United States toward Latin America?
- What has been the response of Latin American countries? And what have been the variations in response?
- What have been the consequent forms of interaction?

I seek to reveal not only recurrent patterns in U.S.–Latin American relations but also the transformation of those patterns over time.

## ANALYTICAL TOOLS

In pursuit of such goals, this study borrows concepts and approaches from a variety of disciplines. One involves a focus on the nation-state. This is a deliberate decision. It has recently been argued that economic imperatives and transnational forces are overwhelming classic nation-states, that territorial boundaries are becoming meaningless, that sovereignty is fading into irrelevance, and that governments, in consequence, are losing power and authority. There is some truth in these claims. Yet there are two strong reasons for using the nation-state as the basic unit of analysis. One is methodological: A consistent framework facilitates historical comparison over time. The second is substantive: Governments establish economic policy, governments impose rules and regulations, governments shape the contexts for transnational behavior, and governments wage wars and make peace. The role of the state has undergone change, of course, and its impact has declined in certain areas, but it is far from withering away.

From this starting point, the book draws on central ideas in international relations—that relationships among nations constitute a "system," a pattern of regularized interaction that entails and enshrines tacit codes of behavior. These codes are analogous to the notion of an international "regime," which political scientist Stephen Krasner some time ago defined as "implicit or explicit principles, norms, rules and decision-making procedures around which actors' expectations converge in a given area of international relations." "Principles," he continues, "are beliefs of fact, causation, and rectitude. Norms are standards of behavior defined in terms of rights and obligations. Rules are specific prescriptions or proscriptions for action. Decision-making procedures are prevailing practices for making and implementing collective choice."[1] As frequently applied, the idea of regime usually pertains to specific and limited issue-areas—such as trade, environment, petroleum ("in a given area of international relations," in Krasner's phrase). In this study, by contrast, I am referring to norms and principles that establish patterns of behavior within broad and general *international systems*, not just with regard to particular issues. Construed in this fashion, the logical content of norms and principles for international systems depends upon a variety of factors: the number of major powers, the nature of resources available to them, and the scope of competition.

Within such contexts leaders and decision makers often pursue relatively long-term, consistent policies—"grand strategies," in the argot of international relations theory—to protect and promote the interests of nation-states. Fundamental interests are either *geopolitical* (the pursuit of military security) or *economic* (the pursuit of prosperity). These two sets of interests often overlap. Security interests are typically advanced by governmental bureaucracies; in capitalist societies, economic interests usually represent the goals of private sectors, which might have direct or indirect representation within the apparatus of the state. While national interests are often cloaked in the uplifting idiom of moral purpose, it is the quest for geopolitical and economic advantage—not idealism—that provides the driving force behind foreign policy and international behavior.

The articulation and pursuit of grand strategy requires some form of cost-benefit calculation. Policy choices respond to logical evaluation of likely outcomes, of predictable losses and gains. Within the context of the prevailing international system and their own power capability, countries and their leaders tend to behave in reasonable ways. There is method in what often appears to be madness.

The definition of strategy depends not only on the objective nature of prevailing conditions but also on the subjective perception of those conditions by decision makers. Therefore I place significant emphasis on the social construction of reality—on general worldviews, or *weltanschauung*. In the idiom of contemporary social science, rationality tends to be "bounded" by ideology, sometimes seriously so. Prevailing assumptions are often unstated, partly because they are presumed to be self-evident, and they do not always lead to the explicit formulation of coherent doctrine. Ideological and attitudinal factors play essential roles in

---

[1]Stephen Krasner, "Structural Causes and Regime Consequences: Regimes as Intervening Variables," in Stephen Krasner (ed.), *International Regimes* (Ithaca, NY: Cornell University Press, 1983), p. 2. See also Stephan Haggard and Beth A. Simmons, "Theories of International Regimes," *International Organization* 41, 3 (Summer 1987): 491–517.

international relations, however, and they require occasional excursions into such fields as cultural studies and intellectual history.

It is elites, not citizens, who forge national strategies and fashion foreign policies. For this reason it is essential to consider the ulterior motivations of policy-making groups within the nation-state and of nonstate actors as well. As often as not, public policy represents the interests of the ruling classes, not of the "nation" as a whole, and policy outcomes reflect the power and effectiveness of dominant alliances. This factor is especially pertinent to Latin America, where patterns of socioeconomic development have resulted in wide discrepancies between social classes and their respective interests. As a general rule, dictatorial governments in Latin America have tended to serve and support privileged elites. And even in democratic settings, official policy does not always represent the greatest good for the greatest number of national citizens.

## Concepts of Power

Throughout this study I devote special attention to the distribution of power. Ever since the early nineteenth century, the United States has been stronger and richer than its Latin American neighbors. The nature and degree of this asymmetry has varied over time, but it has been a pervasive and persistent reality. This means, among other things, that the United States has almost always held the upper hand: There has been little bargaining among equals, and the sovereignty of Latin nations has been under frequent threat. The United States has enjoyed by far the most freedom of action among countries in the Americas. And precisely for this reason, the study of U.S.–Latin American relations becomes a meditation on the character and conduct of the United States: It provides an opportunity to examine, over time, how the United States has chosen to apply and exercise its perennial predominance.

Things seem to have changed in recent years. The Cold War has come to an end, globalization has accelerated processes of interdependence, the attacks of 9/11 and the war on terror have unleashed bitter conflicts, and the rise of China and other powers has begun reshaping geopolitical arrangements. Within the Western Hemisphere, the United States has been conducting itself with aloof detachment and apparent uncertainty. In colloquial form, the question thus arises: Has the United States lost control of its backyard?

The answer depends, of course, on the meaning of *power*. We might begin with the still-classic formulation of Robert Dahl, who defined power as a relationship: "*A* has power over *B* to the extent that he can get *B* to do something that *B* would not otherwise do." It involves not only the use or threat of force but rational calculation of self-interest. As Leslie Gelb has written,

> Power is mental arm wrestling. It derives from establishing psychological and political leverage or advantage by employing resources (wealth, military capability, commodities, etc.), position (such as geographic regional balancer, or a political protector), as well as maintaining resolve and unity at home. These are embodied in a process whereby *A* convinces *B* that *A* can and will help or harm him, give him pleasure or pain, relieve his difficulties or increase them—whatever

the costs to *A* himself. Power thus varies with each and every relationship and changes with each and every situation. It has to be developed and shaped in almost each and every situation, and will vary over time and place. And critically, the wielder of power must take great care to be credible, to be taken seriously, both at home and abroad.[2]

Power is thus relational, situational, and changeable. Classic resources include demographic size, economic wealth, military prowess, and technological achievement.

The study of power has produced a proliferation of undefined terms. Among them is the concept of *hegemony*, which means different things to different people. It has been used to indicate a virtual monopoly of power. It can refer to a self-appointed right to rule.[3] And borrowing from the work of Antonio Gramsci, it can mean acceptance by actor *B* of the right to rule by actor *A*. In this sense, *A*'s power over *B* is seen as right and proper, as a suitable expression of values and realities. Domination and subordination thus become legitimate. Widespread acceptance of reality thus justifies asymmetry. (In this book the term "hegemony" refers to the capacity of an actor—or nation—to impose its will on others without significant challenge.)

Variations on this theme have crystallized in the notion of *soft power*. As framed by Joseph Nye, soft power represents the ability to achieve objectives not through threats, payments, or force, but through cooptation and attraction. Attraction, in turn, can lead to acquiescence. "When you can get others to admire your ideals and to want what you want, you do not have to spend as much on sticks and carrots to move them in your direction."[4] Or, in Dahlian terms, if you are *A* and you can narrow the gap between your objectives and what *B* "would otherwise do," then you don't have to work so hard.

Such benefits come from appreciation and admiration for the society as a whole—for its culture ("from Harvard to Hollywood" plus Michael Jordan), its political values (if it lives up to them), and its foreign policy (if seen as legitimate). The underlying proposition seems self-evident: The more positive the evaluation of a society, the more effective are its claims to leadership.

Soft power is controversial. It exists in the eye of the beholder. High-minded idealists have embraced the concept, since it brings normative and ethical dimensions into the analytical equation. Hardheaded realists have dismissed the notion as wishful and fanciful. Methodologists have worried about operationalization. In my view, it is a mushy but meaningful construct. It improves understanding of, let us say, the paramount role of the United States in various time periods. It is

---

[2]Leslie H. Gelb, *Power Rules: How Common Sense Can Rescue American Foreign Policy* (New York: HarperCollins, 2009), pp. 32–33. Dahl first presented his formulation in the 1950s.

[3]Abraham F. Lowenthal, "The United States and Latin America: Ending the Hegemonic Presumption," *Foreign Affairs* (Fall 1976): 199–213.

[4]Joseph S. Nye, *Soft Power: The Means to Success in World Politics* (New York: Public Affairs, 2004), p. x.

especially helpful in the conceptualization of day-to-day influence in the absence of military force.

## OVERVIEW

Systems and their codes are global in scope, embracing all nations in the world arena. They are of relatively long duration; individual powers might rise and fall, whereas rules of operation tend to stay the same. They are nonetheless subject to change, especially if leading powers arrive at the conclusion that maintenance of a given system will be more costly than its alteration. For implementation they depend on subjective perceptions, especially mutual perceptions of major powers, as well as on objective realities.

My interpretation of inter-American relations stresses both the *character* and the *transformation* of international systems and their corresponding codes. Given the subject of this volume, however, I make no pretense of examining all variations and types of global arrangements. Instead I focus on those systems that have provided relevant frameworks for the conduct of U.S.–Latin American affairs.

There have been, in my view, three broad systems that have guided the management of inter-American relations. The first stretched from the 1790s to the 1930s, when the prevailing regime corresponded to the logic of balance-of-power competition and multilateral rivalry. Imperialism—the quest for land, labor, and resources—provoked rivalry among major European powers and defined the relationship between metropolitan centers and subordinate colonial holdings. It was this logic that shaped the "great war of the mid–eighteenth century," culminating in the Seven Years' War, and it was this logic that determined the rules of international engagement throughout the nineteenth and early twentieth centuries. The United States entered this contest shortly after achieving independence. Leaders of the young republoic would seek to extend territorial reach at the expense of former European colonies, to prevent other powers from challenging this expansion, and to establish a sphere of uncontested influence within the Western Hemisphere. In effect, the fledgling United States was working out the logic of the eighteenth-century wars.

The second system lasted from the late 1940s through the 1980s, corresponding to the Cold War. The prevailing logic of this regime reflected the preeminence of bilateral rivalry between the United States and the Soviet Union on a global scale, intensified by mutual capacity for nuclear destruction. The Cold War altered the basis of inter-American relations, elevating the concept of "national security" to the top of the U.S. agenda and turning Latin America (and other Third World areas) into both a battleground and a prize in the conflict between communism and capitalism, East and West, the Soviet Union and the United States. The doctrine of "containment" led the United States to extend and consolidate its political supremacy throughout the hemisphere. By the early 1950s Washington had laid down policy lines in accordance with the terms of this regime, and they persisted through the 1980s.

Third has been the era following the Cold War. The United States emerged as the world's only military superpower, especially in the wake of the Soviet collapse, and after the Gulf War of 1991 the United States appeared to enjoy a "unipolar moment." At the same time U.S. relative strength appeared to be declining in the economic arena, where the rise of Japan and Europe fostered a multilateral geo-economic competition that relied on implicit "rules of the game." The disjuncture between the military and economic power provoked considerable uncertainty; it also discouraged, and may even have prevented, the articulation of a clear and coherent American "grand strategy."

The post–Cold War era entered a new phase in response to the attacks of September 11, 2001. To avenge its losses the United States unleashed a "global war on terror," an attempt to crush fundamentalist movements that were willing to take innocent lives in the name of Islamic redemption. This U.S.-led campaign began with a military expedition to Afghanistan in 2001 and extended to Iraq in 2003. Because of its scope and intensity the campaign came to dominate global agendas, redefine power, reshape alliances, and alter the rules of world politics. The apparently wanton destruction, mounting casualties, and revelations of human-rights abuses made the campaign increasingly unpopular. And because the United States took the lead, it found itself increasingly alone.

As a quintessentially geopolitical conflict, the war on terror laid down corresponding rules of the game—rules that overlapped and interacted with the still-operative codes of geoeconomic conduct dating from the 1990s. The simultaneous coexistence of geoeconomic and geopolitical international regimes adds complexity to the analysis, but it also helps explain the contradictions and confusions of the post-9/11 period. If and as the war on terror winds down, one might expect increasing attention to geoeconomic concerns.

The antiterror war placed Latin Americans in a curious predicament. Their initial reaction was to express heartfelt sympathy over the loss of life at the World Trade Center and the Pentagon. As Washington focused its attention on South and Central Asia, however, hemispheric leaders felt slighted by neglect of their concerns. As popular opposition mounted within their countries against the U.S. deployment of massive military force, some began to distance themselves from the American cause. A few condemned it altogether. And for many, Washington's preoccupation with distant parts of the world provided an opportunity to forge bonds of solidarity among themselves, seek new allies abroad, and expand their room for maneuver in the international arena.

Broad shifts in international contexts have continually shaped and revised the terms and nature of inter-American diplomacy. A central interpretation of this book thus takes counterintuitive form: The fundamental determinants of U.S.–Latin American relations have been the role and activity of *extrahemispheric* actors, not the United States or Latin America itself. In other words, the inter-American relationship has formed a subsystem with the global system as a whole.

Interests have varied over time. Among U.S. policymakers, the relative weight of economic and geopolitical motivations has undergone cyclical change. During the nineteenth and early twentieth centuries economic considerations were more important; during the Cold War, political considerations were uppermost; in the post–Cold War decade, economic considerations once again returned to the fore; and now, in the post-post–Cold War environment, security concerns are uppermost.

In response to the presence and power of the United States, Latin America has conducted a persisting and creative search for policy options. Leaders from the region—statesmen and politicians, economists and businessmen, students and revolutionaries, poets and essayists—all have attempted to define, expand, and implement the range of plausible alternatives. For the most part they have done so in a realistic fashion. United States observers frequently comment, derisively, on the curious "psychology" of Latin America, on its love-hate relationship with the United States, and on its emotional penchant for populistic nationalism. This condescension utterly misses a fundamental point: For weaker participants in an unequal world, nationalism may be one of the few options available.

The area we know as "Latin America" is far from monolithic, however, and it stoutly denies facile generalization. There are elements that countries and peoples of the region have in common, of course, and to this extent these nation-states can be considered as a group. But there are sharp distinctions among them as well—in population size, demographic composition, economic resources, geographical location, cultural traditions, and political attributes. As a result they often have differing interests. And to put it most succinctly, some countries of Latin America are stronger than others. These simple facts have spawned a wide range of intraregional relationships—associations, alliances, rivalries, wars. They have also bestowed different countries with differing incentives and capabilities for facing up to the United States.

## Caveats and Limitations

This is a pretty ambitious book, but it does not quite do everything. First, it does not offer a detailed examination of policymaking processes in the United States or in Latin America, though it explores this subject near the end. Instead, my principal concern is with the ultimate content of policy, rather than with struggles over its formation. Of course there is ample testimony that governmental decisions emerge from a welter of confusion, disorder, and bureaucratic intrigue—but if there exists a broad commitment among all actors to an underlying strategy or set of shared assumptions, this will tend to show up in the final result. Grand strategies are more evident in the shape of policy than in its shaping, more apparent in deeds than in words.

Further, this book does not make firm predictions about the future. It traces the evolution of inter-American relations from the past to the present and lays a solid foundation for anticipation of the years ahead—but it does not offer omniscient forecasts. Indeed, one of my principal contentions is that uncertainty in the contemporary global arena creates uncertainty within the hemispheric arena. The best we can do, I think, is to develop alternative scenarios for eventual relationships between the United States and Latin America. Outright prediction is bound to founder on the shoals of hard reality.

I am painting here with a very broad brush. My central concerns focus on the character of international systems, on the distribution of power, on the perception and pursuit of national interests, and on the resulting interaction between Latin America and the United States. My goal is to uncover recurrent regularities within the inter-American relationship, to identify long-term trends and transitions, and to analyze continuity and change. Only in this fashion will it be possible to assess the prospects for U.S.–Latin American relations in this new era of uncertainty and strife.

---

**BOX I-1**

### Where Are We?

Geographical terminology can be confusing. Let's get things straight:

- *North America* embraces Mexico, Canada, and the United States.
- *Central America* includes countries of the isthmus from Guatemala through Panama.
- *South America* is the continent that stretches from Venezuela and Colombia down through Argentina and Chile.

What has come to be known as the "Southern Cone" of South America consists of Chile, Argentina, and Uruguay; in colloquial usage, the term sometimes includes Paraguay and even Brazil.

The "Caribbean" includes all island countries that lie within the Caribbean Sea, such as Cuba. The "Caribbean area" or "circum-Caribbean region" usually includes all countries that border on the Caribbean Sea plus the Gulf of Mexico, so it includes Mexico and Central America as well as nations of the Caribbean.

*Latin America* embraces all countries from Mexico to the southern tip of Argentina/Chile, including Spanish- or French-speaking societies of the Caribbean. By convention, it does not include English-speaking islands of the Caribbean.

As used in this book, the adjective *regional* embraces all of Latin America; *subregional* applies to portions of Latin America (such as Central America or South America); and the term *hemispheric* refers to all of Latin America plus North America.

Got that? Find all these locations in the map on the following page.

**Contemporary Latin America**

# PART I

# The Imperial Era

And by and by comes America, and our Master of
the Game plays it badly—plays it as Mr. Chamberlain
was playing it in South Africa. It was a mistake to do
that . . . he played the European game, the Chamberlain
game. It was a pity; it was a great pity, that error; that one
grievous error, that irrevocable error.

MARK TWAIN (1901)

# CHAPTER 1

# The European Game

I have always wished that this country should exhibit to the
nations of the earth the example of a great, rich, and powerful
republic which is not possessed by a spirit of aggrandizement.

DANIEL WEBSTER (1845)

Yes, more, more, more! . . . till our national destiny is fulfilled
and . . . the whole boundless continent is ours.

JOHN L. O'SULLIVAN (1845)

Imperialism established a framework for the conduct of international relations throughout the nineteenth and early twentieth centuries. As a fledgling
power, the United States took active and increasing part in the global competition
that provoked continuous rivalry between major European powers and defined
the relationship between metropolitan centers and subordinate colonial holdings. Over time this imperial contest developed an implicit logic that shaped the
international system as a whole and the roles of contending nations in particular.
Recurrent episodes of conflict led to rearrangements of power relations. Until the
1800s this system reflected both dominance and competition among leading powers of Europe, which continually sought to expand their holdings in Africa, Asia,
and the New World.

The United States entered this contest shortly after achieving independence
("playing the European Game," as Mark Twain would acidly observe). Having
established national sovereignty, U.S. leaders would seek to extend territorial reach
over European colonies and prevent other powers from challenging this expansion. As a result, U.S. relations with Latin America during the nineteenth century represented a continuation and culmination of European incursions into and
struggles over the New World that dated back to the late fifteenth century.

From the outset, in other words, the United States was an aspiring imperial
power. It entered the international arena as a relatively minor, almost insignifi-
cant actor; within a century the young nation became a formidable contender.
The United States embarked on its imperial course by neither impulse, miscalcu-
lation, nor accident. Its behavior represented long-term policy and national purpose. As historian William Appleman Williams has observed, "Americans thought

of themselves as an empire at the outset of their national existence. . . . Having matured in an age of empires as part of an empire, the colonists naturally saw themselves in the same light once they joined issue with the mother country." In an ethical sense, U.S. conduct was neither better nor worse than that of other ambitious powers. All played the game by the same rules.

Once engaged in this contest, the United States adapted its policy in accordance with conditions and circumstances particular to the New World. While European powers engaged primarily in colonization of overseas possessions, the United States tended to rely, first, on territorial acquisition and absorption and, second, on the establishment and preservation of informal spheres of influence. The means thus varied, but the ends were much the same.

## EUROPEAN RIVALRY IN THE NEW WORLD

European powers began to compete for control of the New World almost immediately after Christopher Columbus announced his earth-shattering "discovery" in 1492. Protesting Spanish claims to total monopoly over the Americas, King João II of Portugal convinced the "Catholic kings" in 1494 to accept the Treaty of Tordesillas, which ceded to Portugal dominion over the eastern half of South America—much of present-day Brazil. Theoretically, Spain and Portugal thus possessed exclusive title to the newly found territories. According to terms laid down by the pope, it was the religious obligation of Spain and Portugal to spread the Catholic gospel to the heathen. So long as they fulfilled this missionary duty, Spain and Portugal would have complete control of lands and peoples of the New World.

The Iberian monopoly did not last long. Protestantism took hold throughout much of Europe as a result of the Reformation, and its anti-Catholic adherents saw no reason to respect the Treaty of Tordesillas or any papal declaration. Seeking economic access to the riches of the New World, merchants and buccaneers from rival European countries initiated a thriving trade in contraband. According to then-prevailing mercantilist theory, moreover, the goal of economic activity was to enhance the power of the nation-state. The accumulation of power was to be measured through the possession of precious bullion—that is, gold or silver. Mercantilist policymakers thus sought to run a favorable balance of trade, with exports exceeding imports, since this would increase the storage of coinage or bullion. (The emphasis on trade gave the doctrine its name.) Mercantilist theory tended to assume that nations were engaged in a "zero-sum" game, with one state's gain entailing a loss for another state. Discovery of the New World gravely threatened prevailing power relations, since it placed massive and unforeseen quantities of gold and silver at the disposal of Spain and its crusading Catholic monarchs, Charles I and Philip II. Given the assumptions of the time, other powers had no choice but to react.

By the mid-sixteenth century England emerged as Spain's principal rival. Legendary pirateers John Hawkins and Francis Drake made raids on ports around the Caribbean. Philip II decided to retaliate by invading England. Drake roared into the harbor of Cádiz and destroyed a number of ships, "singeing the beard of the king of Spain," and the English fleet then crushed the Spanish armada in 1588. War extended beyond Philip's death and peace finally came in 1609, when the Netherlands were divided in two: the north was set free from Spain and became Holland; the south remained under Spanish control and is now Belgium.

Spain's setbacks in Europe were soon reflected in the New World. The English settled at Virginia in 1607 and at Massachusetts in 1620. The Dutch reached New York in 1612. The French began moving into Canada in the 1620s. More significantly, from the standpoint of the era, English, French, and Dutch settlements appeared in the Antilles—in the middle of what had been up to then a Spanish lake. In 1630, moreover, the Dutch seized control of the Brazilian northeast—with its extensive sugar plantations—an acquisition that for Holland vastly overshadowed the purchase of Manhattan Island a few years before. The Dutch remained in Brazil until 1654.

By the late seventeenth century Europe was seeking to establish an effective counterweight to France. In 1700 Louis XIV's efforts to impose a family relative on the Spanish throne prompted a coalition of three partners—England, Holland, and the Holy Roman Emperor—to respond with a declaration of war. The War of the Spanish Succession dragged on until 1713. At the war's end Austria gained control of Milan, Naples, Sicily, and Belgium; Philip V (Louis XIV's nephew) was made King of Spain, under the stipulation that the crowns of France and Spain would never be held by the same individual; and England, the biggest winner, gained control of Gibraltar, Newfoundland, Nova Scotia, and—most important—the commercial contract (*asiento*) for the African slave trade with Spanish colonies in the New World. This lucrative privilege gave Britain a secure foothold in Spanish America.

Competition for empire intensified throughout the eighteenth century. A series of skirmishes stretched from 1739 to 1763 (with an uneasy truce from 1748 to 1756) and comprised what has come to be known as "the great war of the mid-eighteenth century." The first part of the contest, usually known as the War of the Austrian Succession, ground to a halt in 1748 when England and France reached agreement to restore the status quo ante bellum. The second stage came with the Seven Years' War, in which Britain and Prussia joined forces against the combined strength of the Hapsburgs and Bourbons. When the dust finally cleared in 1763, the Treaty of Paris codified the results: Britain remained in India; France ceded to Britain all French territory on the North American mainland east of the Mississippi River; France retained its slave stations in Africa plus the cash-producing Caribbean islands of Guadeloupe and Martinique (leading one observer to exult, in classic confirmation of mercantilist economic doctrine, "We may have lost Canada, but we have retained Martinique!"); and Spain retained its North American holdings west of the Mississippi and at the river mouth. The Seven Years' War thus achieved a new political and economic equilibrium. England replaced France as the preeminent colonial power, a position she would extend and consolidate through the *pax britannica* of the nineteenth century.

As England was celebrating its diplomatic triumph, Prime Minister George Grenville took a series of steps to consolidate British rule in North America and to improve imperial finances. His most notorious measure was the Stamp Act, which in 1765 imposed taxes on all legal documents, newspapers, pamphlets, and almanacs. Eventually, and in many instances reluctantly, British colonists rose up in protest against these impositions and against the monarchy. Proclaiming their independence in 1776, they finally achieved sovereignty and recognition in 1783. The emergence of their new nation would have fundamental and far-reaching impacts on the international arena.

## IMPERIAL ORDER: THE RULES OF THE GAME

Imperialism entailed the policy, practice, or advocacy of the extension of control by a nation over the territory, inhabitants, and resources of areas outside the nation's boundaries. Typically, nations engaged in imperialistic behavior for two basic reasons: first, to gain access to economic benefits—such as land, labor, and minerals; and second, to increase political strength and military capability—often through the improvement of geopolitical position in relation to other contending powers. Almost always, the pursuit of imperial advantage evoked elaborate ideological justification, ranging from the religious mission of sixteenth-century Spain to the civilizing mission of eighteenth-century France and the "white man's burden" that would be borne by nineteenth-century England.

As it evolved over time, imperialism spawned an informal but coherent code of international rules. The keystone of this system was the idea of a balance of power. First articulated by the Peace of Westphalia in 1648, this principle assumed that international politics would consist of relations among nation-states. The ultimate purpose of a balance of power was to prevent domination by any single European nation. In practice the principle led to a constantly shifting pattern of alliances and coalitions, as weaker nations often sought to achieve an appropriate balance by combining their forces in opposition to the stronger ones. Alignments would be based not on religion, ideology, culture, or values. They would respond to momentary contingencies and power calculations.

Second, this international system supported the sovereignty of established European nation-states and accepted the state as the primary actor in the global arena. Indeed, the whole idea of a "balance" among nations tended to assume and ensure their individual survival. By definition, equilibrium precluded the possibility of elimination or extinction. Of course this stipulation applied only to recognized powers in Europe, not to other parts of the world.

Third, and partly as a result of this understanding, European nations focused much of their competitive energy on imperial expansion. Preservation of a balance among metropolitan powers tended to limit the scale and scope of wars within the European theater. During the seventeenth and eighteenth centuries, battlegrounds shifted from the European continent itself toward the colonized areas. In effect, the extension of imperial possessions provided nations with an opportunity to enhance their power positions without having always to engage in direct hostilities with other European states. Colonization created a "positive-sum" game, or so it seemed at the time, a means of tilting the balance of power without upsetting the system as a whole.

Fourth, imperial holdings became integral elements in the calculation of the power balance. Especially under the mercantilist doctrines of the period, the ultimate rationale for imperial possessions was to strengthen the economic and political position of the metropolitan state. Consequently, European powers went to considerable lengths to maintain monopolistic control over their dominions, from Spain's elaborate complex of legalisms and regulations to England's maritime enforcement of its *pax britannica*. The point was not only to maximize direct exploitation of the dominions; it was to make sure that no other rival power would seize part of the booty and in so doing revise the prevailing balance of power.

Various methods existed for the pursuit of imperialistic advantage. One was the conquest and incorporation of territory, leading to effective enlargement of the boundaries of the nation-state. After the Peace of Westphalia most European powers tended to shy away from this method, at least in regard to each other's terrain, since it threatened to violate the whole idea of a balance of power. And with regard to overseas territories, the prospect of incorporation raised complex juridical and philosophical questions about the relationship of colonial inhabitants to metropolitan society. Even so, it became the policy of France to regard its imperial possessions in Africa, Asia, and the New World as integral parts of the nation—as *départements d'outre mer,* in theoretical possession of the legal rights and obligations pertaining to the provinces of France.

Another technique involved subjugation and colonization. Through this method, imperial dominions attained special status as subordinate appendages to the metropolitan nation and, usually, to its central government. While adding to the power of the metropole, colonization did not lead to effective enlargement of national boundaries. Nor did it raise awkward questions about the rights or roles of colonial subjects. For such reasons this approach was favored by most European competitors in the imperial contest. The British empire and its contemporary remnants (the so-called Commonwealth) offer perhaps the most notable and elaborate example of this option.

Still another alternative entailed the creation of a "sphere of interest," or sphere of influence, over which an imperial power would exert de facto hegemony through informal means. This could stem from economic domination or, in politics, the installation of client regimes or protectorates. One advantage of this approach was economy of effort: It did not entail the enormous expenditures of military, administrative, and financial resources that formal colonies required. (Indeed, there now exists substantial doubt about the net profitability of colonial possessions for European powers.) A central disadvantage was, of course, insecurity: Precisely because they were informal, spheres of influence were subject to intrusion by rival powers. Stability could prevail only if major powers agreed to recognize each other's spheres of domination. Such was the case in nineteenth-century Africa, where European rivals agreed to a "partitioning" of the continent, and to a lesser extent in turn-of-the-century China, where European nations attempted to carve out exclusive spheres of influence. It also applied to locations where the ever-resourceful British constructed what have come to be known as "informal empires."

## ENTER THE UNITED STATES

The newly independent United States joined the contest for imperial extension soon after achieving constitutional stability in the late 1780s. Two schools of thought quickly emerged with regard to foreign policy. One, championed by George Washington, held that the United States should avoid "entangling alliances" with European powers and should separate itself as much as possible from the Old World. The other, associated with Alexander Hamilton, argued that the United States should actively take advantage of European conflicts: If the new nation were to develop a powerful navy, he wrote, "a price would be set not only upon our friendship, but upon our neutrality. By steady adherence to the Union we may hope ere long to become the Arbiter of Europe in America; and to be able to incline *the balance of European competitions* in this part of the world as our interest may dictate" (emphasis added). Despite these differences, however, U.S. policymakers were in full agreement on one fundamental premise: European influence in the Americas should be reduced and restricted. It was this concern that directed their attention toward Spanish America. As Rufus King said of South America in a letter to Hamilton in 1799: "I am entirely convinced if it [South America] and its resources are not for us that they will speedily be against us."

American statesmen employed several strategies to prevent this negative outcome. First was to insist, at least in the short run, that these colonies remain in possession of Spain, which had the desirable quality of being a weak and declining power. Spain presented no threat; France or England, by contrast, would represent a powerful challenge. As a result, the United States vigorously and consistently opposed the transfer of Spanish dominions in the New World to any other European power.

Second, U.S. leaders would support campaigns for independence by Spanish American colonies in the 1810s and 1820s. They reached this position after a substantial amount of controversy and debate. One concern was that newly independent nations of Spanish America might forge diplomatic and commercial ties with England or France. A second preoccupation was that the resulting nations would be susceptible to instability, authoritarianism, and, as a result, extrahemispheric intervention. Another was that it would be politically difficult for the United States to take territory away from sister republics in the hemisphere. In the end, the United States faced little practical choice—and concluded that Spanish American independence would promote long-term national goals. As Thomas Jefferson wrote in 1808, "We consider their interests and ours as the same, and that the object of both must be to exclude all European influence from this hemisphere."

Third, U.S. policymakers sought to establish their own hegemony within the region. Without the power to back up their statements, they brazenly asserted that the continents of the Americas comprised a U.S. sphere of interest—to the exclusion of European powers. As Secretary of State John Quincy Adams declared, the United States was willing to leave Great Britain in "indisputed enjoyment" of all her colonial possessions so long as Britain would accept "every possibility of extension to our natural dominion in North America." In a similar vein, Jefferson insisted that Europe comprised "a separate division of the globe," while "America," he contended, "has a hemisphere to itself. It must have a separate system of interest which must not be subordinated to those of Europe. The insulated state in which nature has placed the American continent should so far avail that no spark of war kindled in the other quarters of the globe should be wafted across the wide oceans which separate us from them."

Claims to hemispheric hegemony became full-fledged policy with proclamation of the Monroe Doctrine in 1823. Partly aimed at czarist Russia's territorial claims in the American northwest, the doctrine asserted that the American continents "are henceforth not to be considered as subject for future colonization by any European power." It did not condemn colonization as a matter of principle; it inveighed only against colonization by European powers in the Americas. Taking note of an apparent design by the Holy Alliance to help Spain regain her colonies, President Monroe in addition warned against reinstatement of monarchical rule:

> We owe it, therefore, to candor, and to the amicable relations existing between the United States and those powers, to declare that we should consider any attempt on their part to extend their political system to any portion of this hemisphere as dangerous to our peace and safety. . . . We could not view any interposition for the purpose of oppressing [the newly independent nations], or controlling in any other manner their destiny, by any European power in any other light than as the manifestation of an unfriendly disposition toward the United States.

In one sense this statement declared the United States to be the guardian of independence and democracy throughout the hemisphere. But in another, more fundamental sense, it was an assertion of *realpolitik*. Not only would the United States oppose colonization by Europe in America; it would also oppose political *alliances* between newly independent nations of Spanish America and European powers.

## U.S. IMPERIALISM I: TERRITORIAL EXPANSION

The first phase of U.S. imperialistic policy involved territorial acquisition and absorption. Circumstances were propitious in the early nineteenth century. England and France were distracted by internal strife and by continental wars. Spain was in a process of precipitous decline. New nations in the hemisphere, especially in Spanish America, would be unable to offer much resistance. As Thomas Jefferson prophesied as early as the 1780s, it would eventually become possible for the United States to take over remnants of Spain's once-formidable empire "peice by peice [sic]."

## Pocketbook Diplomacy

The acquisition of Louisiana marked the U.S. entry into the imperial contest. In 1763 France lost its possessions west of the Mississippi to Spain—fortunately for the United States, the weakest of the European powers. In 1795 the United States obtained commercial rights along the Mississippi River. In 1800 Napoleon suddenly took title to Louisiana on behalf of France. Thomas Jefferson expressed shock and dismay over this development. "It completely reverses all the political relations of the U.S.," he declared. Shortly afterward Jefferson emphasized the importance of "one single spot" on earth—the port of New Orleans—the possessor of which would necessarily become "our natural and habitual enemy." The United States and France were on a collision course.

England came to the rescue, at least indirectly, as British–French tensions threatened to erupt in war. A beleaguered Napoleon decided to sell off the Louisiana territory: Better it go to the United States, he must have calculated, than to the English. By the terms of the 1803 purchase arrangement, the United States paid about $15 million in exchange for a massive span of land, one that not only included the present-day state of Louisiana but almost doubled the territorial size of the then United States.

Florida came next, through a combination of guile and force. In 1817 Secretary of State John Quincy Adams opened talks with his Spanish counterpart, after which General Andrew Jackson seized Spanish forts at St. Marks and Pensacola. Instead of reprimanding Jackson, as one might have expected, Adams demanded reparations from Spain to cover the cost of the military expedition—allegedly undertaken against Indians whom the Spaniards could not control. Unable to obtain diplomatic support from Great Britain, the king of Spain agreed in 1819 to cede "all the territories which belong to him situated to the eastward of the Mississippi and known by the name of East and West Florida." In return the U.S. government would assume the claims of its citizens against the Spanish government in the amount of $5 million. This money was to be paid to American citizens, not to the Spanish government: technically speaking, the United States did not "purchase" Florida, as is often said. In addition Spain renounced her claim to territory north of the forty-second parallel from the Rockies to the Pacific, while the United States gave up its claims to Texas. America's renunciation of interest in Texas did not, of course, endure the test of time.

England's refusal to support Spanish claims in the New World resulted from political calculations about the European theater. In the mid-1820s, with French troops occupying parts of a much-weakened Spain, British foreign minister George Canning began to worry about the possibility that France might assume control of Spain's holdings in the New World. That would upset the balance of power. To prevent this outcome he extended diplomatic recognition to the struggling republics of Spanish America, a gesture that earned accolades and gratitude throughout the continent. But Canning's motive was less than charitable, as he immodestly declared in 1826: "Contemplating Spain, such as our ancestors had known her, I resolved that if France had Spain, it should not be Spain with the Indies. I called the New World into existence to redress the balance of the Old." Rarely had the logic of the Imperial Era found such pristine expression.

## Military Conquest

In the 1820s Mexico won independence from Spain and jurisdiction over the province of Texas, then a largely unpopulated wilderness. (Mexico's achievement of sovereignty presumably freed the United States from its 1819 commitment to Spain.) After its long and bitter struggle for independence, Mexico was in a greatly weakened state. Economic production was anemic, especially in the mining and agricultural sectors; governmental budgets ran consistent deficits, taxes were steadily raised, properties were confiscated, old currencies were recalled and new ones issued; politics fell prey to chronic instability. Between 1821 and 1860 the country had more than fifty presidents, approximately one per year, and the military comprised by far the nation's strongest political force. Through this turmoil there emerged the mercurial Antonio López de Santa Anna, hero of Mexico's rejection of Spain's attempted *reconquista* in 1829 and of the expulsion of French troops during the so-called *guerra de los pasteles* in 1838. Santa Anna would both precipitate and personify Mexico's disintegration and vulnerability during its first quarter-century of independence.

Recognizing their inability to protect the country's northern frontier, Mexican leaders in the 1820s permitted colonists, most of them slaveholding planters from the United States, to settle in the province of Texas. A group led by Stephen F. Austin agreed to profess the Roman Catholic religion, to conduct official transactions in Spanish, and to abide by Mexican law. Yet the colonists soon began chafing under Mexican rule. They particularly complained about the fact that Texas was appended to the state of Coahuila, where the provincial delegation was in a small minority, and demanded that Texas should become a state within Mexico, with its own legislature and local government. Publicists in the United States began to clamor for Texan independence. Afraid that its control of Texas was slipping, the Mexican government attempted first to discourage immigration (by emancipating slaves in 1829) and then to prohibit immigration altogether (through a proclamation in 1830). Shortly afterward Santa Anna annulled the federalist constitution of 1824 and sought to concentrate effective power in the central government.

Texans rebelled in the name of independence. In March 1836 Santa Anna overwhelmed Texan forces in the Battle of the Alamo; later, captured and defeated, he consented to the secession. When word of his capitulation reached Mexico City, nationalist intellectuals and politicians expressed outrage and disbelief. The Mexican legislature refused to receive a peace commission from Texas or to extend recognition to the Lone Star Republic.

The United States recognized Texas as a sovereign polity in 1837. And in 1845, after the expansionist James K. Polk became president, it annexed the republic of Texas. This was a direct affront to Mexico, which still regarded Texas as an outlaw province of its own. Mexico and the United States severed diplomatic relations.

A boundary dispute fanned the flames of contention. While North Americans claimed that the southern border extended to the Rio Grande, Mexicans insisted that the limit should end, as it always had, at the Nueces River. In 1846 President Polk dispatched U.S. troops under General Zachary Taylor to the disputed area, in what many historians interpret as a deliberate move to provoke a fight. In hopes of relieving tension the harried Mexican president, José Joaquín Herrera, agreed to receive a diplomatic mission so long as the discussions "should appear to be always frank, and free from every sign of menace or coercion." Polk withdrew a U.S. naval force from the coast of Veracruz but authorized the U.S. mission under John Slidell to discuss not only Texas but the acquisition of New Mexico and California as well. As bitterness mounted in Mexico, General Mariano Paredes overthrew the hapless Herrera, installed himself as president, and refused to accept Slidell's credentials.

Polk was now looking for war. On May 9, 1846, he called a cabinet meeting to discuss "definite measures" to be taken against Mexico. That same evening news arrived of military hostilities at a place called Matamoros, on the southern bank of the Rio Grande. Seizing this excuse, Polk promptly called for war. In his message to Congress he praised the United States for its "strong desire to establish peace" and condemned Mexico for treachery. The Mexican government had broken its "plighted faith" by refusing to receive the Slidell mission, and had responded without reason when "Texas, a nation as independent as herself, thought proper to unite its destinies with our own." Tacitly confessing his predetermination for war, Polk insisted that "the cup of forbearance had been exhausted" even prior to the skirmish at Matamoros—which he described as a Mexican invasion of U.S. soil. "As war exists, and, notwithstanding all our efforts to prevent it, exists by the act of Mexico herself," Polk urged Congress to "recognize the existence of the war" and give him full authority to wage the necessary campaigns.

Although the logic of his message was preposterous, Polk received approval for his war. General Zachary Taylor swept into the city of Monterrey, rebels in California took sides with the United States, and in 1847 American troops under General Winfield Scott advanced from Veracruz to Mexico City, seizing the capital after subduing the resistance of young Mexican cadets. The following year, in the Treaty of Guadalupe Hidalgo, Mexico was obliged to surrender a huge span of land—from New Mexico and Colorado to California, as revealed in Map 1-1, more than a million square miles—in exchange for a modest $15 million. Several years later the United States extended its holdings by obtaining an additional section of New Mexico and Arizona through the Gadsden Purchase—a transaction remembered in Mexico for the application of American pressure and therefore known as "the imposition of Mesilla" (*el tratado impuesto de la Mesilla*), so named after the valley that passed to U.S. hands.

Ironically, one eventual consequence of the U.S. defeat of Mexico was a flagrant breach of the Monroe Doctrine. Humiliated by the "war of the North American invasion" and unable to achieve a semblance of stability, political conservatives in Mexico came to the unhappy conclusion that the country could achieve national unity and strength only through a vigorous reassertion of Hispanic, Catholic, and

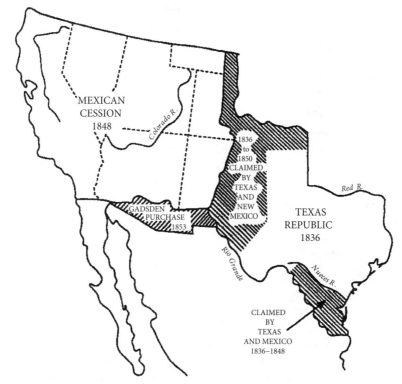

**Map 1-1  U.S. Territorial Acquisitions from Mexico, 1836–1853**
Source: From *Mexican Americans/American Mexicans*. Copyright © 1972, 1993 by Matt S. Meier and Feliciano Ribera. Reprinted by permission of Hill and Wang, a division of Farrar, Straus & Giroux, Inc.

royalist traditions. They also maintained that Mexico would be able to resist further encroachments by the United States only with protection from a European power—in this case France. (It was in this context, incidentally, that the whole concept of "Latin America" emerged: It was a deliberate effort by France to emphasize its solidarity with nations of the region.) In the 1860s Mexican representatives conspired with European sponsors to bring an Austrian prince, Maximilian von Hapsburg, to occupy a newly created "imperial" throne. The ill-starred reign of Maximilian and Carlota led to the exacerbation of an already bitter civil war between "conservatives" and "liberals" in Mexico and concluded with the emperor's execution in 1867.

### Eyes upon Cuba

The United States coveted Cuba throughout the nineteenth century. With its tobacco and sugar production, its thriving commerce, and—especially—its strategic location in the Caribbean, "the pearl of the Antilles" offered numerous and tempting advantages. Over time, the United States developed a two-pronged policy: One goal was to prevent the transfer of Cuba to any European power other than Spain; the other was to take over the island directly.

Thomas Jefferson confidently regarded Cuba as a proper limit for U.S. territorial expansion, proposing the erection of a sign at the southern tip of the island saying *Nec plus ultra* ("Not beyond here"). And as Secretary of State John Quincy Adams viewed the hemisphere in 1823, he observed that Cuba and Puerto Rico comprised "natural appendages to the North American continent." "It is scarcely possible," he wrote, "to resist the conviction that the annexation of Cuba to our federal republic will be indispensable to the continuance and integrity of the Union itself." Eventually, Adams surmised, this would occur as a result of natural forces:

> . . . there are laws of political as well as physical gravitation; and if an apple severed by the tempest from its native tree cannot choose but fall to the ground, Cuba, forcibly disjoined from its own unnatural connection with Spain, and incapable of self-support, can gravitate only towards the North American Union, which by the same law of nature cannot cast her off from her bosom.

In other words, the United States had only to await Cuba's liberation from Spain. Once that occurred, laws of political gravitation would bring the island naturally and inevitably into the fold of the United States.

Campaigns for outright annexation surged in the 1840s and 1850s. Celebrating the conclusion of the Mexican War, journalist John L. O'Sullivan wrote to Secretary of State James Buchanan in March 1848: "Surely the hour to strike for Cuba has come. . . . Fresh from our Mexican triumphs, glories and acquisition, the inevitable necessity for which the United States must sooner or later have Cuba, will force itself on the minds of the Spanish Ministry." Having staked his presidency on expansionist principles, President Polk promptly authorized negotiations for the purchase of Cuba.

Complications ensued. A Venezuelan adventurer, General Narciso López, proposed to conquer the island and present it to the United States. Though López was defeated by Spanish forces, England and France expressed alarm over American filibustering and proposed a tripartite agreement to guarantee that Cuba would stay under Spain. Serving as secretary of state under President Millard Fillmore, Edward Everett not only declined to participate but seized the opportunity to reflect upon the situation of the hemisphere. English and French acquisitions in Africa and elsewhere "have created no uneasiness on the part of the United States," Everett explained, just as U.S. accessions "have probably caused no uneasiness to the great European powers, as they have been brought about by the operation of natural causes, and without any disturbance of the international relations of the principal states." To this extent, Europeans and Americans were complying with the informal codes of the imperial contest. Everett contended that the transfer of Cuba to any European power other than Spain would disturb this equilibrium, however, since "it would indicate designs in reference to this hemisphere which could not but awaken alarm in the United States." The destiny of Cuba was therefore "mainly an American question," and the idea of a tripartite convention was

As legislator, diplomat, secretary of state, and president, John Quincy Adams (1767–1848) played a major role in shaping U.S. policy toward Latin America—helping formulate the Monroe Doctrine and predicting that Cuba would fall to the United States through the force of gravity.
Source: Library of Congress Prints and Photographs Division, Washington, D.C.

wholly inappropriate. Europe should refrain from pronouncements or actions on Cuba. Yet the United States was unwilling to renounce all possibility of future claims. The island was of such strategic importance, Everett insisted, that annexation someday "might be almost essential to our safety." In modern parlance, Cuba was a national security issue.

The United States continued its search for opportunities. In 1854 the otherwise undistinguished President Franklin Pierce instructed the U.S. minister to Spain, Pierre Soulé of Louisiana, to make a new offer to purchase the island or, if unsuccessful, to initiate efforts to "detach" Cuba from Spain. Consequently plotting to overthrow the Spanish monarchy, Soulé received instructions to consult with U.S. ministers to England and France. This ebullient threesome embodied its recommendations in a dispatch known as the Ostend Manifesto. The ministers began with a solemn vow that the United States should make every effort to acquire Cuba with Spanish "consent," presumably through purchase. If this could not be accomplished, however, "we shall be justified in wresting it from Spain if we possess the power; and this upon the very same principle that would justify an individual in tearing down the burning house of his neighbor if there were no other means of preventing the flames from destroying the home." As demonstrated by Haiti's continuing intimidation of the Dominican Republic, a slave revolt in Cuba could also pose a menace to racial purity. The ministers continued:

> We should be recreant to our duty, be unworthy of our gallant forefathers, and commit base treason against posterity, should we permit Cuba to be Africanized and become a second St. Domingo, with all its attendant horrors to the white race, and suffer the flames to enter our own neighborhood shores, seriously endanger or actually to consume the fair fabric of our Union.

To maintain the "fair fabric" of American society and to protect its shores from hostile intrusions, the United States must acquire Cuba without delay. If Spain stubbornly rejected U.S. overtures, it would bear responsibility for the result. The Ostend Manifesto was an ultimatum.

Confronted by news leaks and anxious to maintain good public relations with Spain, the Pierce administration promptly disavowed the document. Yet the ensuing embarrassment proved to be short-lived: One of its signatories, James Buchanan, became the next president of the United States.

By the late 1850s the whole question of Cuba became embroiled in domestic sectional controversy, as the North objected to the prospect of admitting a new slave state. The U.S. Civil War and its outcome temporarily removed the issue from the political agenda. Cuba returned to the forefront in the late 1860s, when rebels launched the Ten Years' War against Spanish colonial rule and prompted Ulysses S. Grant to proclaim in 1869 what came to be known as the "no-transfer principle." Casting a nervous eye on England and France, the president huffed: "These dependencies are no longer regarded as subject to transfer from one European power to another." The issue faded with Spain's defeat of rebels in the Ten Years' War. It was not until the 1890s that Cuba would recapture national attention.

## U.S. IMPERIALISM II: COMMERCIAL EMPIRE

Toward the end of the nineteenth century the United States shifted its strategy toward Latin America. After intense soul-searching and debate over principles and methods of expansion, Washington turned principally from the acquisition of territory to the creation of a sphere of interest, extending U.S. hegemony through an informal network of economic and political relations. There were several reasons for this change. One was demographic reality: These new areas were either unsuitable for European immigration or already populated by peoples of indigenous, African, or Iberian heritage. According to the racist doctrines of the era, to be explored in chapter 2, this made them unfit for incorporation into the predominantly Anglo-Saxon society of the United States. Second was a reevaluation of the global imperial contest, with its growing emphasis on commercial advantage instead of territorial reach. Third was a realization that imperialism, in the European sense, was an expensive proposition. As the British would discover in India and elsewhere, it required substantial expenditures of military and administrative capacity. By the late nineteenth century it was becoming apparent that with foresight and fortune it might be possible to obtain the benefits of imperialism without assuming all its costs.

United States leaders confronted two key challenges within the hemisphere. One was Europe's political domination of the Caribbean Basin. In the mid-1890s, as shown in Map 1-2, the Caribbean was essentially a European lake. With the exception of Hispaniola (shared by Haiti and the Dominican Republic), every single island was a European colony. Spain still held possession of Cuba and Puerto Rico; Britain held Jamaica, part of the Virgin Islands, Grenada, and several of the leeward islands as well as the mainland dominions of British Honduras and British Guiana; France held Martinique, Guadeloupe, and French Guiana; the Dutch held several islands, including St. Maartens, plus Dutch Guiana on the northern fringe of South America. No wonder European leaders ridiculed the Monroe Doctrine.

The second challenge came from Europe's commercial position. The United States had a strong presence around the greater Caribbean Basin, especially in Cuba and Mexico, but Europe was preeminent in South America. As of 1913 Great Britain was the leading overall trade partner for Argentina, Chile, and Peru, and it was the largest source of imports for Brazil. Germany and France both had important commercial relations with Argentina and Brazil. Throughout southern South America, the United States was a relatively minor source of commerce—and of political influence. As writer and publicist William Eleroy Curtis would exclaim to the U.S. Congress in 1886, the benefits of economic growth in that southernmost region were going almost exclusively to "the three commercial nations of Europe"—England, France, and Germany—which "have secured a monopoly of the trade of Spanish America . . . [and] the Englishmen," Curtis gravely warned, "have the Brazilians by the throat."

Investments offered a similar picture. During the nineteenth century the United States, itself a debtor nation, was in no position to export much capital to Latin America. England had taken up the slack, making long-term investments in Brazil and Argentina—and following through with spurts of new investment in the 1870s and the 1890s. By 1914 Britain alone held more than half of all foreign investments in Latin America. France and Germany also supplied substantial capital during the 1880s and after the turn of the century.

In the meantime, U.S. policymakers insisted on the need to expand export markets. As the post–Civil War economy continued its headlong rush toward industrial growth, U.S. exports had grown from a minuscule $392 million in 1870 to $1.3 billion by 1900. This was only a promising start. "But today," cried Senator Albert J. Beveridge of Indiana in 1899, "we are raising more than we can consume. Today, we are making more than we can use. Therefore, we must find new markets

CENTRAL AMERICA AND THE CARIBBEAN

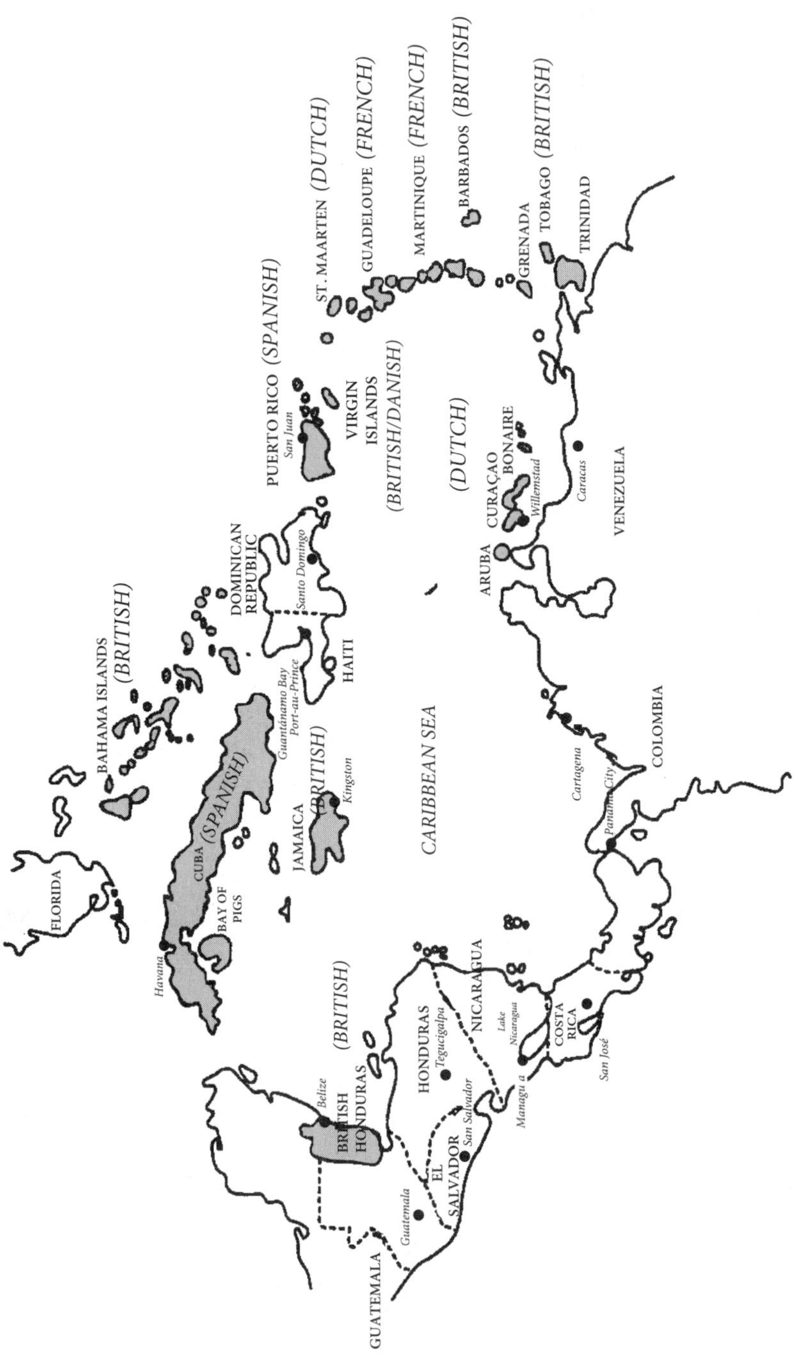

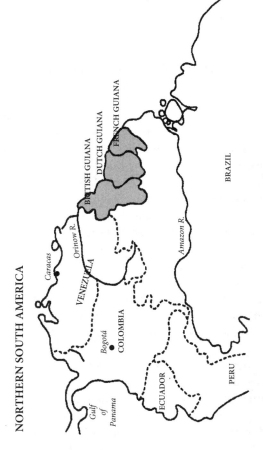

**Map 1-2  European Possessions in Latin America, mid-1890s**
(The Falkland Islands, off the southern coast of Argentina, were also held by the British.)

for our produce, new occupation for our capital, new work for our labor." The hope was that increased trade would sustain steady growth, thereby avoiding the cycles of depression that had devastated the economy in 1873–1878, 1882–1885, and 1893–1897.

To achieve this goal, polemicists and politicians called upon the U.S. government to develop and sustain a clear-cut economic policy, rather than laissez-faire reliance on the workings of the market. They argued that it was up to the Department of State to represent American commercial and financial interests in foreign lands, especially in Latin America. As the New York *Commercial Advertiser* asserted in 1898, we can now speak of "a new Monroe Doctrine, not of political principles, but of commercial policy. . . . Instead of laying down dogmas, it figures up profits."

## A SPHERE OF ONE'S OWN: THE PAN-AMERICAN COMMUNITY

In the late nineteenth century the United States began making vigorous efforts to institutionalize its rising claim to hegemony within the Western Hemisphere. In 1881 Secretary of State James G. Blaine, the "Plumed Knight" from Maine, issued invitations for an international conference to consider "the means of preventing war among the nations of America." (During 1865–1870, countries of the Southern Cone had fought the long and bitter Paraguayan War, and in 1879 Chile and Peru had initiated their War of the Pacific.) As Blaine would later explain, he had two purposes in mind: "first, to bring about peace . . . ; second, to cultivate such friendly commercial relations with all American countries as would lead to a large increase in the export trade of the United States. To obtain the second object the first must be accomplished." To assuage concern among Latin Americans and to distinguish the United States from England, Blaine explained that "Our great demand is expansion" but only of trade, rather than of territory. What he was seeking, in other words, was "what the younger Pitt so well called annexation of trade."

After President James A. Garfield's assassination Blaine was replaced as secretary of state, and his successor, Frederick T. Frelinghuysen, expressed open skepticism about any meeting where Latin American nations might outvote the United States. Yet Frelinghuysen supported the basic idea of consolidating a U.S. sphere of influence: "I am thoroughly convinced," he said in 1884, "of the desirability of knitting closely our relations with the States of this continent . . . in the spirit of the Monroe Doctrine, which, in excluding foreign political interference, recognizes the common interest of the States of North and South America." Commenting on recently concluded reciprocity pacts with Spain for increased trade with Cuba and Puerto Rico, Frelinghuysen expressed satisfaction that the accord would bring "those islands into close commercial connection with the United States [and] confers upon us and upon them all benefits which would result from annexation were that possible." The secretary also looked forward to a series of comparable agreements with nations of Latin America that "opens the markets of the west coast of South America to our trade and gives us at our doors a customer able to absorb a large portion of those articles which we produce in return for products which we cannot profitably raise." Like Blaine, Frelinghuysen saw the principal goal of U.S. policy toward the region as expansion of trade.

With Benjamin Harrison elected to the presidency in 1888, Blaine returned as secretary of state and took the opportunity to issue a second invitation for what had come to be known as a "Pan-American" conference. The agenda included not only the preservation of peace within the hemisphere but also commercial development and economic integration. Topics ranged from construction of a Pan American railway to the adoption of a common monetary standard. There was to be no contemplation of political or military alliances. At the conference itself considerable discussion focused on the possible formation of a customs union— which would oblige nations of the hemisphere to erect common tariffs on commercial products from outside the region. The idea was voted down, however, as delegates expressed concern over potential threats to national sovereignty.

The conference yielded scant material results. One was the creation of a Commercial Bureau of the American Republics—parent of the Pan American Union and, much later, the Organization of American States. Another, indirect consequence was a series of bilateral reciprocity treaties between the United States and nations of Latin America. Yet another outcome drew little notice at the time. During congressional debates over reciprocity, Eugene Hale, a U.S. senator from Maine, proposed a measure that would have included Canada as well as Latin America in a common zone for free trade in raw materials. The idea gained few adherents, and Hale himself quietly withdrew it from consideration. It would reemerge in the century ahead.

## Obtaining John Bull's Acquiescence

During the 1890s America's principal rival in Latin America was Great Britain. A number of episodes heightened tensions between the two powers. In the Chilean port of Valparaíso, for instance, two American sailors from the vessel *Baltimore* were stabbed to death during a saloon brawl in 1891. At first unable to obtain full satisfaction from Chilean authorities, President Benjamin Harrison threatened to take military action. But the real issue was not so much financial indemnity; it was international power. Chile was in the midst of political upheaval, and the United States and Britain found themselves on opposite sides: Washington sided with the existing government, while the British supported anti-American rebels. The New York *Tribune* offered a clear view of the interests at stake:

> The danger to the United States in these crises arises from the disposition of Europeans to interfere, the while pretending that they are merely defending their own commercial interests. In Chili and the Argentine, the most progressive commercial countries of South America, we have permitted England to obtain monopoly of trade. We have talked lustily about the "Monroe Doctrine" while Great Britain has been building ships and opening markets. British subjects today

hold a chattel mortgage over Chili and the Argentine. . . . No American who
wishes his country to possess the influence in commerce and affairs to which its
position among nations entitles it can be pleased with this situation.

The *Baltimore* affair was eventually settled in early 1892 when the Chilean government paid $75,000 as indemnity, but the implications lingered on: The United
States and Britain were wrestling for supremacy in the Americas.

Subsequent encounters took place in Brazil and Nicaragua, but the most
serious British–American confrontation resulted from the Venezuelan crisis of
1895–1896. The precipitating conflict was a boundary dispute between Venezuela
and British Guiana. At specific issue was control over the mouth of the Orinoco
River, the trade artery for the northern third of South America. Venezuela requested
international arbitration. Great Britain responded by augmenting its claims—now
to include a region rich in gold deposits. Venezuela broke off diplomatic relations
with England and appealed to President Grover Cleveland in Washington.

The United States had two major interests in this controversy. One was access
to the Orinoco River. The other was political influence. In February 1895 the U.S.
Congress announced its opposition to the British claims. Months later Secretary
of State Richard Olney couched a message to Whitehall in unusually blunt and
provocative language:

> Today the United States is practically sovereign on this continent, and its fiat is
> law upon the subjects to which it confines its interposition. Why? It is not because
> of the pure friendship or good will felt for it. It is not simply by reason of its high
> character as a civilized state, nor because wisdom and justice and equity are the
> invariable characteristics of the dealings of the United States. It is because, in
> addition to all other grounds, its infinite resources combined with its isolated
> position render it master of the situation and practically invulnerable as against
> any or all other powers.

This passage has earned for Olney a dubious reputation in the history of inter-
American relations. It is rarely remembered that after all this bluster the note concluded with a call for peaceful arbitration.

---

**BOX 1-2**

### Architects of Empire: U.S. Presidents, 1789–1909

American presidents played major parts in forging and shaping the nation's imperial holdings in Latin America. As explained in the text, they relied not so much on
European-style colonialism as on territorial acquisition via diplomacy, threats, and
military force.

George Washington, 1789–1797

John Adams, 1797–1801

Thomas Jefferson, 1801–1809

James Madison, 1809–1817

James Monroe, 1817–1825

John Quincy Adams, 1825–1829

Andrew Jackson, 1829–1837

Martin Van Buren, 1837–1841

William Henry Harrison, 1841

John Tyler, 1841–1845

James K. Polk, 1845–1849

Zachary Taylor, 1849–1850

Millard Fillmore, 1850–1853

Franklin Pierce, 1853–1857

James Buchanan, 1857–1861

Abraham Lincoln, 1861–1865

Andrew Johnson, 1865–1869

Ulysses S. Grant, 1869–1877

Rutherford B. Hayes, 1877–1881

James Garfield, 1881

Chester Arthur, 1881–1885

Grover Cleveland, 1885–1889

Benjamin Harrison, 1889–1893

Grover Cleveland, 1893–1897

William McKinley, 1897–1901

Theodore Roosevelt, 1901–1909

Especially prominent roles fell to John Quincy Adams, James K. Polk, William McKinley, and Theodore Roosevelt.

---

The British foreign minister, Lord Salisbury, responded with two separate messages. One refuted the assertion by Olney that the Monroe Doctrine comprised a part of international law; the other consented to the principle of arbitration. Ongoing crises in Europe, South Africa, and the Middle East finally compelled Lord Salisbury to consent to the creation of an arbitration board—with two Americans, two British citizens, and one Russian authority on international law. (No one had consulted Venezuela in the meantime.) After protesting, Venezuela was reluctantly allowed to have one member of the board.

By accepting arbitration, Great Britain was tacitly recognizing Olney's claim to American preeminence throughout the Western Hemisphere. And from that point forward, Britain would tend to align itself on the side of the United States, using U.S. power whenever possible to protect British interests in Latin America. Through the Venezuelan controversy, the United States had taken a major step toward the achievement of de facto hegemony in the Americas.

**Accepting the Monroe Doctrine.** This cartoon gleefully depicts Britain's acknowledgment of rising U.S. preeminence in the Americas.
Artist: Homer Davenport, 1867–1912.

## SECURING THE CARIBBEAN

The Caribbean Basin remained a focal point for U.S. policy. As always Washington was eager to reduce, if not eliminate, the European presence in the area. The United States wanted to take advantage of promising opportunities for investment and trade. A related goal was the creation and protection of shipping lanes for U.S. commerce. Also compelling was a longstanding desire to construct a canal in Central America that would establish a link between the east and west coasts of the United States and, equally important, provide access to the alluring markets of the Far East. In view of widely accepted military doctrine, this plan bore geopolitical significance as well: As historian-publicist Alfred Thayer Mahan forcefully argued in such magisterial books as *The Influence of Sea Power upon History* (1890), naval power was the key to international influence, which meant that the United States required a two-ocean navy. A transisthmian canal would make this possible.

### Spanish-Cuban-American War

The Cuban question returned to the fore largely because of efforts by anti-Spanish forces. The U.S. response to the depression of 1893 had major repercussions on the island: When the protectionist tariff of 1894 removed provisions for reciprocity, the Cuban economy collapsed. Plantations discharged workers in 1894 and 1895, owing to the loss of the North American market, and rebellion quickly ensued. Led by the Maceo brothers in Cuba and inspired by writings of the exiled José Martí in New York, Cuban forces mounted a determined drive for independence from Spain. Chaos resulting from the military campaigns offered a short-lived pretext for intervention by the United States. In 1896 Congress declared that the U.S. government "should be prepared to protect the legitimate interests of our citizens, by intervention if necessary." By this time North Americans had invested more than $30 million in the island, including $8 million in mines and $12 million in plantations. A clamor for war was steadily intensifying. William Randolph Hearst, the creator of "yellow journalism," reportedly warned an overly scrupulous newspaper artist: "You furnish the pictures, and I'll furnish the war."

Resisting popular opinion, President Grover Cleveland refused to intervene. In June 1895 the White House issued a declaration of neutrality, tacitly acknowledging a state of belligerency in Cuba. And in April 1896, going one step further, Secretary of State Olney offered to mediate the conflict. The move was rejected by Spain, which then sought support from other European powers to forestall U.S. intervention. Madrid's overture fell on deaf ears: Britain was reevaluating its American policies in light of the Venezuelan crisis, France was unconcerned, and Russia was attempting to consolidate its growing influence in Korea and Manchuria.

As events unfolded, this became a triangular conflict—involving Spain, the United States, and the Cuban independence movement. The United States initially supported autonomy for Cuba under a reformed colonial regime, but this was not acceptable to Spain or to the Cubans. Spain wanted to maintain its empire, but this was not acceptable to the Cubans or to Washington. And the Cubans fought for independence, but this was not acceptable to Spain or the United States. In fact Madrid and Washington firmly agreed on denial of power to the Cubans. As the American consul wrote to the State Department in 1897, "All classes of Spanish citizens are violently opposed to a real or genuine autonomy because it would throw the island into the hands of the Cubans—and rather than that they prefer annexation to the United States or some form of American protectorate." He later observed that upper-class supporters of the Cuban rebellion were apprehensive as well: "They are most pronounced in their fears that independence, if obtained, would result in the troublesome, adventurous, and non-responsible class" seizing power.

By late 1897, with William McKinley as president, prospects for a negotiated settlement seemed fairly bright. Then struck two thunderbolts in early 1898. First, the White House came into possession of a confidential but careless letter from the Spanish consul, Dupuy de Lôme, who delivered himself of the opinion that McKinley was a weak, venal, and vacillating politician. Second, an explosion ripped through the U.S. battleship *Maine* in Havana harbor and took the lives of more than 260 American seamen. McKinley responded with an ultimatum, demanding an immediate cessation of hostilities by Spain and full reparations for the sinking of the *Maine*. As Madrid was preparing to accede, McKinley proceeded to recommend war anyway— "in the name of humanity, in the name of civilization, on behalf of endangered American interests." To his other terms McKinley now added a call for Cuban independence, which he knew the Spanish government could not accept.

As McKinley declared war on Spain, the question immediately arose as to whether Washington should extend recognition to the rebel forces. The president finally proclaimed, with uncommon clarity:

> To commit this country now to the recognition of any particular government in Cuba might subject us to the embarrassing conditions of international obligation toward the organization so recognized. In case of intervention our conduct would be subject to the approval or disapproval of such government. We would be required to submit to its direction and to assume to it the mere relation of friendly ally.

Recognition of an independent government might impose unwelcome restrictions on the United States. Like his predecessors, McKinley wanted to preserve complete freedom of action in Cuba.

Under orders from Theodore Roosevelt, assistant secretary of the navy, Commodore George Dewey promptly launched an attack on the Spanish fleet at Manila harbor in the Philippines. The rambunctious Roosevelt himself joined the fray, leading his "Rough Riders" in a much-publicized assault on Cuba's San Juan Hill. The exhausted Spaniards proved to be no match for their American opponents, and the "splendid little war" lasted only a matter of months. According to the peace terms, Cuba attained independence from Spain. The United States assumed outright control of Puerto Rico and Guam and, for a payment of $20 million, the Philippine Islands as well (in these specific cases the United States established European-style colonies). What had started as a war to liberate Cuba, in the eyes of many, became a war to expand the American empire.

Cuba's independence from Spain did not mean independence from the United States. As the hostilities faded, Cuba fell under the direct administration of the U.S. War Department. And as Cuban leaders worked to establish a government, the United States in 1901 attached to Cuba's new constitution the so-called Platt Amendment, permitting the United States to intervene in the affairs of the island "for the preservation of Cuban independence, and the maintenance of a government adequate for the protection of life, property, and individual liberty." This provision was further ratified in a treaty of 1903. A sovereign nation in name, Cuba was in fact a protectorate of the United States.

### Taking Panama

Major powers had long contemplated the possibility of constructing a canal through Central America that would connect the Atlantic and Pacific oceans, eliminate the need for time-consuming and dangerous voyages around Cape Horn, accelerate commerce and trade, and revise the prevailing distribution of geopolitical influence. Initial plans dated back to the seventeenth century. By the middle of the nineteenth century, the United States and Britain sought to minimize friction

**BOX 1-3**

## How Come Gitmo?

Despite a half-century of hostilities with Cuba, the United States continues to retain a large-scale naval base at Guantánamo Bay (fondly known as "Gitmo") on the southeast corner of the island. With over 9,500 troops, it is the oldest U.S. overseas base and the only one in a communist country. How could this possibly be?

It all goes back to the war of 1898, when American forces (including Teddy Roosevelt and his "Rough Riders") helped drive the Spanish out of Cuba and imposed a military government. In 1901 the United States declared that its troops would not leave the island unless Cuba's constitutional convention adopted the Platt Amendment authorizing U.S. intervention. The Cubans reluctantly agreed.

In 1903 Mr. Roosevelt, now president, signed a lease with the new Cuban government for exclusive and perpetual use of Guantánamo Bay and the surrounding areas. Article II stipulated that the United States was to use these locations "exclusively as coaling or naval stations, and for no other purpose." The annual rent was fixed at $2,000, payable in gold coins.

Thirty years later another Roosevelt, FDR, proclaimed his Good Neighbor policy and dissolved the Platt Amendment. He wanted to protect Guantánamo, however, and secured a new treaty after dispatching a fleet of warships to Cuban waters in 1934. The annual payment was changed to 4,085 American dollars—and has remained at that level over the years. FDR visited the facility in 1939 and 1940, as did President Harry Truman in 1948.

After the triumph of the Cuban Revolution in 1959, Fidel Castro cashed the first rent check—and since that time has refused, as a matter of honor, to accept any subsequent payments. United States government lawyers have argued that his cashing of that first check signifies a de facto ratification of the lease, thus obviating questions about violation of sovereignty and illegal military occupation.

Despite the terms of the lease, the Guantánamo base was used to house rafters from Cuba and Haiti and refugees from Kosovo near the end of the twentieth century. And since 9/11, it has served as a prison for hundreds of suspected terrorists and enemies of the United States.

Use of the base as a detention center has sparked intense and angry controversy. Classified as "nonlegal combatants," instead of prisoners of war, detainees have been denied basic rights. They have been subjected to torture, including waterboarding. Amnesty International has denounced the prison as "a human rights scandal," and international organizations around the world have called for its closure.

Upon taking office in January 2009 President Barack Obama issued an executive order to shut down the facility—which would require the transfer or release or detainees. The U.S. Congress refused to authorize funds for these purposes, however, so nothing was accomplished. As of September 2012 there were 167 prisoners still at the base.

Over the years, the Castro regime has chosen not to make Guantánamo a major issue. It has not wanted to risk forceful retaliation by a wrathful American government. And within the international arena, Cuba's tolerance of the base has become a convenient sign of its diplomatic flexibility. Besides, the negative publicity surrounding America's use (or misuse) of the facility has worked to Cuba's political advantage. Why change that?

resulting from their own competing claims by concurring, in the Clayton-Bulwer treaty of 1850, that any such canal would be a joint Anglo-American project. Like so many diplomatic accords, this one was made to be broken.

Attention focused principally on Nicaragua, whose lakes and rivers offered a promising site, and on Panama, a province of Colombia at the narrowest point on the isthmus. In 1878 the Colombian government authorized a French group under Ferdinand de Lesseps, builder of the Suez Canal, to dig a route through Panama. United States engineers continued to favor Nicaragua, and a North American firm received a contract to begin excavation in that country. Then came the financial Panic of 1893, when both groups ran out of money and quit.

Popular interest in Central America quickened as a result of the Spanish-American War. As a bitter internal struggle within Colombia was nearing its end in 1903, Washington dispatched troops to quell disorder in Panama. The resulting crisis eventually led to the Hay-Herrán treaty, an agreement that authorized the United States to build a canal in Panama. The U.S. Congress eagerly approved the document—but the Colombian legislature, unwilling to compromise national sovereignty, refused to go along.

The United States then fomented insurrection. With Roosevelt's full knowledge, Philippe Buneau-Varilla (the de Lesseps chief engineer) started laying plans for a separatist rebellion in Panama. As the uprising began, U.S. ships prevented Colombian troops from crossing the isthmus to Panama City. Within days Washington extended recognition to the newly sovereign government of Panama and received Buneau-Varilla (still a French citizen) as its official representative. United States Secretary of State John Hay and Buneau-Varilla hastily signed a treaty giving the United States control of a ten-mile-wide canal zone "in perpetuity . . . as it if were sovereign." A pliant Panamanian legislature soon approved the document. As Roosevelt would reportedly boast: "I took the Canal Zone."

Opened in 1914, the canal immediately became a major international waterway, and the Panamanian government began receiving steady annuities. The Canal Zone became a de facto U.S. colony, an area of legal privilege and country-club prosperity that stood in sharp and conspicuous contrast to local society. Outside the Zone, Panama developed the characteristics that typified Central America as a whole: dependence on agricultural exports (especially bananas), reliance on the U.S. market, and domestic control by a tightly knit landed oligarchy. Washington had established a protectorate that would help promote, protect, and extend its commercial empire. With possession of the canal, the United States completed its century-long efforts to gain territorial footholds around the Caribbean Basin.

## RECIPE FOR INTERVENTION

Effective maintenance of the U.S. sphere of influence required the exclusion of powers external to the hemisphere. In flagrant contravention of the Monroe Doctrine, however, naval forces from Germany and Great Britain launched an armed intervention against Venezuela in December 1902 to collect debts due their citizens. Italy soon joined the assault. As fighting intensified the Argentine foreign minister, Luis María Drago, urged Washington to proclaim its opposition to the use of armed force by any European power against any American nation for the purpose of collecting debts. It was Drago's intention, however naive, that this stipulation would become a multilateral inter-American policy, not a unilateral U.S. assertion.

The Roosevelt administration was unhappy with the European incursion, especially after an arbitral court decided largely in favor of the interventionist powers, but was also cool to Drago's idea of multilateral consultation. In 1904 the president finally responded with a proclamation:

> Any country whose people conduct themselves well can count upon our hearty friendship. If a nation shows that it knows how to act with reasonable efficiency and decency in social and political matters, if it keeps order and pays its obligations, it need fear no interference from the United States. Chronic wrong-doing, or an impotence which results in a general loosening of the ties of society, may in America, as elsewhere, ultimately require intervention by some civilized nation, and in the Western Hemisphere the adherence of the United States to the Monroe Doctrine may force the United States, however reluctantly, in flagrant cases of such wrong-doing or impotence, to the exercise of an international police power.

To avoid any pretext for intervention by Europe, in other words, the United States would assume responsibility for maintaining order in the hemisphere. And despite Drago's hopes, the United States would act on a unilateral basis.

This statement of policy became instantly known as the "Roosevelt Corollary" to the Monroe Doctrine. It was aimed at major extrahemispheric powers, assuring them that the United States would guarantee order (and fulfillment of obligations on debts) throughout the region, and also at the governments of Latin America, warning them that the United States would take military action in the face of "wrong-doing or impotence." The United States thus proclaimed itself a hegemon.

The mere proclamation of U.S. hegemony throughout the Western Hemisphere did not, of course, bring it into effect. Throughout the early twentieth century, European interests would continue to play a major role throughout the region. Great Britain still held colonies in the Caribbean and maintained close commercial ties with Chile and especially Argentina. Germany would attempt to lure Mexico to its side during World War I through the Zimmerman Telegram, offering to restore lands lost during the "war of the North American invasion" in return for diplomatic and logistical support. With possessions of its own in the Americas, France would nurture cultural and intellectual ties throughout the region. Ultimately, it was a chain of events and processes in the global arena at large, not boisterous declarations of U.S. intent, that led to the eventual fulfillment of America's imperial pretensions.

## QUESTIONS FOR REVIEW

1. What were the basic rules of the "European game"? How did colonial expansion relate to the geopolitical balance of power among major nations?
2. What led the United States to enter the global competition for imperial power? Was there any serious choice in the matter? And how did U.S. imperial strategies differ from those of European countries?
3. What was the immediate purpose and ultimate significance of the Monroe Doctrine?
4. What explains U.S. ambivalence about Latin America's independence from Spain?
5. Why did Cuba occupy such a special place in the minds of U.S. policymakers? What prevented Cuba's annexation to the United States?

# CHAPTER 2

# The Gospel of Democracy

We must Consider that we shall be a City upon a Hill, the eyes
of all people are upon us.

JOHN WINTHROP (1630)

Cabalistic phrases [are designed to hold the citizenry] spell
bound, as if the lies of magic were realities and a syllable or
two of gibberish could reverse all the laws of nature and turn
human intelligence into brutishness. One of these is "Our
manifest destiny," a shallow and impious phrase. Who shall
assure that it is not of the "Devil's fetching." . . . Oh, miserable
humbug of History!

NATIONAL INTELLIGENCER (1848)

A central tenet in America's national creed has endowed the United States with
a political mission: spreading the gospel of democracy throughout the world.
During the nineteenth century this belief served to legitimize imperial behavior
and dignify unseemly conquests, at least in the eyes of the beholders. Implicitly,
the credo sustained the argument that Europe, monarchical and unrepublican,
should stay out of the Western Hemisphere. During the early twentieth century
it provided a rationale for intervention in the affairs of sovereign nations of Latin
America. Under the rubric of the "Good Neighbor" policy, the United States
throughout the 1930s relaxed its efforts to export democracy.

## ROLES OF IDEOLOGY

The basic purpose of these intellectual acrobatics was to provide an explanation
and *justification* for U.S. imperialism, territorial and commercial. Though ideas can
acquire a life of their own, the driving goals of U.S. policy toward Latin America
were economic and political expansion. In this context the role of ideology was to
provide a cohesive interpretation of U.S. behavior, to imbue it with a higher purpose, and to present the issues at hand in satisfying and self-serving terms.

This was not merely an academic exercise. The persistent invocation of the
ideals of democracy represented efforts to redefine the substance of conflict, to seize
control of the agenda, to capture the terms of debate, and to shape the outcome of

the struggle itself. Ideology tends toward simplification. By providing a "cognitive map" of reality, ideology reduces complex issues to straightforward and usually simplistic terms that not only provide a pleasing and coherent explanation but also suggest a prescription for action.

Regarding U.S. relations with Latin America, this rhetoric was aimed at three main audiences. One consisted of domestic society. For national leaders, the definition of U.S. policy as fulfillment of a higher mission could assist in the mobilization of resources. Everything else being equal, American citizens preferred to believe that their efforts were serving some noble purpose rather than material self-interest. Ideology could also provide leaders with weapons for weakening and silencing domestic opposition. Objections to official policy would not merely express disagreement on tactics or strategy; they would constitute disloyalty.

The second audience consisted of rival powers, especially in Europe. The deployment of ideological rhetoric served to emphasize the importance of the matter at hand, warning outside rivals that interference on their part would tread on hallowed ground. Ideology underlined national purpose and will. At the same time it presented would-be rivals with an intellectual challenge. Unless they could produce an ideological rationalization of their own, one that was plausible if not superior, they would be discouraged from action. Throughout history, of course, imperial powers justified their actions in terms of a higher mission. Either they struggled for monopoly over claims to a single shared mission, as in the case of sixteenth-century Portugal and Spain; or they confronted each other and the international community with alternative declarations of purpose. In either event, ideological disputation remained part and parcel of imperialistic rivalry and contestation.

A third audience consisted of the subjugated societies. In this context, the role of ideological indoctrination—epitomized by missionary activities and educational campaigns—was to engender a rationale for acceptance by local peoples of new power arrangements. The colonized could interpret the new situation not so much as national (or societal) defeat but as a march toward higher truth. Special emphasis was placed on leadership groups and those who could serve as go-betweens (and who would usually benefit handsomely as a result). Ultimately, the achievement of voluntary acquiescence within the subordinate society was crucial to imperial power and to the imposition of durable hegemony. Otherwise, rule must rest on the perpetual use or threat of force—which was costly, inefficient, and counterproductive. Ideology was serious business.

## THE MEANINGS OF MANIFEST DESTINY

Every nation has its own mythology. For the United States, the capstone idea has defined American purpose as a quest for national greatness and the promotion of political democracy. As Thomas Paine declared in *Common Sense*, his famous call for independence in 1776, "We have it in our power to begin the world all over again." This was not a modest claim. In the eyes of British (and other European) observers of the time, such brash expressions of self-importance must have looked preposterous.

America's emerging ideology drew a fundamental distinction between the New World and the Old, between America and Europe. These were to be two separate spheres. An early exponent of U.S. views on the world, Paine gave explicit formulation to this credo by stressing, first, the fact that immigrants had crossed the ocean precisely to escape from Europe: "This New World has been the asylum for the persecuted and the lovers of civil and religious liberty from *every* part of Europe." Second, Paine took notice of geography, especially the Atlantic Ocean, observing that "even the distance at which the Almighty has placed England and America is a strong and natural proof that the authority of the one over the other was never the design of heaven." And third, he combined historical with religious interpretation: "The time likewise at which the continent was discovered adds weight to the argument, and the manner in which it was peopled increases the force of it. The Reformation was preceded by the discovery of America—as if the Almighty meant to open sanctuary to the persecuted."

A central element in this mythology was belief in providential benediction. It was God in Heaven, not just earthly mortals, who endowed American society with its virtues and its purposes. The pursuit of national greatness therefore could not be a matter of choice. It was a sacred *obligation*. Just as sixteenth-century Spaniards persuaded themselves that they were performing God's will, so did eighteenth-century Americans and their descendants. It was incumbent upon them to act as they did; otherwise they could be committing sacrilege as well as treason.

This sense of heavenly mission led to an emphasis on national uniqueness, a fundamental belief in the exceptionalism of the United States. Not only was America distinct from Europe; as the bastion of democracy, it stood apart from other nations as a City on a Hill. With regard to foreign policy, this conviction encouraged contradictory impulses. On the one hand, it gave rise to the notion that the United States was exceptional, superior, a truly chosen land whose political ideals and institutions could (by definition) never flourish anywhere else. This was an isolationist idea. On the other hand, the sense of uniqueness shaped and defined the political obligation to spread the gospel of democracy. This was an activist idea. Imbued with this conviction, many American leaders could not rest content with the construction of a working democracy at home. They felt charged to *extend* the virtues of this idea to other parts of the globe, thus carrying out the divine task of political civilization.

Territorial expansion in the nineteenth century required and reinforced a righteous definition for U.S. national purpose. As President James K. Polk contested Britain's claim to the Oregon territory and prepared for war in Mexico during the 1840s, a young newspaper editor named John L. O'Sullivan invoked providential will. The U.S. claim, he asserted in the *New York Morning News,* "is by the right of our manifest destiny to overspread and to possess the whole of the continent which Providence has given us for the development of the great experiment of liberty and federated self-government entrusted to us." Cast in these terms, it was America's mission to democratize the continent.

Thus emerged the idea of "manifest destiny." This was more than a catch-phrase or slogan. It was a concept that crystallized a sense of national purpose, providing both an explanation and a rationalization for U.S. territorial expansion. The seizure of lands represented not avarice but "destiny," a heaven-sent fate that mere mortals could neither prevent nor ignore. This destiny was, moreover, clearly "manifest," a self-evident truth that was plain for all to see. Of course this assertion was not subject to empirical proof or verification. It was held to be transparently true, and it was therefore not a subject for argumentation.

O'Sullivan's newspaper eagerly applied the implications of the doctrine to the Texas question. As debate mounted over the possible incorporation of Texas into the Union, the *New York Morning News* in 1845 blithely interpreted its annexation as a logical expression of historical processes:

> From the time that the Pilgrim Fathers landed on these shores to the present moment, the older settlements have been constantly throwing off a hardy, rest-less and lawless pioneer population, which has kept in advance, subduing the wilderness and preparing the way for more orderly settlers who tread rapidly upon their footsteps . . . As their numbers increased, law and order obtained control, and those unable to bear constraint sought new homes. These latter have rolled forward in advance of civilization, like the surf on an advancing wave, indicative of its restless approach. This is the natural, unchangeable effect of our position upon this continent, and it must continue until the waves of the Pacific have hemmed in and restrained the onward movement.

Thus did the *Morning News* resolve doubts about the validity of annexation. Tongue in cheek, the editorial also proffered an olive branch to Mexico: If the country permitted itself to be overtaken by the "Anglo-Saxon race," it, too, would become able to apply for admission to the United States.

Not surprisingly, there existed some uncertainty about precise boundaries for the extension of the nation's mission. Some commentators cast longing eyes on Canada; others claimed that the United States should take all of Mexico. As Daniel S. Dickinson of New York proclaimed in the Senate, during deliberations over the Treaty of Guadalupe Hidalgo, the United States still had some way to go: "New territory is spread out for us to subdue and fertilize; new races are presented for us to civilize, educate and absorb; new triumphs for us to achieve for the cause of freedom. North America presents to the eye one great geographical system . . . And the period is by no means remote, when . . . [North America] shall be united . . . in one political system, and that, a free, confederated, self governed Republic." Others went even farther. Editor James Gordon Bennett would assert in the *New York Herald,* in 1845, that "the arms of the republic . . . must soon embrace the whole hemisphere, from the icy wilderness of the North to the most prolific regions of the smiling and prolific South." Anglo-Saxons and their "free institutions" were plainly on the march.

The prospect of manifest destiny encompassed significant subthemes. One stressed the notion of America's youth, in implicit contrast to the decrepit Old World of Europe. "Too young to be corrupt," in the words of the *United States Journal,* "it is Young America, awakened to a sense of her own intellectual greatness and her soaring spirit." Fresh, eager, innocent, the United States was coming into its own as a power. Another subtheme challenged European principles of international law, codes that had arisen to regulate intercourse among nations and to sustain the post-Westphalian balance of power. Indeed, O'Sullivan explicitly dismissed "all those antiquated materials of old black-letter international law" in his initial promulgation of the doctrine. Within the Western Hemisphere, in short, the United States would not be constrained by classical rules of law. They applied to Europe, not to the Americas.

Yet another claim stressed the institutional virtues of states' rights. According to O'Sullivan and his cohorts, governmental federation offered an ideal formula for territorial expansion through the incorporation of new states, one at a time: "How magnificent in conception!" O'Sullivan exclaimed. "How beneficent in practice is this system, which associates nations in one great family compact, without destroying the social identity, or improperly constraining the individual genius of any; and cements into elements of strength and civilization those very sources of difference which have heretofore destroyed the peace of mankind!" New states could join the Union without upsetting the structure of government. Added a writer in the *Democratic Review,* the discovery of such a benevolent prescription could only be "an emanation from Providence." God spoke in clear as well as mysterious ways.

Despite its vigor, the summons to manifest destiny contained a good deal of ambiguity. One source of uncertainty concerned the question of inevitability versus agency, passivity versus activism. To what extent was the American future already foreordained and therefore bound to occur as the result of automatic processes? Or would it require decisive action on the part of leaders and citizens? Characteristically, the issue acquired its most explicit form in debates over the need for military action. In discussions over the Oregon question, John C. Calhoun, soon to oppose the war with Mexico, gave clear expression to the passive school of thought:

> *Time* is acting for us; and, if we shall have the wisdom to trust its operation, it will assert and maintain our right with resistless force, without costing a cent of money, or a drop of blood. . . . Our population is rolling toward the shores of the Pacific with an impetus greater than what we realize.

After all, one might have argued, if the nation truly had a "destiny," and a "manifest" one at that, why not simply await its arrival?

On the other side, war hawks expressed no apprehensions about military intervention. Destiny was something to be seized, not passively awaited. As hostilities mounted with Mexico, the definition of national purpose broadened in scope. In his annual message of 1847, Polk declared that U.S. action now had a political goal, the prevention of monarchy in Mexico. That same year the *Boston*

*Times* proclaimed that military conquest by the United States "must necessarily be a great blessing to the conquered. It is a work worthy of a great people, of a people who are about to regenerate the world by asserting the supremacy of humanity over the accidents of birth and fortune." Echoed Moses Y. Beach, editor of the New York *Sun*: "The [Mexican] race is perfectly accustomed to being conquered, and the only lesson we shall teach is that our victories will give liberty, safety, and prosperity to the vanquished, if they know enough to profit by the appearance of our stars. To *liberate* and *ennoble*—not to *enslave* and *debase*—is our mission." War thus offered the key to fulfillment of national ideals.

The greater the degree of military action, in other words, the more expansive the definition of national purpose. At the outset of the Mexican War, the concept of manifest destiny applied to areas of Mexico—ultimately from Texas to California— that would be taken from the country and incorporated into the United States. As U.S. troops hammered their way into Mexico City, however, there emerged yet another intention, the liberation and democratization of Mexico. Years later a sophisticated and skeptical observer, James Russell Lowell, would neatly capture this relationship: The deeper and deeper the military penetration, he wrote in the *Biglow Papers*, "our Destiny higher an' higher kep' mountin.'"

## OBSTACLES TO DEMOCRACY

Spreading the gospel of democracy would be no easy task, as U.S. leaders clearly recognized. And in nineteenth-century perspective, Latin America looked like unpromising soil. One line of reasoning focused on the trajectory of Latin America's history, on the forces giving shape to what would now be called political culture. Prominent among these were the character of Spain, the influence of Catholicism, and the effects of climate. And absolutely crucial, as later explained, was the difficult question of race.

### History and Character

A skeptical view of Latin America's capacity for democracy came from Thomas Jefferson as early as 1811, as he reflected on the wars for independence from Spain. "Another great field of political experiment is opening," Jefferson wrote to DuPont de Nemours, and yet "I fear the degrading ignorance into which their priests and kings have sunk them, has disqualified them from the maintenance or even knowledge of their rights, and that much blood may be shed for little improvement in their condition." It would take at least a generation to uproot the legacies of monarchism and Catholicism. Jefferson was particularly harsh on the impact of the Catholic Church. In 1813 he would surmise that "History, I believe, furnishes no example of a priest-ridden people maintaining a free civil government. This marks the lowest grade of ignorance, of which their civil as well as religious leaders will always avail themselves for their own purposes."

John Quincy Adams, eventual author of the Monroe Doctrine, advocated a constructive but cautious stance toward Spanish American independence. The promotion of democracy "by all the moral influence which we can exercise, whether by example, of friendly counsel, or of persuasion, is among the duties which devolve upon us in the formation of our future relations with our southern neighbors." Faced with pressure to extend diplomatic recognition to the new republics, the secretary of state expressed doubt that U.S. influence would have much positive effect: "I wished well to their cause," he carefully explained, "but I had seen and yet see no prospect that they would establish free or liberal institutions of government. . . . They have not the first elements of good or free government." The less the contact, the better for the United States. Intercourse could only bring contamination.

A more optimistic assessment came from Henry Clay of Kentucky, who consistently promoted the granting of diplomatic recognition to the newly independent countries of the region. His argument had two contentions. One focused on the international arena, maintaining that new governments throughout the region "would be animated by an American feeling, and guided by an American policy," even if dictatorial in form. They would thus provide a bulwark against European influence. The other focused on domestic political processes, holding that cooperation would lead to democratization in Spanish America through a kind of demonstration effect. By granting diplomatic recognition, Clay predicted,

> We should become the center of a system which would constitute the rallying point of human wisdom against all the despotism of the Old World. Did any man doubt the feelings of the South toward us? In spite of our coldness toward them, of the rigor of our laws, and the conduct of our officers, their hearts still turned toward us, as to their brethren; and . . . if our Government would take the lead and recognize them, they would become yet more anxious to imitate our institutions, and to secure to themselves and their posterity the same freedom which we enjoy.

Recognition would lead to diplomatic cooperation, which would in turn promote democracy. When all was said and done, however, Clay's grandiose formula called for relatively modest measures by the United States.

Territorial expansion, especially the war with Mexico and anticipations of Cuba, required an activist doctrine. It was essential, in light of national mythology, for newly acquired lands and peoples to experience the blessings of democracy. In 1854 one enthusiastic legislator justified a potential military takeover of Cuba as an uplifting missionary enterprise:

> We absorb to elevate; we rule by bestowing on the governed a share of political power. Sir, we are destined to expand by assimilation, and by elevating those who have been misgoverned and oppressed to the rank of freemen. . . . We conquer that we may raise the conquered to an equality with ourselves; we annex to assimilate others with us on a higher scale of humanity.

Acquisition was thus an act of liberation for the "misgoverned and oppressed." Once incorporated into the United States, they would be free to climb upward to "a higher scale of humanity." Others saw persisting problems with the pearl of the

Antilles. "The people of Cuba speak a different language," one congressman later recounted, "they profess a different religion, and they are of different extraction from us; and our people have regarded them as aliens and outlaws from the pale of humanity and civilization. . . . I think I have been at more respectable weddings than it would be to bring her into the household [Laughter]."

In the late 1890s the imminence of the Spanish-American War prompted denunciation of Spain's historical record and, particularly, its cruelty to native populations, thus reviving the "black legend" espoused by rival imperial powers in the sixteenth and seventeenth centuries. As one war hawk proclaimed:

> Spain has been tried and convicted in the forum of history. Her religion has been bigotry, whose sacraments have been solemnized by the faggot and the rack. Her statesmanship has been infamy: her diplomacy, hypocrisy: her wars have been massacres: her supremacy has been a blight and a curse, condemning continents to sterility, and their inhabitants to death.

This condemnation possessed a double edge. On the one hand, it provided a rationalization for war against Spain. On the other, it suggested that the legacy of such perfidious rule would severely impede the installation of democracy. This confronted U.S. leaders with an unsolvable dilemma: the worse the qualities of the society at hand, the greater the need for military intervention—and the less the chance for democratic rule.

Climate presented yet another obstacle. Carl Schurz and other respected authorities forcefully argued that the tropics were unfit for democracy; instead they were conducive to laziness, licentiousness, and irresponsibility. When the U.S. Congress was considering how to deal with new territorial acquisitions, Richard F. Pettigrew, senator from the temperate state of South Dakota, rejected annexation of Hawaii in 1898 on the ground that "republics cannot live" in "tropical countries." And in subsequent debates on Puerto Rico, Representative James L. Slayden of Texas took it upon himself to formulate pseudoscientific principles, observing that "The Tropics seems to heat the blood while enervating the people who inhabit them." People who live within twenty degrees of the equator, Slayden solemnly concluded, "neither comprehend nor support representative government constructed on the Anglo-Saxon plan."

## The Problem of Race

More pervasive than concerns about historical formation and national character were preoccupations about race. These issues were closely interrelated, since racial composition was interpreted as a central feature of national character. In the view of nineteenth-century Americans (and many of their descendants), the conviction was unshakeable: Nonwhite peoples were incapable of responsible self-government and were therefore unsuited to democracy.

The intellectual foundation for this conclusion rested not only on racial prejudice, as it did, but also on a hierarchical notion of competence that reflected and expressed God's manifest will. At the top of this pyramid were Anglo-Saxons, the hardiest and strongest of all whites: "Out of all the inhabitants of the world," one polemicist boasted in the late nineteenth century, "a select stock, the Saxon, and out of this the British family, the noblest of the stock, was chosen to people our country." John W. Burgess, a well-known professor at Columbia University in this same era, confirmed as indisputable fact the contemporary notion that "there are vast differences in political capacity between the races, that it is the white man's mission, his duty, and his right to hold the reins of political power in his own hands for the civilization of the world and the welfare of mankind."

Asians of pure heritage, Chinese and Japanese, fell in the middle of this scheme, as did Spaniards and other southern Europeans. At the bottom were blacks and Indians, widely regarded as hopelessly beyond redemption. Mixed-bloods occupied an ambivalent position. Some observers regarded the mixture of races as a means of uplifting character and quality over generations; others denounced it as a path to degradation and perdition. In 1848 the *Cincinnati Gazette* expressed its considered opinion that, in general, mixed races "unite in themselves all the faults, without any of the virtues of their progenitors; as men they are generally inferior to the pure races, and as members of society they are the worst class of citizens." Standards for judgment not only involved racial background; they also demanded racial purity.

War with Mexico raised the problem of racial assimilation in clear and forceful fashion. Early in his career James Buchanan had denounced "the imbecile and indolent Mexican race." And as debate mounted in the late 1840s over ratification of the Treaty of Guadalupe Hidalgo, the *New York Evening Post* went straight to the heart of the problem:

> The Mexicans are *Indians*—Aboriginal Indians. Such Indians as Cortez conquered three thousand [*sic*] years ago, only rendered a little more mischievous by a bastard civilization. The infusion of European blood whatever it is, and that, too, infused in a highly *illegitimate way*, is not enough, as we see, to affect the character of the people. They do not possess the elements of an *independent* national existence. . . . Providence has so ordained it, and it is folly not to recognize the fact. The Mexicans are *Aboriginal Indians*, and they must share the destiny of their race.

Whatever its longevity, European and Spanish influence was negligible. As Indians, the Mexican people were beyond redemption—and therefore suitable only for conquest and servitude.

At the same time, racist formulations provided arguments for opposition to the war. John C. Calhoun, that redoubtable champion of states' rights and slavery, foresaw nothing but trouble in the annexation of Mexico, proclaiming that "we have never dreamt of incorporating into our Union any but the Caucasian race—the free white race. To incorporate Mexico, would be the very first instance of the kind, of incorporating an Indian race. . . . I protest against such a union as that! Ours, sir, is the Government of a white race." Only the "free white race" was capable of democratic government. The United States should therefore resist the temptation to seize control of Mexico.

Departing from similar racist premises, others came to advocate a compromise: Their solution was to take as much land from Mexico with as few people as possible. The purpose of the Treaty of Guadalupe Hidalgo was acquisition of territory, according to the *Louisville Democrat*, not incorporation of citizens:

> Besides, we have by this treaty, not the best boundary, but all the territory of value that we can get without taking the people. The people of the settled parts of Mexico are a negative quantity. We fear the land, minus the people, is not worth much. We think all Mexico will fall, piece by piece, into this government; but then it must first be settled by a different population, and the union effected by other means than the sword.

In the long run, the United States could confidently await alteration of the ethnic composition of Mexican society. With this accomplished the entire country would fall, "piece by piece," into the control of the United States. Racial rearrangements would provide the key to imperial expansion.

Decades later the issue would again emerge. In reference to potential annexation of the Philippines, John W. Daniels, a senator from Virginia, expressed horror in 1899 over the prospect of assimilating "this mess of Asiatic pottage" into American society. Unfazed by such logic, annexationists turned the racist argument to their own advantage. Filipinos were indeed "a decadent race," according to Senator Albert J. Beveridge, but this simply defined the nature of the imperialist challenge. After Rudyard Kipling's notorious ditty on the "White Man's Burden" appeared in *McClure's Magazine* in 1899, Teddy Roosevelt concluded that it was "very poor poetry but made good sense from the expansion point of view." As Roosevelt and others saw it, empires around the world were engaged in the task of uplifting inferior races. In this respect, Roosevelt conceded, the United States was just like any other imperial power.

Fulfillment of divine obligation nonetheless raised a fundamental question: how to incorporate the newly subjugated peoples. The prospect of eventual citizenship ran directly into the problem of race. As Senator Henry M. Teller of Colorado explained, "I would a great deal rather make the Philippine Islands a colony, a province, a dependency, or whatever you may choose to call it, than to make their inhabitants citizens of the United States . . . that they shall stand before the law on an equality with all other citizens of the United States." Cuba, with its large black population, posed an even greater challenge. Southerners were especially quick to express apprehensions. Benjamin F. Tillman, a rural populist from South Carolina (fondly known as "Pitchfork Ben"), explained his opposition to outright annexation after the Spanish-American War in frankly racist terms:

> It was not because we are Democrats, but because we understand and realize what it is to have two races side by side that cannot mix or mingle without deterioration and injury to both and the ultimate destruction of the civilization of the higher. We of the South have borne this white man's burden of a colored race in our midst since their emancipation and before.

The burden, he warned colleagues from the North, would be heavier than they might expect.

Senators were listening. Orville H. Platt, author of the Platt Amendment, expressed fervent opposition to the incorporation of Cuba because "The people of Cuba, by reason of race and characteristic, cannot be easily assimilated by us.... Their presence in the American union, as a state, would be most disturbing." A few years later John W. Foster, who had served as secretary of state in 1892–1893, would draw a clear connection between domestic and foreign policies: "With the negro problem in our Southern States pressing upon us for solution . . . do we desire to aggravate the situation by adding a million more of the despised race to our voting population?" Partly in response to such concerns, Cuba was granted independence—of the most nominal kind—in 1902. There continued to be occasional talk of annexation or incorporation after a due process of "Americanization," but the racial barrier presented a persisting obstacle. Commenting on an insurrection by Cuban blacks in 1911, one observer noted that "Cuba may need us, but we do not need the Cubans. They, as a mass, are a degenerate race lacking in all the instincts of civic pride or honor and utterly disregarding all moral obligations to themselves." Better to keep a safe distance.

In the end, racism bore a paradoxical relationship to U.S. imperialism. On the one hand, prejudicial disdain for colored peoples offered justification for the forceful acquisition of influence and territory. Since the resident nonwhite population was (by definition) unsuited to develop the land and construct a civilized society, that obligation—that "burden"—fell to members of the more highly endowed Anglo-Saxon race. On the other hand, the presence of nonwhite peoples in newly dominated lands posed the unwelcome possibility that they might have to be incorporated into American society, thus altering its racial composition and lowering its quality. Racism thus *promoted* imperialist expansion by the United States but also *restricted* it as well.

It was largely because of these ideological contradictions that, by the turn of the century, U.S. leaders turned away from the outright annexation of territory toward the construction of protectorates and colonies, which offered a permanent source of influence; or toward periodic episodes of military intervention, which provided regular (if intermittent) sources of influence. A commercial empire did not necessarily require a permanent military or administrative presence. By contrast, invasions and protectorates would prove cost effective.

## INTERVENTION FOR DEMOCRACY

Between 1898 and 1934 the United States launched more than thirty military interventions in Latin America. (According to one quaint but telling definition, a military intervention consists of the dispatch of armed troops from one country to another "for other than ceremonial purposes.") There were varied motivations for these actions. One was the protection of U.S. economic interests, especially private loans to local governments. Another was the assertion of geopolitical hegemony,

Table 2-1  U.S. Military Interventions in the Caribbean Basin, 1898–1934

| COUNTRY | INTERVENTIONS |
| --- | --- |
| Costa Rica | 1921 |
| Cuba | 1898–1902, 1906–1909, 1912, 1917–1922 |
| Dominican Republic | 1903, 1904, 1914, 1916–1924 |
| Guatemala | 1920 |
| Haiti | 1915–1934 |
| Honduras | 1903, 1907, 1911, 1912, 1919, 1924, 1925 |
| Mexico | 1913, 1914, 1916–1917, 1918–1919 |
| Nicaragua | 1898, 1899, 1909–1910, 1912–1925, 1926–1933 |
| Panama | 1903–1914, 1921, 1925 |

Source: Adapted from William Appleman Williams, *Empire as a Way of Life* (New York: Oxford University Press, 1980), pp. 136–142, 165–167.

in keeping with the Roosevelt Corollary, thus assuring European powers that they need not meddle in the hemisphere; during and after World War I, protection of the Panama Canal assumed special importance. In all cases, the perpetual rationalization was that the judicious application of military force by the United States would lead to the promotion of democracy throughout the region.

This component of U.S. policy focused exclusively on the greater Caribbean Basin, including Mexico and Central America. As shown in Table 2-1, the United States launched major operations during this period in Cuba, the Dominican Republic, Haiti, Honduras, Mexico, Nicaragua, and Panama. (There were threats of intervention on other occasions as well.) Some of these, as in Mexico, were relatively short-lived episodes. Others led to military occupations of several years' duration. In Nicaragua, American forces occupied the country almost constantly from 1909 to 1934; in Haiti, U.S. troops lingered from 1915 to 1934; in the Dominican Republic, they established military rule from 1916 to 1924. The basic goal of U.S. policy, as commentators repeatedly said, was to convert the Caribbean into an "American lake."

At the same time, Washington insisted that it was fulfilling a high-minded political mission. The principal exponent of this view was Woodrow Wilson, who eventually defined his purpose in World War I as making the world safe for democracy. As for the hemisphere, Wilson would exclaim: "We are the friends of constitutional government in America; we are more than its friends, we are its champions." And then he sternly vowed: "I am going to teach the South American republics to elect good men!" Viewing democracy as a universal possibility, the southern-born Wilson was implicitly rejecting prejudicial theories about historical, religious, and geographical limitations on the spread of political civilization. Through instruction, example, and the judicious application of force, even Latin Americans could learn the rules of democratic conduct.

Yet the conception of Latin American democracy, even for Wilson, had clear-cut limits. This was a period, it should be remembered, of substantial constraints on American democracy: Women acquired the right to vote only in 1920, organized labor was struggling to assert itself, and racial segregation meant the virtual exclusion of blacks from political life. And in view of popular skepticism about the political capability of Latin American peoples, the United States had precious little interest in promoting highly participative politics throughout the region. Instead, the preference, as political historian Paul W. Drake has pointed out, was for an "aristocratic republic." The insistence was on the maintenance of law and order. The one thing to avoid was mass-based social revolution. One of the nation's leading diplomatic experts on the region, Adolf A. Berle, Jr., would sum up this point succinctly: "I don't like revolutions on principle."

Most U.S. interventions displayed a consistent pattern. Military forces would arrive amid considerable fanfare; depose rulers, often with minimal force; install a hand-picked provisional government; supervise national elections; and then depart, mission accomplished. The political key to these operations was the holding of elections—which, as tangible signs of democracy at work, justified both the fact of intervention and the decision to lift the occupation. United States supervision of these contests was often overbearing, sometimes to the point of preselection of the winner, but the holding of elections was an essential step in the process. As one U.S. ambassador explained to his bewildered British counterparts, the United States would intervene as necessary in Latin America to "make 'em vote and live by their decisions." If rebellions follow, "We'll go in and make 'em vote again."

This sequence first took clear shape in 1906, when Teddy Roosevelt used the Platt Amendment as justification for dispatching troops to Cuba and installing William Howard Taft as provisional governor. The United States undertook to annul the elections of 1905, enact electoral legislation, and monitor a vote in 1909. As TR defined the mission to Taft in 1907: "Our business is to establish peace and order on a satisfactory basis, start the new government, and then leave the island." The United States followed a similar course in Panama, diligently overseeing elections in 1906, 1908, and 1912 (at this point dispatching troops for this purpose). Nicaragua received the same treatment and provided an opportunity for expostulation of U.S. policy toward the region as a whole. According to an official declaration in 1912: "The full measure and extent of our policy is to assist in the maintenance of republican institutions upon this hemisphere, and we are anxious that the experiment of a government of the people, for the people, and by the people shall not fail in any republic on this continent." Tacit reminiscence of the rolling cadences in Lincoln's Gettysburg Address could only serve to emphasize the point.

There were efforts to enshrine promotion of democracy as hemispheric principle. In 1907 an Ecuadorean diplomat named Carlos Tobar proposed the so-called Tobar Doctrine, under which American nations would refuse recognition to de facto regimes that had entered office by deposing constitutional governments. And in 1913 the United States would propound the Wilson Doctrine, which went one step farther by calling for the nonrecognition of all unconstitutional governments in Latin America. The U.S. stand was resisted by former Argentine foreign minister Estanislao Zeballos, among others, who saw it as a pretext for continuing and arbitrary North American intervention in domestic affairs of the region. Multilateralism did not flourish in this political arena.

## Taking Sides: The Mexican Revolution

The outburst in 1910 of a revolutionary movement in Mexico was deeply disturbing to Washington. American investors had profited handsomely under the decades-old government of Porfirio Díaz, which had, under the slogan of "peace and administration," promoted economic growth and political stability. Mexico was a source of special concern to the United States—because of its size, its resources, and its geographical proximity. And as a result of its presence and power, the United States exerted considerable influence in Mexican affairs. Uncertain and hesitant, Washington first resisted the Mexican Revolution and then took halting steps to direct its political course.

Ambassador Henry Lane Wilson (no relation to Woodrow) began overtly meddling in Mexican national politics as early as July 1911. Expressing his contempt for the newly installed government of Francisco Madero, the U.S.-educated idealist who had prompted the overthrow of Díaz, Wilson complained bitterly of "disrespect for constituted authority . . . a defiance of the law . . . lack of respect for property rights, violence, and rapine." A year later the United States officially protested crimes against American citizens in Mexico. Ambassador Wilson avidly sought Madero's resignation from the presidency and threatened U.S. military intervention in the event that he refused (President Taft would not, however, endorse this act of blackmail). Unchastened, the ambassador then undertook negotiations with Madero's counterrevolutionary opponents, Victoriano Huerta and Félix Díaz. Shortly thereafter Huerta deposed and murdered Madero. While not directly responsible for this assassination, an accredited U.S. diplomat had campaigned actively against an elected president of Mexico and expressed no palpable remorse over his demise. This is not remembered as a happy chapter in U.S.–Mexican relations.

To its credit, the Taft administration withheld recognition from Victoriano Huerta. Woodrow Wilson continued this policy after his election in November 1912, vowing: "I will not recognize a government of butchers." When Huerta refused to succumb to U.S. pressure, President Wilson in April 1914 lifted an embargo on arms shipments to Mexican rebels, secured British cooperation for economic sanctions against the Huerta regime, and authorized a naval occupation of the port of Veracruz. His ultimate goal, Wilson proclaimed, was the installation of "an orderly and righteous government in Mexico."

The action proved counterproductive, as political groups throughout Mexico denounced the invasion as an unwarranted assault on national sovereignty. Huerta resigned in July 1914, more as a result of his deteriorating military position than because of U.S. pressure, and Wilson seized the face-saving opportunity to

THE WHITE MAN'S BURDEN.

**The White Man's Burden.** This 1914 caricature manages to blend Woodrow Wilson's crusade for democracy with prevailing racist doctrine.
ARTIST: Rollin Kirby, 1875–1952.

withdraw the troops from Veracruz. Perhaps as a result of this experience, Wilson began to comprehend the complexity of the Mexican situation and the logic behind its revolutionary imperative. A year later the U.S. president observed, "The first and most essential step in settling the affairs of Mexico is not to call general elections. It seems to me necessary that a government essentially revolutionary in character should take action to institute reforms by decree before the full forms of the constitution are resumed." In Mexico, social justice would become a necessary prelude to democracy.

At a later stage in the Mexican Revolution, Wilson would dispatch another military mission. In March 1916 armed forces under Pancho Villa, who was feeling betrayed by lack of U.S. support, conducted a raid on the otherwise-insignificant town of Columbus, New Mexico, killing eighteen American citizens and burning the town beyond recognition. In retaliation Wilson launched a punitive expedition under General John J. ("Black Jack") Pershing, who scoured the inhospitable countryside for months in an unsuccessful effort to apprehend the villainous Villa. The goal of this expedition was not to overtake a government or oversee elections, however; it was simply to capture and punish Villa. In early 1917 the fruitless expedition was withdrawn, and Pershing was rewarded for his failure with promotion to leadership of U.S. forces in Europe after Wilson finally entered World War I.

United States military responses to the Mexican Revolution had three related goals: inflicting punishment on transgressors Huerta and Villa, and weakening their political position; protecting U.S. interests; and promoting political stability. What is perhaps most striking about these episodes, in light of the high stakes involved, was the timidity of U.S. incursions. They were profoundly offensive to Mexican patriots, understandably so, but they were remarkably limited in scope. But as other countries in the Caribbean were discovering, the pursuit of economic interests by the United States could result in long-term military occupations.

## Dollar Diplomacy I: The Dominican Republic (1916–1924)

As implied by the Roosevelt Corollary, the United States expressed continuing concern over the prospect that European creditors would persuade their governments to take military action against financially delinquent countries of the Caribbean Basin in order to permit collection on debts. In this sense, economic instability threatened U.S. designs on consolidation of an "American lake." Military incursions by British, German, or French forces would clearly undermine U.S. hegemony.

To forestall such possibilities, Washington developed a strategy that came to be known as "dollar diplomacy"—the deployment of private financial resources for the sake of geopolitical advantage. Specifically, the U.S. government encouraged American banking concerns to assume the debts of beleaguered countries in and around the Caribbean and promised to assist the financiers in the collection of their payments. One standard procedure was for U.S. officials to take charge of customs houses, a step that guaranteed timely payment on the rescheduled debts. The strategy served the interests of both Wall Street and Washington. President William Howard Taft was only half right when he described the policy as "substituting dollars for bullets"—relying on financiers instead of on marines. In actual fact, these tactics often led to long-term military occupation: Dollars and bullets went hand in hand.

One site for this scenario was the Dominican Republic, struggling under the weight of public debts owed to European creditors. When it failed to keep up with payments, rumors began circulating that French and Italian vessels were on their way to collect their debts by force. Alarmed by this prospect, Secretary of State John Hay instructed the U.S. representative in Santo Domingo, Thomas C. Dawson, to suggest that the Dominican government "request" the United States to take over management of the customs houses. The Dominicans reluctantly assented, and Teddy Roosevelt eventually reached an "executive protocol" in February 1907 stipulating that the U.S. president would appoint a customs collector for the Dominican Republic, the U.S. government would afford military protection, and the Dominican government would neither increase debts nor lower taxes without the consent of the United States. Moreover, the American receiver-general was to pay off the Dominican debt with $20 million borrowed through the brokerage firm of Kuhn, Loeb & Co. To ensure its payments to Kuhn, Loeb, the United States was entitled "to collect customs for fifty years." Under the terms of this 1907 agreement, the National City Bank of New York agreed to float a subsequent loan of $1.5 million to the Dominican government in 1914.

American financial control led to close political supervision. An uprising in 1911–1912 led U.S. representatives to propose, for the sake of stability, the resignation of a provisional president. In September 1913, William Jennings Bryan, Wilson's secretary of state, assured Dominican rulers that the United States would uphold the country's "lawful authorities." If rebellious factions took power, Washington would withhold diplomatic recognition and impound the Dominican share of customs receipts. Amid mounting tension the American minister in Santo Domingo arranged for new elections, which were held under the watchful eye of U.S. naval warships.

In 1916 a major insurrection prompted the landing of U.S. marines. Washington refused to recognize the temporary government of Francisco Henríquez y Carvajal unless he signed a new treaty granting U.S. control not only of customs but also of the treasury, the army, and the police. The president refused, customs payments stopped, and deadlock ensued. In November 1916, Captain H. S. Knapp, in command of the U.S. marines, declared outright martial law. Knapp summarily ousted Dominican officials, dissolved the legislature, forbade elections, levied taxes, imposed censorship, and declared himself "supreme legislator, supreme judge, and supreme executor." This was, in fine, a military dictatorship.

Under the U.S. regime additional bonds followed in 1921 and 1922. Invoking the 1907 agreement, U.S. naval authorities took it upon themselves to assure American bankers that customs duties "shall be collected and applied by an official appointed by the President of the United States and that the loan now authorized shall have a first lien upon such customs duties." Since the 1922 loan was repayable over a twenty-year period, this implied that the United States would retain control of the Dominican customs houses until 1942. After another election U.S. troops withdrew from the country in 1924, but only when the new Dominican leaders agreed to ratify the acts of the military government and to place the command of local armed forces under American officers.

## Dollar Diplomacy II: Nicaragua (1909–1925)

A special consideration about Nicaragua was the ever-present issue of a transisthmian canal. There were questions about financial stability and American loans, as in the Dominican Republic, but the prospect of a waterway tended to dominate the bilateral agenda. Even after completion of the Panama Canal, Washington continued to express interest in Nicaragua—if for no other reason than to prevent an extrahemispheric power from winning a rival concession. United States authorities were also eager to secure a naval base in the Gulf of Fonseca. Nicaragua entailed security interests.

The Taft administration frequently conveyed displeasure over the rule in Nicaragua of José Santos Zelaya, a Liberal who strongly resisted foreign control in negotiations over a canal route. In 1909 the capricious Zelaya ordered the execution of two North American adventurers. Secretary of State Philander C. Knox denounced Zelaya as "a blot upon the history of his country" and expelled Nicaragua's ambassador from the United States. The following year U.S. support for an anti-Zelaya revolt helped force the president to resign. Nicaragua was in chaos; the treasury was empty; European creditors were clamoring for payment on their bonds.

In October 1910 the State Department appointed Thomas C. Dawson, fresh from his exploits in the Dominican Republic, as a special agent to Nicaragua, with instructions to rehabilitate the nation's finances and "to negotiate a loan secured by a percentage of the customs revenues to be collected . . . in such a way as will certainly secure the loan and assure its object." Brown Brothers offered to float the Nicaraguan loan. Aboard an American warship, anti-Zelaya leaders consented to the so-called Dawson Pact, under which the United States would recognize their new Conservative government under several conditions: a constituent assembly would elect Juan José Estrada president and Adolfo Díaz vice president; a U.S.–Nicaraguan mixed commission would arbitrate outstanding financial questions; and a loan would be guaranteed by administration of the customs house in ways "satisfactory to both governments." News about the Dawson Pact unleashed a storm of controversy in Nicaragua, and the nation's constituent assembly promptly adopted a charter expressly prohibiting such arrangements as the customs house clause; under pressure from Washington, Estrada dissolved the assembly and called for new elections. Virulent protests forced Estrada to resign in favor of Adolfo Díaz. To keep Díaz in office, the United States responded by dispatching a warship.

By June 1911 a new bilateral agreement specified terms for authorization of $15 million in loans to Nicaragua, reaffirming U.S. control of customs. Nicaragua also pledged not to alter customs duties without U.S. approval. Later in the year Colonel Clifford D. Ham arrived to take charge of customs, in violation of the constitution, and in May 1912 the American bankers assumed all liabilities for debts owed to a syndicate in London. In exchange for this favor the New York financiers insisted on their right to "apply to the United States for protection against violation of the provisions of this agreement and for aid in the enforcement thereof."

---

### BOX 2-1

## Dollar Diplomacy and Social Darwinism

Rationalizations for U.S. policy toward Latin America have ranged far and wide. In this excerpt, F. M. Huntington Wilson (1875–1946), who served as assistant secretary of state during the Taft administration, draws a connection between American supremacy and laws of evolution.

Suffice it to say that the object of the Central American policy was "to substitute dollars for bullets," to create a material prosperity which should wean the Central Americans from their usual preoccupation of revolution. Those countries have great natural wealth. Lack of capital, lack of skill, and still more the absence of any guarantee against confiscation and destruction due to the frequent revolutions when law and order are thrown overboard, prevent the development of their natural wealth by the people themselves. The same conditions throttle their export trade and destroy their purchasing power. Attacks upon American interests, and even upon the personal safety of American planters and others engaged in those countries, call for our government's protection. . . .

The public revenues, especially the customs dues, must be placed out of reach of the revolutionary robber or the dictator. Capital must be brought in to establish peaceful husbandry and unmolested industry. Education and civilization must bring justice. A guiding hand must prevent foreign entanglements, which, under the Monroe Doctrine, straightway involves us. Even if the Monroe Doctrine had never been announced, common prudence would today force upon us the same policy from our southern border throughout the zone of the Caribbean. . . .

There are so many analogies between biology and international evolution that one may invoke a sort of "international biology." The march of civilization brooks no violation of the law of the survival of the fittest. Neighboring countries comprise an environment. The strongest will dominate that environment. Sentimental phrases about the sovereignty of weaker countries will no more permit them to run amuck with impunity than ranting about individual rights will permit an outrageous citizen to annoy a municipality and escape the police. The biological law of the tendency to revert to the lower type as the higher attributes are disused is at work among nations; and nature, in its rough method of uplift, gives sick nations strong neighbors and takes its inexorable course with private enterprise and diplomacy as its instruments. And this course is the best in the long run, for all concerned and for the world.

SOURCE: Robert H. Holden and Eric Zolov (eds.), *Latin America and the United States: A Documentary History*, 2nd ed. (New York: Oxford University Press, 2011), pp. 112–113.

Liberals continued to reject Conservative rule. An uprising in July 1912 brought the arrival of U.S. troops under the colorful Smedley Butler and then led to a full-scale intervention. United States Marines crushed the Liberal insurrection, established order, and oversaw elections—which were won, not surprisingly, by the congenial Adolfo Díaz. For twenty out of the next twenty-one years, U.S. marines would remain on Nicaraguan soil.

Combining concerns over debts and the canal route, the Bryan-Chamorro treaty in February 1916 called for a $3 million payment by the United States to Nicaragua in return for three concessions: (1) the exclusive right to construct a transisthmian canal, (2) a ninety-nine-year lease on two islands plus a naval base in the Gulf of Fonseca, and (3) a U.S. option to renew the naval base lease for an additional ninety-nine years. The $3 million would enable Nicaragua to pay off a large share of current debt. And for the United States, according to Colonel Ham, the Bryan-Chamorro agreement would forever eliminate "the danger of a foreign power seeking and obtaining those concessions," while it also forged "an important link in the chain . . . of preparedness and national defense, and the protection of our investment in the Panama Canal." In 1918 the two countries established a high commission on finances—with two Americans and one Nicaraguan. In effect, the United States created a protectorate in Nicaragua.

United States military occupation of Nicaragua led to conflict and tension. In February 1921 a group of U.S. marines wrecked the offices of a prominent newspaper. A clash in January 1922 resulted in the death of four Nicaraguan civilians. After payments to U.S. bankers were completed in 1924, Washington proceeded the next year to withdraw its troops, which were replaced by a constabulary—a force that was created, trained, and officered by Americans.

### Dollar Diplomacy III: Haiti (1915–1934)

As the crusading Wilson struggled with problems in Mexico, the Dominican Republic, and Nicaragua, he came to launch a long-term occupation in Haiti. The country was in disarray. With plantations long ago destroyed, wild coffee was the only export crop. The government had no money and was borrowing from anyone that would lend. Between 1908 and 1915 there were seven presidents and about twenty uprisings and insurrections. When President Vilbrun Guillaume Sam was torn limb from limb by a mob in Port-au-Prince in mid-1915, the U.S. Marines invaded.

There were three reasons for the intervention. One had to do with the ubiquitous National City Bank of New York, which possessed a 5 percent share in a new loan of 1910—and which served as agent for a number of German and French bondholders as well. When Haiti showed signs of defaulting on payments, National City representatives persuaded the Banque Nationale (the country's central bank) to freeze all government accounts—in hopes of provoking U.S. intervention. Irate Haitian authorities responded by issuing paper currency and then tried to retrieve a $2 million deposit from the Banque Nationale. Distraught local bankers requested assistance from Washington, and U.S. Marines aboard the cruiser *Machias* obligingly transported $500,000 for safekeeping to National City Bank headquarters in New York.

A second motivation concerned foreign influence. France held the largest share of Haitian debt and therefore possessed a clear incentive to invade. At this point in World War I there was, as well, concern that Germany might attempt to take over Haiti. As Secretary of State Robert Lansing explained to Congress, the U.S. action was "designed to prevent the Germans from using Haiti as a submarine base." In the event, of course, both France and Germany were much too preoccupied with the European theater to devote much time or attention to Haiti.

A third concern focused on the Panama Canal, the protection of which was a national security interest. As in Nicaragua, U.S. authorities took action in Haiti with an eye toward Panama.

Thus the U.S.S. *Washington* steamed into Port-au-Prince, oversaw elections, and ensured the victory of the obsequious Philip Sudre Dartiguenave. By August

1915 the State Department pressed by-now-familiar treaty terms on the new government: United States control of the customs house, U.S. appointment of a financial adviser, a gendarmerie manned by Haitians but commanded by U.S. officers, and U.S. control over sanitation and public works. Haiti further agreed not to sell or surrender any territory "to any foreign government or power, not to enter into any treaty or contract with any foreign power or powers that will impair or tend to impair the independence of Haiti." And "should the necessity occur," according to the document, "the United States will lend an efficient aid for the preservation of Haitian independence and the maintenance of a government adequate for the protection of life, property and individual liberty." The treaty was to be in force for ten years, renewable for a second term "if, for specific reasons presented by either of the high contracting parties, the purpose of the Treaty has not been fully accomplished." Within a year of its ratification it was extended to 1936.

Acting through the gendarmerie, the so-called Garde d'Haiti, the United States erected an indirect form of military rule. In the midst of constitutional debates, American officers of the gendarmerie dissolved the national assembly in 1916 and arranged for new elections in 1917. When the resulting assembly refused to ratify a U.S.-sponsored constitution, reportedly drafted by the assistant secretary of the navy, Franklin Delano Roosevelt, the Garde dissolved the congress for a second time. To gain approval for the constitution, U.S. authorities then arranged for a national plebiscite in June 1918—an utterly farcical exercise that resulted in the charter's approbation by a vote of 98,294 to 769.

Indirect rule by American forces promoted precious little progress. United States–supported governments acquiesced in the imposition of Jim Crow–style segregation rules and reinstituted the long-hated corvée law, under which peasants could be drafted for road building. While accumulating a surplus on government accounts, thanks to careful management of customs receipts, U.S. authorities concentrated all their energies on debt repayment rather than on investments in infrastructure and education. The United States failed to train a civil service, improve agriculture, or change the political culture. "In fact," as historian Robert Rotberg has observed, "the marine occupation simply prepared Haiti for a renewal of dictatorship and instability."

One justification for extension of the military occupation, and also for the inattention to democracy, came from racist doctrine. A U.S. diplomat carefully explained to his superiors key differences between peoples of the Dominican Republic and Haiti:

> The former, while in many ways not advanced far enough for the highest type of self-government, yet have a preponderance of white blood and culture. The Haitians on the other hand are negro for the most part, and, barring a very few highly educated politicians, are almost in a state of savagery and complete ignorance. The two situations thus demand different treatment. In Haiti it is necessary to have as complete a rule within a rule by Americans as possible.

The political difficulty posed by such racist contentions was that they offered no prospect for a gracious exit by U.S. troops. Here again was the principal conundrum of contemporary imperialism: how to exert effective control with minimal administrative and military costs.

Ultimately, the United States would welcome the chance to withdraw from Haiti. In 1930 Herbert Hoover appointed a joint U.S.–Haitian commission that recommended the holding of new elections, won by Stenio Vincent (1930–36). A relieved Hoover then began to expedite withdrawal, and in 1934 Franklin Delano Roosevelt ordered the complete evacuation of U.S. forces. The financial mission nonetheless stayed until 1941.

## PROMOTING DEMOCRACY?

From the 1830s to the 1930s, despite high-minded rationalization and ostensible nobility of purpose, not a single U.S. intervention led to the installation of democracy in Latin America. What can account for this dismal record?

One explanation stemmed from the goals of U.S. policy. Stripped of rhetoric, Washington's actions had geopolitical and economic motivations. A primary purpose was to assert U.S. influence throughout the greater Caribbean Basin and, in so doing, to reduce if not eliminate the European presence. An additional and related purpose was to protect the business investments, especially the banking interests, that had become vital instruments of imperial expansion. When push came to shove, the promotion of democracy was a secondary consideration.

A second explanation related to strategies and methods. In keeping with the political myopia of the era, U.S. occupation forces made little effort to construct, strengthen, or bolster democratic practices or institutions. From time to time they oversaw elections, sometimes patently fraudulent ones, as much for the purpose of extricating themselves from unpleasant situations as for the purpose of promoting pluralistic competition. And in each of the three countries with the longest U.S. occupations—Nicaragua, the Dominican Republic, and Haiti—Washington supervised the creation of local constabularies that would eventually become the agents of dictatorial repression. Not only did the United States fail to promote democratic development in Latin America, but also, it could even be argued, with considerable reason, U.S. military interventions tended to retard the prospects for democracy.

A third explanation was ambivalence and prejudice. While Woodrow Wilson and his cohorts espoused the universal applicability of democracy, policymakers in Washington—and U.S. citizens in general—had severe reservations about the political suitability, capability, and desirability of Latin American peoples. As a result of history, religion, and race, many Americans believed, Latin America was incapable of sustaining true democracy. Rather than waste time and effort on illusory hopes, analysts commonly argued, it made more sense to concentrate on law and order. The goal of stability thus came to replace the ideal of democracy. And if stability required an iron hand, that was neither the fault nor the responsibility of the United States.

From the formulation of "manifest destiny" to the adoption of Wilson's democratic crusade, American policymakers, legislators, scholars, and journalists justified the application of military power as a means of propagating the gospel of democracy. It was Herbert Hoover, of all people, who would articulate the fundamental contradiction underlying these efforts. During a goodwill tour of South America in 1928, the then-popular president-elect promised that the United States would be respectful of Latin American sensibilities. In fact, he said somewhat disingenuously, domination of neighboring nations was alien to America's political tradition. "True democracy," he said, "is not and cannot be imperialistic."

## QUESTIONS FOR REVIEW

1. What was the doctrine of "manifest destiny"? Did it represent deeply held values of American society, or was it a cynical attempt at ideological manipulation?
2. What factors led to a change in U.S. policies toward Latin America around the turn of the twentieth century? What explains the rising emphasis on military intervention?
3. From the standpoint of the United States, what were the principal obstacles to democracy in Latin America? How important was racial prejudice?
4. What was the significance of international debt in evolving relations between the United States, Europe, and Latin America?
5. What was the meaning of "dollar diplomacy"?

# CHAPTER 3

# Latin America: Responses to Imperialism

I have lived inside the monster and know its entrails—and my
weapon is only the slingshot of David.

José Martí (1895)

Each day the United States advances farther in its imperialistic
pretensions against Latin America. We cannot stand by with
folded arms. We must devise our own master plan for resisting
United States aggression.

Joaquín Walker Martínez (1906)

I will not sell myself, nor will I surrender. I must be conquered.

Augusto César Sandino (1927)

Participation by the United States in the global imperial contest had serious
implications for Latin America. As political and intellectual leaders throughout the region attempted to forge strategies for national development, they needed
to take explicit account of the inexorable expansion of U.S. power. Around the
turn of the nineteenth century, from the American Revolution through the Wars
of Independence, there existed a genuine sense of confraternal solidarity between
statesmen of North America and Latin America, bound by their common cause
against European rule. Yet the subsequent U.S. quest for hemispheric hegemony,
increasingly successful from the 1830s to the 1930s, presented Latin America with
a challenging combination of incentives, restrictions, and opportunities. This new
situation seemed a bitter pill: Having cast off colonial bonds to Spain and Portugal,
at considerable cost, Latin America now had to confront a rising imperial power
within the Western Hemisphere.

What could Latin America do? What strategic options were available to
countries of the continent? What was *possible* and *plausible*? The range of feasible
alternatives for Latin America embraced not only diplomacy, geopolitics, and foreign policy. It included schemes for economic development, political change, and
intraregional cooperation. Not surprisingly, the breadth of these programs often

provoked substantial internal disagreement, and for this reason the struggle over Latin America's destiny reached far into the domestic political arena. The continental predicament also provoked intellectual discourse and ideological debate, entering realms of popular culture. This is not to exaggerate the role of the United States: A great deal of conflict and contention in Latin America reflected purely domestic interests, forces, and purposes, especially as peoples of the region struggled to establish national and collective identities in the wake of independence. The century-long extension of U.S. power would nonetheless have fundamental ramifications for countries of the region.

Capitulation offered one expedient solution. Latin Americans could align themselves with U.S. power and/or succumb to U.S. pressure in hopes of salvaging as much as possible; this option was especially tempting for social oligarchies and political elites needing external support in order to survive. This reaction became especially commonplace in countries around the Caribbean Basin, where the United States established neocolonial protectorates in the wake of military intervention. Tomás Estrada Palma in Cuba and Adolfo Díaz in Nicaragua, among others, realized that their political fortunes depended directly on U.S. sponsorship. The extension of U.S. economic influence, through trade and investment, provided additional incentives for collaboration. Juan Vicente Gómez in Venezuela and a host of lesser-known executives in Central America made personal fortunes by consenting to lucrative contracts with U.S. petroleum, banana, and mining companies. Corruption could help pave the way for empire. A tacit rule thus emerged: the more informal the U.S. penetration, the greater the likelihood of local collaboration.

Yet most Latin American leaders made efforts to resist, or at least deflect, the rise of U.S. power. With the exception of extremely small minorities (and occasional secessionist movements), virtually all sectors of Latin American society opposed the forcible seizure and incorporation of territory throughout the nineteenth century; even Mexico's faithless Santa Anna claimed to have succumbed to U.S. pressure only under duress, and just a few voices in turn-of-the-century Cuba called for outright annexation by the United States. Similarly, military intervention and the imposition of protectorates between 1898 and 1934 provoked widespread condemnation and denunciation. The expansion of economic influence created a more equivocal circumstance, allowing local elites to benefit from complicity with the United States without explicit endangerment to political sovereignty, but it also met with apprehension and concern throughout the region. In all its various forms, U.S. imperialism confronted Latin America with a real and rising threat.

Over time, Latin American leaders developed a range of responses to the realities of U.S. power. Ultimately, they faced distinct choices:

- They could attempt to unify themselves, thus creating a continental counterweight to the United States.
- They could attempt to strengthen ties with (and seek protection from) European powers.

- They could attempt to establish subregional hegemony, thus challenging the United States or sharing power with it.
- They could fashion doctrines of international law that would impose constraints on the United States.

And in addition, more as an expression of feeling than as a strategy, they could formulate nationalistic cultures of resistance. These options were not all mutually exclusive, and they would appear in a variety of combinations, settings, and times. They reflected realistic appraisals of and reactions to the changing configurations of power throughout the Imperial Era. As such, they revealed an underlying, systematic logic in the conduct of U.S.–Latin American relations.

## OPTION 1: THE BOLIVARIAN DREAM

The ideal of Latin American unity captured the continental imagination from the outset of independence. It was none other than Simón Bolívar, *El Libertador,* who first gave expression to this hope. In his famous "letter from Jamaica," written in 1815 at the height of the struggle for independence from Spain, Bolívar expounded on the possibility of forging Spanish America into a single new nation:

> It is a grandiose idea to think of consolidating the New World into a single nation, united by pacts into a single bond. It is reasoned that, as these parts have a common origin, language, customs, and religion, they ought to have a single government to permit the newly formed states to unite in a confederation. But this is not possible. America is separated by climatic differences, geographic diversity, conflicting interests, and dissimilar characteristics. How beautiful it would be if the Isthmus of Panama could be for us what the Isthmus of Corinth was for the Greeks!

"Surely," he continued,

> unity is what we need to complete our work of regeneration. . . . I shall tell you with what what we must provide ourselves in order to expel the Spaniards and to found a free government. It is *union,* obviously; but such union will come about through sensible planning and well-directed actions rather than by divine magic.

In practical terms, Bolívar at this point envisaged the formation of three Spanish American federations: Mexico plus Central America; northern Spanish South America, including Peru and Bolivia; and southern South America. But the ultimate goal, what became known as the "Bolivarian dream," was the unification of all Spanish America.

External pressure provided motivation for the movement. Throughout the 1820s there persisted the fear that Spain, with help from the Holy Alliance, would attempt to regain its empire in America. In December 1824 the government of Colombia, led by Bolívar, extended formal invitations to a conference to be held in Panama (then a Colombian province) for the purpose of establishing a Spanish

American union. As preparations continued, Bolívar exulted that the upcoming congress "seems destined to form a league more extensive, more remarkable, and more powerful than any that has ever existed on the face of the earth." Delegates finally convened in mid-1826, but with representation from only four states: Mexico, Colombia, Peru, and the Central American federation. (Brazil and the United States were invited, over Bolívar's own objections, but to his relief Brazil declined the invitation, and the U.S. delegates never attended the meeting.) The congress reached agreement on a treaty "to uphold in common, defensively and offensively, if necessary, the sovereignty and independence of all and every one of the confederated powers of America against all foreign domination." But the threat from Spain was subsiding, a spirit of nationalism within Spanish America was increasing, and the United States was not yet challenging Mexico. Only Bolívar's Colombia actually ratified the document.

The first attempt at unity thus ended in failure. It was perhaps this outcome, as much as the dissolution of Gran Colombia (a confederation of Colombia, Ecuador, and Venezuela), that led Bolívar to sketch out "a few sure conclusions" while en route to exile in November 1830: "First, America is ungovernable for us; second, he who serves a revolution ploughs the sea. . . . [and] the Europeans will not deign to conquer us." Yet the Panama Congress managed to bring together official representatives from a geographical area stretching from Mexico to Peru, it reached agreement on a compact for mutual defense, and, most of all, it placed the question of unification on the continental agenda. By giving credence to the dream, Bolívar ignited aspirations that would long endure.

The spread of U.S. power provoked additional appeals for Spanish American unity. Expressing fear of the United States and opposition to the Monroe Doctrine, Juan Bautista Alberdi, a leading intellectual of Argentina, wrote in 1844 a *Memoria sobre . . . un Congreso General Americano* that called for an "American union" for the peaceful settlement of disputes, creation of a common coinage, and the elimination of trade barriers throughout Latin America. A few years later the U.S.-Mexican war added a sense of urgency to such demands. North Americans are the "Islamites" of the nineteenth century, fumed Mexico City's *El Universal* in 1853, and they can be stopped only by "an alliance of all peoples of Hispanic origin."

A second Latin American conference took place in Lima in 1847–1848. The gathering came in response to two threats: renewed Spanish designs upon the west coast of South America, and U.S. incursions into Mexico. Official delegates took part on behalf of Bolivia, Chile, Ecuador, Colombia, Peru; Venezuela, Argentina, Brazil, and the United States all declined. (Mexico, then under military siege, was unable to dispatch a delegation.) The conference agreed on a mutual defense treaty, as had the Panama Congress more than twenty years before, but it was never ratified by the signatories. The only practical achievement was approval of a consular convention among those countries in attendance.

Largely in reaction to William Walker's infamous filibustering in Nicaragua, there followed a third meeting in 1856 that was attended by Chile, Ecuador, and Peru. Delegates approved a continental treaty—later adhered to by Bolivia, Costa

Rica, Nicaragua, Honduras, Mexico, and Paraguay—to respect the integrity of national territories, to refrain from hostile acts, and to adopt uniform procedures for trade and commercial law.

A fourth gathering, in Lima again, took place in 1864–1865. By this time Latin America was facing multiple pressures from abroad: in 1861 Spain had retaken Santo Domingo; having occupied the Chincha islands (off Peru) in 1864, Spain was at war with both Chile and Peru; and France was supporting a European monarchy in Mexico. In response Chilean patriots formed a Sociedad de la Unión Americana de Santiago, published a two-volume set of documents on the movement for unification, and depicted the United States as a major source of danger. Warned Francisco Bilbao: "The United States extends more each day the predatory hunt which it has already undertaken. We see fragments of America falling into the Saxon jaws of the voracious serpent. Yesterday, Texas. Soon, northern Mexico will accept a new sovereign," and, eventually, all of Spanish America could be reduced to a U.S. protectorate. Representatives came from Bolivia, Chile, Colombia, Ecuador, El Salvador, Guatemala, Peru, and Venezuela; reflecting their desires to maintain close ties with Europe, Argentina and Brazil declined to attend. Peru explored the possibility of inviting the United States but met with disapproval. Delegates approved a resolution denouncing Spain's seizure of the Chincha islands but produced no treaties of any kind.

The Lima conference was perhaps the last institutional embodiment of Bolívar's exalted dream. Subsequent efforts would founder on the lack of complete consensus among countries of the region and, in particular, on the historic rivalry between Chile and Argentina. Ambivalence about Brazil posed yet another obstacle, since it was unclear whether the project should embrace a Luso-American nation or focus only on Spanish America. Nonetheless the idea of regional unification would appear, time and again, throughout the twentieth century. It would remain a fundamental aspiration of the region.

## OPTION 2: EXTERNAL POWERS

Complications in the quest for unity encouraged a search for alternatives. One of the most straightforward options for confronting the United States was to seek protection from one of its major rivals. This tactic was entirely consistent with rules of the prevailing imperial contest, and it offered weaker states (in Latin America) the opportunity of aligning themselves with stronger nations (in Europe) to counter the influence of the United States. As shown in chapter 1, several European states were pressing for advantage in the Western Hemisphere throughout the nineteenth century. The task was persuading them to embrace the Latin American cause.

### Pax Britannica?
Simón Bolívar recognized the opportunity. In his conception there was one nation that presented itself as an exceptionally desirable ally, patron, and protector—a nation with colonial possessions in the Caribbean, territorial holdings in Central

and South America, and extensive commercial and financial interests throughout the region: Great Britain, which offered the additional advantage of being the preeminent power in the nineteenth-century world. From the outset, Bolívar's plans for continental unification included the explicit hope that Great Britain would join the confederation. As he wrote to General Santander in March 1825, while preparing for the upcoming Panama congress: "Believe me, my dear General, we shall save the New World if we come to an agreement with England in *political and military matters. This simple sentence ought to tell you more than two whole volumes.*" And as time for the congress approached, Bolívar emphasized his hopes: "Should Great Britain agree to join it as a constituent member, the Holy Alliance will be less powerful than this confederation. Mankind will a thousand times bless this league for promoting its general welfare, and America, as well as Great Britain, will reap from it untold benefits." Bolívar's reasoning was crystal clear: A British protectorate over Spanish America would discourage attempts at reconquest by the Holy Alliance, it would protect the newly independent region from the expansionist United States, and it would utterly demolish the Monroe Doctrine.

The Liberator's scheme was not as farfetched as it might in hindsight seem. English statesmen were acutely concerned about the prospect of U.S. hegemony within the Western Hemisphere. In December 1824, the prime minister, the 2nd Earl of Liverpool, wrote one of his colleagues: "I am conscientiously convinced that if we allow these new states to consolidate their system and their policy with the United States of America, it will in a very few years prove fatal to our greatness, if not endanger our safety." The foreign minister, George Canning, expressed particular unease over U.S. ambitions toward Cuba: "The possession by the United States of both shores of the channel through which our Jamaica trade must pass . . . would amount to a suspension of that trade, and to consequent total ruin." Latin America was thus of considerable interest to the British and their imperial policy. Congratulating himself on his master stroke of gaining British recognition for the newly independent countries of Spanish America, Canning summarized the outlook succinctly: "The fight has been hard," he wrote in 1826, "but it is won. The deed is done. Spanish America is free; and if we do not mismanage our matters sadly, she is English, and *Novus saeclorum nascitur ordo.*"

Canning nonetheless resisted Bolívar's overtures, dispatching only a British observer (rather than a conference delegate) to the Panama congress. For the remainder of the century Britain chose to protect its growing economic interests in Latin America through diplomatic pressure and, on occasion, military operations. Indeed, British vessels blockaded the port of Buenos Aires in 1846–1847 and the port of Rio de Janeiro in 1894; British troops entered Venezuela and Nicaragua in the 1890s; and British authorities maintained tight hold on valued colonial possessions throughout the Caribbean. On mainland Latin America, however, Britain relied on commercial and financial prowess to consolidate an "informal empire." By the mid-1890s the British foreign office consented to Washington's resolution of the Venezuelan crisis, tacitly accepting America's claim to hemispheric hegemony, and a few years later Britain took refuge behind Teddy Roosevelt's corollary to the Monroe Doctrine. In the end, Latin America was simply not important enough to tempt Britain into open alliance with countries of the region. At least as envisioned by Bolívar, the *pax britannica* would never come to pass.

## Opposition to Pan Americanism

The U.S. promotion of Pan Americanism in the 1880s met stiff resistance throughout the hemisphere. In literary journals and diplomatic forums, in private and public arenas, spokesmen for Latin America developed three related reasons for opposition to Washington's plan: apprehension about the rise of U.S. power, resentment of the Monroe Doctrine, and insistence on retaining ties to Europe.

As preparations were under way for the first Pan American conference in Washington, the Cuban writer and patriot José Martí in 1889 urged Latin America to proceed with caution:

> Never in America, from its independence to the present, has there been a matter requiring more good judgment or more vigilance, or demanding a clearer and more thorough examination, than the invitation which the powerful United States (glutted with its unsalable merchandise and determined to extend its dominion in America) is sending to the less powerful American nations (bound by free and useful commerce to the European nations) for purposes of arranging an alliance against Europe and cutting off transactions with the rest of the world. Spanish America learned how to save itself from the tyranny of Spain; and now, after viewing with judicious eyes the antecedents, motives, and ingredients of the invitation, it is essential to say, for it is true, that the time has come for Spanish America to declare its second independence.

The congress, Martí warned, was meant to usher in "the frank and forthright achievement of an era of United States dominion over the nations of America."

During the conference itself, delegates from Latin America sought ways to resist demands by the United States. They fought successfully against James G. Blaine's pet proposal for a customs union, which, in the words of one assessment, entailed "the proposition of excluding Europe from the advantages accorded to its commerce. . . . The present convocation has as its object the erection of an American Zollverein." Moreover, they maintained, the setting of tariffs was a prerogative of national sovereignty. Insistence on self-determination was thus identified with maintenance of commercial ties to Europe. The plan for a customs union met an early death in a conference committee, which came out with a lukewarm recommendation in favor of bilateral or reciprocity treaties—signed by the United States, Mexico, Brazil, Nicaragua, Colombia, and Venezuela, over a minority dissenting report from Chile and Argentina. And as the conference was preparing to adjourn, in April 1890, Argentine representative Roque Saenz Peña (later his country's president) uttered an elegant demurral to demands for hemispheric solidarity. "What I lack is not love for America," declared the future president, "but suspicion and ingratitude towards Europe. I cannot forget that in Europe are Spain, our mother; Italy, our friend; and France, our elder sister." Instead of "America for the Americans," he proclaimed, the congress should uphold the principle of "America for all humanity."

Condemnation of the Monroe Doctrine went hand in hand with celebration of the European connection. As early as the mid-1820s, Diego Portales of Chile issued a stern admonition about Monroe's pronouncement: "Be careful," he wrote, "of escaping one domination at the price of falling under another. We must distrust those who take advantage of the work of our champions of freedom, without having helped us in any way." Alberdi of Argentina would later urge Spanish American states to forge commercial links to Europe, "so as to defend themselves against Brazil and the United States. Their peril is in America; their safeguard in Europe." And at a 1916 financial conference, Chilean representative Armando Quesada Acharán emphasized the value of the European connection: "Closer economic ties between the United States and Latin America must not, in any way, interfere with the maintaining and increasing of economic relations with Europe." Reformers and nationalists would continue to denounce the Monroe Doctrine, its corollaries, and its applications well into the twentieth century.

The Pan American movement and the Monroe Doctrine thus became twin symbols of U.S. preponderance. In the 1920s the Argentine sociologist José Ingenieros neatly summarized the challenge for Latin America:

> We are not, we do not want to be any longer, we could not be Pan Americanists. The United States is to be feared because it is great, rich, and enterprising. What concerns us to is find out whether there is a possibility of balancing its power to the extent necessary to save our political independence and the sovereignty of our countries.

For Washington, keeping Europe out of the hemisphere meant keeping Latin America under U.S. control; for Latin America, the protection of national sovereignty required the maintenance of ties with Europe.

## Hispanidad and Francophilia

A frequent corollary of this general position stressed the importance of Latin America's cultural, social, and intellectual connections with Europe rather than with the United States. During the nineteenth century the quest for self-identity meant not *indigenismo,* a movement that would emerge later in the twentieth century, but appreciation of European ancestries. In practice this pattern took two forms: *Hispanidad,* or glorification of things Spanish, and unabashed Francophilia.

Veneration for Spain implied a celebration of Catholic, conservative values that placed dignity, status, and manners above talent and tangible accomplishment, religious faith above mundane achievement, dogma above curiosity, the traditional over the novel, the graceful and artistic over the functional and practical. In 1845 former president Joaquín Pinto of Chile stressed the Hispanic legacy in declaring that "we will never utilize the methods of democracy as practiced in the United States of America, but rather the political principles of Spain." And in the wake of Mexico's calamitous mid-nineteenth-century war with the United States, conservative writer-politician Lucas Alamán spoke disdainfully of a conflict that had resulted from the ambitions "not of an absolute monarchy, but of a republic which claimed to be in the vanguard of nineteenth-century civilization." Alamán went on to condemn U.S. culture as derivative, a place where religion was mixed with commercial spirit, where the cult of individualism led to systematic disregard for morality, order, and good customs. By contrast, he wrote,

> We are not a people of merchants and adventurers, scum and refuse (*hez y desecho*) of all countries, whose only mission is to usurp the property of the miserable Indians, and later to rob the fertile lands opened to civilization by the Spanish race. . . . We are a nation formed three centuries ago, not an aggregation of peoples of differing customs.

In due course Alamán and his conservative associates would turn for salvation toward France, importing ill-starred Emperor Maximilian from the House of Hapsburg.

Democracy and capitalism came under attack as vehicles for the promotion of alien and materialistic values. Uruguayan writer José Enrique Rodó penned a consummate statement of this position in *Ariel,* a turn-of-the-century essay that extolled the lofty morality of Spanish America and denounced the grasping materialism of the United States. Invocation of Hispanic virtue intensified during and after the Spanish-American War, which provoked widespread fear of U.S. imperial ambitions. Although the motherland might suffer defeat, one Chilean proclaimed, "Spanish valor was still worth more than all the gold of the United States." United States materialism came in for particular scorn. If Argentina were to become merely a colossal *estancia,* crisscrossed by railroads and bursting with wealth, said Juan Agustín García, "I would rather live in the most miserable corner of the earth where there still lives a feeling for beauty, goodness, and truth."

For these generations, France represented the center of civilization and *haute couture.* Boulevards in bustling capitals, from Mexico City to Buenos Aires, were copies of the Champs Elysées. Stately mansions were erected in imitation of Parisian models. Opera houses, even in such removed locations as the Amazonian city of Manáus, were carbon copies of L'Opéra. Oligarchs took vacations in France and sent their sons to study at the Sorbonne. When Victor Hugo died in 1885, *Sud América* in Buenos Aires devoted its entire front page to recapitulating his career.

Such insistent evocation of European legacies had several implications for Latin America's ruling elites. One was to stress their cultural superiority over the United States. Another was to deemphasize the importance of the economic realm, where the United States was rapidly increasing its advantage. Third was to demonstrate the continuing affinity between Latin America and Europe and, by so doing, to affirm the foundation for joint political collaboration.

## OPTION 3: RIVALRY AND SUBREGIONAL HEGEMONY

A third strategic option was for individual countries of Latin America to achieve subregional hegemony and compete on a more or less equal basis with the United States. Nationalism thrived on visions of grandeur. This aspiration was in fact unavailable to small nations around the Caribbean Basin, where the United States was steadily gaining the upper hand over Europe, or to Mexico, humiliated and dismembered by the war of 1847–1848. By virtue of geographical location, size, and resources, only two nations could seriously entertain such an ambition: Argentina and Brazil.

---

**BOX 3-1**

### Beauty or Progress?

Seeking to assert their cultural identity, Latin Americans have often claimed superiority over the crass materialism of the United States. A treatise entitled *Ariel* by the Uruguayan writer José Enrique Rodó (1871–1917) has become a classic of this genre:

> Prodigal with his riches . . . the North American has with his wealth achieved all the satisfaction and vanity that come with sumptuous magnificence—but good taste has eluded him. In such an atmosphere, true art can exist only in the form of individual rebellion. . . . They ignore in art all that is selfless and selective. They ignore it, in spite of the munificence with which private fortunes are employed to stimulate an appreciation of beauty; in spite of the splendid museums and exhibitions that their cities boast; in spite of the mountains of marble and bronze they have sculptured into statues for their public squares. And if a word may some day characterize their taste in art, it will be a word that negates art itself: the grossness of affectation, the ignorance of all that is subtle and exquisite, the cult of false grandeur, the *sensationalism* that excludes the serenity that is irreconcilable with the pace of a feverish life.
>
> The idealism of beauty does not fire the soul of a descendant of austere Puritans. Nor does the idealism of truth. He scorns as vain and unproductive any exercise of thought that does not yield an immediate result. He does not bring to science [or knowledge] a selfless thirst for truth, nor has he ever shown any sign of revering science for itself. For him, research is merely preparation for a utilitarian application. His grandiose plans to disseminate the benefits of popular education were inspired in the noble goal of communicating rudimentary knowledge to the masses; but although these plans promote the growth of education, we have seen no sign that they contain any imperative to enhance selective education, or any inclination to aid in allowing excellence to rise above general mediocrity. Thus the persistent North American war against ignorance has resulted in a universal *semi*-culture, accompanied by the diminution of high culture. To the same degree that basic ignorance has diminished in that gigantic democracy, wisdom and genius have correspondingly disappeared. This, then, is the reason that the trajectory of their intellectual activity is one of decreasing brilliance and originality. While in the period of independence and the formation of their nation many illustrious names emerged to expound both the thought and the will of that people, only a half century later de Tocqueville could write of them, *the gods have departed.*

SOURCE: Robert H. Holden and Eric Zolov (eds.), *Latin America and the United States: A Documentary History,* 2nd ed. (New York: Oxford University Press, 2011), pp. 80–81.

## Argentina's Manifest Destiny

During the late nineteenth century, Argentina saw itself as similar to the United States and therefore its natural rival. The winning of the American West had its counterpart in Argentina's Conquest of the Desert and settlement of the pampa, routinely referred to in presidential statements as *nuestro "Far West"* (with deliberate employment of the English phrase). Both countries received mass waves of immigrants from Europe between 1870 and 1910. In keeping with racist assumptions of the day, Argentine leaders took pride in the Caucasian composition of its ethnic stock, which made it feel comparable to the United States and vastly superior to neighbors with large indigenous or black populations. Geopolitically, too, many Argentines believed that location in the southern cone of South America placed the country in a natural position to impose subregional hegemony.

It was in this sense that Domingo Sarmiento, the great reformer of the nineteenth century, evolved his own view of the United States. Initially a Francophile, he became disenchanted with Europe and at one point embraced the Monroe Doctrine. While serving as minister to Washington, from 1865 to 1868, he even appeared to accept U.S. claims to manifest destiny: "It is the province of the United States," he once told an American audience, "the highest mission entrusted by Providence to a great people, that of conducting others through the new paths opened by mankind to advance firmly to their great destinies." As Argentina gained political stability and enjoyed rapid economic growth, however, Sarmiento's attitude changed from awe to rivalry. His final written words, in 1888, presented his compatriots with a prediction and a challenge: "We shall reach the level of the United States. We shall be America as the sea is the ocean. We shall be the United States."

Many of Sarmiento's colleagues were supremely confident. The Buenos Aires newspaper *La Prensa* anticipated that Argentina could achieve both political democracy and economic prosperity. "The Argentine Republic ought to aspire to grow like the United States," declared its editors in 1886, "and not in the manner, and with the elements, of France, England, and Germany." Thus appeared the elements of a national strategy, or at least of a national aspiration: Argentina would be to South America what the United States had become in North America. Each would enjoy continental hegemony; in tandem, they would dominate the hemisphere.

For Argentina this project did not imply alliance or collaboration with the United States. On the contrary, Argentine leaders intended to maintain extremely close ties to European powers, especially to England. These European connections would assert and emphasize Argentina's distance and independence from Washington. As rivals of the United States, both Europe and Argentina would have a natural interest in diplomatic and economic partnership.

Foreign observers gave further credence to the dream. After a brief visit, journalist William Eleroy Curtis predicted in 1888 that "the Argentine Republic will some day become a formidable rival of the United States." A French economic geographer, M. E. Vavasseur, wrote in 1890: "The Argentine Republic, which occupies in the temperate zone of South America a position analogous to that of the United States in North America, may dream, if not of equal power, at least of a similar future." To complete the picture, some Argentine commentators even developed a vision of "manifest destiny," analogous to pretentious claims made on behalf of the United States. As the only white, prosperous, and democratic nation on the continent, Argentina would have an obligation to spread the gospels of development through South America: According to *La Prensa* in 1893, Argentina has "a great civilizing mission in the New World."

Predictably enough, Argentine leaders looked upon Brazil with a mixture of fear and contempt. According to one nationalist just after the turn of the century: "The natural enemy of all the Hispanic-American nations is Brazil. It is our born enemy. . . . Speaking a different language, differently oriented in culture and politics, entirely different because of the mixture with the Negro race . . . Brazil forms a foreign element within our body." Racist criteria thus assured Argentina of social superiority over its principal rival on the continent.

By the early twentieth century Argentina seemed to be heading for its predestined greatness. In the late 1920s it was ranked as the seventh-richest country in the world. It was also one of the world's most democratic nations, having institutionalized a system of genuinely competitive elections in 1912. Ably, and energetically, Argentina successfully resisted the U.S. drive toward regional hegemony in a variety of diplomatic settings. Political and economic setbacks during the 1930s began to unravel the dream, however, and it would later come apart at the seams. The notion of Argentina's manifest destiny may look, in retrospect, like a quaint historic artifact; but for generations of *argentinos*, from the 1860s to the 1930s, it offered a vision of national grandeur.

## God Is a Brazilian

The other country aspiring to emulate the United States was Brazil. Even during the colonial period, love of land and a sense of natural majesty had inspired a feeling of greatness, as suggested by the titles of such books as Ambrósio Fernandes Brandão's *Diálogos das Grandezas do Brasil* (1618) and André João Antonil's *Cultura e Opulência do Brasil* (1711). Indeed, the beauty and vastness of the land gave rise to the not-always tongue-in-cheek assertion that "God is a Brazilian." In 1838, with an independent monarchy in place, the Visconde de São Leopoldo, president of the recently founded Brazilian Geographical and Historical Institute, offered an optimistic prediction: "Everything points to the fact that Brazil is destined to be not accidentally, but by necessity, a center of enlightenment and civilization and an arbiter of the politics of the New World." Sargento Albuquerque echoed this theme in 1917: "The historic and political superiority of Brazil is manifest: united, colossal, irreducible. . . . It is destined to occupy in South America within a century the same preponderant place that the United States occupies in North America."

Noting with asperity the condescension expressed by Argentines, Brazilians responded with their own contempt. "Whether the [Argentines] like it or not," in the words of one Brazilian, "we have already proved the superiority of our organizational talents by systematizing juridical, economic, and intellectual forces, while the Hispanic inferiority becomes obvious in the fragmentation of states all more or less weak, all more or less turbulent." The Baron of Rio Branco, Brazil's legendary diplomat, likewise condemned "those political evils which so greatly hurt the South American nations. There is nothing more ridiculous and extravagant than the manifestations of dictators, the pronouncements, the revolutions for possession of power, the military demagoguery."

In contrast to Argentina, which sought alliances in Europe, Brazil cultivated close connections with the United States. Rio Branco once explained that Brazil "prides itself on the spontaneous and affirmed friendship of that American nation and its great president [Cleveland]. There is no friendship more coveted in the world." And in 1906, just before the third Pan American conference, he expressed public support for the Monroe Doctrine and the Roosevelt Corollary. These principles guaranteed that the Americas "cannot be touched by any European greed or conquest," in his words, "because the Monroe Doctrine is not an abstraction. It has for its base the prodigious ascendancy of the United States." Rio Branco continued:

> Latin America has nothing to fear from Anglo-Saxon America. The United States is a nation of English origin and principles and therefore beneficial for the civilization of other people because the sentiment of individualism is so much a part of their race that English or North American imperialism, if it should manifest itself, never would be of the same type as German or Latin imperialism, which seeks to destroy and annihilate everything, contorting everything, in order to create from the incompatibilities and irreconcilables the same kind of country in all the regions of the world. Nothing, absolutely nothing, in the policies of the United States would be able to cause uneasiness to the national sensitivity of the other American countries. Just the opposite, these nations find in the preponderance of the first nation of the continent support for their causes and aspirations.

United States power was a benefit for Latin America, not a threat to sovereignty. In a world of major-power rivalries, Washington would shield the region from continental Europe.

Thus the Brazilian strategy took shape. Brazil would gain ascendancy in South America, following the U.S. model, and would forge a partnership with the United States. In effect, the two countries would establish a joint condominium over the Western Hemisphere. They would sustain their greatness and subregional superiority through mutual collaboration. For Brazil, and especially for Rio Branco, emulation of the United States had practical meaning as well. Like its partner to the north, Brazil was busily engaged in expanding its territorial reach, usually at the expense of increasingly resentful neighbors. Under Rio Branco's leadership, Brazil proclaimed the doctrine of *uti possidetis* and triumphed in successive territorial disputes over Argentina, France, Bolivia, and Peru. All in all, Rio Branco managed to delineate 9,000 miles of frontier and to add nearly 115,000 square miles to the national domain. It seemed only fitting that, as expansionist powers, Brazil and the United States should give support to one another.

Dreams of Brazilian *grandeza* later foundered on hard times. Political instability, economic stagnation, and persistent poverty created uncertainty and apprehension about the nation's destiny throughout the twentieth century. Positive recent developments have revived the idea that, with its vast natural and human resources, Brazil is a great power in the making, a sleeping giant, a nation destined for fulfillment. Coequal partnership (or rivalry) with the United States may seem like a distant prospect, perhaps for the next generation, but it remains a vital part of national mythology.

## OPTION 4: DOCTRINES AND DIPLOMACY

A fourth alternative for Latin America took the form of a quest for protection under international law. Legal codes represented a positive asset for weaker nations in their dealings with stronger powers. Theoretically, international law obliged all countries to abide by universal principles of conduct. Since the rules applied to all members of the international community, great and small, the rules imposed constraints upon the powerful. Within the context of inter-American relations, therefore, international law came to be seen as a means of curtailing the United States.

International jurisprudence was undergoing intense development during this era. In practice, the expansion of imperial holdings and pursuit of major-power rivalries reflected raw demonstrations of power; in response, idealists sought to strengthen the corpus and meaning of international law. The Permanent Court of International Arbitration was established at The Hague in 1899. And nearly thirty years later, in 1928, U.S. Secretary of State Frank P. Kellogg and his French counterpart, Aristide Briand, would announce their own grand faith in legal principles: Through the Pact of Paris, they proposed to outlaw the use of war as an instrument of national policy. It was a touching declaration, overwhelmingly naive in retrospect, but a fitting expression of the hopes and contradictions prevailing in the world arena at this time.

A principal contribution of Latin American jurists was the doctrine of sovereign immunity from external intervention. First formulated in the mid-nineteenth century by Andrés Bello of Chile and by Carlos Calvo of Argentina, the basic idea insisted on the absolute equality of sovereign states—regardless of size, position, or power. As a logical result, courts of one country should not be subject to appeal in cases involving rights of foreign nationals. Out of this emerged what came to be known as the Calvo clause, typically applied to foreign (especially U.S.) companies with investments in Latin America: The foreign party would agree to the settlement of disputes by courts of the host country and forswear any right of appeal for special assistance from its own government.

In support of this principle, Venezuela offered a proposal at the first Pan American conference denouncing diplomatic representation for economic claims by foreign nationals. As reported out of committee—with the support of Argentina, Chile, Ecuador, and Guatemala—the resolution stipulated that foreigners were "entitled to enjoy all the civil rights enjoyed by natives," but no more than that:

"A nation has not, nor recognizes in favor of foreigners, any other obligations or responsibilities than those which in favor of the natives are established, in like cases, by the constitution and by the laws." The conference adopted the majority report by a vote of 15–1, with the United States alone in opposition. Equally revealing were the terms of debate, where the U.S. representative sharply criticized the concept of an "American" or hemispheric international law. Stressing the differences between Europe and the Americas, Latin American delegates were attempting to fashion a special body of international law for the Western Hemisphere; the United States insisted that there could only be a single and universal code of conduct.

Another central issue at the 1889–1890 conference concerned a U.S. proposal for compulsory arbitration of legal disputes. Latin American delegates regarded the plan with suspicion, as an effort to circumvent national courts through international tribunals or panels that would inevitably reflect the interests of the United States. In particular, Chileans feared that such a mechanism would deprive them of hard-won spoils from the War of the Pacific (1879–1883). More generally, José Martí condemned the project as a transparent scheme to create a hemispheric institution under Washington's control. Manuel Quintana offered an eloquent statement of the Latin American view:

> In the eyes of international American law there are neither great nor small nations. All are equally sovereign and independent, all equally worthy of consideration and respect. The arbitration proposed is not, consequently, a compact of abdication, of vassalage, or of submission. Before as well as after its conclusion, all and each of the nations of the Americas will preserve the absolute direction of their political destinies, absolutely without interference by the others.

At this point the proposal for final arbitration included a "point of independence," allowing any country to exclude from arbitration any matter appearing to endanger its own vital interests, but even this watered-down version did not gain the approval of the conference. Latin America thus upheld the principles of sovereignty and equality of nations.

The question of international arbitration resisted resolution. Essentially, Latin America upheld the sovereignty and integrity of national courts; the United States held out for international arbitration in cases of dispute. The two sides reached a compromise at the 1902 Pan American conference, in Mexico City, accepting the idea of voluntary arbitration through the international court at The Hague. Latins agreed because adherence would be voluntary; Americans consented because the world court would apply principles of universal law, not a regional or hemispheric doctrine. Also at the Mexico conference, Brazil proposed creation of a legal panel to begin work on a specifically regional or inter-American system of arbitration, on private international law, and on a code of public international law "to govern the relations between American republics." Essentially, Latin Americans were attempting to find a way to enshrine the principles of national sovereignty and nonintervention; the United States wanted to preserve the rights of intervention, then recognized under some circumstances by international law. The impasse continued for years.

Another key development in legal circles emerged from the Venezuelan crisis of 1902–1903 (during which Great Britain, Germany, and Italy began taking military action in order to collect outstanding debts). As reported in chapter 1, the foreign minister of Argentina, Luis María Drago, dispatched a note to U.S. Secretary of State John Hay proposing "that the public debt gives no place for armed intervention, and less still to the material occupation of the soil of American nations by a European power." Revealingly, Drago invoked both the Monroe Doctrine and the principle of national sovereignty, concepts that would soon be at odds with each other. Hay responded noncommittally, and the Europeans soon consented to arbitration in their dispute with Venezuela. There the matter rested until 1904, when Teddy Roosevelt laid bare the implicit contradiction in Drago's proposition by announcing his "corollary" to the Monroe Doctrine, proclaiming that the United States would act as hemispheric policeman in cases of "chronic wrong-doing or impotence." Quickly sensing the danger, *La Prensa* denounced Roosevelt's proclamation as "the most serious and menacing declaration against South American integrity which has come out of Washington."

After William Howard Taft's election as president, however, the United States decided to support a diluted version of Drago's proposal at a 1907 conference on international law at The Hague. United States delegates agreed that the use of force should be in principle prohibited for the collection of "contract debts claimed from the government of one country by another," but they insisted that force could be admissible if countries refused to abide by the results of arbitration. Latin Americans greeted the Hague protocol with justifiable skepticism. Not a single South American country agreed to it. Several countries ratified it—Mexico, Panama, Guatemala, Nicaragua, Haiti, and El Salvador—and only Panama (a U.S. protectorate) and Mexico (under Porfirio Díaz) without reservation. Years later, in 1931, postrevolutionary Mexico denounced the convention and gave notice of its intent to withdraw.

World War I interrupted these legal and diplomatic maneuvers. At a 1923 Pan American conference in Santiago, Alejandro Álvarez, a distinguished Chilean jurist, renewed the debate by taking a clear position on the existence of a unique body of inter-American law. Declared Álvarez:

> The States of America, even before reaching a mutual agreement, have proclaimed certain regulations or principles different from and even contradictory to those ruling in European countries, and which these latter are compelled to respect in our Continent, for instance, nonintervention and the nonoccupation of territories of the States of America by ultra-continental countries.

Firmly supporting the doctrine of nonintervention, the American Institute of International Law, a private organization, drafted a resolution for a 1925 meeting that stipulated: "No Nation has the right to interfere in the internal or foreign affairs of an American Republic against the will of that Republic. The sole lawful intervention is friendly and conciliatory action without any character of coercion." With U.S. troops still stationed in Haiti and poised for a return to Nicaragua, Washington was cool to these proposals.

The minuet continued. In 1927 a legal conference at Rio discussed a resolution that "No State has the right to interfere in the internal affairs of another." The next year, at a Pan American conference in Havana, chief U.S. delegate Charles Evans Hughes disputed this idea:

> What are we going to do when government breaks down and American citizens are in danger of their lives? Are we to stand by and see them killed because a government in circumstances which it cannot control and for which it may not be responsible can no longer afford reasonable protection? . . . Now it is a principle of international law that in such a case a government is fully justified in taking action—I would call it interposition of a temporary character—for the purpose of protecting the lives and property of its nationals.

In effect, Hughes was recasting the Roosevelt Corollary, justifying "interposition of a temporary character" as a principle of international law.

In the early 1930s Argentina launched an aggressive diplomatic offensive against the U.S. position. Under its flamboyant foreign minister, Carlos Saavedra Lamas, Argentina pressed repeatedly for an absolute statement of prohibition against intervention. Seeking to mediate the Chaco War (between Bolivia and Paraguay), Saavedra Lamas in September 1932 unveiled a proposal for an Anti-War Treaty condemning "wars of aggression," denying territorial acquisitions or occupations by force, and prohibiting all forms of intervention, "either diplomatic or armed." The key clause was, of course, the absolute stricture against intervention.

On the eve of the 1933 Pan American conference, in Montevideo, Saavedra Lamas induced six Latin American nations to accede to his proposal. It now had the standing of an actual treaty, backed by multilateral calls for accession. The newly inaugurated administration of Franklin Delano Roosevelt, about to embark on its Good Neighbor policy, agreed not only to support the Anti-War Treaty but also to approve a resolution that "No State has the right to intervene in the internal or external affairs of another." Thus triumphant, Saavedra Lamas presided over the commission—technically associated with the League of Nations—that brought an end to the Chaco War. For this accomplishment and for his Anti-War Treaty, he received the Nobel Peace Prize in 1936.

## CULTURES OF RESISTANCE

An additional development in Latin America during this period was the formulation of cultural and rhetorical codes for resisting U.S. power in the hemisphere. This was not a strategic option or policy guideline so much as an expression of popular feeling, the adoption of a general stance, and the construction of a national and regional discourse. Yet these "cultures of resistance" grew in complexity and intensity from the mid-nineteenth century through the early twentieth century. They would have considerable impact on the tenor and tone of inter-American relations. In time, they would provide both a basis and a resource for populist and nationalist movements throughout the region.

The creeds of resistance contained a series of interlocking assumptions. To uphold the sovereignty of young and fragile republics in Latin America was to be a nationalist. To be a nationalist was to be anti-imperialist. To be anti-imperialist, as U.S. power grew, was to become anti-American, anti-*gringo*, and anti-*yanqui*. Paradoxically, however, nationalism also implied solidarity with other countries of Latin America: Victims of a common enemy, according to this view, they must band together for the sake of mutual support. In one form or another this outlook appeared in virtually every part of the region, finding particularly acute expression in countries most directly affected by the application of U.S. power: Mexico, Cuba, and Nicaragua. Not coincidentally, each of these countries eventually underwent social revolution.

## Mexico: War and Invasion

Mexico felt the presence of its neighbor in frequent, profound, and often painful ways. Most deeply etched in the national memory are recollections of the "war of the North American invasion," the mid-nineteenth-century military conflicts that resulted in the loss of nearly half the country's territory. For Mexicans this episode began in the 1820s, when the newly independent republic granted permission for colonists under Moses and Stephen Austin to settle in what was then the northern province of Texas. When Texans began demanding self-government, the U.S. government lent moral support to the rebels by dispatching a military expedition into Mexican territory. This itself was cause for war; but when Mexico desisted, the United States responded by recognizing Texan independence and then, in the mid-1840s, by approving its annexation as a state. This was not, in the Mexican outlook, an accidental series of spontaneous events, but the expression of long-held expansionist ambitions. As José Vasconcelos would write in his *Breve historia de México,* "The Texas colonists were the advance guard for Yankee imperialism."

As recounted in chapter 1, boundary disputes persisted in the 1840s. Under Mexican rule the western frontier of Texas had stretched to the Nueces River, well north of the Rio Grande, but U.S. authorities began disputing this fact. In 1846 troops under General Zachary Taylor moved across the Nueces, in defiance of Mexican sovereignty, and a U.S. naval force moved near the coast of Veracruz. Mexico's embattled president José Joaquín Herrera agreed to talks about the Texas question, but U.S. emissary John Slidell scuttled the negotiations by proclaiming his intent to discuss not only Texas but also the purchase of New Mexico and California. In frustration, General Mariano Paredes overthrew Herrera and canceled the Slidell negotiations. One thoughtful Mexican observer left this record of the affair:

> While the United States seemed to be animated by a sincere desire not to break the peace, their acts of hostility manifested very evidently what were their true intentions. Their ships infested our coasts; their troops continued advancing upon our territory, situated at places which under no aspect could be disputed. Thus violence and insult were united: thus at the very time they usurped part of our territory, they offered us the hand of treachery, to have soon the audacity to say that our obstinacy and arrogance were the real causes of the war.

In May 1846 Polk went on to declare war against Mexico, and U.S. troops swiftly overwhelmed Mexican forces. In 1847 General Winfield Scott invaded Mexico City, where young cadets fought to the death in defense of their country and, in an act of heroic bravado, hurled themselves off a parapet in Chapultepec rather than surrender the national flag. The *niños héroes* came to symbolize the noble struggle of Mexico against impossible odds, obtaining a place of mythic honor in the pantheon of Mexican patriots. The disastrous defeat at the hand of the United States carved a deep scar on Mexico's national soul.

Additional traumas came through the Mexican Revolution, when the United States would intervene in a variety of ways. Even while Francisco Madero was in the process of ousting Porfirio Díaz, U.S. representatives reported widespread anti-Americanism. Consul Samuel E. Magill at Guadalajara reported to Secretary of State Philander Knox in 1911 that "the anti-American sentiment is almost universal among rich and poor alike." Consul Charles M. Freeman at Durango wrote that "this district is 95 percent anti-American, and that is a most conservative estimate for I have yet to meet a Mexican who has any love for the people of the United States as a whole." M. S. Largey, a banking and mining operator, returned to the United States in 1913 with a report that "the great masses of the population hate Americans with an intensity that is awful to contemplate." The logic was ineluctable: Virtually by definition, a nationalist movement in quest of social justice would have to be anti-American.

There existed a constant, understandable fear that the United States would take advantage of rising unrest in Mexico. As Madero mounted his drive against Díaz, commentators expressed apprehension about U.S. troop movements along the northern border and naval operations off the coast. Posters and billboards summoned compatriots to resist: "Death to the Yankees!" "Down with Gringos!" "Kill Díaz and his Yankee friends." Once in office, the mild-mannered Madero dismissed American workers from the Mexican railroad system, out of fear that they might comprise a fifth column. Anticipating a U.S. invasion, in April 1912 the newspaper *El Tiempo* called for the Mexican people to rise up, repel the aliens, and make sure that "each bullet fired goes to strike the heart or the forehead of the profaner of our soil."

Conservatives joined in this chorus as well. After Woodrow Wilson refused to recognize the administration of Victoriano Huerta (following the assassination of Madero), a pro-Huerta spokesman claimed that a resistance movement in Sonora was in fact the first step in a plan formulated by Teddy Roosevelt and "Yankee bankers" to partition Mexico into small republics that would then be at the mercy of the United States. In 1914 Wilson authorized a naval occupation of the port of Veracruz, after Mexico had refused to fire a twenty-one-gun salute of respect; bloody confrontations led to at least 200 Mexican dead and 300 wounded, compared with 19 American deaths and 71 additional casualties.

Later in the revolution, as the Wilson administration began to favor the forces of Venustiano Carranza, an outraged Pancho Villa massacred fifteen American citizens at Santa Ysabel in January 1916. Two months later he conducted a daring cross-border raid on the town of Columbus, New Mexico, resulting in the death of eighteen Americans. As noted in chapter 2, Wilson responded by mobilizing 150,000 militia along the southern frontier and dispatching 12,000 troops under General John Pershing to pursue and punish Villa. Pershing never came close to capturing Villa in the mountains of Chihuahua, U.S. troops were routed in a battle at Carrizal, and after ten months of frustration the expedition returned to the United States. For his successful defiance of the *gringos,* Villa would become a national hero.

Thus did Mexico develop its culture of resistance, a fierce pride in *lo mexicano* and resentment of U.S. depredations. In 1924 a Catholic priest, José Cantú Corro, spoke of underlying strength in the national character. Because of its Indian and Spanish strains, he wrote in *Patria y raza,* "There throbs in our heart the spirit of El Cid and of Cuauhtémoc." Continued Cantú Corro: "Mexico must not be for foreigners; no, a thousand times no. . . . Mexico, idolized Motherland, nest of affections, mansion of happiness, noble Republic; Mexico, my Motherland, let the Saxons never assault your soil, nor implant their false religion, nor tarnish your flag."

## Cuba: Inside the Monster

One of the most revered patriots in Cuban history is José Martí. A passionate advocate of Cuban independence from Spain, a writer, publicist, and essayist, Martí went into exile in the United States from 1880 to 1895. While acknowledging respect for the United States, he expressed continual apprehension about its annexationist tendencies and its longstanding designs upon Cuba. In a reference to Francis Cutting, one of the most noted militants in the American Annexationist League, Martí once observed that "We love the land of Lincoln just as we fear the land of Cutting." What he condemned most was *ultraguilismo,* as he called it, the policy of "extending over much of the earth the wings of the American eagle."

In Martí's view, the U.S. drive toward empire had an economic basis. American producers were in desperate need of new markets:

> The manufacturers of North America . . . have come to produce more articles than the country needs, but are unable, as a result of the cost of production . . . to place their excess production in foreign markets, [and] today they urgently and actually need to display and sell their surplus at low cost in the nearby American markets; and with their additional production, in the absence of a corresponding demand to absorb it, the surplus will continue to accumulate on top of the current surplus. People here, thus, need someone to display their products. People there need someone to explain and point out to them the appropriateness and advantages of their purchases. *La América* is a timely answer to both needs.

Here was precisely the problem. For Martí, U.S. imperialism was not a whimsical impulse or a partisan cause. It was a fundamental requirement for continued development of the North American economy.

Equally hazardous, in Martí's eyes, was the power and presence of pro-annexationist forces in Cuba. As he explained in 1882:

There is still a greater danger, perhaps greater than all others. In Cuba there has always been an important group of cautious men, quite bold in their rejection of Spanish domination, but yet quite reserved in endangering their own personal comfort to combat it. This kind of man, aided by those who would enjoy the benefits of freedom without paying its high price, vehemently favors the annexation of Cuba to the United States. All these shy, irresolute men, all these shallow observers, so attached to their possessions, are tempted to support this solution, which they believe to be cheap and easy. In this way they satisfy their patriotic conscience and appease their fears of real patriotism. But, since this is human nature, we must not look upon their temptations with stoic contempt, we must stop them.

Martí thus formulated an enduring element in Latin America's emergent political culture: the detection and identification of turncoats, of pro-U.S. traitors ready to forswear national dignity for the sake of personal and private gain. This would be a persistent theme in the continental culture of resistance.

In a fashion reminiscent of Bolívar, Martí summoned progressive elements throughout the region to the dream of unification. It was essential, he wrote in a famous essay entitled "Nuestra América," for Latin American nations to acknowledge their common cause with Cuba: "The urgent task for our America is to reveal itself for what it is, united in purpose and soul, rapidly triumphant over its suffocating past, its hands stained only by blood spent in the struggle against [colonial] ruins, blood from the veins pricked by our masters. The disdain of a powerful and unknowing neighbor is the greatest danger for our America . . . because this ignorance could inspire greed." Regional unification faced an intimidating array of internal obstacles and external threats, mainly from the United States; all the more reason to realize Bolívar's noble dream.

Martí expressed continuous fear that, once the Spaniards were ousted, the United States would attempt to annex Cuba. In 1895 he wrote,

Every day my life is in danger. I am in danger of giving up my life for my country, for my duty—as I understand it and must execute it—so that Cuba's independence will prevent the expansion of the United States throughout the Antilles, allowing that nation to fall, ever more powerfully, upon our American lands. Everything I have done, everything I will do, is toward this end. It has been a silent and indirect process, for there are things which must be kept hidden if they are to take place. . . . I have lived inside the monster and know its entrails—and my weapon is only the slingshot of David.

The independence of Cuba, he insisted once again, was essential to the sovereignty and integrity of the remainder of Latin America.

Once back in Cuba, Martí met an early death on the battlefield. The "pearl of the Antilles" lost one of its most devoted and capable leaders, and Latin America gained a martyr for the continental cause.

## Nicaragua: Origins of Sandinismo

Nicaragua was long the object of imperial intrigue. As early as the seventeenth century, European powers began to contemplate the possibility of constructing a transisthmian canal through Nicaragua, thus connecting the Atlantic with the Pacific; in the mid-nineteenth century the United States and Britain agreed to keep the project to themselves. After a filibustering expedition in the 1850s, William Walker, an American citizen, proclaimed himself to be the president of Nicaragua. In response to an insult (and an outstanding debt) the United States occupied the country from 1909 to 1925, controlling national politics through local minions. In 1926, after a fraudulent election, the United States invaded again. This time a young guerrilla leader named Augusto César Sandino took to the hills in order, in his words, "to fight the Yankee piracy." He organized an effective military unit, which he called the Army in Defense of the Sovereignty of Nicaragua, and he adopted a powerful slogan: *Patria y Libertad.*

In letters and testimonials, Sandino described American soldiers and leaders in scathing terms. His prose dripping with vituperation, he referred in April 1927 to "drug-dependent Yankees." Months later he wrote of "Yankee cowards and criminals" and went on to denounce "the adventurous Yankees, who are trampling Nicaragua's sovereignty under foot." In December 1927 he railed against "Yankee imperialism" once again, openly decrying "the monstrousness of the crimes committed by the *patricides and Nordic punitive army* upon the Nicaraguan people." On occasion he ridiculed the "blond beasts" and "blond pirates" from the north; at times he criticized "Wall Street magnates" and "North American piratical assassins." Sandino aimed his scorn not only at the U.S. government and military. Though he welcomed support from some groups in the United States, such as the All-America Anti-Imperialist League, he concluded by January 1930 that "the North American people support and will always support the expansionist policies of their unprincipled governments." "The North American people," he observed in another communiqué, "are as imperialistic as their own leaders."

Sandino reserved his sharpest criticism, however, for traitorous groups within Nicaragua. Shortly after initiating his campaign, Sandino claimed that partisan divisions had divided national society into three groups: "Puritanical and honorable Liberals," meaning himself and his followers; "Chicken Liberals (or eunuchs)," meaning José María Moncada and others who agreed to abide by the U.S.-sponsored election pact of 1928; and "Sellouts of their country, in other words, Conservatives." Time and again he heaped scorn on the political leaders who collaborated with U.S. occupation forces: Moncada, Adolfo Díaz, and Emiliano Chamorro, "the unholy trinity of miserable sellouts of their country." And against these forces, the guerrilla leader vowed unending resistance: "*We swear before the symbol of the fatherland to die rather than to sell ourselves or to surrender to the offers of the invaders, oligarchs, and traitors who for so many years have trafficked with the Nation's honor.*"

His avowed mission was the achievement of national sovereignty. "My obsession," Sandino said in September 1927, "is to repel with the dignity and pride of our race every imposition that, with the cynicism derived from strength, the assassins of weak nations are imposing upon our country, and you may be firmly convinced that as long as I possess bullets, I will make them understand that their audacity will

Rebel, patriot, and political martyr, César Augusto Sandino stoutly resisted the U.S. military presence in Nicaragua.
Source: Copyright Bettmann/Corbis/AP Images.

cost them dearly." In view of the strength of the opposition, victory could come only through force. Antedating Mao Zedong's later dictums in China, Sandino proclaimed in October 1927: "Freedom is not won with flowers! It is with bullets that we must drive the enemy from power! The revolution is synonymous with purification!"

As did Martí for Cuba, Sandino asserted that the cause of Nicaragua was the cause of all Latin America. Invoking the struggles "of all the Latin American peoples against the imperialist policies of the Anglo-Saxon colossus," he warned leaders of Latin America about U.S. ambitions to reduce the entire region to the status of "an Anglo-Saxon colony." And like Martí, he sought to reawaken the Bolivarian dream. In March 1929, after drafting a proposal for a continental congress to "assure the sovereignty and independence of our twenty-one Indo-Hispanic republics and friendship between the America of our race and the United States of America, upon a basis of equality," Sandino developed a multipoint "plan for the realization of Bolívar's highest dream":

> Profoundly convinced, as we are, that North American capitalism has arrived at its last stage of development, transforming itself as a result into imperialism; and that it no longer has any respect for theories of right and justice, ignoring the inexorable principles of independence of the divisions of the Latin American nationality, we view as indispensable, and even more so, undelayable, the Alliance of our Latin American states as a way to maintain that independence before the designs of U.S. imperialism, or before that of any other power that may wish to subject us to its interests.

"There is nothing more logical, nothing more decisive or vital," Sandino asserted, "than the fusion of our twenty-one states of our America into one unique Latin American nationality." Calling for the abolition of the Monroe Doctrine, establishment of a Latin American court, organization of a continental army, regional control of the Panama Canal, and other collaborative measures, Sandino addressed his appeal to heads of government throughout the region. "We are proposing an alliance," he assured them, "and not a confederation." He was also seeking a gesture of continental solidarity in his struggle against the U.S. Marines.

Despite his radical-sounding appeals to the working classes and furious condemnations of imperialism, Sandino was not a Marxist. (Indeed, he stoutly resisted attempts at socialist indoctrination.) He displayed, instead, a mystical faith in religion and in God. But there would be, he predicted, no messianic arrival during the twentieth century. Instead:

> What will happen is the following: The oppressed people will break the chains of humiliation, with which the imperialists of the earth have sought to keep them in backwardness. The trumpets that will be heard will be the bugles of war, intoning the hymns of the freedom of the oppressed peoples against the injustice of the oppressors. The only thing that will be submerged for all time is injustice, and Love, king of Perfection, will remain, with his favorite daughter, Divine Justice.

Partly in recognition of Sandino's political and military strength, Franklin Delano Roosevelt withdrew U.S. forces from Nicaragua in 1933. The next year Anastasio Somoza masterminded the assassination of Sandino and then proceeded to install a dictatorial regime conspicuous for its brutality, venality, and nepotism. It was hardly surprising that, decades later, youthful leaders of a guerrilla movement against the Somoza dynasty would christen themselves as "*sandinistas.*"

## Continental Solidarity

Calls for pan-Latin American solidarity steadily mounted in response to U.S. power. Despite the unattainability (and perhaps implausibility) of the Bolivarian dream, writers and essayists took frequent note of common cause against the United States. Even in Brazil, perhaps the most pro-American country in the region, Eduardo Prado attacked "the absorbent, imperialist, and tyrannical policies of North American diplomacy" as early as 1893, concluding bitterly: "There is no Latin American nation that has not suffered in its relations with the United States." José Enrique Rodó (of Uruguay) and Rubén Darío (of Nicaragua) would sound anti-American themes around the turn of the century, a tradition soon followed by Manuel Pesqueira (of Mexico).

In 1912 an articulate and irascible Argentine, Manuel Ugarte, wrote a letter congratulating Woodrow Wilson on his election to the presidency and enumerating a long list of grievances that Latin Americans held in common. He lectured the president-elect:

> We desire that Cuba be freed from the painful weight of the Platt Amendment; we desire that there should be granted to Nicaragua the ability to dispose of their soil, *leaving to the people to depose those who govern them with the aid of a foreign army, if they deem it necessary;* we desire that the status of Porto Rico [*sic*] be settled in accordance with the rights of humanity; we desire that the abominable injustice committed against Colombia be repaired so far as possible; we desire that Panama, which today suffers the consequences of a temporary displacement, be ceded the dignity of a nation; we desire that the pressure being exerted on the port of Guayaquil shall cease; we desire that the archipelago of the Galápagos be respected; we desire that liberty be conceded to the heroic Filipinos; we desire that Mexico shall not always see suspended above her flag Damocles' sword of intervention; we desire that the disorders of Putumayo shall not serve as a pretext for diplomatic dexterities; we desire that the companies which go beyond their authority shall not be supported in their unjust demands; we desire that the Republic of Santo Domingo be not suffocated by unjust oppression; we desire that the United States abstain from officiously intervening in the domestic politics of our countries and that they discontinue the acquisition of ports and bays on this continent; we desire that measures of sanitation shall not serve to diminish the sovereignty of nations of the Pacific; we ask, in short, that the star-spangled banner cease to be a symbol of oppression in the New World.

It was a stirring challenge, more effective in rallying Latin America than in deterring the United States. During his first term in office Woodrow Wilson, the professorial idealist, would send U.S. troops headlong into Cuba, Mexico, Haiti, and the Dominican Republic.

Dollar diplomacy gave further impetus to the drive for cultural and political unity in Latin America. In 1925 a prominent Mexican philosopher, José Vasconcelos, would proclaim that the *mestizo* combination, or "cosmic race," provided Latin America with a social identity, a legacy different from North America, and an inherently virtuous ethnic stock. And from an entirely different quarter, outgoing president Arturo Alessandri of Chile would in 1926 express frustration with U.S. diplomacy: "During my five years in office, I worked to give true life to Pan-Americanism," he reflected bitterly. "But now I will devote all the energies that remain to me in preaching that. . . . we [Latin American republics] must arise, and together, in union, proclaim: Latin America for the Latin Americans."

During the 1920s and 1930s, anti-U.S. argumentation began to acquire a sharp analytical edge. A young Peruvian reformer, Víctor Raúl Haya de la Torre, would sound a clarion call for the continental solidarity of "indo-America" in its "international struggle against Yankee imperialism in Latin America" as he launched his program for the Alianza Popular Revolucionaria Americana (APRA), the keystone for the *Aprista* party in his native country. Around the same time his brilliant compatriot, José Carlos Mariátegui, developed an explicitly Marxist analysis of social and racial inequities in a famous tract, *Siete ensayos de interpretación de la realidad peruana* (1928). Spreading out from intellectual circles, Marxism would eventually become a major component of the continental cultures of resistance.

## IN RETROSPECT

Notwithstanding constancy of effort, Latin America had relatively little success in curtailing the rise of U.S. imperial power. Conspicuously ineffective were attempts to establish subregional hegemony, as on the part of Argentina and Brazil, which simply lacked the necessary capabilities for such an enterprise. Equally ineffective were efforts to induce extrahemispheric powers to step into the hemisphere and provide protection for nations of Latin America. European policymakers gradually relaxed their resistance to U.S. advances during the course of the nineteenth century, and by the early twentieth century most became willing to allow Washington to guarantee their loans, investments, and commerce. As major powers accepted U.S. participation in the worldwide imperial contest, in other words, they became increasingly prepared to regard Latin America as Washington's backyard.

The Bolivarian pursuit of continental unification produced ambiguous results. In one sense, the ideal proved a quixotic failure: Despite several attempts, leaders of the region were unable to create any kind of meaningful organization. But in another sense, the notion had significant impact: It drew on beliefs in common origins, it defined a sense of collective purpose, and on occasion it played a crucial political role. Its diplomatic significance was especially apparent in the decades-long promotion of hemispheric international law, most notably with regard to doctrines of sovereignty and nonintervention. To a considerable extent, inculcation of these provisions in FDR's Good Neighbor policy represented a triumph for Latin America and a vindication of its quest for solidarity. Of course this outcome was only as meaningful as international law itself, but at the time it represented a remarkable achievement.

**BOX 3-2**

### An Anti-Imperialist Manifesto

One of Latin America's most important twentieth-century figures was Víctor Raúl Haya de la Torre (1895–1979). Exiled in Mexico from his native Peru during the 1920s, he launched a movement called APRA (*Alianza Popular Revolucionaria Americana*, or Popular Revolutionary American Alliance) as a call for broad political reform and resistance to U.S. hegemony. As Haya de la Torre explained, APRA's international program had five basic points:

1. Action of the countries of Latin America against Yankee Imperialism.
2. The political unity of Latin America.
3. The nationalisation of land and industry.
4. The internationalisation of the Panama Canal.
5. The solidarity of all the oppressed people and classes of the world.

The APRA organises the great Latin American Anti-Imperialist united front and works to include in its ranks all those who in one way or another have struggled and are still struggling against the North American danger in Latin America. Until 1923 this danger was regarded as a possible struggle of races— the Saxon and the Latin races—as a "conflict of cultures" or as a question of nationalism. . . .

The history of the political and economic relations between Latin America and the United States, especially the experience of the Mexican Revolution, leads to the following conclusions:

1. The governing classes of the Latin American countries—landowners, middle class or merchants—are allies of North American Imperialism.
2. These classes have the political power in our countries, in exchange for a policy of concessions, of loans, of great operations which they—the capitalists, landowners or merchants and politicians of the Latin American dominant classes—share with Imperialism.
3. As a result of this alliance the natural resources which form the riches of our countries are mortgaged or sold, and the working and agricultural classes are subjected to the most brutal servitude. Again, this alliance produces political events which result in the loss of national sovereignty: Panama, Nicaragua, Cuba, Santo Domingo, are really protectorates of the United States. . . .

The experience of history, especially that of Mexico, shows that the immense power of American Imperialism cannot be overthrown without the unity of the Latin American countries . . . The overthrow of the governing classes is indispensable, political power must be captured by the workers, and Latin America must be united in a Federation of States. That is one of the great political objects of the APRA.

Upon returning to Peru, Haya de la Torre founded the APRA or Aprista Party, which continues to exist today.

Source: Robert H. Holden and Eric Zolov (eds.), *Latin America and the United States: A Documentary History*, 2nd ed. (New York: Oxford University Press, 2011), pp. 122–123.

Ultimately it was the formulation of cultures of resistance that left the most enduring legacy. Throughout this historical era Latin America's search for self-identity became profoundly, inextricably, and necessarily entwined with its relationship to the United States. The rise of U.S. power, and its application to the region, left no other choice for Latin Americans. They could embrace the U.S. claim to hegemony, as many of them did, they could tolerate the U.S. role, as more of them did, or they could resist advances by the Colossus of the North, as most of them did. The unavoidable reality of U.S. power led some *pensadores* to denigrate American culture and to celebrate Latin America's lofty appreciation for faith, beauty, and nobility; it prompted others to issue urgent appeals for support and solidarity; it led still others to compose trenchant critiques of U.S. imperialism and its underlying purposes. Resistance to the United States became an integral part of national and continental self-assertion. This connection would persist in times to come.

## QUESTIONS FOR REVIEW

1. What were the main strategies available to Latin America for responding to U.S. hegemony?
2. What was the "Bolivarian dream," and what were the leading obstacles to its fulfillment?
3. What hopes did Latin American leaders have for partnerships with Europe? How did they pursue these possibilities? What might have been accomplished by close alliances with Europe?
4. Why were Brazil and Argentina uniquely positioned to present themselves as subregional powers? What were the long-term legacies of their efforts?
5. Why did Latin Americans place such strong emphasis on international law? What specific ideas or doctrines did they seek to promote?

# CHAPTER 4

# Mr. Roosevelt's Neighborhood

That is a new approach that I am talking about to these South
American things. Give them a share. They think they are just as
good as we are and many of them are.

FRANKLIN DELANO ROOSEVELT (1940)

A new era of colonial ambitions, determined more by
economic factors than strictly political ones, is going to take
charge of universal destinies.

OSWALDO ARANHA (1935)

The decade of the 1930s stands out as a golden era of U.S. relations with Latin America. President Franklin Delano Roosevelt's proclamation of a "Good Neighbor" policy marked an abrupt change in U.S. policy toward the region. Washington withdrew military troops, refrained from intervention, and initiated a process of consultation and cooperation. The United States began treating Latin American nations as sovereign entities rather than as subordinates, as equal partners engaged in the collective promotion of hemispheric interests. This new stance promoted goodwill and mutual respect among countries of the Americas, according to conventional accounts, and its practical consequence was the achievement of nearly unanimous support for the United States throughout World War II. Being a Good Neighbor turned out to be good policy.

There is another way of viewing these events. Within the imperial context, the Good Neighbor policy can be seen not as a departure from past practices but as the *culmination* of trends in U.S. policy toward the region. In effect, FDR's stance reflected a hardheaded sense of *realpolitik* that promoted and protected the longstanding U.S. quest for hegemony throughout the hemisphere. In the name of nonintervention, the Good Neighbor policy constituted yet another attempt to achieve, impose, and consolidate American supremacy.

The policy stemmed from a recognition that political intervention and democratic proselytization à la Woodrow Wilson were ineffective, that the costs were greater than the benefits. At a time when most European powers were reducing their involvement in the Americas, it was no longer necessary or advantageous for the United States to engage in heavy-handed intervention. And to an increasing extent, the United States could apply economic leverage over countries in the hemisphere. As a result, Washington could now extract voluntary cooperation from Latin American governments through diplomatic and economic means. Instead of seizing territory or creating colonies or nurturing protectorates, the United States was using new instruments in behalf of time-honored goals. In essence, the Good Neighbor policy would amount to a declaration of triumph in the imperial contest.

At the same time, the policy implicitly renounced the missionary goal of democratization. Respect for the sovereignty of Latin American nations implied acceptance of their political systems—including authoritarian regimes. During the 1930s the hemisphere was swarming with dictatorships. As a "good neighbor," Washington chose not to meddle in the domestic affairs of governments nearby. Unable to impose democracy, the United States decided to conduct business with whomever held the power. Beneath the warmth of diplomatic rhetoric, the U.S. stance revealed a cold-blooded calculation.

The Good Neighbor policy reflected major changes in the global arena. As a result of World War I, which severely interrupted commercial flows between Latin America and Europe, the economic influence of European powers was in marked decline. The United States seized the opportunity to accentuate links to the region: Between 1919 and 1929, direct U.S. investments in Latin America climbed from $2.0 billion to $3.5 billion. The Depression intensified this pattern. Latin American trade with Europe dropped sharply in the early 1930s, and, despite the crisis in its own economy, the United States moved in to fill the gap.

Another major factor was the imminence of war. The rise of Adolf Hitler in Germany and his alliance with Benito Mussolini of Italy confronted Europe with the specter of fascism. Similarly, the emergence of a military-led government in Japan posed a looming threat to all of Asia. In this setting, extrahemispheric powers were hardly in a position to expand their influence in the Western Hemisphere— with the exception of the Nazis, who made vigorous efforts to establish footholds in South America. Most European nations had to concentrate their energies on grave and immediate challenges, including Hitler's military aggressions. This left the United States with a relatively free hand in its dealings with the hemisphere.

As a result of these developments, inter-American relations assumed primary importance for Washington. In the language of a State Department document of 1933, "Among the foreign relations of the United States as they fall into categories, the Pan American policy takes first place in our diplomacy." Contrary to historical stereotype, the United States did not adopt an isolationist stance toward all world regions throughout the 1930s. While Washington refrained from major involvement in the European theater and strident voices in support of "America First" called for strict isolationism, the United States steadily increased its level of commitment and concern with regard to Latin America. The United States was consolidating its own sphere of influence.

## CRUCIBLES: NICARAGUA AND CUBA

As often occurs, the inception of a new U.S. policy emerged from the exhaustion of a prior policy. During the 1920s, the United States dispatched troops frequently to

Central America and the Caribbean, with long-term occupations in Haiti and the Dominican Republic—for the ostensible purpose of promoting democracy and (especially) imposing economic order. None of these episodes proved to be an unqualified success. It was the outcome of two other adventures, however, that marked a turning point in Washington's views away from military intervention. The first, and more important, took place in Nicaragua.

### Nicaragua, 1927–1933

After World War I Washington was casting wary eyes on Mexico, still emerging from its "Bolshevist" revolution of 1910. In 1923 the administration of Warren Harding agreed to provide diplomatic recognition to Mexico in exchange for assurances to U.S. investors, especially petroleum companies. Shortly afterward the Calvin Coolidge administration expressed concern over prospects for large-scale land reform, while American Catholics expressed vehement opposition to anticlerical tendencies within the revolution and the constitution of 1917. Perceived as a source of manifold dangers, Mexico also sought to take advantage of instability in Nicaragua. Costa Rican officials reported to Washington that "Mexico is attempting to develop a sphere of influence in Central America," while a State Department analysis argued that the government of Plutarco Elías Calles was making "an unmistakable attempt...to extend Mexican influence over Central America with the unquestionable aim of ultimately achieving a Mexican primacy over the Central American countries." The United States and Mexico thus found themselves on a collision course.

Within Nicaragua, the United States continued to support the Conservatives against the Liberals. Coolidge had withdrawn U.S. Marines in 1925 only after the patently fraudulent election of 1924 extended Conservative rule. With Americans gone, the Liberals, who probably enjoyed the majority of popular support, staged a rebellion in 1926. To promote stability, Washington persuaded Emiliano Chamorro to step down in favor of Adolfo Díaz, who was then elected president by a pliant legislature. Mexico continued to recognize the would-be Liberal government of archrival Juan Sacasa. In response, a State Department spokesman publicly charged that Mexico "was seeking to establish a Bolshevist authority in Nicaragua in order to drive a 'hostile wedge' between the United States and the Panama Canal."

As Díaz's grasp on power weakened, President Coolidge dispatched a contingent of U.S. Marines in December 1926. Explaining his action to Congress, Coolidge argued that conditions in Nicaragua "seriously threaten American lives and property, endanger the stability of all Central America, and put in jeopardy the rights granted by Nicaragua to the United States for the construction of a canal." Denouncing Sacasa's "Mexican allies," Coolidge surmised that the Díaz government would be unable to protect foreigners "solely because of the aid given by Mexico to the revolutionists." Concluded the president: "The United States can not, therefore, fail to view with deep concern any serious threat to stability and constitutional government in Nicaragua tending toward anarchy and jeopardizing

American interests, especially if such state of affairs is contributed to or brought about by outside influences or by any foreign power."

European observers quickly denounced the U.S. intervention as "frankly imperialist." Responded the *New York Times,* with an air of sanctimonious defiance: "All that we do has at least the motive of aiding and protecting the weaker republics on this continent, rather than of overriding or despoiling them. If this be Imperialism, make the most of it."

A decision to arbitrate land and petroleum rights led to an easing of U.S. bilateral tensions with Mexico. In Nicaragua, however, Liberal forces continued their relentless advance on Managua. Faced with difficult choices, Coolidge eventually assigned Henry L. Stimson to negotiate a settlement that would permit a face-saving exit. Having no prior experience in Nicaragua—"So far as ignorance would free it from prejudices or commitments," he would later recall, "my mind was a clean slate"—Stimson chose to supervise elections in hopes of bringing order to the country. He also convinced Conservatives and Liberals to accept a power-sharing arrangement. There were 5,500 U.S. Marines on hand for the election in 1928 of José María Moncada, a Liberal who had consented to the Stimson compromise.

Governmental authority proved tenuous, however, so U.S. troops remained in Nicaragua. César Augusto Sandino denounced the Liberal-Conservative bargain and took to the mountains, where he led an armed rebellion. By April 1931 Stimson was forced to proclaim that the United States was unable to ensure "general protection of Americans" in Nicaragua. Attempts to capture Sandino merely made him a national hero. United States troops supervised yet another presidential election in 1932, but instability continued to mount. In recognition of this fact the United States helped develop the Guardia Nacional, which promptly fell under the leadership of Anastasio Somoza.

Armed intervention was not achieving its goals. As one American coffee planter in Nicaragua wrote to Stimson:

> Today we are hated and despised and in danger of massacre any time the Marines are withdrawn. This feeling has been created by employing the American Marines to hunt down and kill Nicaraguans in their own territory. This was a fatal mistake. The intervention of the U.S. government in the internal affairs of Nicaragua has proved a calamity for the American coffee planters doing business in this Republic.

Appointed by Herbert Hoover as secretary of state, Stimson decided to withdraw the marines after the election of 1932. Asked if he would advocate the dispatch of American troops elsewhere in Latin America, Stimson replied: "Not on your life. . . . If we landed a single soldier among those South Americans now, it would undo all the labor of three years, and it would put me in absolutely wrong in China, where Japan has done all of this monstrous work under the guise of protecting her nationals with a landing force."

In short, the seven-year episode in Nicaragua conveyed sobering lessons for Washington. By the end of 1932, 135 U.S. soldiers had lost their lives. Financial costs were mounting. Neither Congress nor the White house was prepared to authorize funding to sustain the American presence. American troops withdrew in January 1933. Somoza had Sandino murdered in February 1934. Two years later Somoza would take power for himself.

### Cuba, 1929–1933

Cuba presented a different kind of challenge. Reelected for a six-year term in 1929, President Gerardo Machado y Morales reacted harshly to social agitation caused by the economic Depression. In February 1931 he suspended constitutional guarantees and shut down the University of Havana.

Washington found itself obliged to respond to these developments. Ironically enough, these policy deliberations were greatly complicated by the fact that the Platt Amendment specifically authorized precisely the kind of U.S. intervention that Stimson had come to oppose. Besides, Machado had achieved for foreign investors the political and economic stability that the amendment was designed to ensure. Eventually, Washington decided that the amendment guaranteed "the protection of life, property, and individual liberty" of *foreigners only,* especially Americans, and not of anti-Machado Cuban nationals.

Consequently there would be no intervention. As Stimson later explained, "We should make ourselves extremely unpopular with every country in Latin America if we adopted such a course of action." Contending that a request for Machado to resign would be "a very serious intervention," Stimson pondered the possibility of supervising an election:

> that would be even more of an intervention on our part. We have done it in Nicaragua in order to bring to a termination a long period of civil war and anarchy and, in that case, we only did it upon the request of all parties and factions in Nicaragua. Even then, we found the expense and difficulty involved in such an operation, even in such a small country as Nicaragua, a very serious burden. Under present conditions, it would be quite out of the question in Cuba.

It was the precedent of Nicaragua as much as the reality of Cuba that argued against direct U.S. action.

By the early 1930s, in summary, the practice of military intervention appeared to have outlived its usefulness. There was need and opportunity to forge a new approach. It was at this moment and in this context that Franklin Delano Roosevelt swept to victory in the presidential election of 1932.

## THE GOOD NEIGHBOR POLICY:
## POLITICAL DIMENSIONS

In his inaugural address of 1933 Roosevelt coined the phrase that would define the lines of policy. "I would dedicate this nation to the policy of the Good Neighbor," he said, "—the neighbor who respects his obligations and respects the sanctity of his agreements in and with a world of neighbors." Though vague in content, this formulation directly challenged isolationist sentiments that would continue to gain strength during the course of the Depression. And while the idea was initially intended for the world as a whole, it would acquire its most specific meaning in relation to Latin America.

The cornerstone of the Good Neighbor policy was nonintervention. This began to take shape at the inter-American meeting of 1933 at Montevideo, where delegates concurred in a resolution firmly asserting that "No state has the right to intervene in the internal or external affairs of another." United States Secretary of State Cordell Hull not only assented to this language but further explained that "the United States government is as much opposed as any other government to interference with the freedom, the sovereignty, or other internal affairs or processes of the governments of other nations." As a result, Hull pledged, "no government need fear any intervention on the part of the United States under the Roosevelt administration."

Nonintervention sharply modified the Monroe Doctrine. More particularly, it amounted to a rejection of the 1904 Roosevelt Corollary, which had proclaimed that the United States possessed not only a right to intervene but also a moral duty (in cases of "impotence" or "chronic wrongdoing"). According to the Buenos Aires protocol, military intervention was henceforth prohibited "for whatever reason." At least on this one issue, Franklin Roosevelt repudiated the legacy of cousin Theodore.

By upholding the principle of national sovereignty, the doctrine of nonintervention supported the juridical equality of states. Under Good Neighbor precepts, large countries were supposed to respect the integrity of smaller countries. As Latins came to say with pride: "Now there are no little nations." Moreover, nonintervention meant that force should no longer be used for the protection of property or citizens abroad. It thus overthrew Calvin Coolidge's dictum that the U.S. government was obliged to protect the property rights of U.S. citizens in foreign lands. In effect, the Good Neighbor position held that U.S. citizens and investments overseas must obey the sovereign laws of host societies. In addition, the policy called for consultation among the states of the Americas. At a 1936 meeting in Buenos Aires, delegates concurred in a resolution that hemispheric states "shall consult together for the purposes of finding and adopting methods of peaceful cooperation." In translation, this meant that the United States would no longer act in unilateral fashion. And as a result, it was imagined, the hemisphere would become a cooperative community of states.

A final component was the principle of noninterference. Going much further than the idea of nonintervention, which held that countries should refrain from the deployment of military force, noninterference meant that nations should abstain from *any* form of meddling in the internal affairs of sovereign states— through coercion, enticement, manipulation, or other means, which might range from unsought advice to economic pressure to the threat or show of force.

## Cuba, 1933–1936

The concept of noninterference evolved not from presidential declaration but from the passage of events, especially in Cuba. Taking office as FDR's secretary of state, Cordell Hull immediately initiated diplomatic negotiations that led to abrogation of the Platt Amendment by May 1934. The United States thus forfeited its longstanding right to intervention within Cuba. But this did not imply total disengagement. On the contrary, Hull replaced the threat of outside intervention with more subtle efforts to direct the course of Cuban affairs.

The principal agent of this new approach was Sumner Welles, who arrived as U.S. ambassador to Havana in May 1933. As opposition mounted against the relentless rule of Machado, Welles took it upon himself to present the ruler with a five-point plan that included his taking a leave of absence from office. Machado dissented but lost the support of his army and departed Cuba in August. Subsequent conditions under Carlos Manuel de Céspedes rapidly deteriorated, however, and Welles responded with a plan for new elections. And then, in September 1934, rank-and-file army elements under Sergeant Fulgencio Batista imposed a junta that included five civilians. Becoming apoplectic as his plans unraveled, Welles denounced the ruling leadership as representing "a group of the most extreme radicals of the student organization and three university professors whose theories are frankly communistic." This was not the first occasion, and by no means the last, when U.S. officials would denounce the threat of communism in the Western Hemisphere.

Welles pursued several courses of action. First, he urged Washington to intervene. The cautious Hull rejected this advice, warning that "if we have to go in there again, we will never be able to come out and we will have on our hands the trouble of thirty years ago." Second, Welles persuaded the State Department to withhold recognition of the new government, eventually led by Ramón Grau San Martín, a university professor, on the grounds that the regime was incapable of maintaining law and order. In the meantime, Welles continued to denounce the Grau San Martín administration as "an undisciplined group of individuals of divergent tendencies representing the most irresponsible elements in the city of Havana with practically no support whatsoever outside the capital." Despite FDR's claim that the U.S. decision on nonrecognition was wholly impartial, it was, of course, a highly partisan act—yet it failed to topple the government. Third, Welles courted and supported domestic opposition to the new regime, proclaiming in September 1934 that "a social revolution" was in progress against the government. His successor as ambassador, Jefferson Caffery, openly encouraged Batista to overthrow Grau. Shortly thereafter Grau resigned, to be replaced by Carlos Mendieta. Greatly relieved by this turn of events, the United States followed with swift diplomatic recognition.

No longer meddling outright in Cuban affairs, the United States continued to press its interests and its preferences. When Mendieta suspended constitutional guarantees in mid-January 1935, Caffery interpreted the move as strictly anticommunist: "The Mendieta government has been fighting for its life against the communistic elements, and, although it has strengthened its position in the country by its recent firm attitude, the communists have by no means given up hope and will continue to be a menace for some time to come." After presidential elections in 1936, won by Miguel Mariano Gómez, the U.S. government continued its close communications with Fulgencio Batista, inviting him to Washington in 1938 for high-level discussions with FDR as well as Cordell Hull and others. Such displays of tacit support no doubt influenced Batista's decision to run for the presidency in 1940.

From 1933 to 1936, in other words, U.S. diplomats made persistent attempts to interfere in Cuban politics—and eventually chose to desist. This does not quite mean that all their efforts met with failure. As a Mexican official recalled, the succession of threats and enticements during this period was "one of the most effective and skillful interventions ever carried out by the American government." But from Welles' blustering to Caffery's persuasion, the methods for exerting U.S. pressure underwent visible change. At this point, open interference was no longer part of the diplomatic arsenal.

By the end of the 1930s, much of Latin America had fallen under the sway of long-lived dictatorships: Maximiliano Hernández Martínez in El Salvador, Jorge Ubico in Guatemala, Rafael Trujillo in the Dominican Republic, Fulgencio Batista in Cuba, and Anastasio Somoza in Nicaragua. Somewhat conspicuously, these regimes emerged precisely in those countries where the United States had intervened or intermeddled to the greatest degree. As FDR is alleged to have said of Somoza during a visit to Washington in 1939: "He's a son of a bitch, but at least he's our son of a bitch." More serious, and more damning, was the comment of Víctor Raúl Haya de la Torre, the aspiring young reformist from Peru, who proclaimed in 1938 that FDR had made himself "the Good Neighbor of tyrants."

## THE GOOD NEIGHBOR POLICY:
## ECONOMIC DIMENSIONS

Roosevelt's policy toward Latin America entailed not only political accommodation but also economic influence. In 1933 FDR maintained that the stimulation of trade was "the most important item in our country's foreign policy," and as secretary of state he appointed Cordell Hull, a zealous proponent of trade liberalization. Hull believed that commercial opening would not only expand U.S. exports and stimulate production, but that, as a general principle, it would diminish tendencies toward conflict and strengthen prospects for world peace. He also detected geopolitical advantage in the consolidation of commercial ties: The political lineup followed the economic lineup, according to his oft-quoted homily, and Washington could greatly enhance its international position through the artful pursuit of trade policy.

After a hesitant start, the Roosevelt administration began to implement Hull's approach. In 1934 the government established an Export-Import Bank to extend commercial loans to U.S. exporters. That same year Congress approved the Reciprocal Trade Agreements Act (as FDR affixed his signature to the bill, Hull

Revealing a dark side of the Good Neighbor policy, FDR received Nicaraguan dictator Anastasio Somoza on a formal state visit.
Source: Thomas D. McAvoy/Getty Images.

would later recall that "each stroke of the pen seemed to write a message of gladness on my heart"). In effect, this legislation authorized the negotiation of bilateral agreements for trade liberalization, which Hull interpreted as the mutual reduction of tariffs and, if possible, the unconditional extension of most-favored-nation status. Paradoxically, the Smoot-Hawley Tariff Act of 1930 strengthened the U.S. bargaining position, since the reduction or elimination of its protectionist barriers offered major incentives to potential trading partners.

Latin America became a starting point and testing ground for U.S. commercial strategy. The region offered a strong potential market. Between 1929 and 1932 American exports to Latin America declined by 78 percent; recuperation of these sales would help promote U.S. recovery. Moreover, imports from Latin America—which dropped by 68 percent between 1929 and 1932—would not displace American goods. On the contrary, over 80 percent of these goods were raw materials used in manufacturing (for industrial production) or noncompetitive foodstuffs (such as coffee, cocoa, and bananas). Under these conditions customs duties and excise taxes were mutually disadvantageous. And for Hull, especially, successful agreements to liberalize trade with Latin America could set a precedent for negotiations with Europe and other parts of the world. "In carrying out our policies toward Latin America," he later recalled, "it was never my wish to make them exclusively Pan-American."

BOX 4-1

### Sentinels of Empire: U.S. Presidents, 1909–1945

Territorial expansion of the United States came to an end around the turn of the twentieth century, with the colonization of Puerto Rico and the Philippines and the takeover of the Canal Zone in Panama. American presidents thereafter relied on military occupation, "dollar diplomacy," and the invocation of a democratic mission. During the 1930s, FDR's Good Neighbor policy marked a sharp break with the past—and signified the ultimate consolidation of an informal U.S. empire within the hemisphere. They were:

William H. Taft, 1909–1913

Woodrow Wilson, 1913–1921

Warren Harding, 1921–1923

Calvin Coolidge, 1923–1929

Herbert Hoover, 1929–1933

Franklin D. Roosevelt, 1933–1945

FDR oversaw the massive mobilization of U.S. military resources during World War II, which led to the nation's emergence as a global superpower. That wartime effort has been hailed as the signature achievement of America's "greatest generation"—which struggled through economic depression, defeated fascist governments, and elevated the country to a position of international leadership.

True to his convictions, Hull went to the Montevideo conference of 1933 with the avowed intention to "introduce a comprehensive economic resolution calling for lower tariffs and the abolition of trade restrictions." The administration simultaneously initiated bilateral trade discussions with Argentina, Brazil, and Colombia. In view of Colombia's dependence on the U.S. coffee market, one-sided negotiations with Bogotá promptly led to the signing of an advantageous treaty for the United States; "it actually costs us nothing," in the revealing judgment of a State Department memorandum. Passage of the Trade Agreements Act in 1934 required subsequent revisions that led to considerable tension, and it was not until 1936 that the two governments exchanged ratification. Ever gracious, Colombia's exhausted foreign minister expressed appreciation for the Good Neighbor policy with its "new criterion in the diplomatic sphere, and commercial relations based on liberal principles which consecrate the operation of the most-favored-nation clause."

With its tariff legislation in place, Washington next turned to Cuba. As a result of the Depression, the island's sugar income in 1933 had declined to 30 percent of its 1929 level (and merely 12 percent of the 1924 level). Cuba badly needed secure access to the U.S. market; for its part, the United States sought protection for its $1.5 billion in investments. In 1934 Congress fixed quotas among domestic and foreign suppliers for the U.S. sugar market, granting Cuba a 28 percent share.

Soon afterward Washington reached a series of commercial agreements with nations of Central America: Honduras in 1935, Guatemala and Costa Rica in 1936, El Salvador in 1937. As with Colombia and Cuba, these negotiations revealed a common pattern: The United States managed to reach trade agreements only with countries that were heavily dependent on U.S. markets for agricultural (usually monocultural) exports. During the course of the decade, Washington was unable to conclude agreements with Argentina, Chile, Uruguay, Peru, Bolivia, Paraguay, or Mexico.

By far the most dramatic trade negotiations focused on Brazil, the world's fifth-largest supplier to the United States and the source of 60 to 65 percent of its coffee imports. Even more significantly, Brazil was a cornerstone for Adolf Hitler's attempts to augment Germany's political and economic presence throughout Latin America. During the 1930s, Germany launched an economic offensive in the Americas, aggressively promoting the sale of German industrial products in exchange for raw materials from Latin America. Under bilateral arrangements, Germany would often arrange to pay handsome prices for imports with "compensation marks," a special currency that could only be used to purchase German goods in return (this was, fumed Cordell Hull, "a cut-throat double-dealing method of trade"). From 1936 to 1939, imports from Latin America came to 7 percent of Germany's total, whereas German exports to Latin America climbed to over 14 percent of the regional total. Ominously, too, Germany held military instructorships in over half the countries of Latin America. As one U.S. chargé reported back to Washington, Nazi Germany was "conducting a well-organized and astute campaign . . . to discredit in every way possible American efforts on this continent."

Because of its size, location, and importance, Brazil became a central object of the U.S.–German rivalry. For Germany it represented not only a substantial market but also an important source of raw materials, especially cotton (which could be used in the manufacture of explosives). Moreover, the country had a sizable Germanic community, consisting of around 100,000 German nationals and 800,000 German-Brazilians or *teuto-brasileiros*. Seeking to maximize its own commercial exports and its political room for maneuver, the Brazilian government managed to steer an artful middle course. In 1935 the Getúlio Vargas administration announced a Reciprocal Trade Agreement with the United States, which placed over 90 percent of Brazilian imports on its duty-free list; the following year it reached a secret "gentlemen's agreement" with Nazi Germany. Between 1933 and 1938 the German share of Brazilian imports climbed from 12 percent to 25 percent, while the German share of Brazilian exports jumped from just over 8 percent to nearly 20 percent.

United States politicians took notice of the Third Reich's campaign. In the spring of 1938 New York Mayor Fiorello La Guardia sounded a public alarm:

> For the maintenance of our economic well-being, for the preservation of peace, it is vital that we take immediate steps to eliminate this new growing sore on the soil of the Western Hemisphere. In this way, we may lay the foundation of peace and

security for our world of the future. A united people in the Western Hemisphere, without invasion of the sovereign rights of any government. The Americas for the Americans.

Shortly afterward an experienced U.S. businessman speculated about the commercial implications of German penetration of the Western Hemisphere: "Markets would be closed to our exporters. Political, naval and aviation concessions would be linked to commerce. We should soon find a European 'sphere of influence' creeping up toward us from the south, and outposts of the Empire appearing closer and closer to the Panama Canal." President Roosevelt added his own commentary on the possibility of Axis influence in Latin America: "Do you think that the United States could stand idly by and have this European menace right on our own borders? Of course not. You could not stand for it."

As a result of governmental policy, the United States steadily improved its commercial position in the hemisphere. By 1938 the United States had become the leading overall trade partner for every major country of Latin America—with the sole exception of Argentina, which continued to sell large quantities of high-quality beef in the British market, and with the partial exception of Chile. Germany was making substantial headway, especially in the ABC countries, but it was nowhere predominant. In South America as well as in the Caribbean Basin, the United States was gaining the upper hand.

In the end, it was neither diplomatic pressure nor neighborly sentiment that blunted the German offensive in South America. It was the eruption of World War II and, more particularly, the British naval blockade against Hitler's vessels. Commerce with Germany ground to a virtual halt. "What the commercial policy of the United States failed to achieve with its relentless opposition to the expansion of our compensation trade," one Rio de Janeiro newspaper remarked in 1940, "the war brutally realized from one moment to the next."

## Applying Leverage

In its promotion of U.S. economic interests, the Roosevelt administration encountered serious challenges against American oil companies. The first conflict erupted in Bolivia, where the government in March 1937 annulled its concession to the Standard Oil Company and confiscated its properties. The decree alleged that the company had defrauded the government by failure to pay taxes and by the illegal exportation of oil to Argentina in 1925–1926. Technically speaking the governmental decision was not an expropriation, for which compensation might have been offered, but an outright cancellation, which would entail no compensation at all.

The announcement immediately led to wrangling in the Bolivian courts. By February 1938, Sumner Welles, now assistant secretary of state, decided to advocate some form of arbitration, explaining to a Bolivian representative that "the only way in which public opinion in this country was going to support the 'Good Neighbor' policy as a permanent part of our foreign policy would be for the policy to be recognized throughout the continent as a completely reciprocal policy and not one of a purely unilateral character." In March 1938 Standard Oil filed a suit under protest, after consultation with the Department of State, which promised to support a claim for arbitration once legal remedies were exhausted in Bolivia. A year later the Bolivian Supreme Court decided unanimously that Standard Oil did not possess a legal status in that country that entitled it to sue the government.

As the U.S. Department of State pondered its next steps, Cordell Hull issued a blunt warning that:

> in this dangerous, chaotic world situation there was never such a ripe plum dangled before a hungry person than Latin America appears to be to…lawless nations, hungry as wolves for vast territory with rich underdeveloped natural resources such as South America possesses; that it is all-important for the American nations to pursue a lawful, friendly and reasonable course with each other; and that the dollars and cents involved in the oil seizure were small compared to the great injury that would result to Bolivia, as well as to my own and other countries, if that sort of an act should go uncorrected and the friendship between the two countries should be seriously impaired.

The allusion to Germany was as transparent as the threat to Bolivia itself. The petroleum dispute was being drawn into the worldwide arena.

In June 1939 the Department of State offered to act as intermediator. Subsequent news leaks from Bolivia scuttled this idea, and the U.S. government retaliated with two forms of economic pressure: First, the United States tried to prevent Bolivia from obtaining help from immediate neighbors (an effort that was partly successful with Paraguay but less so with respect to Argentina, which continued to purchase Bolivian oil); second, and more important, the United States blocked loans and technical assistance. To emphasize this point, heads of the Reconstruction Finance Corporation and the Export-Import Bank told the U.S. Senate that they would refuse to make loans to "a country that is confiscating our property."

Bolivian officials began seeking a way out of the impasse by August 1940. And as World War II approached, U.S. diplomats began to fear inroads by Germany— implicated in a plot to overthrow the Bolivian government in July 1941—and soon began drawing up plans for a resumption of economic assistance. Under these changing circumstances, Bolivia and Standard Oil eventually agreed on a settlement in January 1942: a payment of $1.5 million (plus 3 percent interest) for sale of the company to the Bolivian state under conditions "freely entered into." A check arrived on April 22. Washington achieved its goal.

The second challenge came in Mexico. Disputes over wages and working conditions in the foreign-owned oil industry led to a strike in May 1937. Unions found backing for their position from the Board of Conciliation and Arbitration, a mixed-member body on which the Mexican government held the balance of power between workers and management. The Mexican Supreme Court thereafter upheld the board ruling. Foreign companies refused to comply, however, rejecting the offer of a guarantee from President Lázaro Cárdenas against further tax or wage demands. On March 18, 1938, a frustrated Cárdenas announced expropriation of Dutch, British, and U.S. companies. Delirious crowds throughout Mexico expressed jubilant support for the government action, and the newspaper *El Nacional* captured the popular mood: "First, political independence, then internal emancipation, today the inexorable rupture of this umbilical cord which ties us to imperialism.... The country writes its history with its own blood."

The stakes in this conflict were high. The total value of oil lands came to approximately $500 million (in dollar amounts of that time). The U.S.-held concession was worth about $200 million, and U.S. direct investments amounted to $60 million. Given interests of this magnitude, the Mexican crisis was bound to set a precedent for U.S. policy.

The American position took time to evolve. Shortly after Cárdenas' announcement, Cordell Hull issued an ultimatum, demanding to know "what specific action with respect to payment for the properties in question is contemplated by the Mexican government, what assurance will be given that payment will be made, and when such payment may be expected." Apprehensive about the tone of this missive, U.S. ambassador Josephus Daniels exceeded customary bounds of diplomatic discretion and urged the Mexicans to consider the note as "not received." He also reported to Washington that Mexico would be willing to pay compensation. Daniels' bold action endangered his career and cost him the confidence of Hull and Welles, but it managed to prevent a damaging break in U.S.–Mexican relations.

The United States renounced the use of force but was quick to apply economic pressure. Barely one week after the expropriation, the U.S. Department of Treasury terminated a 1936 agreement for the purchase of 5 million ounces of silver from Mexico at slightly above the world price. This was an important blow to Mexico: Exports of silver were almost as large as those of oil, and the purchase arrangement represented a significant source of governmental revenue. After a three-month hiatus, Treasury resumed the purchase of Mexican silver on a day-to-day basis at the world level. On balance, suspension of the silver deal had a more symbolic than practical impact.

More significant were efforts by the oil companies to prevent the export of Mexican oil. In open collusion, the companies sought to obstruct the acquisition of tankers and drilling equipment. The result was a highly effective boycott of Mexican petroleum in major markets, including the United States. In May 1939 the U.S. State Department endorsed the boycott of Mexican oil, issuing a statement that it would be "undesirable" for U.S. government agencies to purchase Mexican oil and encouraging Latin American governments to take a similar stand. (For its part, Mexico responded by making deals with Axis powers: As war approached, Mexico was earning over $1.2 million per month from petroleum exports, over half from Germany and Italy.) United States government lending agencies also refrained from making loans to Mexico between August 1937 and November 1941.

The Dutch and British governments and all the oil companies—with the exception of Sinclair, which was breaking ranks to negotiate its own agreement—called for arbitration by an international tribunal. In 1939, FDR, too, wrote directly to Cárdenas with a proposal for international arbitration. After Mexico rejected this overture, favoring instead a two-person bilateral commission, Welles proposed arbitration again. It was the fall of France in mid-1940 that ultimately led the United States to accept the Mexican position. Under pressure from the War Department, in fact, the State Department consented to the idea of a two-person commission in late 1941. "In the event the United States is attacked and must enter the war," one U.S. official noted, "Mexico's oil resources might be of importance from the point of view of national and even hemispheric defense." For the United States it thus became urgent not only to settle the controversy but also to sustain Mexico's capacity for production. The decision came in April 1942, just after the creation of a joint U.S.–Mexico defense commission: Mexico would pay to U.S. companies compensation of $24 million plus 3 percent interest since the date of expropriation, for a total of $29 million.

The third instance of petroleum politics occurred in Venezuela, where the United States applied lessons that it may have learned in Bolivia and Mexico. After the death of long-time dictator Juan Vicente Gómez in 1935, the Venezuelan labor movement began to assert its independence and power—achieving an eight-hour day, rights to collective bargaining, and the imposition of export taxes on petroleum—steps that the oil companies would normally oppose. At the same time, the government of Eleazar López Contreras granted new concessions to Socony and Standard Oil of New Jersey. In view of the Mexican crisis there was no effective threat of governmental expropriation. On the contrary, the Venezuelan goal was to capture market share—thus taking advantage of the boycott on Mexican oil.

In an effort to prevent recurrence of the Bolivian or Mexican scenarios, the Department of State in 1940 decided to consult with U.S. oil companies on strategies for negotiation and representation. Discussions followed from December 1942 through March 1943 on provisions of a new Venezuelan law that raised the royalty on petroleum from a range of 7.5–11 percent to a uniform 16–2/3 percent, established a new base for calculation of taxes, and reduced customs exemptions. In this the oil companies freely concurred. Washington thus secured another wartime goal: maintaining the flow of petroleum to allied forces.

## Extending Assistance?

The Roosevelt administration began to rethink its policy on economic assistance toward Latin America in 1939. Prior to that time the United States had employed a carrot-and-stick approach, withholding loans from Bolivia and Mexico in order to protect American investments in petroleum. As war loomed on the international horizon, however, Washington started to emphasize hemispheric security instead of economic interests.

In the absence of centralized coordination, changes in U.S. foreign economic policy faced substantial inertia and resistance. Harry Dexter White, a monetary expert in the Treasury Department, encouraged Roosevelt "to use our great financial strength to help safeguard future peace for the United States, and to make your 'Good Neighbor' policy really effective." Unless the United States were to embark on "a program of assistance to Latin-American countries on a scale appropriate to the problem with which we are faced," White continued, "Latin America will gradually succumb to the organized ideological and economic campaign now being waged by aggressor nations." Eventually the president concurred, indicating in a speech at the Pan American Union in April 1939 that the United States would "give economic support, so that no American nation need surrender any fraction of its sovereign freedom to maintain its economic welfare." Implicitly contradicting then-current policy toward Mexico, a State Department memorandum contended in June 1939: "Our national interests as a whole far outweigh those of the petroleum companies." Economic assistance would be used to keep Latin American nations on the U.S. side in case of war.

That same year the State Department began laying plans for a commercial cartel that would handle Latin American exports and take up the slack caused by the closing of European markets. The idea met resistance in Latin America, but Washington eventually backed off for reasons of its own: It feared a backlash in Asia, since Japan would be likely to demand comparable commercial hegemony over China, and it came to the conclusion that the scheme was unworkable. As U.S. trade official Will Clayton noted: "Cartels must be world cartels—not Hemisphere cartels." The United States decided to continue its reliance on bilateral arrangements.

Also in 1939, the Export-Import Bank initiated transactions with governments, greatly enlarging its role. In short order the bank was making substantial loans for broad-based development projects. Especially significant was support for construction of the Volta Redonda steel mill in Brazil. Bernard Baruch, ever the businessman, expressed skepticism about the wisdom of this venture: "After the property is developed," he wondered aloud, "will they pull a Mexican stunt on us?" But Washington went ahead with the loan, and the Eximbank embarked on an ambitious program of lending throughout the region. William Culbertson, former ambassador to Chile, observed the appearance of a new kind of diplomacy: "to use Federal funds in order to conserve and develop the economic life of the Latin American countries, I presume with the idea in mind that we are to keep them lined up politically for the purpose of economic defense of the hemisphere. You are really witnessing the entrance of the American Government into the field of political loans."

As flows of aid increased, the U.S. government displayed considerable uncertainty over proposals for a regional inter-American Bank. Latin Americans espoused "the creation of an inter-American financial institution of a permanent character," one that would adopt multilateral policies rather than the bilateral methods of the Eximbank. Differences arose over potential provisions for enabling Latin American governments to repay loans they might acquire. What the Latins wanted was preferential access to U.S. commercial markets. Without enhanced trade, said Pedro Larránaga of Peru, the result would be counterproductive: "Why obscure the meaning of this solution, which instead of giving the Americas a new independent and neutral credit structure is merely going to increase our indebtedness to the United States?"

Latin American representatives objected to a February 1940 draft proposal that insisted on government guarantees for loans to Latin American private citizens, gave a veto power to the United States in voting rules, and provided no assurance about commercial access to the U.S. market. Even so, U.S. bankers and financiers were reluctant. "I hope," said Bernard Baruch, that "our Latin-American efforts will not have too much government action, but rather more by individuals." The proposal died in committee. In 1947 President Harry S. Truman finally withdrew the convention from the U.S. Senate.

## THE GOOD NEIGHBOR POLICY: IDEOLOGICAL DIMENSIONS

The Good Neighbor policy rested on ideological foundations, as the Roosevelt administration continually emphasized the mythical unity of the New World and its differences from the Old World. While Europe was falling prey to totalitarian dictatorship, according to this litany, nations of the Americas stood for justice and democracy. "We and the other American Republics have distinguishing ideals and beliefs which bind us together in contrast with other, non-American powers," insisted a State Department memorandum of 1939; among these were "faith in republican institutions, loyalty to democracy as an ideal, reverence for liberty, acceptance of the dignity of the individual and his inviolable personal rights, belief in peaceable adjustment of disputes." Invoking what historian Arthur P. Whitaker described as "the Western Hemisphere idea," U.S. officials maintained that the New World was culturally unified, ideologically unique, and politically superior to other realms of the globe. It stood apart from Europe—and, by implication, was under the leadership and guidance of the United States.

United States representatives pressed this argument in forum after forum. At the Pan-American gathering in Montevideo in 1933, the American delegation supported a series of resolutions designed to advance "mutual knowledge and understanding of the peoples of the Americas." At Buenos Aires in 1936, U.S. delegates supported the Declaration of Principles of Inter-American Solidarity and Cooperation, which proclaimed that American republics shared a "common likeness in their form of democratic government." And at Panama in 1939, the United States sponsored a resolution recommending that "in view of the democratic ideal which prevails in the American hemisphere," it was necessary "to eradicate from the Americas the spread of doctrines that tend to place in jeopardy the common inter-American democratic ideal." Alien doctrines were unwelcome. In keeping with the Monroe Doctrine, Washington must lead the fight against extrahemispheric ideologies.

In this diplomatic effort, cultural connections received high-level attention. The assumption was that mutual respect arising from a sympathetic understanding of history, literature, and the arts would not only bind together countries of the hemisphere but would also promote trade and commercial cooperation.

For such reasons the Roosevelt administration established a cultural division in the Department of State "to promote mutual progress and understanding in the Americas." And it was to counteract the growing Axis menace that FDR created, in August 1940, the Office of the Coordinator of Inter-American Affairs (OCIAA) and placed it under the leadership of the youthful Nelson Rockefeller. Invested with a broad mandate, OCIAA oversaw economic cooperation, cultural exchange, and public information; its primary purpose was to counter "subversive, insidious, destructive Nazi propaganda." The budget for the OCIAA's first year of operation was $3.5 million; by the end of the war it was $45 million. As Rockefeller reflected in 1945: "The United States came in with a program of truth in answer to enemy lies."

From the outset, the OCIAA worked with a broad range of media. It distributed articles to magazines and newspapers throughout the hemisphere. OCIAA produced and distributed the magazine *En Guardia* in Spanish and Portuguese, on sale at newsstands and sent without charge to about 40,000 prominent Latin Americans each month. OCIAA sponsored art exhibitions, musical concerts, and literary translations (but not of John Steinbeck's *The Grapes of Wrath,* which it deemed inappropriate). The office cooperated with major radio networks, enticing the industry through tax benefits to increase its number of shortwave broadcasts and to improve the quality of programs aired to Latin America. By 1941 U.S. news broadcasts had expanded from a handful of shortwave programs a week, mostly in English, to eighteen reports in Spanish and eight in Portuguese. OCIAA purchased advertising space in pro-U.S. newspapers announcing the time, wavelength, and call letters of American broadcasts and blacklisted Latin American radio stations that carried pro-Axis programs.

It was in the motion picture industry that OCIAA had its most remarkable influence. As explained by the director of the agency's film department, John Hay ("Jock") Whitney:

> The Office of the Coordinator of Inter-American Affairs has a share in the task of imparting the full force of the meaning of freedom and sovereignty to a quarter of a billion people in the Americas. The menace of Nazism and its allied doctrines, its techniques and tactics, must be understood from Hudson Bay to Punto Arenas. Wherever the motion picture can do a basic job of spreading the gospel of the Americas' common stake in this struggle, there that job must and shall be done.

To pursue this goal OCIAA installed in Hollywood a consultant to the Motion Picture Association who could offer advice on scripts, censor films, and encourage distribution of movies that would display "the truth about the American way." In practical terms, OCIAA became the clearinghouse and censor for all films sent to Latin America.

The OCIAA was highly effective. It successfully opposed distribution in Latin America of a film entitled *Mr. Smith Goes to Washington,* starring Jimmy Stewart, because of its adverse commentary on the U.S. political establishment.

It persuaded Twentieth Century Fox to spend $40,000 to remove potentially offensive scenes from *Down Argentine Way* (1940), which featured one Argentine character as a gigolo, depicted another with a Mexican accent, and revolved around an allegedly crooked horserace at the Buenos Aires Jockey Club. And it urged the producers of *Juarez* (1939), a cinematic classic comparing Mexico's Benito Juárez with Abraham Lincoln, to eliminate a scene in which an American diplomat notified Napoleon III that France must get out of Mexico because of the Monroe Doctrine, thus minimizing the role of Mexican resistance. In a variety of ways, Rockefeller and Whitney urged Hollywood to reiterate the messages of hemispheric solidarity.

The industry responded with alacrity. There were several reasons for Hollywood's cooperation. One was political: Leading movie producers, many of them Jewish, strongly opposed Nazism and objected to U.S. calls for isolationism. Another was creative, particularly musical: In the words of one executive, swing music of the big-band era was on the way out and "the rhumba stuff is jumping into the number one position in American taste." Third, and perhaps most critical, was the need for a new export market. As World War II closed off commercial access to Europe and Japan, there was no alternative to Latin America. Political imperatives and economic calculations thus neatly converged, creating a powerful partnership between Hollywood and Washington.

As reported by historian Allen Woll, "Hollywood's attitude toward the Latin countries suddenly bordered on reverence." No longer did U.S. films depict Latins as uncouth greasers or ignorant peasants. In *They Met in Argentina* (1941), gauchos on the pampas sang the same song as had the American hero as a youth in Texas. And in *That Night in Rio* (1941), Don Ameche warbled a tune called "Chica Chica Boom Chic" with touchingly ludicrous lyrics:

My friends, I extend felicitations,
To our South American relations.
May we never leave behind us
All the common ties that bind us.
One hundred and thirty million people
Send regards to you. . . .

It sounded more like a speech at the Pan American Union than a Hollywood song, but it seemed to accomplish its purpose.

Rockefeller's OCIAA was not reluctant to propose specific themes. "Right now," its oversight committee urged at one point, "we need to create 'Pan-Americana,' a noble female figure, bearing a torch and cross, subtly suggesting both the Virgin Mary and the Goddess of Liberty." What they got instead was pulsating music and throbbing sensuality, from the song-and-dance routines of Brazil's Carmen Miranda to the passionate outbursts of Lupe Vélez, who gained renown as "the Mexican spitfire." Throughout U.S. popular culture, Latin America came to be seen as provocative, thrilling, cooperative—and desirable. Hollywood films drew mixed reactions in Latin America, even after OCIAA-sponsored amendments, but on balance they strengthened popular support for U.S. foreign policy. According to a State Department memorandum on OCIAA's overall activity as of 1942: "It was the greatest outpouring of propagandistic material by a state ever."

## SIZING UP THE NEIGHBORHOOD

The crowning achievement of Roosevelt's Good Neighbor policy was hemispheric solidarity during World War II. During the quest for this goal, however, the precepts of nonintervention and noninterference posed dilemmas for U.S. policymakers. Assistant Secretary Welles expressed opposition to the idea of open intervention against pro-fascist governments in Latin America. As Hitler's troops stormed into Poland and the Netherlands, diplomatic observers expressed serious concern about the Good Neighbor policy itself. How could the United States forestall Axis influence on the basis of noninterference?

The fall of France in mid-1940 led to intense concern over the fate of overseas territories in the Americas, such as Guadeloupe and French Guiana, then in danger of Nazi takeover. The State Department promptly drafted a nontransfer resolution that passed unanimously in the Senate and by an overwhelming vote (380 to 8) in the House. Cordell Hull notified Berlin that "the United States would not recognize any transfer, and would not acquiesce in any attempt to transfer, any geographic region of the Western Hemisphere from one non-American power to another non-American power." German foreign minister Ribbentrop replied with an appeal for equal treatment, noting that England and France still had colonies in the Western Hemisphere, but Hull replied that the Monroe Doctrine proscribed not the *possession* of historic colonies but their *transfer* from one European power to another.

The Japanese attack on Pearl Harbor in December 1941 raised immediate questions about the hemispheric response. During World War I only eight Latin American states, most U.S. protectorates, declared war on Germany; the majority assumed neutrality. Within days of Pearl Harbor, however, all nine Central American and Caribbean republics (as before, virtual U.S. protectorates) declared war on Japan. Colombia, Venezuela, and Mexico promptly severed relations with the Axis. Shortly thereafter the 1942 Meeting of Ministers of Foreign Affairs of the American Republics sought to reinforce solidarity in the war effort. Two countries were decidedly unenthusiastic: Chile, which feared Japanese hit-and-run attacks along its coastline, and Argentina, which harbored strong pro-Axis sympathies. Delegates nonetheless supported a resolution asserting that "The American Republics . . . recommend the rupture of their diplomatic relations with Japan, Germany, and Italy, since the first of these states has attacked and the other two have declared war upon an American country." Peru, Uruguay, Bolivia, and Paraguay quickly complied, and Oswaldo Aranha of Brazil announced his country's adhesion in a dramatic closing session. Looking back on the Rio meeting, a U.S. observer opined that "It was excellent statesmanship—and damned fine showmanship, too." Chile eventually succumbed to U.S. threats to cut off economic assistance and broke relations with the Axis in January 1943. On the eve of Allied victory, in March 1945, Argentina finally agreed to declare war on Germany and Japan. Hemispheric solidarity was at last complete.

In retrospect, Franklin Roosevelt's Good Neighbor policy was not so much a departure from past practice as an adaptation and extension of it. The United States continued to pursue hegemony within the Western Hemisphere, in keeping with the imperialist codes of the international system, but now employed new tactics in response to changing circumstances. Instead of relying on Teddy Roosevelt's "big stick," on military force and intervention, the United States could now rely on economic strength and diplomatic persuasion. The policy was not an exercise in charity. After undoing the Platt Amendment and withdrawing troops from Nicaragua and Haiti and the Dominican Republic, for instance, Washington continued to interfere in Cuban and Nicaraguan politics and to retain control over customs houses on Hispaniola to protect returns on American investments. "In actuality," one scholar has written, "the United States abrogated what was obsolete and retained what it considered vital to the national interest." Tactics had changed, but goals were much the same.

With its emphasis on hemispheric unity—and on consolidation of a U.S. sphere of influence—the Good Neighbor policy came to be seen as a cloak for isolationism during the 1930s. Its ideological emphasis on the uniqueness of the Americas and on differences with Europe and Asia appeared to justify indifference to world affairs. As Congressman Joe Henricks (D-Florida) proclaimed in late 1939: "The future of the United States lies to the south, and if we bend our efforts to effecting closer relationships with Latin America we will never worry about getting entangled with the petty quarrels of old Europe." But if the United States was relatively passive in Asia and Europe, it was highly activist with regard to Latin America. Hemispheric affairs assumed topmost priority in U.S. foreign policy, and leading figures in U.S. diplomatic circles—from Cordell Hull to Sumner Welles and Adolf Berle—devoted great energy and attention to relations with Latin America. It is only in European (or Asian) perspective that U.S. policy during this period might be construed as isolationist; in the perspective of the Americas, it most decidedly was not.

To be sure, the "Western Hemisphere idea" declined sharply after World War II. United States policy took on a global cast, with strong commitments to European affairs, and the postwar world witnessed new kinds of division—between communist and noncommunist, North and South. In this context the notion of hemispheric solidarity became irrelevant and obsolete.

An epitaph for the Good Neighbor era came from Philip Jessup, a professor at Columbia University who made a tour of Latin America in 1941. At the end of his visit, Jessup reported with confidence:

> A decade of the Good Neighbor policy has helped enormously to overcome the
> results of mistaken policies of the past, but the postwar situation will be a great

challenge to our intelligent self-restraint. We shall meet that challenge success-fully because the government and people of the U.S. are irrevocably committed to the sound conclusion that the old, stupid type of imperialist policy can never be used again.

## QUESTIONS FOR REVIEW

1. What led FDR to proclaim the Good Neighbor policy? What benefits did the United States attain from this new diplomacy?
2. Did the Good Neighbor policy promote democracy, or did it promote dictatorship?
3. What was the principal ideological message of the Good Neighbor policy?
4. What was the policy's principal achievement?
5. The 1930s is now widely remembered as a time of inter-American harmony. Why?

# PART II

# The Cold War

Soviet Communism is not only the gravest threat that ever faced the United States, but the gravest threat that has ever faced what we call Western civilization or, indeed, any civilization that was dominated by a spiritual faith.

JOHN FOSTER DULLES (1953)

# CHAPTER 5

# Closing Ranks

Conditions in Latin America are somewhat comparable
to conditions as they were in the mid-thirties when the
communist movement was getting started. . . . Well, if we
don't look out, we will wake up some morning and read in the
newspapers that there happened in South America the same
kind of thing that happened in China in 1949.

JOHN FOSTER DULLES (1953)

The Cold War altered the logic of inter-American relations, elevating the protection of "national security" to the top of the U.S. foreign policy agenda and turning Latin America (and other developing areas) into a battleground and prize in the conflict between communism and capitalism, East and West, the USSR and the United States. In response to Soviet challenges, the United States sought to extend and consolidate its political supremacy throughout the hemisphere. Launching an anticommunist crusade, the United States institutionalized military and political alliances with nations of the region; offered to collaborate with authoritarian regimes so long as they were anticommunist; encouraged (or compelled) friendly governments to crush leftist labor movements and to outlaw communist parties; and orchestrated the military overthrow of elected governments that seemed "soft" on communism. Fear of a "Soviet menace" in the Americas was greatly exaggerated, but it nonetheless had crucial implications for U.S. policy. By the mid-1950s Washington had laid down policy lines that would continue through the 1980s.

## UNITED STATES AS SUPERPOWER

World War II transformed global arrangements and elevated the United States to the status of a superpower. By the late 1930s the United States had a very small military establishment, with only 185,000 combat-ready troops; no military alliances at all; and, after the withdrawals from Haiti and Nicaragua, no troops on foreign soil. The centerpiece of U.S. foreign policy was Roosevelt's Good Neighbor stance toward Latin America and cultivation of a "sphere of influence" within the Western Hemisphere but not in other parts of the world. In the Atlantic and Pacific theaters, the United States was a relatively unimportant actor.

This would suddenly change. One consequence of World War II was to weaken classic European powers—not only the defeated Axis countries, but triumphant Allies as well. Overall, the fighting and associated devastation took the lives of approximately 55 million people, at least 35 million in Europe. The Soviet Union alone lost more than 21 million soldiers and civilians. Poland and Germany (including Austria) suffered 6 million deaths each; Yugoslavia, 1.6 million; France, about 600,000; Britain, around 400,000. Whole cities were destroyed and thousands of villages were reduced to rubble. Economic production on the European continent ground to a virtual halt.

At the same time, World War II greatly strengthened the United States. Despite the sacrifice of service personnel, there were no bombings of U.S. cities, no occupations of U.S. territory. Economic production climbed to unprecedented levels: It was wartime mobilization, in fact, that lifted the United States out of the Depression of the 1930s. At war's end the United States enjoyed a position of extraordinary economic preponderance. By 1947 the United States accounted for one-third of the world's total exports and nearly one-half of the world's industrial output. Washington applied this leverage to establish a postwar economic order that would avoid repetition of the Depression by promoting international trade and stabilizing monetary exchange.

Moreover, the war altered international alignments and the structure of relative power. The United States did not enter the war until December 1941, nearly a year and a half after the Nazi conquest of France, and did not cross the English Channel until June 1944. Until that time the Soviet Union bore the brunt of the land war with Germany, and, as the Red Army pushed toward Berlin, the USSR slowly gained control of Eastern Europe. Joseph Stalin succinctly summarized the political implications of these military developments: "Whoever occupies a territory," he once proclaimed, "also imposes on it his own social system."

In the Pacific theater, as well, the United States did not have troops on the most important land masses—China, Korea, and Japan. Atomic bombs at Hiroshima and Nagasaki cut the campaigns short in August 1945, leading to Tokyo's unconditional surrender. Allied forces under U.S. leadership promptly occupied Japan and South Korea, but not China or North Korea. In keeping with Stalin's dictum, this would have profound results on politics.

In addition to its economic and military power, the United States possessed a monopoly on a new instrument of warfare—the atomic bomb. To consolidate its advantage, Washington built a stockpile of these deadly weapons, each capable of destroying a city at a time. The U.S. arsenal contained 7 atomic bombs in 1946, 13 in 1947, 50 in 1948, nearly 300 by 1950, and around 1,000 in 1953. In 1950 the government initiated development of the even more powerful hydrogen bomb, carrying out the first test in 1952. Nuclear capacity gave the postwar United States an enormous sense of power. First, it appeared to offer an efficient and inexpensive key to military security without the need for military mobilization. Second, it was thought, the bomb conferred on the United States both the right and the duty to control processes of change throughout the world.

The United States retained its military dominance in years to come. By the late 1960s the United States had 2 million soldiers in the armed forces, forty-eight military alliances with other countries, and 1.5 million troops stationed in 119 countries of the world. It was, beyond doubt, the strongest power on earth.

## COLD WAR: THE RULES OF THE GAME

Unilateral triumph soon gave way to bilateral tension. Stalin tightened his grip on Poland. In March 1946 Winston Churchill denounced the lowering of an "iron curtain" in the midst of continental Europe and called for liberation from communist rule. In 1948 there came a Soviet-sponsored coup in Czechoslovakia; later in the year Stalin sought to cordon off the occupied city of Berlin, which required a months-long airlift of food and supplies by the Allies. In 1949 the USSR announced successful detonation of its own atomic bomb, thus shattering America's postwar monopoly. On front after front, the Soviet Union appeared to provoke confrontation with the United States.

What would Washington do? The answer came in 1947, when President Harry S. Truman decided to support the government of Greece in its struggle with a leftist insurgency. As heir to the anti-Nazi partisan movement, it should be noted, this insurrection reflected political realities evident throughout the continent. During the war, centrist and monarchist leaders generally fled their countries for the relative safety of Great Britain; those who remained to lead the resistance—fabled as *la resistance* in France—tended to come from the political left. And, not surprisingly, in view of their heroic sacrifices, they strongly resisted claims by conservative exile leaders to reclaim power at war's end.

In response to crises in Turkey and Greece, the American president launched what became known as the Truman Doctrine in a momentous address to Congress: "I believe it must be the policy of the United States to support free peoples who are resisting attempted subjugation by armed minorities or by outside pressures." This phrasing implied a remarkably capacious mandate. It committed the United States to assist "free peoples" (however defined) in struggles against external *or internal* foes. This called for both defense against outside threats and intervention against domestic challenges. In effect, the Truman Doctrine proclaimed that the United States would assume the role of global policeman.

In fact, the doctrine—and the policy that it defined—rested on a series of crucial assumptions. One was that the Soviet Union was seeking to conquer the world in the name of international communism. A second was that these Soviet ambitions would produce a long and continuous struggle with the capitalist world, not a military conflagration but a "cold war." And this conflict, as George F. Kennan wrote in 1947, would require from the United States "the adroit and vigilant application of counterforce at a series of constantly shifting geographical and political points, corresponding to the shifts of Soviet policy." Washington's principal goal, in other words, would be to halt the spread of communism. The policy thus came to be known as one of *containment*.

This strategy initially focused on Europe. One key component was a massive program of economic assistance, launched as the Marshall Plan in 1947. Since communism thrived amid despair and poverty, in Washington's official view, economic recovery would bolster the forces of capitalism and democracy. In support of this belief the United States provided $19 billion in foreign aid to Western Europe in 1945–1950. A second pillar of the policy was the North Atlantic Treaty Organization (NATO), a military pact established in 1949. Its principal effect was to commit U.S. military forces to the defense of Western Europe. In the phrase of Senator Tom Connally, "The Atlantic Pact is but the logical extension of the principle of the Monroe Doctrine." United States power now stretched far beyond the limits of the Western Hemisphere.

During the 1950s the doctrine of containment extended to Asia as well. American occupation forces quickly built up Japan as a pro–United States bulwark in the fight against international communism. Concern mounted rapidly after the "loss" of China in 1949 to revolutionaries under Mao Zedong, an event that gave rise to Senator Joseph McCarthy's infamous accusations against "traitors" in the U.S. State Department. The invasion of South Korea by North Korea in 1950 provoked a three-year conflict ending in a virtual stalemate, reestablishing the line of demarcation between North and South at the 38th parallel.

Developments in Asia had several fundamental implications for U.S. policy. One was abandonment of the idea of "liberation." First in Korea and later in Europe, the United States came to acknowledge the practical limits of containment—tacitly accepting the existence of a Soviet sphere of influence in 1956, when Western powers failed to provide support for an anti-Soviet uprising in Hungary. Second was a conviction within U.S. society and government that the communist movement was worldwide, coherent, and monolithic—led by Moscow, in close collaboration with Beijing. Third was a perception of the entire world as a single theater; events in Europe and Asia were inextricably linked together by the fact of global struggle. Fourth was unremitting hostility toward the Soviet Union, the People's Republic of China, and all their "stooges" or "puppets" (whether or not they were consciously acting on behalf of communist goals). Finally, the invasion of South Korea supported the view that communist tactics would consist not only of internal subversion, as in Greece, but also of outright military aggression. This led to the formation in 1954 of the Southeast Asia Treaty Organization (SEATO), in principle (if not in practice) a Pacific counterpart to NATO, and it also prompted an intensive rearmament campaign that lasted throughout the 1950s.

In paradoxical ways, the waging of the Cold War led to a series of tacit understandings or rules of the game. Each side strove mightily to establish military superiority over the other, yet there existed no plausible chance of military victory. In view of the potential for nuclear retaliation, neither side could take the risk of attacking the other. The United States and the USSR thus found themselves locked in a nuclear standoff, accumulating arsenals they could never use. Instead they could merely resort to threats, saber-rattling, and ever-larger military budgets. The Cold War promised neither victory nor peace.

Each side defined its purpose in the name of high and principled causes. The Soviet Union sought to extend communist influence in support of social solidarity and economic justice. The United States positioned itself as leader of the "free" and democratic world. Despite the grandeur and intensity of this ideological conflict, however, both powers tended to accept each other's established sphere of influence.

There could be constant conflict—but always on the periphery, not in the central arena. The principal contenders never fought among themselves; they assigned that task to clients and/or surrogates. In the 1950s hostilities thus erupted in Korea, Iran, and Lebanon. Such struggles were assumed to represent a "zero-sum" game, in which one side's gain would be another's loss. Even more worrisome was the U.S. notion of a "domino theory," in which the loss of one country would immediately and automatically endanger its neighbors. Conflicts within or among small countries were therefore resistant to negotiation; because these entailed symbolic contests between the superpowers, neither side had much interest in accommodation.

By the 1960s Washington had explicitly extended the doctrine of containment to what became known as the Third World. As President John F. Kennedy would say: "The great battleground for the defense and expansion of freedom today is the southern half of the globe, . . . the lands of the rising peoples." The United States and the Soviet Union thus engaged in competition for political allegiance among the poorer regions of the world. The principal target for U.S. policy would be so-called wars of liberation, a diagnosis that eventually led to a decade-long involvement in Vietnam. Around this same time, as we shall see, U.S. policy sharpened its focus on Latin America as well.

The Cold War bore some resemblance to traditional balance-of-power politics and spheres of influence, but there were important differences as well. One defining feature of the post–World War II era was the bipolar structure of world power, whereas the imperial quest for a balance of power relied on a multipolar system. The Cold War was utterly dominated by two superpowers, the United States and the Soviet Union. "Not since Rome and Carthage," U.S. Secretary of State Dean Acheson once claimed, "had there been such a polarization of power on this earth."

A second key characteristic was the emphasis on ideological factors. To be sure, traditional powers justified the subjugation of other peoples in the name of religious conversion or cultural mission or some other uplifting purpose. But the *intensity* of East–West ideological competition, of the contest between Karl Marx and Adam Smith, added a special ingredient to the Cold War. This was not only an academic contest for intellectual superiority but also a struggle for the allegiance of society at large. Ideology magnified the stakes of competition.

Third was its worldwide scope. While the principal actors never challenged each other in direct military fashion, their frequent use of surrogates—and their constant invocation of ideology—extended their rivalry to all corners of the globe. By the late 1940s and early 1950s, policymakers saw the entire world as consisting of a single theater; no countries or regions were exempt from participation. Unlike classic big-power contests, this was not confined to a specific area or based on territorial acquisition. It was a geopolitical and ideological contest that covered the world as a whole.

Partly because of its breadth, the Cold War provoked systematic tension between the superpowers and their allies (or client states). Often haughtily, policymakers in both Moscow and Washington presumed and asserted that only they, not their allies, could truly understand the nature of the global conflict under way; only they could comprehend the challenges and stakes. To the undisguised irritation of the British and French especially, this conviction fostered the idea that only the United States could accurately ascertain genuine threats to the West. And within the Western Hemisphere, it implied that Washington possessed an inherently superior perspective on international matters; U.S. policymakers could identify, analyze, and eradicate communist threats more effectively than local leaders. Such presumptuousness not only offended Latin Americans, including reformers and dedicated anticommunists; it could also result in grievous miscalculations by the U.S. government.

Policymaking during the Cold War became a special prerogative of political and bureaucratic elites. The U.S. Congress quickly reached a bipartisan consensus on foreign policy that prevailed from the late 1940s through the 1980s. Encouraged by the Red-baiting tactics of Joseph McCarthy and alarmed by the realities of Soviet power, the American public fervently supported anticommunist positions. Partly in reflection of this unanimity, governmental elites—political appointees (usually from the East Coast establishment), career foreign service officers, and longtime senior legislators—assumed control of the policymaking apparatus. The business community played occasional but supportive roles, displaying neither the initiative nor the power wielded during the foregone era of "dollar diplomacy." Organized labor entered the international arena, also in staunch support of official policy, as did other interest groups from time to time. Throughout this era, however, responsibility for and control of U.S. foreign policy rested almost exclusively within the political and bureaucratic apparatus. The center of decision making was neither in corporate boardrooms nor on the electoral hustings; it was in the nation's capital—and the name of the city, "Washington," became synonymous with the sinews of power.

Ultimately, the waging of the Cold War was bound to result in frustration. The doctrine of containment called for vigilance, persistence, and sacrifice, but it could not bring victory in any classical sense of the term. From the late 1940s through the 1980s it was nonetheless the Cold War, with its curious logic, that defined and enforced the rules of the game for international competition.

## THE COLD WAR IN LATIN AMERICA

Latin America commanded significant attention from U.S. policymakers during and just after World War II. In December 1943 the Joint Army and Navy Advisory Board established its Western Hemisphere Defense Program. The State Department pressed Latin countries to join the Allied cause throughout the course of the war.

## BOX 5-1

### Generals in the Cold War: U.S. Presidents, 1945–1993

The principal challenge for all U.S. presidents from the 1940s through the 1980s was the worldwide geopolitical struggle with the Soviet Union and, more generally, with international communism. This struggle led each and every one of them to take decisive action in Latin America.

Harry S. Truman, 1945–1953

Dwight D. Eisenhower, 1953–1961

John F. Kennedy, 1961–1963

Lyndon B. Johnson, 1963–1969

Richard M. Nixon, 1969–1974

Gerald Ford, 1974–1977

Jimmy Carter, 1977–1981

Ronald Reagan, 1981–1989

George H. W. Bush, 1989–1993

At the founding of the United Nations, in 1946, U.S. diplomats accorded special attention to the region—which at that time controlled nearly two-fifths of the votes in the General Assembly (twenty out of fifty-one). Latin America also offered U.S. producers a major export market and site for direct investment. In 1946–1947 one-quarter of U.S. exports flowed to Latin America; in 1950 U.S. investments in the region amounted to more than one-third the country's global total of $12 billion overseas.

As World War II drew to a close, Washington seems to have envisioned a continuation of (or reversion to) the Good Neighbor policy—including its assertion of hemispheric hegemony. "I think that it's not asking too much to have our little region over here which never has bothered anybody," Secretary of War Henry L. Stimson once remarked. His assistant John J. McCloy agreed, casting an eye across the Atlantic and insisting that "we ought to have our cake and eat it too; that we ought to be free to operate under this regional arrangement in South America, [and] at the same time intervene promptly in Europe."

In this spirit the United States supported Latin America's push for an endorsement of regional security organizations at the founding conference of the United Nations in 1946. Article 51 of the UN charter thus provided a juridical basis for the Rio Pact of 1947, a mutual defense treaty between Latin American nations and the United States. There would be differing views on the significance of this

October 1962: In one of the most dramatic moments of the Cold War, John F. Kennedy announced the presence of Soviet missiles in Cuba (see page 158).
Source: AP Photo.

development. Secretary of War Stimson interpreted Article 51 as a preservation of "the unilateral character of the Monroe Doctrine," since the United States could take action in Latin America without being "at the mercy of getting the assent of the Security Council." Latin Americans, by contrast, imagined that Article 51 would encourage the formation of a regional security agreement that could provide protection for existing governments and, at the same time, place constraints on the United States. In essence, their hope was that international organization could accomplish the goals they had earlier pursued through international law.

The principle of nonintervention received further expression at the founding meeting of the Organization of American States in Bogotá in 1948. Seeking to bolster their autonomy, Latin American delegates won approval of key language in Chapter 15: "No state or group of states has the right to intervene, directly or indirectly, for any reason whatever, in the internal or external affairs of any other state." This stipulation expressly prohibited not only armed intervention, so common in the prewar period, but also "any other form of interference or attempted threat." Thus the United States continued to forswear the use of force in its relations with Latin America and to cultivate cooperation in the name of hemispheric unity. As historian Steven Rabe has remarked, both the Rio Treaty and the OAS "reflected the spirit of the Good Neighbor policy."

Global crises turned U.S. official attention away from Latin America. From Greece to Berlin, events in Europe came to dominate the Washington agenda; the fall of China and hostilities in Korea focused concern on Asia as well. One of the most experienced Latin American specialists at the State Department, Adolf A.

Berle, noted growing lack of interest in the region with dismay. "Men [in high office] who know the hemisphere and love it are few," he said in 1945, "and those who are known by the hemisphere and loved by it are fewer still." By 1949 the situation had grown still worse: Complaining about "sheer neglect and ignorance," Berle declared that "we have simply forgotten about Latin America."

Gradually, however, the Cold War came to the Americas, and the United States braced itself to contend with communist threats. In 1950 President Truman approved a National Security Council memorandum on "Inter-American Military Collaboration" insisting that "the Cold War is in fact a real war in which the survival of the free world is at stake." (Millions of dollars for military assistance would soon be flowing to Latin America.) Later in the year an official statement declared that "U.S. security is the objective of our worldwide foreign policy today," and "U.S. security is synonymous with hemisphere security."

Around this same time, George Kennan, chief architect of the containment policy, offered his conception of the goals of U.S. policy in Latin America:

1. The protection of our [*sic!*] raw materials,
2. The prevention of military exploitation of Latin America by the enemy, and
3. The prevention of the psychological mobilization of Latin America against us.

Communists "represent our most serious problem in the area," Kennan insisted, and they "have progressed to the point where they must be regarded as an urgent, major problem." Under no circumstances could they be allowed to take power. "The final answer might be an unpleasant one," Kennan conceded, "but . . . we should not hesitate before police repression by the local government. This is not shameful since the Communists are essentially traitors. . . . It is better to have a strong regime in power than a liberal one if it is indulgent and relaxed and penetrated by Communists." Danger to U.S. security came not only from declared Marxists but also from their unwitting accomplices. Eternal vigilance must be extended to the Americas.

Electoral politics intensified public concern about communist threats within the hemisphere. During the 1952 presidential campaign, Dwight D. Eisenhower, the Republican candidate, accused the Truman administration of disregarding Latin America and creating "terrible disillusionment" throughout the region, where economic distress was "followed by popular unrest, skillfully exploited by Communist agents there." The president's brother, Milton S. Eisenhower, echoed this sentiment in a November 1953 report on conditions in the region:

> The possible conquest of a Latin American nation today would not be, so far as anyone can foresee, by direct assault. It would come, rather, through the insidious process of infiltration, conspiracy, spreading of lies, and the undermining of free institutions, one by one. Highly disciplined groups of communists are busy, night and day, illegally or openly, in the American republics, as they are in every nation of the world. While many persons may now think of Latin America as not being in the line of attack in the modern world struggle, success by the communists in these nations could quickly change all the maps which strategists use in calculating the probabilities of the future.

Himself a university president, Milton offered a philosophic rumination on the incompatibility of East and West: "The greater the differences in the cultures of nations, the more arduous cooperation becomes. This is the basal difficulty between the communist countries of the East, with their rejection of God and their adherence to a militant dialectic materialism, and the West, with its long adherence to the cardinal principles of the Judeo-Christian philosophy." There could be no dealing with communists. They would have to be purged, hounded, driven, and excluded from the hemisphere.

## COURTING DICTATORS

A central goal of U.S. policy was to foster and strengthen anticommunist regimes in Latin America. This often led to acquiescence in dictatorship. Just after World War II, in fact, Latin America experienced a broad surge of democratic rule. Civilian governments gained strength in Chile, Costa Rica, and Colombia. Relatively free elections took place in Ecuador, where José María Velasco Ibarra won the presidency in the wake of a popular uprising; in Cuba, where Ramón Grau San Martín (once again) emerged triumphant; in Peru, where José Luis Bustamante y Rivero was victorious; and, perhaps most important, in Venezuela, where the Acción Democrática party finally managed to win the presidential election of 1947. In the meantime dictatorships abandoned power in Guatemala, where Juan José Arévalo took over from a military junta; in Brazil, where elections took place in December 1945; and in Argentina, where a sharp increase in popular participation characterized the presidential elections of 1946. While these shifts toward democracy were for the most part incomplete, they represented significant departures from the blatant repressions of the past.

There were several key features in these political transitions. One was the appearance of "progressive" political parties or movements dedicated to social reform (the Auténticos in Cuba, the Apristas in Peru, Acción Democrática in Venezuela, even Peronists in Argentina). A second was participation of the political left, including the communist left. During the war Latin America's communist parties joined in antifascist activities, and at war's end they benefited from the temporary prestige of the Soviet Union; because they increasingly tended to act as integral parts of national popular movements rather than as members of an international network, communist parties were legalized or at least tolerated in virtually every country. Their total membership, less than 100,000 in 1939, reached close to 400,000 by 1947. A third feature was the political mobilization of organized labor; by the war's end about 3.5 million to 4.0 million workers were unionized throughout the region. Fourth was a shift in ideological discourse, with a notable emphasis on the virtues and superiority of Western-style "democracy" as a result of the Allied triumph over Nazism.

As this process of democratization began, the United States found itself in an awkward position. During the course of the war, as historian Leslie Bethell has pointed out, "Washington actively cooperated with *all* stable, cooperative regimes in Latin America, dictatorships and democracies, that opposed the Axis powers." A 1944 cable from U.S. ambassador Walter Thurston captured the dilemma as it applied to El Salvador, still under the authoritarian grip of Maximiliano Hernández Martínez: It is "difficult," said Thurston, to reconcile pronouncements about democracy "with the fact that the United States tolerates and apparently is gratified to enter into association with governments in America which cannot be described as other than totalitarian. . . . The principal defect of a policy of nonintervention accompanied by propaganda on behalf of democratic regimes," he continued, "is that it simultaneously stimulates dictatorships and popular opposition to them." Intervention might not provide the answer, but something needed to be done.

Preference for democracy gained momentum as the war drew to a close. At the Chapultepec conference of February–March 1945, the U.S. delegation led Latin America in declaring "fervent adherence to democratic principles." In May 1945 an official document prepared by prominent diplomat Spruille Braden recommended "aloof formality" toward dictatorships, including termination of financial assistance and military aid. In October 1945, Eduardo Rodríguez Larreta, the foreign minister of Uruguay, proposed that Pan American nations consider taking multilateral action against any member states violating elementary human rights; within a month, James F. Byrnes, the U.S. secretary of state, gave his endorsement to this doctrine.

In the immediate postwar environment it was fascism, not communism, that was seen as the principal challenge to democracy in Latin America—and to U.S. interests. Accordingly the United States focused attention on South American countries with pro-Axis tendencies. Argentina, which joined the Allied cause only at the last minute, came in for special criticism. United States diplomats were especially exercised over the emergence of a nationalist, populist, working-class movement in that country and spared no efforts to derail Juan Perón's bid for the presidency in 1946. Briefly appointed as ambassador to Argentina, Spruille Braden campaigned openly and avidly against Perón. According to *peronista* publicists, the ambassador's antics offered Argentine voters with a clear-cut choice: "Braden or Perón!" By a stunning 54 percent majority, the electorate favored Perón.

Abruptly, the political cycle then turned from democracy toward authoritarian rule. Military coups took place in Peru, where Manuel Odría seized power (and repressed the APRA party) in October 1948; in Venezuela, where Marcos Pérez Jiménez overturned a democratic government in November 1948; and in Cuba, where Fulgencio Batista reasserted direct control in 1952. In Nicaragua, Anastasio Somoza took steps to perpetuate his one-man rule. In Colombia, meanwhile, a state of siege in November 1949 led to a decade-long closure of congress. By the end of 1954 there were only four democracies remaining in Latin America, even by generous standards for classification: Uruguay, Costa Rica, Chile, and Brazil.

The turn toward dictatorship reflected primarily political reactions by Latin America's dominant classes (and their military forces) against progressive movements for social reform. Changing U.S. policy appeared to support this turn toward the right, however, especially as Washington began to mount its assault on communist influence. In 1947 the United States renewed licenses for arms sales to the ruthless regime of Rafael Leonidas Trujillo Molina in the Dominican Republic; refused to provide support (moral or otherwise) to a fledgling "Caribbean Legion" of exiled democrats; and finally came to terms with Peronist Argentina. As James Reston of the *New York Times* aptly noted that same year, "The administration is concentrating not on catching fascists but on stopping communists." The wheel had come full circle.

Continuing its accommodation with right-wing authoritarians, the State Department in 1948 granted prompt diplomatic recognition to coup masters Odría of Peru and Pérez Jiménez of Venezuela (and, after some hesitation, to Somoza of Nicaragua). A few years later, as though to rub salt in the wounds of democratic opponents, the United States bestowed the Legion of Merit on both dictators, who had proclaimed themselves firm anticommunists. The bemedaling of Pérez Jiménez took place in a particularly ostentatious ceremony in Caracas in October 1954. It was an occasion that Venezuelans would not forget.

While Cold War perceptions hardened in Washington, the United States placed increasing emphasis on ties with Latin American military establishments. As President Eisenhower argued, apparently with reference to a potential conventional war (rather than a nuclear exchange), it was important to strengthen armed forces throughout the region because "we can't defend South America if this Communist war starts." By mid-1954 Congress had approved $105 million in military aid for Latin America. In fact the strategic benefits were slight, notwithstanding Eisenhower's military judgment, but the anticipated political benefits were substantial. As U.S. Army Chief of Staff J. Lawton Collins explained, "The Latin American officers who work with us and some of whom come to this country and see what we have and what we can do are frequently our most useful friends in those countries."

As was so often the case, Secretary of State John Foster Dulles had the last word on this issue. "Do nothing to offend the dictators," he instructed U.S. diplomats throughout the region; "they are the only people we can depend on." In the cause of anticommunism, the Eisenhower administration nurtured exceptionally close relations with Pérez Jiménez, Batista, and Trujillo. The consummate expression of this policy came in 1955, when Vice President Richard M. Nixon offered a toast to Batista and compared him with Abraham Lincoln.

## CLEANING HOUSE

The U.S. embrace of dictatorship in Latin America did not reflect a value judgment in favor of authoritarianism over democracy. It represented, instead, a cold-blooded calculation: that dictatorial regimes would be more predictably and efficiently anticommunist than other types of governance, including democratic systems. As the Cold War unfolded, the United States and military rulers in Latin America joined together in a three-part crusade to stanch the influence of communists through: (1) virtual elimination of Latin American communist parties,

(2) assertion (or reassertion) of state control over labor movements, and (3) diplomatic exclusion of the Soviet Union from the Western Hemisphere.

The first assault declared the existence of communist parties to be against the law. Throughout Latin America, support for communist parties peaked in 1944–1947, partly as a result of euphoria over the Allied victory and partly as a result of democratization. Overall membership climbed to 375,000—some say as high as half a million—while many citizens and voters cast ballots for communist candidates in local and national elections. Communist parties polled an aggregate of well over a million votes to elect their candidates to local, state, or national offices in more than half of the twenty republics. In Cuba, Ecuador, and later in Chile, communists received cabinet positions and took active part in the formulation of national policies.

Upper-class strata and conservative groups in Latin America regarded this trend with fear and distaste. In democratic and pseudodemocratic political arenas, they mounted challenges against communist parties for leadership of labor and student organizations and for electoral support. In campaigns and contests throughout the region, centrist and rightist groups denounced communist parties for their identification with Stalin, their allegiance to an international movement, and their abstract ideology. And with the advent of the Cold War, reactionary forces throughout the region found a strong and willing ally in their confrontation with the left: the United States.

As a result of this collaboration, there began a concerted campaign to outlaw communist parties (many of which had been previously outlawed in the 1920s and 1930s as well). In one country after another—in Brazil in May 1947, in Chile in April 1948, and in Costa Rica in July 1948—communist parties were declared to be against the law even though they had played by the rules of the democratic game. Elected party members were removed from the cabinet and from congress in Chile in 1947 and from congress (as well as state and municipal assemblies) in Brazil in 1948. Before the end of 1948 the communist movement had again been outlawed in eight nations of the region, including Nicaragua and Peru; in Mexico the party was technically legal but unable to register for elections. "By 1956," as one historian has noted, "most Communists had been removed from public office, the party had been stricken from the electoral lists, and Communist propaganda outlets had been closed or restricted in fourteen of the twenty countries."

Evisceration of communist parties represented a clear triumph for the United States. It also offered an opportunity for dictators in Latin America: Outlawing communist parties was a quick and certain way to curry favor from Washington. By one count, there were a dozen authoritarian regimes in Latin America by 1954—and all but one (Perón's Argentina) had banned communist parties. Prosecution of the Cold War thus entailed not so much protection from extrahemispheric threats as penetration into the domestic realm of national politics.

The crackdown extended to labor unions as well as to political parties. The industrial working class was presumably more receptive to leftist appeals than other sectors of Latin American society (as Marx himself would have predicted), and communist organizers sought to establish their institutional base within the labor movement. Postwar governments took stern measures in response: In Brazil, the Dutra administration introduced new legislation to bring labor under state control in 1946; in Chile, the government helped break a crucial strike by coal miners in 1947; in Mexico, the ruling PRI crushed independent labor leaders and installed pliant collaborators in the so-called *charrazo* of 1948. Similar events took place in Cuba, Costa Rica, and elsewhere. Throughout the region labor confederations in the postwar period were intervened, marginalized, disbanded, or placed under state control.

The United States joined this campaign directly, through the appointment of labor attachés to embassy staffs, and indirectly, through the anticommunist efforts of the American Federation of Labor. Under the leadership of George Meany and the remarkable Serafino Romualdi—the gregarious, rotund, Italian-born deputy in charge of Latin American operations—the AFL launched a militant campaign against the World Federation of Trade Unions, regarded as a "communist front organization," and its regional affiliate, the Confederación de Trabajadores de América Latina (CTAL), established in 1938 under the leadership of Mexican labor leader Vicente Lombardo Toledano, whom Romualdi denounced in 1943 as a "well-known follower of the Communist Party line." The CTAL represented a broad front of democratic forces throughout the region, especially during the war, and it accordingly accepted the participation of communist groups. Romualdi firmly declared the CTAL to be "the Communist front designed to control the Latin American labor movement."

With the active support of the U.S. State Department, Romualdi set out to organize an anticommunist movement that could challenge both the WFTU and the CTAL. His tireless efforts came to fruition in January 1948 with the creation of what came to be known as the Organización Regional Interamericana de Trabajadores (ORIT). Drawing on strong international support, plus fervent backing from Washington, ORIT and its local affiliates steadily took over the labor movement in Latin America. In his memoirs, Romualdi narrates a tale of unceasing struggle against communist influence among working-class syndicates. By the mid-1960s ORIT had reached 28 million workers grouped in fifty-two affiliated organizations located in thirty-nine republics, territories, and possessions of the hemisphere.

Yet another component of hemispheric Cold War strategy was diplomatic isolation of the USSR. The idea was to seal the Americas off from Soviet influence and thus to prevent its contamination by Marxist thought or Leninist agents. In a sense, a diplomatic cordon around Latin America would amount to reassertion of the Monroe Doctrine.

Prior to World War II, in fact, only three Latin American nations had granted de jure recognition to Soviet Union: Mexico (1924), which later broke relations in 1930; Uruguay (1926), which ruptured relations in 1935 partly at the behest of Brazil; and Colombia (1935), with Bogotá the only host to a Soviet diplomatic mission anywhere in the region until 1942. At the wartime urging of the United States, however, thirteen nations recognized the USSR between 1942 and 1945.

By 1946 the Soviet Union enjoyed diplomatic relations with fifteen out of twenty Latin American republics, with resident missions in eight countries of the region.

Then came the Cold War. By the mid-1950s all but three of the fifteen governments that had recognized the Soviet government had severed relations with the USSR. "In each case," as analyst Rollie Poppino has said, "a specific grievance was cited as justification for the action taken. In most instances, however, the decision to cut formal ties with the Communist power reflected broad anticommunist policies being adopted by the Latin American governments, at least in part to win favor with the United States." Brazil and Chile broke relations in 1947; Colombia followed suit in 1948; Venezuela (under Pérez Jiménez) and Cuba (under Batista) did the same in 1952. Guatemala became a special case in 1954.

Economic ties with the Soviet bloc were no stronger than political links. In commerce as well as in diplomacy, the United States for the most part succeeded in keeping the Soviet Union out of the Western Hemisphere. Cold War policies insulated the Americas from alien, dangerous, subversive Soviet influence.

## THE NIXON TRIP

Through the mid-1950s the Eisenhower administration came to regard its Latin American policy with self-satisfaction. In late 1957 John Foster Dulles assured a group of journalists that "we see no likelihood at the present time of communism getting into control of the political institutions of any of the American Republics." And in February 1958 Allen Dulles of the CIA admitted to Congress that there might be "soft points" within the region, but he nonetheless concluded that communism in Latin America was not "a situation to be frightened of as an overall problem."

It was with confidence, then, that Vice President Nixon undertook a tour through South America in May 1958. Originally planned as a courtesy call at the inauguration of newly elected Arturo Frondizi in Argentina, the trip gradually expanded into a two-and-a-half-week tour of eight countries. On "a bleak and drizzly day," Nixon later recalled, he and Patricia Nixon left Washington's National Airport on what was shaping up as a tedious and time-consuming exercise in diplomatic protocol.

To his evident surprise, Nixon met an unruly reception. In Uruguay, the first stop on his tour, the vice president noticed a mild demonstration against U.S. imperialism. A defiant Nixon then went straight to the university, a hotbed of leftist ideology, and engaged a crowd of students in spirited but friendly debate. In Argentina, too, Nixon spoke to labor groups and to university students—engaging in a confrontation with Gregorio Selser, "a well-known Communist newspaper writer" (actually, Selser was a widely respected social scientist)—and emphasizing the danger of communist threats to the region. In neighboring Paraguay, still in the iron grip of General Alfredo Stroessner, Nixon saluted the government for its "strong opposition . . . to Communism." So far, so good.

In Peru things started to change. The night before a scheduled visit to the University of San Marcos, in Lima, Nixon received warnings of possible violence.

"It was apparent that the Communists, after the failure of their efforts to disrupt my tour in Uruguay, Argentina, or Bolivia, had decided to make an all-out effort to embarrass me and the United States at San Marcos University, an institution so well known throughout Latin America that whatever happened there would be front-page news everywhere." As Nixon decided whether to keep his appointment, a crowd kept up a steady chant outside his hotel: *Fuera Nixon, Fuera Nixon, Fuera Nixon.* Approaching the students at San Marcos, Nixon claimed to pick out the leaders—"the usual case-hardened, cold-eyed Communist operatives"—and then retreated when the crowd began throwing stones. Back at his hotel he encountered another angry mob, and "one of the most notorious Communist agitators in Lima" spit directly in his face. Having challenged the demonstrators directly, Nixon would look back on the visit to Lima as a personal triumph.

Ecuador and Colombia provided pleasant interludes, and then Nixon headed for Caracas. Only five months before, the detested right-wing dictator of Venezuela, Marcos Pérez Jiménez—recipient of the Legion of Merit from the Eisenhower administration for his anticommunist efforts—had fled the country and, together with his notorious chief of secret police, found exile in the United States. En route to Caracas Nixon heard rumors of plans for huge anti-American manifestations and even an assassination plot. As Nixon would later remember, "the Communist high command in South America had made a high-level decision to regain the ground they had lost in Lima by mounting a massive payoff demonstration in Caracas."

Venezuelans lost no time in expressing their anger over U.S. policy. A taunting, jeering crowd greeted the Nixons at the airport. The motorcade to the city ran into a blockade, and a mob surged toward the Nixons' automobile. Rocks filled the air, and, as Nixon graphically recalled, "The spit was flying so fast that the driver turned on his windshield wipers." The crowd rocked the car, threatening to turn it over, but then the driver managed to escape. Heading for the U.S. embassy, Nixon remembered, "I felt as though I had come as close as anyone could get, and still remain alive, to a firsthand demonstration of the ruthlessness, fanaticism and determination of the enemy we face in the world struggle."

Astonished by these expressions of popular hostility, Washington immediately denounced the anti-Nixon demonstrations as the result of communist agitation. Nixon himself expressed "no doubt that the riots were Communist-planned, Communist-led, and Communist-controlled." Senator Homer Capehart, Republican of Indiana, proclaimed that the vice president's reception was "a 100 percent Russian penetration." Bourke Hickenlooper, Republican senator from Iowa, said that it revealed a "worldwide pattern of Communist stimulus." Concurred Serafino Romualdi, leader of the anticommunist ORIT: The anti-Nixon demonstrations "clearly indicated a prearranged plan of unquestionable Communist organization and direction."

The Nixon tour prompted an immediate (but incomplete) reassessment of U.S. policy toward Latin America. Nixon himself suggested that Washington distance itself from authoritarian rulers, explicitly recommending a "formal handshake for dictators; an *embraso* [sic!] for leaders in freedom." By February 1959 Eisenhower appeared to accept the spirit of this idea, despite resistance from John Foster Dulles, approving gestures of "special encouragement" toward representative governments. The following year Eisenhower even endorsed a plan to persuade the ruthless Rafael Trujillo to step down from the presidency of the Dominican Republic.

Opposition to dictatorship was, however, equivocal at most. In the midst of a discussion about military assistance, for which the United States sent approximately $400 million during the 1950s, Christian Herter, Dulles' successor as secretary of state, framed the key rhetorical question: "Is the country on our side?" In view of communist threats, he asserted, "a more urgent value—security and survival—must take precedence over an absolute commitment to the promotion of democracy." Unless they were becoming fragile, unpopular, or inconvenient, anticommunist dictators could expect continuing support from Washington.

A second reassessment concerned economic assistance. In the wake of his South American tour, Nixon declared: "We must develop an economic program for Latin America which is distinctively its own. . . . There must be a new program for economic progress for the hemisphere." The proposal met with time-honored skepticism throughout the U.S. government. As one frustrated embassy official blurted out in 1959, looking back on the $129 million in economic assistance that Washington had granted to Bolivia since 1953: "We don't have a damn thing to show for it. We're wasting money. The only solution to Bolivia's problems is to abolish Bolivia."

With cautious hesitation, Eisenhower moved ahead. In 1959 the United States supported the creation of an Inter-American Development Bank (IDB), thus realizing one of the early visions for a Pan American community. And in July 1960 the government announced in Bogotá a Social Progress Trust Fund, with $500 million earmarked for health, education, housing, and land reform throughout the region, to be administered through the new IDB. By the end of his term, observers noted, Eisenhower had forged a two-pronged policy toward Latin America: the 1954 Declaration of Caracas, with its renunciation of Marxism, and the 1960 Act of Bogotá, with its assault on poverty and underdevelopment. At long last, the United States was seeking to eradicate what it took to be the underlying causes as well as the political expressions of communism in the hemisphere.

## QUESTIONS FOR REVIEW

1. What was the Truman Doctrine, and what was the policy of "containment"? How did they shape U.S. policy toward Latin America?
2. Why did the United States forge alliances with right-wing dictators?
3. What did Vietnam have to do with Latin America?
4. Why did the Untied States attempt to gain control over organized labor in Latin America?
5. What was the importance of the Nixon trip?

# CHAPTER 6

# Making Friends

The U.S. can win wars, but the question is can we win revolutions.

HENRY CABOT LODGE (1959)

There are three possibilities in descending order of preference: a decent democratic regime, a continuation of the Trujillo regime, or a Castro regime. We ought to aim at the first but we really cannot renounce the second until we are sure that we can avoid the third.

JOHN F. KENNEDY (1961)

Geopolitical dimensions of the U.S.–Soviet competition obliged both superpowers to seek allies, friends, and clients throughout the world, especially in unaligned parts of the globe. Enlistment of new partners not only increased the relative strength of each side, but, if the inscription could be portrayed as voluntary, it also testified to the presumed superiority of the rival social systems. The extension of economic assistance by Washington offered an excellent means for making friends, through the dispensation of material benefits, and a promising method for weakening foes, since the alleviation of poverty would presumably undercut the social base of communist movements. From the 1960s through the 1980s Washington threw its support behind anticommunist regimes in other ways, welcoming the advent of military regimes in Brazil and Argentina and aligning itself with right-wing dictatorships throughout the hemisphere.

The quest for allies coincided with the emergence of the Third World. (According to this hierarchical lexicon, the "first" world contained industrialized capitalist democracies, principally Western Europe and the United States; the "second" world comprised the communist bloc, especially the USSR and Eastern Europe; the "third" world was a residual category, embracing all countries not included in the first or second worlds.) Despite this subjective (and rather presumptuous) classification, it was apparent that Third World countries shared common characteristics. In economic terms, they were poor, disadvantaged, and dependent; many, with small populations, lacked both the consumer market and the human resource bases vital for self-sustaining development. In political terms, especially in Asia and Africa, many had been European colonies or protectorates prior to

World War II, and they earned their independence through a variety of means: often through peaceful negotiation, but in some cases, like India, after decades of resistance, and in others, like Vietnam, after armed struggle. Consequently they were profoundly suspicious of the Western "first" world, they were fiercely proud of their sovereignty, and they were intent on improving their socioeconomic circumstance. During the Cold War, with its struggle for geopolitical and ideological supremacy, these countries also marked a critical arena for U.S.–Soviet rivalry.

Despite sharp contrasts with Asia and Africa, Latin America clearly belonged to this emergent Third World. With the conspicuous exception of small island nations in the Caribbean, most of Latin America had achieved political independence in the 1820s. With the painful exception of Haiti, most countries of the region were considerably more prosperous—or less poor—than sub-Saharan Africa and South Asia. And as a result of their proximity to the United States, leaders of Latin America would find it difficult to claim neutrality in the Cold War and/or to play the two superpowers off against each other. Nonetheless Latin America pertained to this heterogeneous category—if only through a process of elimination, since it could not be regarded as part of the first or second worlds—and regional spokesmen would frequently assert solidarity with other "less developed" areas around the globe. By the outbreak of the Cold War, Latin America had already endured a long and instructive relationship with the United States; as a result of lessons learned from this experience, Latin America could claim leadership among newly independent nations in the developing areas.

The rise of the Third World presented the United States with a pressing challenge. What kind of policy should Washington use for dealing with these emergent areas? And how should it apply to Latin America? What was needed was a doctrine.

## SOCIAL SCIENCE, IDEOLOGY, AND FOREIGN POLICY

The formulation of a long-term strategy emerged from an unusual convergence of academic talent and political purpose. Drawing heavily on a group of "action intellectuals" based primarily at Harvard and MIT, the Kennedy administration developed and implemented a blueprint for U.S. policy toward the Third World. Eventually known as "modernization theory," the argument rested on complex logic and dubious premises. From time to time it also revealed overtly partisan purposes (one of its charter documents, Walt Rostow's famous essay on "The Stages of Economic Growth," carried the subtitle "An Anti-Communist Manifesto"). Espoused by some of the nation's most prominent social scientists, including Gabriel Almond, Max Millikan, Lucian Pye, and Samuel P. Huntington, modernization theory provided a programmatic basis and intellectual rationale for U.S. actions throughout the 1960s and much of the 1970s.

An underlying assumption was that the diffusion of political democracy throughout the developing world would serve and protect U.S. national interests. If governments were freely elected, it was believed, they would support the United States in its titanic struggle with the Soviet Union. Given an opportunity to express an opinion, in other words, citizens of all nations would necessarily and inevitably choose to join and support the "free world." The idea that people might voluntarily choose socialist or communist rule seemed utterly preposterous. Communism, everyone knew, could spread only by conquest, conspiracy, or subversion. Democratic elections would lead to democratic governments that would support the U.S. side in the Cold War.

The operative question then became how to promote political democracy. Modernization theory found ready and congenial answers in processes of economic and social development. In its most essential form, the argument posited simple causal connections. Economic development would create middle-class sectors that would in turn espouse political democracy, either as a tactical means of gaining power or as an expression of enlightened values (this distinction did not seem to matter at the time). Rather than provoking class struggle between the proletariat and the bourgeoisie, as Marxists held, industrial development would lead to reform, transformation, and social harmony. The greater the level of societal modernization, in other words, the greater the likelihood of democratic politics.

Economic development was therefore extremely desirable, in Washington's eyes, and it could be promoted by U.S. foreign aid. During the 1940s and 1950s the Marshall Plan had comprised a crucial element in U.S. efforts to contain communist advances in post–World War II Europe. In the 1960s, analysts thought, foreign assistance could perform a similar function throughout the Third World. Of course there was a world of difference between stimulating a *recovery* of formerly advanced European economies and achieving the *development* of never-industrialized societies, but this discrepancy seemed trivial at the time. Central to the prevailing model of structural change was the idea, associated with Walt Rostow, of an economic "takeoff." Countries underwent uniform stages of economic growth, according to this theory, and fulfillment of sufficient conditions propelled nations through a "takeoff" phase into self-sustaining growth and continuing development. Foreign aid would not have to go on forever. Its task was to help countries reach the moment of liftoff. Once that was done, the process of development would become more or less automatic, and Washington could apply its resources to other needy causes or nations.

As formulated by "the best and the brightest" recruits in Kennedy's administration, the modernization paradigm quickly seized Washington. It enjoyed academic respectability, it offered bright hopes for the future, and it established clear guidelines for policy. Intellectually, it issued a rebuttal to Leninist notions about imperialism as the highest stage of capitalism; politically, it envisioned a convergence of interests between the United States and the Third World. Promote economic development and you promote democracy—which, by definition, would advance U.S. interests in the struggle with the Soviets.

Modernization theory was fraught with ambiguity. Perhaps the most telling failure, evident in academic writings as well as official declarations, was its inadequate definition of political "progress" or "development" or "modernization." At times the concept referred to democratization—that is, to the progressive expansion of meaningful participation in the quest for political power by growing sectors of the population. At other times, and with frequency, it referred to stability—that is, to the continued preservation of political regimes and the imposition of law and order. These were not only differing notions. They could also be in direct conflict with each other.

As appropriated by the U.S. government, modernization theory was at bottom an antirevolutionary doctrine. It stressed the benefits of guided, gradual, evolutionary change. It emphasized the need for peaceful reform rather than violent upheaval. It called upon Third World governments to accept and promote change to ensure their own survival. As John F. Kennedy declared on one occasion: "Those who make peaceful revolution impossible make violent revolution inevitable." According to rigorous definition the idea of "peaceful revolution" represented a contradiction in terms, but Kennedy nonetheless made his point: Gradual reform would provide the antidote to radical revolution. "If the only alternatives for the people of Latin America are the status quo and communism," Kennedy once insisted, "then they will inevitably choose communism."

Revolution itself was held to be a bad thing. It would upset the social order, destroy political institutions, unleash nationalist sentiments, and invite left-wing takeovers. These concerns gave rise to a widespread conviction, virtually an article of faith by the 1960s, that Latin America stood on the brink of massive revolution (it was "one minute to midnight," in the hackneyed language of the time). The prospect of social upheaval contained two forms of political danger. One was that revolutionary leaders would turn out to be Marxists, dedicated agents or pliant "puppets" of the Soviet Union who would align their governments with the communist bloc. Another was that revolutionaries might be well-meaning idealists who nonetheless would provoke political instability, thus opening their movements and their governments to communist subversion. Either way, uprisings by the "have-nots" seemed threatening to the United States.

In addition to opposing revolution, U.S. strategy made strenuous efforts to prevent the rise of leftist movements. Prevention of revolution and suppression of the left would provide time and opportunity for processes of socioeconomic modernization to unfold, for countries to attain the stage of economic takeoff and self-sustaining change. Thus it was Kennedy who urged the development of counterinsurgency strategies within the Pentagon, and it was Kennedy, as well, who established the antiguerrilla unit known as the Green Berets.

The ultimate application of modernization theory, in conjunction with the doctrine of containment, came in Vietnam. As Vice President Lyndon B. Johnson reported after a trip to the region in 1961: "The basic decision in Southeast Asia is here. We must decide whether to help these countries to the best of our ability or throw in the towel in the area and pull back our defenses to San Francisco and a 'Fortress America' concept." As the U.S. Congress approved the fateful Gulf of Tonkin resolution in 1964, presidential adviser Eugene Rostow proclaimed: "It is on this spot that we have to break the liberation war—Chinese type. If we don't break it here we shall have to face it again in Thailand, Venezuela, elsewhere. Vietnam is a clear testing ground for our policy in the world." The Third World, analysts claimed time and again, was like a row of dominoes; if Vietnam fell, according to elementary laws of physics, others would necessarily collapse. The U.S. commitment in Vietnam swelled from 1,400 advisers in 1961 to 541,500 troops in 1969. By 1967 there had been more bombardments in Vietnam than in the European theater during World War II; by 1970, more conventional bombs had been dropped over Vietnam than in the prior history of humankind. Over 58,000 U.S. soldiers were killed, and millions of Vietnamese were killed or maimed. In 1975 the United States finally withdrew the last of its troops in defeat. Ho Chi Minh, nationalist and communist, had achieved his nation's liberation.

Elsewhere in the developing world, U.S. policy evolved according to a two-track strategy: strict opposition to leftist movements, with paramilitary or even military means, and long-term promotion of socioeconomic development and of centrist reform. The idea was relatively clear: Foreign aid would lead to economic development, which led to political stability, which led to eventual democracy. The anticipated results were uniformly benign: more democracy, less communism, greater national independence and greater political stability. All these outcomes would be good for the United States.

## THE ALLIANCE FOR PROGRESS

Latin America's economic relations with the United States turned disadvantageous in the years just after World War II. As wartime suppliers of price-controlled commodities to the Allied cause, Latin countries accumulated $3.4 billion of credits—only to discover that the United States would promptly raise prices on its capital-goods exports. "In effect," as historian Steven Rabe has written, "Latin America made a $3-billion non-interest-bearing loan to the United States and could not collect on the principal." Nor was there much assistance in the offing for the region. Between 1945 and 1952, the era of the Marshall Plan, the entire region received less economic aid from the United States than did Belgium and Luxembourg. The Mutual Defense Assistance Act of 1949 authorized expenditures of $1.3 billion; not a penny went to Latin America. Between 1948 and 1958, under Truman and Eisenhower, Latin America received only 2.4 percent of U.S. foreign economic aid. Asked why Washington was paying such short shrift to the region, veteran diplomat Louis Halle responded with customary candor: "The United States no longer desperately needs Latin America."

The fallout from Richard Nixon's 1958 tour of South America began a shift in priorities. In January 1956 Juscelino Kubitschek, the new president of Brazil, had attempted to persuade Eisenhower that the "way to defeat leftist totalitarianism" was "to combat poverty wherever it may be encountered." Two weeks after the Caracas episode, in 1958, Kubitschek followed up with a letter to Eisenhower, later explaining to U.S. officials that "the problem of underdevelopment will have to be solved if Latin American nations are to be able more effectively to resist subversion and serve the Western cause." For these reasons, the Brazilian proposed a twenty-year development program with $40 billion in economic assistance, to be known as Operation Pan America. Nixon himself advocated "a new program for economic progress in the hemisphere" after his tour of South America, but Eisenhower took only halting steps.

The 1959 triumph of the *fidelista* movement in Cuba created a new sense of urgency. From the outset, long before Fidel Castro declared himself to be a Marxist-Leninist, the United States regarded his regime with apprehension and disdain. Castro's nationalist rhetoric, his confiscation of U.S.-held companies, and his program for land reform—reminiscent of the Arbenz plan in Guatemala— provoked a predictably negative response in U.S. policy circles. Compounded by fears of the "communist threat," the Cuban Revolution became utterly intolerable. To Washington, it was both an insult and a challenge.

## Forming the Alliance

It was in response to the Cuban Revolution that newly elected President John F. Kennedy, an ardent and eloquent Cold Warrior, would launch a bold and new initiative. At a glittering White House reception in March 1961, less than two months after his inauguration, Kennedy observed to Latin American diplomats that "we confront the same forces which have imperiled America throughout its history— the alien forces which once again seek to impose the despotisms of the Old World on the people of the New." To meet this challenge Kennedy proposed a ten-year effort, an Alliance for Progress, or *Alianza para [el] Progreso*, that would promote economic growth, social development, and political democracy. "We propose to complete the revolution of the Americas," Kennedy proclaimed,

> to build a hemisphere where all men can hope for a suitable standard of living, and all can live out their lives in freedom and dignity. To achieve this goal political freedom must accompany material progress. . . . Let us once again transform the American continent into a vast crucible of revolutionary ideas and efforts—a tribute to the power of the creative energies of free men and women, an example to all the world that liberty and progress walk hand in hand. Let us once again awaken our American revolution until it guides the struggle of people everywhere—not with an imperialism of force or fear, but the rule of courage and freedom and hope for the future of man.

It was a stirring address, appearing to mark a dramatic and fundamental reorientation of Washington's policy toward Latin America.

At a historic meeting in August 1961 at Punta del Este, Uruguay, representatives from the United States and Latin America (minus Cuba) gathered to put Kennedy's sweeping vision into practice. A charter established a series of goals for the decade of the 1960s:

- Raising per capita income "to attain, at the earliest possible date, levels of income capable of assuring self-sustaining development"—with minimum growth-rate targets of 2.5 percent per capita per year.

- Social reform, especially focused on "unjust structures of land tenure and use."
- Diversification of trade—by broadening the range of export products and overseas markets.
- Industrialization and increased employment.
- Enhanced education, including the elimination of adult illiteracy by 1970.
- Price stability, so as to avoid either inflation or deflation.

By accelerating development through the 1960s, the Alliance for Progress would bring Latin America through its takeoff stage for economic growth. This would yield social and political benefits both for the region and for the United States.

Delegates at Punta del Este designed a series of measures for achieving these lofty goals. First was a requirement for participating countries to draw up comprehensive plans for national development. These plans were, moreover, to be submitted for approval or amendment by an inter-American board of experts ("the nine wise men," as they promptly came to be known, Walt Rostow among them). This procedure represented a major step for state activism in economic affairs. Said Felipe Pazos, director of the United Nations Economic Commission for Latin America (ECLA/CEPAL): "Planning represented a break with the mentality of an earlier generation which accepted Latin American poverty as a natural consequence of Latin inferiority."

The second measure was an insistence on redistributive reform. Changes in tax codes should demand "more from those who have most." Even more important was a call for land reform. This proved to be a crucial issue. In the early 1960s nearly half the population of Latin America lived in the countryside; as a general rule, 5 to 10 percent of the people owned 70 to 90 percent of the land. Imbued with symbolic and cultural value, land represented a key to subsistence, prosperity, and stability; a significant change in ownership patterns would necessarily entail a major social transformation. As political scientist Tony Smith has pointed out, the United States attempted comparable changes only in postwar Germany and in Japan. "Only in countries occupied after World War II had the United States tried anything so bold."

Third was a U.S. commitment for sustained and large-scale economic assistance. The ambitions of the alliance were to channel $20 billion in foreign assistance within a single decade to Latin America, "with priority to the relatively less developed countries." Of this amount $10 billion was to come from official sources and $10 billion from private sources; the expectation was that this infusion would trigger additional investments by Latin American governments and businesspeople. In the August 1961 declaration from Punta del Este, Washington agreed to shoulder its responsibility, promising to provide "a major part of the minimum of $20 billion, principally in public funds, which Latin America will require . . . in order to supplement its own efforts." The Kennedy administration was committing the United States to a multiyear, multibillion-dollar effort in the Americas. This was utterly unprecedented.

**A Little More Effort, Señor.** Implicitly criticizing the Alliance for Progress, this cartoon employs classic stereotypes of Latin America—as a lazy land of *mañana*.
Artist: Hugh Hutton (1897–1976).

As was so often the case, President Kennedy offered the most clear-cut explanation of U.S. motivations. "Latin America is seething with discontent and unrest," he observed. "We must act to relieve large-scale distress immediately if free institutions are to be given a chance to work out long-term solutions." The point, in other words, was to bolster reformist democratic regimes and to forestall revolutionary threats. Such centrist parties as Acción Democrática in Venezuela and Christian Democracy in Chile offered desirable models for political reform and leadership. Support for the center would prevent the rise of the left.

The Alliance for Progress led to an immediate and substantial increase in U.S. aid to Latin America. Bilateral economic assistance nearly tripled between

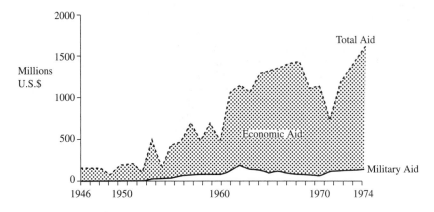

**Figure 6-1  U.S. Bilateral Aid to Latin America, 1946–1974**
Source: Data in Samuel L. Baily, *The United States and the Development of South America, 1945–1975* (New York: Franklin Watts, 1976), p. 74.

FY 1960 and FY 1961, thereafter climbing to well over $1 billion in the mid-1960s (Figure 6-1). Under Kennedy and Johnson, Latin America received nearly 18 percent of total U.S. aid, compared with just 3 percent under Truman and 9 percent under Eisenhower. According to one U.S. official, the United States supplied $1.4 billion per year to Latin America from June 1962 through June 1967; when private investments and other international sources are included, the total for new investments rose to $3.3 billion per year. United States bilateral aid dropped sharply in the late 1960s, especially after Richard Nixon won the presidential election of 1968, but the cumulative amount of assistance was nonetheless substantial. According to another calculation, the total amount of economic aid during the decade of the alliance came to $22.3 billion.

The 1960s witnessed a marked acceleration in economic growth for Latin America. Regional output expanded by 2.4 percent per capita per annum during the 1960s, nearly matching the alliance goal of 2.5 percent, and per capita growth was on a steady rise—reaching 2.7 percent in the latter half of the decade, and climbing to 3.8 percent in 1970–1974. Compared with 2.1 percent in the 1950s, this growth was a major achievement. It stemmed from several factors: the successful implementation of strategies for "import-substitution industrialization," the continuing strength of major commercial markets (especially in the United States), and the stimulation of private investments. Expansion of the industrial sector, especially in Argentina, Brazil, and Mexico, proved to be the driving force behind the region's growth. Overall, seven countries actually reached the target of 2.5 percent per capita per year, twelve nations fell short of the goal, and two countries, Haiti and Uruguay, actually suffered declines in GDP per capita. Foreign assistance under the Alliance for Progress played a relatively minor part in this picture. But with regard to regional rates of per capita growth, according to its own criteria, the alliance nonetheless proclaimed the near-fulfillment of a central goal.

Social reform presented a more discouraging picture. It proved impossible to eliminate adult illiteracy within the decade, as alliance planners projected, but access to secondary and higher levels of education showed a notable increase; in some countries, the number of people going on to higher education doubled or even tripled. Housing projects expanded but could not keep up with population growth, and overcrowding continued to proliferate in urban slums. Provision of potable water and sewage systems became the focus of major efforts, especially in urban areas, but with modest impacts on general welfare. Perhaps the most poignant indicator of public health concerned infant mortality, which the alliance vowed to reduce by one-half within five years. Infant mortality rates declined nearly everywhere (with the exception of Guatemala), but not a single country was able to reach its target under the alliance.

The most intractable issue was, predictably, agrarian reform. As former OAS official Ronald Scheman has written, "The agricultural sector was the problem child of the Alliance." Of more than 15 million peasant families living in Latin America at the beginning of the 1960s, fewer than 1 million benefited from any kind of land reform policy. Determined to maintain their base of power, traditional elites mounted effective resistance to redistributive programs. The ideal of social reform also came into conflict with another of the alliance's declared goals, the increasing of production. When push came to shove, efficiency triumphed over justice.

## Requiem for Failed Expectations

The Alliance for Progress represented an earnest and high-minded attempt by the United States to make friends in Latin America—quite literally, in the sense of creating the friends as well as forming the friendships. There were several basic reasons for its eventual failure. First, perhaps, was the modesty in levels of economic aid. A ten-year injection of $20 billion in a single world region sounded like a massive enterprise, which it was in many respects, but it also amounted to approximately $10 per capita per year. There were limits to what this could achieve.

Second, planners misread social facts of the region. They confidently assumed that Latin America's emerging middle classes would uphold democracy as a matter of moral principle and idealistic conviction. This presumption turned out to be wrong, for in Latin America the so-called middle classes—those whose lifestyle bore essential resemblance to that of middle classes in the United States—belonged to the upper strata of society. They found very little in common with workers in the cities or peasants in the countryside. Lacking in ideological conviction, opportunist at times, Latin America's middle sectors tended to identify their interests with the upper classes. Revealingly enough, it was the middle classes that provided moral and political support for military rulers in Brazil, Argentina, and elsewhere. They did not comply with the prescriptions of the Alliance for Progress.

Third, designers of the alliance misunderstood the relationship between social change and political conflict. It was their anticipation that transformation of Latin American society could come about within a context of political stability (it was their idea, as one analyst has noted, that "all good things go together"). The reality, in contrast, was that upper-class sectors would fight to maintain their privilege and power. This determination was especially evident with regard to land reform, which explicitly called for a redistribution of resources from top to bottom. Ultimately, Washington lost its nerve and backed off from its promises. Agrarian reform, the U.S. government believed, might stir up radical sentiments and play into the hands of communist subversives. Better to leave things as they were.

Finally, alliance planners assumed that social and political change would enhance the strength of a reformist center. This expectation was mistaken for at least two reasons. First, Washington overestimated the significance and ubiquity of reformist forces in Latin America. Acción Democrática in Venezuela and Christian Democracy in Chile were viewed as attractive models, but these types were relatively rare; there was nothing quite comparable in Argentina, Brazil, Ecuador, or most other countries of the region. Second, social change and conflict did not usually benefit moderate reformist tendencies. These processes often led to a political polarization that fortified extremes of left and right rather than the center, thus weakening the prospects for gradual reform. They also undermined a central conviction, especially apparent during the Kennedy era, that the United States would have clear and simple political choices: Washington could circumscribe the left, contain the right, and nurture an enlightened center. Unhappily, this option turned out not always to be available.

## HOLDING THE LINE: DICTATORS AS FRIENDS

The most striking failure of the Alliance for Progress occurred within the political realm. Instead of promoting and consolidating reformist civilian rule, the 1960s witnessed a rash of military coups. There were six *golpes* in 1962–1963 alone, within the early years of the alliance: in Argentina (March 1962), Peru (July 1962), Guatemala (March 1963), Ecuador (July 1963), the Dominican Republic (September 1963), and Honduras (October 1963). Subsequent overthrows led to the installation of new styles and longer-term dictatorial regimes that sought to bring about fundamental transformations in society rather than mediation of disputes through short-term periods of intervention. Military coups in Brazil (April 1964) and Argentina (June 1966) imposed repressive and far-reaching machineries that became archetypes for what came to be known as "bureaucratic-authoritarian" regimes; another coup in Peru (October 1968) installed military leadership with a nationalist outlook and a reformist social agenda. By the end of 1968 dictators were holding sway in Argentina, Brazil, Peru, Paraguay, and most of Central America; Bolivia and Ecuador were controlled by the military; and Mexico remained under the rule of its unique, dominant-party, civilian-led, but unmistakably authoritarian regime.

United States reaction to these developments evolved over time. President Kennedy took particular and somewhat personal umbrage at the overthrow of centrist reformers, precisely the type of leadership that he hoped to nurture and support with alliance programs. Washington accordingly mounted a strong diplomatic offensive in response to the 1962 coup in Peru, where the military intervened to prevent an electoral victory by Víctor Raúl Haya de la Torre and his Aprista party. Kennedy suspended diplomatic relations, cut off economic aid, ordered technical personnel not to go on their jobs—and considered suspension of the Peruvian sugar quota. As the president announced in a news conference: "We are anxious to see a return to constitutional forms in Peru. . . . We feel that this hemisphere can only be secure with free and democratic governments." Washington received precious little support for its position from Latin American governments—Argentina, Brazil, and Mexico protested against the "intervention," while the Chilean foreign minister warned the United States against being "more royalist than the king"— but the Peruvian junta departed from power after supervising another election in 1963. This time, however, the Apristas were not permitted to win.

Similarly, Kennedy expressed considerable displeasure with the overthrow of Ramón Villeda Morales, a moderate civilian who was elected to the presidency of Honduras in 1957. In keeping with the mandate of the Alliance for Progress (and, ironically, with the legacy of Guatemala's Jacobo Arbenz), Villeda Morales designed and promoted a project for land reform. His proposal inspired the wrath of traditional aristocrats as well as the armed forces, of course, and they ousted him from office in October 1963. Kennedy had sharp words for the new ruling junta, but took no meaningful action.

Underlying this position was ambivalence. The undeniable fact is that Kennedy had little to say about the antidemocratic coups taking place in Argentina, Guatemala, Ecuador, or, most fatefully, in the Dominican Republic (as explained in the following chapter). In such cases, the president appeared to follow his own dictum: Do not oppose authoritarian regimes until or unless the communist threat has disappeared. Hardheaded calculations of costs and benefits prevailed.

In keeping with these developments, the U.S. State Department began to soften its opposition to military rule in Latin America. On this subject Assistant Secretary of State for Inter-American Affairs Edward M. Martin composed a key policy statement in October 1963 (when Kennedy was still in office): "We all have respect for motherhood and abhor sin. We may observe, however, that while motherhood has prospered, so has sin. In an increasingly nationalistic world of sovereign states, a U.S. frown doesn't deter others from committing what we consider to be political sins." Military coups had serious negative consequences. In Martin's assessment, they "thwart the will of the people, destroy political stability and the growth of the tradition of respect for democratic constitutions, and nurture communist opposition to their tyranny." Yet the United States could not prevent them from occurring. Under these circumstances, he continued, the U.S. government should engage the ensuing authoritarian regimes in positive ways and encourage the military to concentrate on internal security and civic action programs. In conclusion he wrote,

> I fear there are some who will accuse me of having written an apologia for coups. I have not. They are to be fought with all the means we have available. Rather . . . I

> am insisting . . . that democracy is a living thing which must have time and soil and sunlight in which to grow. We must do all we can to create these favorable conditions, and we can and have done much. But we cannot simply create the plant and give it to them; it must spring from seeds planted in indigenous soil.

Seeking middle ground between "impatient idealists" and "defeatist cynics," Martin attempted to define a realistic and pragmatic approach for U.S. policy.

Even so, the U.S. stance took a sharp turn toward the right after Kennedy's assassination in November 1963. From his own personal experiences in Mexico and Texas, Lyndon B. Johnson concluded that JFK's policy toward Latin America was "a thorough-going mess." Skeptical about prospects for social reform and disdainful of political idealists, Johnson was adamant about the need to avoid a "second Cuba" in the hemisphere. A victory for communism in Brazil, he thought, would confront the United States with "another China." It was time for the United States to get tough.

Abruptly dismissing Martin and Teodoro Moscoso, chief administrator of the Alliance for Progress, Johnson united both State Department and AID functions in the person of Thomas C. Mann, assistant secretary of state for economic affairs in the last years of the Eisenhower administration and ambassador to Mexico. A self-styled "country lawyer" from southwest Texas, Mann embodied Johnson's approach toward the region. ("I know my Latinos," Mann was once reported to have said. "They understand only two things—a buck in the pocket and a kick in the ass.") In March 1964 he convoked a three-day meeting of U.S. ambassadors to Latin America and, in an off-the-record statement, announced the administration's new line. What subsequently became known as the Mann Doctrine propounded four basic objectives: (1) promotion of economic growth with absolute neutrality on questions of social reform, (2) protection of U.S. private investments, (3) display of no preference, through aid or other means, for representative democratic institutions, and (4) opposition to communism. In effect, Mann discarded cherished ideas of the Alliance for Progress, especially its insistence on social reform and political democracy. Indeed, Mann expressed no political or moral reservations about cooperation with military governments. In his view, so long as a government was not communist-controlled or in danger of becoming so, it would be acceptable to the United States.

The Mann Doctrine found virtually immediate application in Brazil, where military officers overthrew the center-left government of João Goulart on April 1, 1964. Concerned about the possibility of a sharp leftward turn by the wavering Goulart, the U.S. government was fully aware of the military conspiracy and even offered assistance (which was never needed). Within hours of the coup, President Johnson dispatched a congratulatory telegram expressing "warmest good wishes" to the titular president of the new regime, stating that "the American people have watched with anxiety the political and economic difficulties through which your great nation has been passing, and have admired the resolute will of the Brazilian community to resolve these difficulties within a framework of constitutional democracy and without civil strife." Johnson's message thus adopted the transparently specious argument that Goulart had voluntarily "vacated" the presidency of Brazil, so the constitutional requirements for succession were maintained. Plainly enough, the U.S. government was establishing a rationale to justify the coup.

Encouraged by the denouement in Brazil, Mann offered a public description of the new U.S. policy in a commencement address at Notre Dame in June 1964. The United States sought to strengthen democratic government and to discourage military intervention, he said, and Washington would promote the return to democracy in cases where coups occurred. But the practice of democracy, Mann continued, was not just a question of civilian rule. It also entailed respect for rights of expression and organization. As a result, Mann contended, the United States should:

> encourage democracy in a quiet, unpublicized way and on . . . [a] day-to-day basis; broaden the scope of collective action in the hemisphere; [make] a careful evaluation of each case of the use of force to overthrow a government; if as a result of this evaluation it is decided not to recognize a regime, it should be made clear that nonrecognition is tied to a breach in established international conduct; and if it is decided to recognize a government, it should be made clear that recognition in no way constitutes approval.

In translation: The United States would offer diplomatic recognition to military regimes that were not in flagrant defiance of minimal standards of international conduct. Washington would henceforth deal with dictators on a practical, pragmatic, and realistic basis.

Mann stipulated one key exception to this policy of nonintervention. "The question of our relations with Communist regimes in this hemisphere is, of course, a separate subject. . . . It raises separate questions, such as our inherent right of self-defense and measures, under existing treaties, to deal with situations which threaten the peace and security of the hemisphere." While the United States would not take action against dictatorships of the right, it reserved the option of deposing left-wing regimes. Intervention would thus be allowable in order to forestall communist rule.

The U.S. posture toward military regimes thenceforth oscillated between passive acceptance and outright endorsement. Washington saw little convincing reason to denounce or oppose authoritarian rule. In June 1966, perhaps emboldened by the Brazilian example, the Argentine armed forces ousted Arturo Illia, installed a general in the presidency, abolished legislative bodies, outlawed political parties, expressed abhorrence for international communism, and embarked on a conservative economic program; the Johnson administration warmly welcomed the new government. In the meantime the United States approved loans to the tyrannical government of François ("Papa Doc") Duvalier in Haiti, continued to support the Somoza dynasty in Nicaragua, and cooperated with the autocratic Stroessner regime in Paraguay.

Washington's acceptance of dictatorship became even more explicit under Richard M. Nixon, one of whose first acts as president after the 1968 election was to commission political rival Nelson Rockefeller to conduct a study of U.S.–Latin

American relations. Rockefeller's expansive entourage made four trips through the region, conferred with more than 3,000 leaders, endured frequent anti-U.S. demonstrations, and submitted its final report in August 1969. "The United States has allowed the special relationship it has historically maintained with the other nations of the Western Hemisphere to deteriorate badly," stated the report. This deterioration stemmed from several causes, in the commission's view, including "narrow special interests," competing foreign-policy priorities, "well-intentioned but unrealistic rhetoric," and a "paternalistic attitude. . . . The United States has talked about partnership," in the view of the commission, "but it has not truly practiced it." Partly as a consequence, Latin America presented a disturbing picture. Expectations were rising but population growth, urbanization, unemployment, nationalism, radicalism, and anti-U.S. sentiment were commonplace: "The seeds of nihilism and anarchy are spreading throughout the hemisphere." Emerging forces for social change included women ("by and large, a middle-of-the-road influence") and the Roman Catholic Church, although, like young people in general, the idealistic priesthood was "vulnerable to subversive penetration." Indeed, the potential for Castroite and Marxist infiltration was powerful: "Clearly, the opinion in the United States that communism is no longer a serious factor in the Western Hemisphere is thoroughly wrong."

In the face of these challenges, the Rockefeller group found one strong and positive influence: the Latin American military. As the commission proclaimed, "a new type of military man is coming to the fore and often becoming a major force for constructive social change in the American republics. Motivated by increasing impatience with corruption, inefficiency, and a stagnant political order, the new military man is prepared to adapt his authoritarian tradition to the goals of social and economic progress." Implicitly referring to the maverick regime in Peru, the report went on to observe that military governments "have an intrinsic ideological unreliability and a vulnerability to extreme nationalism. They can go in almost any doctrinal direction." The question, therefore, was whether they would favor the United States—"Or will they become radicalized, statist, and anti-U.S.?" To prevent this undesirable outcome, the commission called for more training of Latin American officers in U.S.-sponsored programs, more contact and cooperation, and more types of military assistance. As a general proposition, the commission opined, it made much more sense to collaborate with Latin American military rulers "than to abandon or insult them because we are conditioned by arbitrary ideological stereotypes."

Cooperation with dictators would therefore continue to be a basic element in U.S. policy toward Latin America for years to come. The Nixon administration formed close relations with the ruling generals in Brazil, and in 1973, as will be recounted in the next chapter, Nixon warmly welcomed a military takeover in Chile. In 1976 President Gerald Ford granted prompt recognition to an antidemocratic junta in Argentina. In the meantime Washington worked together with dictatorial regimes throughout most of Central America.

A partial exception to this rule came under Jimmy Carter, the only Democrat to occupy the White House during the remainder of the Cold War. Driven by the president's moral convictions and spurred by an activist Congress, the U.S. government launched a major campaign on behalf of human rights that led to the denial of economic and military assistance to regimes in Guatemala, Chile, and Argentina that were flagrantly abusing their citizens. And in 1979, as a *sandinista* rebellion spread throughout Nicaragua, the Carter administration withdrew its support from Anastasio Somoza and allowed his tyrannical regime to come to an end.

It is to be observed, however, that Carter was willing to overlook human-rights violations in countries outside the hemisphere that were viewed as crucial to U.S. security, mostly notably Iran under the shah and the Philippines under the Marcos family. To this degree, even the Carter administration ratified a long-standing principle in U.S. Cold War policy: to oppose dictators in Latin America only if they (1) became a serious embarrassment to Washington, (2) ran a risk of being overthrown by radical or "communist" movements, or (3) provoked both conditions (1) and (2). In such cases the United States would typically seek to persuade the ruler to cede power to a trusted centrist, who (with support from Washington) could prevent a victory by communists. The idea was not so much that dictatorship was inherently bad; it was fear that the alternative would be much worse.

Carter's policy on human rights, cautious as it was, came in for critical excoriation. In a well-known essay entitled "Dictatorships and Double Standards," published in 1979, neoconservative analyst Jeane Kirkpatrick denounced the Carter administration for withdrawing support from the shah of Iran and from Somoza in the face of popular challenges. Because of a naive belief in the feasibility of democratic politics, Kirkpatrick charged, the Carter team allowed both countries to fall under the grip of hostile, totalitarian movements. "The American effort to impose liberalization and democratization on a government confronted with violent internal opposition not only failed," she said, "but actually assisted the coming to power of new regimes in which ordinary people enjoy fewer freedoms and less personal security than under the previous autocracy—regimes, moreover, hostile to American interests and policies." Misconceived American policies had brought about precisely the situations they sought to avoid.

The practical implication was clear: the United States should support traditional authoritarian regimes so long as they promote the cause of anticommunism. The consequence of Carter's high-minded mistakes was, she proclaimed in yet another essay, a serious threat to U.S. security: "The deterioration of the U.S. position in the hemisphere has already created serious vulnerabilities where none previously existed, and threatens now to confront this country with the unprecedented need to defend itself against a ring of Soviet bases on its southern flanks from Cuba to Central America." Once again, eternal vigilance would be the price of liberty. In the name of national security, Washington should back its friends and challenge its foes.

## QUESTIONS FOR REVIEW

1. Does the U.S. preference for democracy stem from moral principle? Or does it stem from political calculation?
2. What was the impact of the Cuban Revolution on U.S. policy toward Latin America?
3. What were the theoretical underpinnings of the Alliance for Progress? Why did they seem to make sense at the time?
4. What were the outcomes of the Alliance for Progress? Could it have succeeded with more effort from the U.S. government?
5. What were the principal differences between Kennedy, Johnson, and Nixon with regard to Latin America?

# CHAPTER 7

# Crushing Enemies

I don't see why we should have to stand by and let a country go communist due to the irresponsibility of its own people.

HENRY KISSINGER (1970)

If the Soviet Union can aid and abet subversion in our hemisphere, then the United States has a legal right and a moral duty to help resist it. This is not only in our strategic interest; it is morally right.

RONALD REAGAN (1984)

Throughout the Cold War the United States considered the installation in Latin America of radical regimes—socialist, Marxist-Leninist, or "leftist" in any way—to be intolerable. Any such development would represent an advance for the communist cause and, in the zero-sum calculus of the time, a vital loss for the West. In view of Soviet strategy, with its presumed domination of clients and puppets, the presence of a socialist government would represent an intrusion of extrahemispheric power within the Americas—and violate the Monroe Doctrine. Acceptance of this outcome could weaken the credibility of the United States as the leader of the West and as a rival for the USSR. In the eyes of Cold Warriors, the consolidation of any left-wing regime in the Western Hemisphere would have dire and dangerous implications for U.S. national security and for the global distribution of power.

It was therefore essential to resist this possibility. As shown in chapters 5 and 6, the United States developed strategies in the 1950s and 1960s to prevent such unfavorable denouements. On occasion, however, Washington found itself face to face with what it regarded as an unacceptably "leftist" regime within the hemisphere. In such cases U.S. policymakers felt obliged to take action—which meant overthrowing the government in question. Exigencies of the Cold War thus led the United States to adopt a tacit but consistent policy of political intervention in Latin America. American officials routinely attempted to justify each episode as singular, exceptional, and nonprecedential, but U.S. interventions occurred with relentless regularity—from Guatemala in 1954 to Cuba in 1961 to the Dominican Republic in 1965 to Chile in 1973 to Grenada in 1983 and to Central America throughout the 1980s. This decades-long sequence was not a serendipitous accumulation of random events; on the contrary, it was a crystal-clear reflection of the logic of the Cold War.

## INTERVENTION IN GUATEMALA

American intolerance for left-of-center politics first became apparent in the otherwise-unlikely context of Guatemala, where Colonel Jacobo Arbenz Guzmán won the presidency through free elections in 1950. A dedicated reformist, Arbenz proclaimed three objectives for his administration: "to convert our country from a dependent nation with a semi-colonial economy to an economically independent country; to convert Guatemala from a backward country with a predominantly feudal economy into a modern capitalist state; and to make this transformation in a way that will raise the standard of living of the great mass of our people to the highest level." Key to this program was agrarian reform. Enacted in June 1952, the bill empowered the government to expropriate only uncultivated portions of large plantations. All lands taken were to be paid for in twenty-five-year bonds bearing a 3 percent interest rate, and the valuation of land was to be determined according to its taxable worth as of May 1952. During its eighteen months of operation the agrarian reform distributed 1.5 million acres to some 100,000 families. The expropriations included 1,700 acres owned by Arbenz himself, who had become a landowner through the dowry of his wife.

Almost immediately, Arbenz and the agrarian reform ran into implacable opposition from the United Fruit Company and from the U.S. government. For its banana production *La frutera* held enormous tracts of land in Guatemala, 85 percent of which was unused—or, as the company maintained, held in reserve against natural catastrophes. And in calculating tax obligations, UFCO consistently undervalued its holdings. On the basis of tax declarations, the Guatemalan government in 1953 offered UFCO $627,572 in bonds in compensation for a seized portion of property; on behalf of the company, the U.S. State Department countered with a demand for $15,854,849!

Washington was deeply involved. Some of the ties were personal. Secretary of State John Foster Dulles and his brother, CIA director Allen Dulles, both came from a New York law firm with close links to United Fruit. The company's Washington lobbyist was Thomas Corcoran, a prominent lawyer who was on close terms with President Eisenhower's trusted aide and undersecretary of state, Walter Bedell Smith, himself once interested in a management position with UFCO.

More important than personal ties, however, was the anticommunist crusade. UFCO publicists and the Dulles brothers accused the Arbenz regime of being "soft" on communism, branding it a threat to U.S. security and to the free world at large. They cultivated fears that defeat in Guatemala might lead to a Soviet takeover of the Panama Canal. They warned that if Guatemala fell, then the rest of Central America might go as well. But the principal issue was agrarian reform. Such writers as Daniel James warned that communists would use the program as a stepping-stone to gain control of Guatemala. ("The battle of the Western Hemisphere has begun," he wrote at one point. "We enter upon a new era in our history. We face, for the first time, the prospect of continuous struggle against Communism on a hemispheric scale. . . . Such is the ultimate meaning of Moscow's first attempt to conquer an American country, Guatemala.") Whatever Arbenz may have intended, from the U.S. viewpoint he was merely a "stooge" for the Russians.

United States policy soon began to take shape. President Eisenhower warned Guatemalan foreign minister Guillermo Toriello that because the United States was "determined to block the international communist conspiracy," he "couldn't help a government which was openly playing ball with communists." The newly dispatched U.S. ambassador, John Peurifoy, offered a succinct impression of his first meeting with Arbenz: "If the president is not a Communist he will certainly do until one comes along."

At an OAS meeting at Caracas in March 1954 John Foster Dulles pressed delegates to support a resolution that "the domination or control of the political institutions of any American state by the international communist movement . . . would constitute a threat" to the entire hemisphere and would require "appropriate action in accordance with existing treaties." His reference was to the Rio Treaty of 1947, which permitted collective action if two-thirds of OAS members concurred that the political independence of any member state was threatened by "an aggression which was not an armed attack." As Dulles explained, the United States wanted to extend "the Monroe Doctrine to include the concept of outlawing foreign ideologies in the American Republics." And as Assistant Secretary John Moors Cabot observed, there was no need to demonstrate conscious intent to serve the Soviet cause: "It is our position that anyone traveling in the interests of communism is in fact part of the whole subversive program of international communism."

Latin American diplomats immediately realized that the U.S. resolution sought to establish a pretext for action against Guatemala. After two weeks of intense debate, the resolution carried by a vote of 17–1–2 (only Guatemala was opposed; Mexico and Argentina abstained). Its impact was greatly softened by an amendment that called for OAS consultations instead of immediate action. Thus the resolution lost its teeth. In summary, opined long-time diplomat Louis Halle, the message of Caracas was "that there was more fear of U.S. interventionism than of Guatemalan communism."

Even so, the Arbenz government concluded that the United States was preparing to intervene. The regime cracked down on domestic opposition and turned to Eastern Europe for small arms, which were en route by May. Meanwhile the U.S. government was demanding, in increasingly blunt language, compensation for U.S. property in Guatemala, meaning, of course, United Fruit.

Unable to obtain OAS sponsorship for direct intervention, the Eisenhower administration turned to covert action. The CIA organized an exile force under an obscure renegade Guatemalan colonel named Carlos Castillo Armas. A rebel column of several hundred men was assembled across the border in neighboring Honduras. They were equipped and directed by the CIA, which set up and operated a rebel radio station and provided a few World War II fighter planes to strafe Guatemala City. Under attack by these planes and convinced that a large army was approaching the capital, Arbenz lost his nerve and gave up. Upon leaving office, however, he delivered a blistering resignation speech:

> The United Fruit Company, in collaboration with the governing circles of the
> United States, is responsible for what is happening to us. . . . In whose name
> have they carried out these barbaric acts? What is their banner? We know very
> well. They have used the pretext of anticommunism. The truth is very different.
> The truth is to be found in the financial interests of the fruit company and the
> other U.S. monopolies which have invested great amounts of money in Latin
> America and fear that the example of Guatemala would be followed by other
> Latin American countries.

The president disappeared behind the walls of the Mexican embassy, and the
Castillo Armas rebels rolled into the capital virtually unopposed.

The Eisenhower administration exulted in its Guatemalan triumph. In July the
White House held a reception for top CIA officials, to whom the president offered
his gratitude: "Thanks to all of you. You've averted a Soviet beachhead in our hemisphere." The redoubtable George Meany, ever the anticommunist, expressed satisfaction in similar language: "The American Federation of Labor rejoices over
the downfall of the Communist-controlled regime in Guatemala, brought about
by the refusal of the Army to serve any longer a Government that had betrayed
the democratic aspirations of the people and had transformed the country into a
beachhead of Soviet Russia in the Western Hemisphere."

In Latin America, however, the U.S. action sparked dozens of protests. In
Mexico, students and workers marched against the United States at rallies in
marketplaces and the university. In Honduras, students held a demonstration
to denounce "Wall St. interests." In Panama, students staged a twenty-four-hour
strike. In Cuba, demonstrators hurled stones at offices of United Press International
and the North American Electric Company. In Argentina, the national congress
passed a resolution backing Arbenz; in Uruguay, the congress enacted a resolution condemning the U.S. "aggression"; and in Chile, the Chamber of Deputies
voted 34–15 to denounce the U.S. operation. While the Guatemalan intervention
provoked nationalist and anti-imperialist outcries throughout the region, the U.S.
mainstream weekly *Life* magazine offered its own interpretation of the protests:
"World communism was efficiently using the Guatemalan show to strike a blow
at the U.S. . . . in the form of Red-run anti-U.S. demonstrations which loudly supported Guatemala and waved the bloody shirt of Yankee imperialism from Mexico
City to Santiago."

Under a temporary military junta, the new government of Guatemala reversed
the expropriation of United Fruit lands and, even more brazenly, wiped out the
banana workers' union. In addition the regime established a National Committee
of Defense Against Communism, followed by a Preventive Penal Law Against
Communism—establishing the death penalty for "crimes" that could be construed
as "sabotage," including union activities. And as part of its ideological crusade,
the Guatemalan junta commanded the banning and burning of such "subversive"
books as *Les Miserables*, by the same Victor Hugo whose death had caused such
mourning among intellectuals in fin de siècle Buenos Aires, as well as novels by the
Nobel Prize–winning author Miguel Ángel Asturias.

On September 1, 1954, the junta stepped down and Castillo Armas assumed power alone. To legitimize his authority, he staged a mock plebiscite the following month: 485,531 favored his continuation as president, 393 were opposed, 655 had no answer. He reestablished ties with the Catholic Church, brought Guatemala back into the OAS, and lifted prohibitions on foreign oil concessions. Eventually assassinated in 1957, Castillo Armas left a dolorous legacy. As later described by one of the CIA operatives who took part in the Arbenz overthrow, "Castillo Armas was a bad president, tolerating corruption throughout his government and kowtowing to the United Fruit Company more than to his own people. The United States could have prevented this with the vigorous exercise of diplomatic pressure on Castillo Armas to assure that he pursued social reform for the many rather than venal satisfaction for a few. Instead, Washington breathed a collective sigh of relief and turned to other problems."

Actually, U.S. indifference would not last for long. As the Cold War spread throughout Latin America, Guatemala plunged into a thirty-six-year-long civil war. This became a murderous time and place. Military governments joined with the historic oligarchy to wage unremitting war on peasants, indigenous communities, political opponents, and guerrilla groups. Paramilitary death squads, most notoriously Mano Blanca ("White Hand") and Ojo por Ojo ("An Eye for an Eye"), sowed a reign of merciless terror. Violence and repression led to the death or disappearance of more than 200,000 citizens—over 90 percent at the hands of progovernment forces. In avid pursuit of its anticommunist goals (plus a retroactive justification for its campaign against Arbenz), the United States threw its wholehearted support behind the right-wing authoritarians. The degree of this collaboration would become apparent only in the 1990s, especially after a Guatemalan truth commission released a massive 3,500-page report that painstakingly documented the source and extent of human-rights abuse. During a state visit in March 1999, President Bill Clinton went so far as to offer a public apology: "For the United States," the president said, "it is important that I state clearly that support for military forces and intelligence units which engaged in violence and widespread repression was wrong, and the United States must not repeat that mistake." He was greeted with heartfelt applause.

## CUBA, CASTRO, AND THE BAY OF PIGS

The Cuban Revolution confronted the United States with the gravest—and most enduring—challenge of the Cold War period. Its economy dependent on sugar exports, its society controlled by a narrow-minded elite, its politics governed by disorder and venality, its history marked by U.S. interference and intervention, Cuba was preparing for upheaval. In March 1952 Fulgencio Batista seized power in order to stave off likely electoral defeat, an action that prompted Fidel Castro, a would-be candidate for a congressional seat, to launch a paramilitary assault against the dictatorship on July 26, 1953. Captured and imprisoned, Castro delivered his famous "History Will Absolve Me" speech; he was released as part of a general amnesty in 1955. Exiled to Mexico, he organized an invasion of Cuba; routed in his abortive December 1956 landing, Castro withdrew to the Sierra Maestra in Cuba and developed a guerrilla force (the 26th of July Movement, named in commemoration of the 1953 attack). During 1958 the Batista government came apart at the seams; on January 1, 1959 Fidel Castro and his M-26 took the reins of power.

Washington had greeted early signs of unrest against the Batista dictatorship with proclamations of support for the ruler. Arthur Gardner, Eisenhower's first ambassador to the island, expressed his opinion that "I don't think we ever had a better friend [than Fulgencio Batista] . . . he was doing an amazing job." But as the Batista regime began to weaken, Washington opted in the late 1950s for an alternative course: *batistianismo sin Batista*—keeping the regime intact but changing topmost personnel. William Wieland, head of the Caribbean desk at the State Department, later explained the U.S. predicament:

> Our problem . . . was a desire to see an effective solution to Cuba's political strife that would ensure a democratic transition and the support of the bulk of the Cuban people [and] that would have eliminated any major threat from the violence which was at that time being waged by the Castro forces. . . . Castro was at that time still a small figure in the east. . . . We were not thinking of dictating on the type of government.

The principal goal was prevention of a *fidelista* triumph. As Wieland would recall: "Fidel Castro is surrounded by commies. I don't know whether he himself is a communist. . . . [But] I am certain he is subject to communist influences."

After Fidel Castro made his triumphant entrance into Havana, Washington greeted his government with undisguised hostility. As anti-Castro émigrés flocked to Florida and other destinations, the American media provided negative coverage to "popular" trials and executions of *batistiano* collaborators. When Castro visited the United States in April 1959, Eisenhower refused to meet with him— and delegated Vice President Nixon to be an intentionally uncongenial host. Government officials railed loudly against Cuba's agrarian reform, which entailed the confiscation (albeit with compensation) of U.S.–owned sugar estates. As animosity mounted in Washington, Castro turned toward the Soviet Union. In early 1960 Cuba signed an economic agreement with the USSR, which promised to purchase 450,000 tons of sugar in 1960 and a million tons per year for the following four years—and to lend 100 million pounds sterling to the struggling young government.

Eisenhower promptly reacted. In March 1960 the president endorsed a CIA recommendation for "A Program of Covert Action against the Castro Regime," a plan that included "the development of a paramilitary force outside of Cuba for future guerrilla action." By October 1960 the CIA was training 400–500 Cubans (in Guatemala) for the purpose of overthrowing Castro's government. Shortly thereafter the Eisenhower administration decided to prepare for an outright invasion, instead of merely supporting a guerrilla underground, and in November 1960 the program began training a paramilitary force of about 1,000 attackers. Estimates that an invasion force of this size would be sufficient rested on either (or both) of two assumptions: First, the arrival of rebels would draw instant and widespread support from the Cuban populace; second, an amphibious landing would establish an opportunity for U.S. armed forces to intervene.

The U.S. presidential campaign of 1960 further intensified America's resolve, as candidates Nixon and Kennedy both sought to demonstrate anti-Castro credentials. (In this Kennedy had the upper hand, since Vice President Nixon was unable to reveal government plans then under way.) In January 1961, just as JFK was about to assume the presidency, Eisenhower severed diplomatic relations with Cuba. In March 1961 Kennedy launched the Alliance for Progress, as described in the preceding chapter, and on April 3, as part of the same overall strategy, the White House published a white paper asserting that "The present situation in Cuba confronts the Western Hemisphere and the Inter-American System with a grave and urgent challenge . . . [and] offers a clear and present danger to the authentic and autonomous revolution of the Americas." Among the Washington elite, only Senator William J. Fulbright had the courage to counsel caution: "The Castro regime is a thorn in the flesh," the lawmaker pointed out, "not a dagger in the heart."

Plans for an invasion went ahead. The CIA placed sixteen B-26 planes at the disposal of the rebel force. The detachments moved from Guatemala (then under Miguel Ydígoras Fuentes) to Nicaragua (under the Somoza dynasty). On April 14 they embarked on ships for Cuba—after receiving a final word of encouragement from Luis Somoza, who challenged them to bring back hairs from Castro's beard. Throughout this operation, the United States was not only undertaking an intervention against a revolutionary regime in the Caribbean; it was also tightening links to right-wing dictatorships in Central America.

At 3:15 A.M. on the morning of April 17, Castro received news that an invasion force was attempting to land at the Bay of Pigs, on the south-central coast of the island. (The choice of this site for disembarkation seemed curious, since it was a hotbed of pro-*fidelista* sentiment: As chronicler Hugh Thomas later remarked, "It would have been hard indeed to have found a region in Cuba in which a rebellion could have been less easily inspired among the local people.") Moving quickly to the invasion site, Cuban forces reacted with power and efficiency. At dawn, two T-33 jet trainers and a Cuban B-26 began to attack landing craft and ships, sinking the *Houston* and causing the *Rio Escondido* to explode. As Cuba's air force chased away supply ships, the hapless invaders awaited help from the United States. An indecisive Kennedy hesitated to authorize air strikes from the U.S. carrier *Essex* lying off Cuba, instead permitting only six unmarked jets to provide cover for a B-26 attack from Nicaragua (in actual fact, the jets never left the *Essex* at all). Eventually Cuban forces took 1,180 prisoners—out of the 1,297 who had landed—and held them for a year and a half, to the great embarrassment of the United States. Castro eventually agreed to release the prisoners in exchange for medical supplies.

The Bay of Pigs would have far-reaching implications. At a cost of $45 million, it represented a humiliating failure for U.S. strategy. It boosted Castro's political stature in Cuba, Latin America, and the developing world. And it helped drive him and his revolution toward the Soviet Union; it was in December 1961, not before, that Castro declared his lifelong allegiance to Marxist-Leninism.

The Bay of Pigs would also affect the Cold War as a whole. In October 1962 the Soviet Union began to install medium-range missiles in Cuba, apparently to deter yet another U.S. attack. Kennedy responded with a naval blockade, and after several days of nuclear confrontation Nikita Khrushchev consented to withdraw the missiles—in exchange, it appears, for a U.S. commitment to desist from further invasions. The Cuban Revolution, U.S.–Cuban relations, and the U.S.–Soviet rivalry thus brought the world to the brink of nuclear holocaust. Paradoxically enough, this episode encouraged both superpowers to pursue eventual détente—and to restrain their rivalries in the Third World.

None of this would prevent the United States from its unrelenting opposition to Cuba's maximum leader. The CIA steadfastly pursued a variety of efforts to eliminate Castro, including premeditated assassination. According to the 1975 report of the Senate Select Committee on Governmental Operations, there came to light

> concrete evidence of at least eight plots involving the CIA to assassinate Fidel Castro from 1960 to 1965. Although some of the assassination plots did not advance beyond the stage of planning and preparation, one plot, involving the use of underworld figures, reportedly twice progressed to the point of sending poison pills to Cuba and dispatching weapons to commit the deed. Another plot involved furnishing weapons and other assassination devices to a Cuban dissident. The proposed assassination devices ran the gamut from high-powered rifles to poison pills, poison pens, deadly bacterial powders, and other devices which strain the imagination.

These plots took place under three successive presidents: Eisenhower, Kennedy, and Johnson. Despite their comic-opera quality, these were serious attempts to eliminate a head of state through deliberate acts of murder. They also represented an exceedingly primitive form of political analysis. According to this view, the problem with Cuba was neither social injustice nor *batistiano* brutality nor the tortured history of U.S.–Cuban relations. The problem was Fidel Castro: Eliminate *El Líder* and all would be well. This was hardly a constructive approach to the reality of social revolution.

## THE DOMINICAN INVASION

Fidel Castro, the Cuban Revolution, and the Bay of Pigs made profound impressions on Washington's assessment of political tendencies in Latin America. The United States became grimly determined to prevent "another Cuba" in the Western Hemisphere—an obsession that fastened itself, in particular, on the Dominican Republic. Superficial parallels between the situations seemed intriguing. Both Cuba and the Dominican Republic had suffered long bouts of political interference by the United States and could therefore be expected to harbor anti-*Yanqui* sympathies.

Both economies were dependent on the cultivation of sugar (largely for export to the U.S. market) on large-scale plantations whose oppressed and downtrodden work forces could be susceptible to clamors against social injustice. And, perhaps most telling, both countries had long been under the heel of brutal dictators, Batista in Cuba and Trujillo in the Dominican Republic. After Castro's triumph, in fact, Washington became deeply concerned that the Trujillo regime would provoke a left-wing opposition and ultimately a communist takeover, a fear that prompted the stoutly anticommunist Eisenhower administration to withdraw support from the dictator and to explore means of removing him through assassination.

After Trujillo fell victim to a gunshot assault (by a Dominican) on May 30, 1961, the Kennedy administration was quick to take action. Washington immediately dispatched a naval task force to the vicinity of Santo Domingo to discourage (or prevent) leftists from moving into the political vacuum, and it kept a close eye on subsequent events. The United States was especially supportive of the Council of State that governed the country in 1962–1963, bolstering the regime with substantial amounts of economic aid, assistance to the national police, development of a "public safety corps" for riot control, and building a counterinsurgency capacity within the national army. As U.S. ambassador John Bartlow Martin would later recall, the preoccupation with a leftist threat in the Dominican Republic was pervasive: "A Castro-Communist takeover was the one thing the United States government, and the American people, would not tolerate."

The Council of State oversaw general elections in December 1962 that gave the presidency to Juan Bosch of the Dominican Revolutionary Party (PDR). Inaugurated in February 1963, Bosch was a respected journalist and intellectual who was committed to social reform and political change. Bosch was not, however, an especially gifted politician, and he proceeded to alienate most key sectors of Dominican society—including the military, the business community, and out-of-office politicians. In September 1963, these groups came together in support of a military coup. Offering little resistance, Bosch went off to Puerto Rico.

The Dominican *golpe* led to installation of a fragile, civilian triumvirate that sought to impose order on the polarized nation. In due course a political split within the Dominican armed forces came to dominate the scene: Calling themselves "constitutionalists," one group demanded the reinstatement of Bosch and a return to constitutional government; calling themselves "loyalists," the other faction (of pro-*trujillistas*) sought to reconstitute some kind of military-dominated junta. The two groups set up rival governments and prepared for serious battle.

The United States government defined its position with care. Taking office after the Kennedy assassination, Lyndon Johnson never gave any serious consideration to the prospect of returning Bosch to the presidency, since he was regarded as being leftist, weak, and unreliable. At the same time, Washington was disinclined to uphold the cause of Reid Cabral and his unpopular junta. By a process of elimination, the United States thus arrived at its policy preference: installation of a provisional junta that would hold a new round of elections (to be won by someone other than Bosch).

Initially, the U.S. embassy and the State Department believed that Dominicans would reach this same conclusion on their own. As "constitutionalist" prospects improved, however, Washington threw its support to the right-wing "loyalist" side. Within days the U.S. ambassador reported that radio broadcasts from the rebel side were exhibiting a "definite Castro flavor" and that communist groups, well armed and organized, were poised to take advantage of the chaos.

As pro-Bosch forces gained ground, the loyalists formed a new junta under Colonel Pedro Benoit—but failed to stem the tide. By 3:00 P.M. on Wednesday, April 28, a besieged Benoit telephoned the U.S. embassy to request a detachment of 1,200 U.S. Marines "to help restore peace." An hour later Benoit submitted a formal written request (in English) emphasizing that the pro-Bosch movement "is directed by Communists and is of authentic Communist stamp, as shown by the excesses committed against the population, mass assassinations, sacking of private property, and constant incitations to fight [that are] broadcast by Radio Havana." The document failed even to mention the need for protection of U.S. citizens.

Events then moved with lightning speed. Johnson huddled with his advisers and instantly approved the landing of 500 Marines. By 6:00 P.M., when the president signed his formal authorization, U.S. forces had already occupied parts of Santo Domingo. By 8:00 P.M., William Raborn, sworn in that same day as new director of the CIA, was warning congressional leaders about the communist threat and explaining that President Johnson had taken action against a "Moscow-financed, Havana-directed plot to take over the Dominican Republic."

The United States undertook an extraordinary buildup of military capacity. For six days after the initial invasion an average of 243 flights landed at the San Isidro airport—one every six minutes around the clock. Within ten days there were nearly 23,000 American troops on Dominican soil, almost half as many as were then serving in Vietnam. The goal was prevention of a leftist takeover. As Secretary of State Dean Rusk would later say, "What began in the Dominican Republic as a democratic revolution was taken over by Communist conspirators who had been trained for and had carefully planned that operation. Had they succeeded in establishing a government, the Communist seizure of power would, in all likelihood, have been irreversible." Assistant Secretary of State Thomas C. Mann echoed this claim, asserting that a large U.S. military presence was necessary "in view of the clear and present danger of the forcible seizure of power by the Communists."

Ever the politician, Johnson sought to prevent diplomatic isolation of the United States by engaging the Organization of American States in the Dominican operation. On April 29, the day after the landing, the council of the OAS met in special session at the request of the United States and asked the papal nuncio in Santo Domingo to keep them informed of developments. That same night the OAS asked all parties to accept a ceasefire. By May 6, a meeting of foreign ministers endorsed a U.S. proposal to request governments of member states to take part in the formation of what became euphemistically known as the Inter-American Peace Force. Although seven nations eventually sent modest contingents, the peacekeeping operation was totally under U.S. control. Throughout the summer of

1965, as in an earlier era, the Dominican Republic was governed through military occupation by the United States.

The OAS played an instrumental role in supporting U.S. policy and lost credibility throughout the hemisphere as a result. One OAS study group dutifully confirmed the claim that communists were active within the Dominican Republic. Another OAS committee helped persuade constitutionalists and loyalists to agree to the Act of Santo Domingo, which formalized a ceasefire and established a security zone within the city. And despite clear evidence of political executions by the loyalist forces, the OAS included a provision for total amnesty as part of an overall Act of Reconciliation. On September 3 the OAS oversaw the installation as president of the unobtrusively moderate Héctor García Godoy. Within a year he would be succeeded by Joaquín Balaguer, a longtime collaborator of none other than Rafael Leonidas Trujillo Molina, and Bosch was removed from the political scene. The United States got what it wanted.

## CHILE: ALLENDE OVERTHROWN

Several years later, electoral politics in Chile would confront the United States with yet another challenge. Results of a three-way presidential race in 1970 bore considerable resemblance to previous national patterns—with left, right, and center each earning about one-third of the votes—but on this occasion the center and right failed to join forces to ensure victory in the election. In consequence a modest plurality of 36.6 percent went to Salvador Allende, leader of the Unidad Popular movement with backing from both socialists and communists. The Chilean constitution stipulated that in cases of elections without majority winners there was to be a runoff in the national congress. And according to longstanding civic tradition, the legislature would decide in favor of the candidate with the most votes.

Even more clearly than with Bosch in the Dominican Republic, the prospect of an Allende presidency in Chile presented Washington with its worst-case scenario—a free and fair election that gave power to the left. Cold War ideology construed this as a logical impossibility: Communists could come to power only through force of one kind or another, either conquest or subversion; given the opportunity, free-thinking citizens— especially within the Western Hemisphere— would always cast their ballots against left-wing radicals. Even worse, from Washington's standpoint, electoral processes in Chile were so notoriously efficient that there was no point in claiming that Allende had triumphed through fraud.

Henry Kissinger, then head of the National Security Council under Richard M. Nixon, sprang quickly to action. Bringing together the Forty Committee (with representatives from the CIA, the State Department, the Joint Chiefs of Staff, and the Department of Defense), Kissinger excoriated the people of Chile for their political "irresponsibility" and oversaw the formation of a two-part strategy to prevent the Chilean congress from ratifying the Allende electoral victory. Track I, as it came to be known, involved maneuvers to reinstate Eduardo Frei, the outgoing Christian Democrat who was constitutionally prevented from direct reelection. According to one variation on this scheme, Frei would resign in favor of a military government, which would promptly call new elections—in which Frei could become the candidate of a center-right coalition. According to another, more promising version of the "Frei gambit," the congress would vote in favor of Jorge Alessandri, not Allende, and soon after his inauguration Alessandri would call for the new elections, to be won by Frei. All that was needed was influence over the Chilean legislature. Toward this end the Forty Committee established a bribery fund of $250,000.

Track II entailed outright promotion of a military coup. A right-wing group in Chile called Patria y Libertad began pressing for a *golpe* right after the election, promptly receiving $38,500 from the CIA on behalf of its efforts. Over the opposition of the U.S. ambassador, Edward Korry, President Nixon threw his support behind Track II. In mid-September 1970 the president demanded measures to "make the economy scream." As Richard Helms, director of the CIA, would later recall: "The President came down hard. He wanted something done and he didn't much care how. . . . If I ever carried a marshal's baton out of the Oval Office, it was that day." Proclaimed a subsequent CIA cable: "It is firm and continuing policy that Allende be overthrown by a coup. We are to continue to generate maximum pressure toward this end utilizing every appropriate resource."

One persistent obstacle to Track II was the resolute opposition of General René Schneider, the Chilean army commander-in-chief who stoutly adhered to constitutional principles. For a successful coup, said Ambassador Korry, Schneider "would have to be neutralized, by displacement, if necessary." Apparently in response to this assessment, the CIA began to contemplate means of removing Schneider in one way or another. As things turned out it was a different group that actually kidnapped Schneider. The commander-in-chief was gravely wounded while resisting his abduction, however, an event that sent shock waves throughout the country. In deference to popular will and Chilean traditions, a horrified Alessandri urged his congressional supporters to cast their ballots for Unidad Popular, and in late October the legislature ratified Allende's presidential victory. Schneider died the next day and received a hero's funeral.

Undaunted by this development, the United States mounted a bitter campaign against the Allende government. One reason, perhaps, was protection of U.S. business interests. American corporations had more than $1 billion invested in Chile; ITT plus Anaconda and Kennecott, two copper companies, had especially sizable holdings. Corporate executives were fearful of nationalization. There were political interests as well. Of minor importance were two clandestine intelligence stations in Chile that had been monitoring the Soviet submarine fleet in the South Pacific. More significant, from the viewpoint of the Nixon White House, was anticipation of a domino effect. As Kissinger declared at one point, "I have yet to meet somebody who firmly believes that if Allende wins there is likely to be another free election in Chile." And on another occasion, he ruminated on the consequences of an Allende regime:

> In a major Latin American country you would have a Communist government, joining, for example, Argentina, which is already deeply divided, along a long

frontier, joining Peru, which has already been heading in directions that have been difficult to deal with, and joining Bolivia, which has also gone in a more leftist, anti-U.S. direction. . . . So I do not think we should delude ourselves that an Allende takeover in Chile would not present massive problems for us, and for democratic forces in Latin America, and indeed to the whole Western Hemisphere.

An Allende "takeover," in Kissinger's words, would thus lead to the long-term installation of a Marxist regime that would conspire to spread its influence throughout the Americas.

Kissinger harbored yet another fear. According to Roger Morris, a policy aide at the NSC, Kissinger held a complex view of Chile. As Morris later recalled,

> I don't think anyone in the government understood how ideological Kissinger was about Chile. I don't think anybody ever fully grasped that Henry saw Allende as being far more serious a threat than Castro. If Latin America ever became unraveled, it would never happen with Castro. Allende was a living example of democratic social reform in Latin America. All kinds of cataclysmic events rolled around, but Chile scared him. He talked about Eurocommunism [in subsequent years] the same way he talked about Chile early on. Chile scared him.

The real problem, in other words, was not that Allende would establish dictatorial control; it was that he would hold free and fair elections in 1976, thus confirming the proposition that socialism could rise and govern through democratic means. It was this, the essence of the *via chilena*, that posed such a threat to Kissinger and to the United States. And it was for precisely this reason that Washington could not permit Allende to succeed.

Once Allende took office, the Nixon administration developed a multifaceted campaign to destabilize politics in Chile. One component consisted of what Allende himself would label an "invisible financial and economic blockade." On November 9, shortly after Allende's inauguration, a national security memorandum outlined the U.S. intent: "Within the context of a publicly cool and correct posture toward Chile," the United States would undertake to "maximize pressure on the Allende government to prevent its consolidation and limit its ability to implement policies contrary to U.S. and hemisphere interests." This involved a shutdown of U.S. economic assistance ($70 million per year in the late 1960s, under the Alliance for Progress), opposition to international credits, discouragement of private investment, and examination of means to disrupt the world copper market. The document also proposed the application of diplomatic pressure "to assure that other governments in Latin America understand fully that the United States opposes consolidation of a Communist state in Chile hostile to the interests of the United States and other hemisphere nations, and to the extent possible encourages them to adopt a similar posture."

A second component of the U.S. campaign entailed covert support for opposition to the Unidad Popular government. In January 1971 the Forty Committee approved the expenditure of $1.2 million by the CIA to finance opposition parties in the April municipal elections (which turned out to be a triumph for Allende).

Chile, 1970s: A firmly committed socialist, Salvador Allende was an insightful thinker and popular orator.
SOURCE: AFP/Getty Images.

Through the rest of 1971 and 1972 the CIA continued to finance anti-Allende elements, including the well-known conservative newspaper *El Mercurio*. United States funds also supported strikes by independent truckers who objected to Allende's proposal for a state-run trucking firm. Especially devastating in an economy so dependent on road transportation, the truckers' strikes drew support from a broad cross section of workers and employees. For the March 1973 midterm elections the Forty Committee approved expenditures of more than $1.4 million in support of opposition candidates and parties.

The military was in the meantime moving over to the opposition. In June 1973 a detachment from the Second Armored Regiment attempted to rescue a captain imprisoned for plotting against the government along with Patria y Libertad; ostentatiously driving tanks through downtown Santiago (and politely stopping for red lights en route!), the rebels eventually withdrew their demands but made their political point. In August 1973 the moderate army commander stepped down, making way for the ascendancy of Augusto Pinochet. On August 22 the congress adopted a partisan resolution denouncing the Allende government for "habitually" violating the constitution and national laws and called on the armed forces to "put an immediate end to all the de facto situations . . . which violate the constitution and the law."

Finally, on September 11, naval units seized the port city of Valparaíso at 7:00 A.M. The city of Concepción fell by 8:15. In Santiago, air force planes began bombing the presidential palace by 11:55 A.M. Most defenders of the palace surrendered by 1:30 P.M. At 4:00 P.M., the armed forces announced that Salvador Allende had committed suicide.

A brutal crackdown followed. The day after the coup, the head of the air force proclaimed the need for Chile to extirpate "the cancer of Marxism." Members of the Allende government were rounded up and placed under detention; thousands of alleged leftists were detained, questioned, and tortured in the national soccer stadium; sweeps were conducted through working-class districts of Santiago and other cities. At least 3,000 Chileans were killed or disappeared in the aftermath of the *golpe*—and this by a conservative count. Soldiers ransacked the headquarters of socialist and communist parties, imposed a strict curfew, dissolved labor unions, and took over once-proud universities.

In retrospect, it appears that the overthrow of Allende was due more to the escalation of political and social conflict within Chile than to the efforts of the United States. It is undeniably true, however, that the United States was making strenuous efforts to undermine and overthrow the Allende regime. It is also true that the U.S. government greeted Allende's overthrow with gleeful enthusiasm. Kissinger and Nixon were ecstatic. Years later, Jimmy Carter, with his concerns about human rights, expressed reserve toward Pinochet, but the Reagan administration quickly abandoned this position and embraced the anticommunist regime. Assistant Secretary of State for Inter-American Affairs Langhorne Motley would proclaim in early 1985: "The democracies of the Western world have a debt of gratitude to the people and government of Chile for what they did in 1973 . . . the destiny of Chile is in good hands, Chilean hands."

Eventually, however, the United States elected to abandon Pinochet—as it had abandoned Trujillo, Batista, and Somoza in the past. The central reason for this switch was fear of "another Nicaragua," a concern that polarization in Chile would lead to instability and pave the way for a leftist takeover. As democratization began taking hold throughout South America, the Pinochet regime became something of an embarrassment. Into this context came Harry Barnes, named ambassador to Chile in 1985, who promptly and publicly established contact with the political opposition and human-rights groups. As a sign of its turnaround, the United States introduced a resolution at the 1986 meeting of the UN Human Rights Commission expressing "profound concern" over human rights abuses in Chile and urging the Pinochet government to "proceed vigorously" in the investigation of "torture, deaths, kidnappings, and other violations of human rights."

But the fundamental basis for the U.S. position was not celebration of democracy itself—it was preoccupation with the left. As archconservative analyst Mark Falcoff proclaimed in congressional testimony, "If the way to democracy is closed and the democratic forces destroyed, there is no doubt that before the end of this century, Chile will be a Marxist-Leninist state, allied to the Soviet Union." Or, as explained in 1986 by the equally strident Elliott Abrams, assistant secretary of the state for inter-American affairs: Those who supported indefinite perpetuation of Chile's military dictatorship were "playing the game of the Communists." Such assertions were dubious at best, but the unstated message was clear: Pinochet had outlived his usefulness. In 1988 the U.S.-funded National Endowment for Democracy openly threw its support to the "no" vote in a plebiscite on continuation of Pinochet's rule. The opposition triumphed, the old man stepped aside, and Washington escaped from its entanglement.

## THE SEIZURE OF GRENADA

The triumph of Ronald Reagan over Jimmy Carter in the 1980 election campaign brought a marked change in the tone and style of U.S. foreign policy. Reagan lost little time in announcing a hard line toward what he perceived as the communist threat. "I know of no leader of the Soviet Union," he said shortly after his inauguration in 1981, "since the revolution and including the present leadership, that has not more than once repeated in the various Communist Congresses they hold, their determination that their goal must be the promotion of world revolution and a one world Socialist or Communist state—whichever word you want to use." Denouncing the Soviet bloc as an "evil empire," Reagan would later consign socialism to the "ashcan of history" in a speech to the British parliament in mid-1982. One way or another, Reagan made clear his intention of challenging Soviet and socialist authority throughout the world.

The new president and his associates quickly sought to demonstrate this resolve within the Western Hemisphere. An opportunity for action soon appeared in 1983 in a most unlikely place—the English-speaking nation of Grenada, with a total population of 90,000 scattered over three small islands in the Caribbean Sea. Established as a British crown colony in 1877, Grenada acquired "associate statehood" in 1967 and full independence in 1974. In legal terms Grenada nominally remained a monarchy, with a resident governor general representing Her Majesty Queen Elizabeth II in her capacity as ruler of Grenada, but in practice it was a sovereign nation.

Political life in the 1950s and 1960s fell under the spell of Eric Matthew Gairy—"Hurricane Gairy," an energetic, charismatic, volatile, and ultimately megalomaniac leader with personal interests in self-aggrandizement and unidentified flying objects. As Grenada's first prime minister, Gairy promptly set out to repress his rivals, to enhance his wealth, and to pursue his quixotic fascination with the occult. Opposition eventually coalesced under the rubric of a "New Jewel Movement" led by Maurice Bishop and Bernard Coard, who proclaimed a vaguely Marxist-Leninist ideology in the mid-1970s. In March 1979, while Gairy was in New York attempting to persuade the United Nations to establish an agency for the investigation of UFOs, the opposition seized power in a near-bloodless coup. A celebrating populace happily chanted a sardonic refrain:

Freedom come, Gairy go,
Gairy gone with UFO.

The gregarious and popular Bishop became prime minister in what soon came to be known as the People's Revolutionary Government (PRG); the intense and taciturn Coard became minister of finance.

Despite its rhetorical flourishes, the PRG pursued a moderate path. It sought to increase tourism. A labor code established the legality of unions and led to a sharp rise in union membership. To diversify the economy, dependent on the export of agricultural goods (principally nutmeg), the PRG sought to develop the country's infrastructure—improving roads and cultivation techniques—and to explore new methods of marketing and packaging. While Bishop and his advisers expanded the role of the state within a mixed economy, they did not impose a socialist regime. They never confronted the question of land reform, for instance, the issue that had toppled Jacobo Arbenz in Guatemala in 1954. Their only radical stance came in the realm of foreign policy, where they proclaimed an alliance with Cuba and other socialist states. At bottom, the PRG under Bishop was national-democratic, reformist, and anti-imperialist.

It was this moderation, in fact, that led to the implosion of the PRG. Bernard Coard and his wife, Phyllis (both educated in the United States), became increasingly critical of Bishop's willingness to compromise. In September 1983 a split within the PRG yielded a proposal for joint leadership by Bishop and Coard. After some equivocation Bishop opposed the plan; Coard and his supporters then placed Bishop under house arrest. A crowd of citizens released Bishop from confinement, but, in a display of stupidity and cruelty, the Coard faction executed Bishop on October 19. Within hours, the People's Revolutionary Government was replaced by a Revolutionary Military Council.

The Reagan administration watched these events with mounting interest. On October 19, the day of Bishop's murder, the U.S. ambassador recommended that Washington consider plans for the possible evacuation of American citizens from Grenada. State Department officials argued that an evacuation would in itself be insufficient; instead, the entire main island would have to be seized "to save American lives and to serve broader goals." Conservative leaders in surrounding microstates began calling for U.S. action. On October 20 Tom Adams of Barbados called for an outright invasion. Two days later the Caribbean Community (CARICOM) voted to suspend Grenada from its roster and to impose economic and diplomatic sanctions.

It proved to be a fateful weekend. On Sunday, October 23, a suicide attack by an Islamic fundamentalist led to the massacre of 241 U.S. Marines in faraway Beirut. This provoked intense concern within the White House about the possible taking of American hostages in Grenada, and it greatly raised the political stakes. As one participant in the planning sessions recalled: "The overriding principle was not to allow something to happen worse than what we were proposing to do. The purpose was to deny the Russians/Cubans a feeling of potency in grabbing small vulnerable states in the region. It had to be nipped in the bud before it developed into another Cuba." The next day Reagan signed an executive order approving an invasion.

At 5:00 A.M. on the morning of October 25, 1983, a detachment of 1,900 U.S. Marines and army airborne troops (plus token contingents from a handful of Caribbean countries) launched an assault on Grenada. Resistance was spotty at most. All significant military objectives were achieved in a couple of days. Reagan justified the operation as an effort to protect 800–1,000 U.S. citizens whose safety was threatened because "a brutal gang of leftist thugs" had seized power and to assist in the restoration of democracy. In an address to the American nation he stressed construction of an airport facility in Grenada "which looks suspiciously suitable for military aircraft, including Soviet-built long-range bombers." As a matter of fact, the president contended, this lovely tropical nation actually "was a Soviet-Cuban colony being readied as a major military bastion to export terror and undermine democracy." He breathlessly concluded, "We got there just in time."

Reagan's invocation of a global communist threat in this tiny island country seemed patently absurd. The airport runway to which he referred was intended for the tourist trade. It was to be 9,000 feet long—shorter than similar runways in Barbados, Guadeloupe, and Martinique. Financing came from Venezuela and the European Community as well as from Cuba. A U.S. firm from Miami did the necessary dredging of an inlet; a British firm had been contracted to install navigation and communication equipment. Washington nonetheless persisted in its grandiose interpretations. One official drew an explicit connection between events in Lebanon and those in Grenada: "Not only has Moscow assisted and encouraged the violence in both countries, but it provides direct support through a network of surrogates and terrorists." Said another spokesperson: "We obviously don't like being put in the position of the heavy. We want to act like a mature, responsible world power. But here's a little country saying insolent things, and we're forced to reply."

The rest of the world did not quite agree. A UN Security Council resolution that "deeply deplored the armed intervention in Grenada" received a favorable vote of 11–1–3—with support from France and the Netherlands and an abstention from Britain—and was vetoed by the United States. An identical resolution passed the General Assembly by a vote of 108–9. Perhaps most stunning to Ronald Reagan was the vociferous criticism of Margaret Thatcher, his ideological soul mate, who pointedly observed that the U.S. government had engaged in the military invasion of a British Commonwealth nation.

Order returned to Grenada. The U.S. occupation force swelled to more than 6,000 troops. A new round of elections took place in 1984. Peace came back to the island. By his own standards, Ronald Reagan had achieved a decisive success.

## CENTRAL AMERICA: THE CONTRA WAR

While Grenada appeared to lend itself to a quick-fix solution, Central America would preoccupy the Reagan administration during its entire eight-year period in office. Convolutions in El Salvador and Nicaragua threatened to change the political order, to spread to neighboring countries, and to pose new challenges to the United States. Reagan's analysts seized upon the opportunity to stress the global implications of this essentially local imbroglio, identifying the isthmus as a fundamental testing ground of national resolve in a worldwide struggle against the forces of communism. As early as 1981 this would lead Jeane J. Kirkpatrick, Jimmy Carter's acerbic critic and Ronald Reagan's ambassador to the United Nations, to make the absolutely remarkable statement that "Central America is the most important place in the world for the United States today."

## El Salvador

Part of the story began in El Salvador, a mountainous coffee-growing country of 5 million citizens ruled by an unholy alliance of large-scale landowners and military officers. Acceleration of agricultural exports during the 1960s led to increased concentration of rural holdings and the rapid displacement of *campesinos*—by the mid-1970s about 40 percent of peasants had no land at all, compared with 12 percent in 1960. A reformist challenge to the status quo came through the Christian Democratic Party, under the leadership of José Napoleón Duarte. As mayor of San Salvador (1964–1970), the dynamic and articulate Duarte built a strong following among intellectuals, professionals, and middle-class groups. As presidential candidate he may well have won the election of 1972, but the military intervened and imposed dictatorial rule. Fraudulent elections in 1977 led to the installation as president of General Carlos Humberto Romero, who promptly imposed a "law to defend and guarantee public order." Duarte himself was imprisoned, tortured, and exiled—but he did not take to the hills.

Others took a revolutionary path. A movement called the Farabundo Martí Liberation Front (FMLN)—named for the leader of a popular uprising in 1932— came to pose a major challenge to El Salvador's right-wing regime. A complex organization, including a political wing as well as a military force, the FMLN developed considerable support among the peasants of the countryside. It would soon expand to the cities as well.

In October 1979 a group of junior officers ousted Romero and attempted to implement long-needed reforms. The junta sought support from "popular organizations" and invited Christian Democrats to join the government. Official repression persisted, however, and killings continued at the astonishing rate of nearly 1,000 per month. On March 24, 1980, Archbishop Oscar Arnulfo Romero, an outspoken critic of the violence, was assassinated in the national cathedral; on December 3, four U.S. churchwomen were murdered on a country road. Civilians protested, and the liberal wing of the PDC defected from the ruling coalition. Now looking undeniably conservative, a beleaguered Duarte took over as titular head of the government. For most of the 1980s, official forces and the FMLN would carry on the struggle in a political stalemate.

Whereas the Carter administration had withdrawn assistance to the Salvadoran regime because of its human-rights abuses, the Reagan White House devoted unequivocal support to the government in its fight against the rebels. Though the uprising had fully indigenous roots, Washington saw the conflict as a sign of alien communist agitation. As explained by Secretary of State Haig, "Our problem with El Salvador is external intervention in the internal affairs of a sovereign nation in this hemisphere—nothing more, nothing less." In February 1981 the State Department released a white paper purporting to offer "definitive evidence of the clandestine military support given by the Soviet Union, Cuba, and their Communist allies to Marxist-Leninist guerrillas now fighting to overthrow the established government of El Salvador." According to this analysis, the Salvadoran insurgency represented a "textbook case" of communist interference within the hemisphere. Not surprisingly, Washington did not look kindly on a joint Mexican-French declaration in August 1981 recognizing the FMLN as a "representative political force."

The logical corollary for U.S. policy was to terminate this external intrusion in El Salvador. With much bravado, the swaggering Haig declared that the United States would have to go to "the source"—by which he meant Cuba. Others focused their attention on nearby Nicaragua. It was this accusation that would provide the rationale for a renewal of U.S. activity within that troubled country.

### Nicaragua

The Somoza dynasty contained the seeds of its own destruction. Coming to power in the wake of the U.S. occupations of 1916–1933, the Somoza family drew support from several sources: the Guardia Nacional, the landed elite, and, of course, the United States. Anastasio Sr., it will be remembered, supported the U.S. conspiracy against Arbenz in Guatemala in 1954; and it was Luis, the elder son, who encouraged the anti-*fidelista* brigade as it set sail for Cuba in 1961. Yet the regime began to weaken in the 1970s. Self-seeking and corrupt, Anastasio Jr. ("Tachito") clamped iron rule over the country but offended thoughtful Nicaraguans by his excesses, most notably his extraction of windfall profits from the reconstruction of Managua after a devastating earthquake in 1972. He also made the mistake of excluding the country's traditional elite from his entrepreneurial activities.

Unlike El Salvador, where the existence of legal institutions encouraged a reformist option, the near-complete absence of representative institutions in Nicaragua meant that opposition to Somoza could take only one form: armed resistance. In the 1960s there emerged a guerrilla movement known as the Sandinista National Liberation Front (FSLN), which took its name from nationalist hero Augusto César Sandino. After years of fighting, the Somoza regime suddenly collapsed in 1979, just as Batista had given way in Cuba two decades before. The triumph exacted an enormous toll. Approximately 45,000 lives were lost during the insurrection; economic output declined by 6 percent in 1978 and by 24 percent in 1979.

Once in power, the youthful *sandinistas* proclaimed two broad policy goals. One called for the creation of a "mixed economy" in order to achieve social justice. The other espoused an "independent and nonaligned" foreign policy. In pursuit of these objectives the FSLN sought economic assistance from other countries of Latin America, from Western Europe, from the United States—and from the Soviet bloc. Between 1979 and 1982 communist countries supplied about 20 percent of Nicaragua's credit; Latin America provided 32 percent, and Mexico alone gave almost twice as much economic aid as the Soviets.

The Reagan administration viewed the *sandinista* government with fervent hostility. The 1980 Republican Party platform openly denounced "the Marxist Sandinista takeover of Nicaragua and the Marxist attempts to destabilize El Salvador, Guatemala, and Honduras. . . . We [Republicans] will support the efforts of the Nicaraguan people to establish a free and independent government"—in other words, to overthrow the *sandinistas*. In early 1981, just after taking office, Reagan formally ended economic aid to Nicaragua. In March 1981 Reagan signed a "presidential finding" authorizing the CIA to undertake covert actions in Central America to interdict arms trafficking by Marxist guerrillas.

True to form, the CIA began to organize a paramilitary opposition—as before, in right-wing Guatemala. This was the origin of a counterrevolutionary movement whose adherents were known as *contrarevolucionarios* in Spanish, "Contras" for short. From the start it included disaffected Nicaraguans of various political per-suasions, but its heart and soul—and its military capability—rested with former members of the Guardia Nacional. In early 1982 a group of pro-Somoza former guardsmen, trained by the CIA, destroyed two bridges in northern Nicaragua. Encouraged by this tangible success, the Reagan administration then made a firm commitment to the Contra cause—and expanded its policy goals. The purpose of U.S. activity was no longer just interdiction of arms shipments to neighboring El Salvador. It became, first and foremost, an attempt to topple the *sandinista* gov-ernment. As the deputy director of the CIA would claim in March 1982, this was necessary because Nicaragua was turning into a "Soviet bastion."

Reagan's policy encountered serious obstacles. One was the U.S. Congress, which, in reflection of public opinion, was reluctant to endorse outright interven-tion in Central America. In December 1982 the House adopted a measure prohib-iting the use of U.S. funds to overthrow the government of Nicaragua. The other obstacle loomed in January 1983, when representatives of four countries—Mexico, Venezuela, Colombia, and Panama—met on the island of Contadora in order to devise a plan for peaceful negotiations among contending parties on the isthmus. This diplomatic initiative would prove to be a constant thorn in Reagan's side.

Seeking to muster popular support, the president addressed a joint session of the U.S. Congress in April 1983. "The government of Nicaragua," he solemnly pro-claimed, "has treated us as an enemy. It has rejected our repeated peace efforts. It has broken its promises to the Organization of American States, and most impor-tant of all, the people of Nicaragua. . . . The national security of all the Americas is at stake in Central America." Moreover, Reagan insisted, the stalemate in Central America threatened to damage the credibility of U.S. commitments elsewhere around the globe: "If the United States cannot respond to a threat near our own borders," the president asked, "why should Europeans or Asians believe we are seriously concerned about threats to them?"

Buildups meantime continued. By 1983 the Contra forces comprised 12,000–15,000 troops, and by 1985, according to some estimates, they may have grown to 20,000 fighters. In response the *sandinista* government expanded the Nicaraguan military from around 5,000 troops in 1979 to 31,000 in 1981 up to 119,000 in 1985.

And not surprisingly, the October 1983 action in Grenada had a profound impact on the *sandinista* leadership: it signaled that Nicaragua would have to prepare not only for the Contras but for a U.S. invasion as well.

Reagan continued his relentless campaign. In September 1983 he skirted opposition through a presidential finding that authorized "material support and guidance to the Nicaraguan resistance groups," not for overthrowing the FSLN government, which Congress had prohibited, but for two other reasons: pressuring the *sandinistas* into negotiations with neighboring countries, and forcing them to terminate support for the FMLN in El Salvador. A month later the *sandinista* government accepted this second condition, offering to pledge that Nicaragua "will not permit [its] territory to be utilized to affect or threaten the security of the United States or to attack any other state." The White House ignored the proposal.

---

**BOX 7-1**

### The Communist Menace in Central America

United States intervention in Central America became a central matter of national debate during the 1980s. In a televised speech President Ronald Reagan—the "great communicator"—delivered a powerful statement in support of his administration's policy:

> Our diplomatic objectives will not be attained by good will and noble aspirations alone. In the last 15 years the growth of Soviet military power has meant a radical change in the nature of the world we live in. This does not mean, as some would have us believe, that we're in imminent danger of nuclear war. . . . [The Soviets] are presently challenging us with a different kind of weapon: subversion and the use of surrogate forces—Cubans, for example. We've seen it intensifying during the last 10 years as the Soviet Union and its surrogates moved to establish control over Vietnam, Laos, Kampuchea, Angola, Ethiopia, South Yemen, Afghanistan, and, recently, closer to home in Nicaragua and now El Salvador. It's the fate of this region, Central America, that I want to talk to you about tonight.
>
> The issue is our effort to promote democracy and economic well-being in the face of Cuban and Nicaraguan aggression, aided and abetted by the Soviet Union. It is definitely not about plans to send American troops into combat in Central America. . . .
>
> Central America is a region of great importance to the United States. And it is so close—San Salvador is closer to Houston, Texas, than Houston is to Washington, D.C. Central America is America; it's at our doorstep. And it has become the stage for a bold attempt by the Soviet Union, Cuba, and Nicaragua to install communism by force throughout the hemisphere.
>
> When half of our shipping tonnage and imported oil passes through Caribbean shipping lanes, and nearly half of all our foreign trade passes through the Panama Canal and Caribbean waters, America's economy and well-being are at stake. . . .
>
> What we see in El Salvador is an attempt to destabilize the entire region and eventually move chaos and anarchy toward the American border. . . . This

communist subversion poses the threat that 100 million people from Panama to the open border on our south could come under the control of pro-Soviet regimes.

If we come to our senses too late, when our vital interests are even more directly threatened, and after a lack of American support causes our friends to lose the ability to defend themselves, then the risks to our security and our way of life will be infinitely greater.

We can and must help Central America. It's in our national interest to do so; and morally, it's the only right thing to do. But, helping means doing enough—enough to protect our security and enough to protect the lives of our neighbors so that they may live in peace and democracy without the threat of communist aggression and subversion .

SOURCE: Robert H. Holden and Eric Zolov (eds.), *Latin America and the United States: A Documentary History,* 2nd ed. (New York: Oxford University Press, 2011), pp. 305–306.

Amid continuing skepticism, Reagan resorted to yet another means of quieting his critics: appointment of a bipartisan, blue-ribbon panel to study the problem and produce policy recommendations. Chaired by Henry Kissinger, the commission consisted largely of pliant Republicans and conservative Democrats. Its explicit purpose was to build a national consensus around a single policy. The commission produced a meandering report that advocated a large-scale program of economic assistance to Central America, conditional support of the military forces in El Salvador, and—in rather opaque prose—continued support for the Contras. To justify this conclusion, the commission engaged in fanciful speculation:

A fully militarized and equipped Nicaragua, with excellent intelligence and command and control operations, would weigh heavily on the neighboring countries of the region. This threat would be particularly acute for democratic, unarmed Costa Rica. It would have especially serious implications for vital U.S. interests in the Panama Canal. We would then face the prospect, over time, of the collapse of the other countries of Central America, bringing with it the specter of Marxist domination of the entire region and thus the danger of a larger war.

Here again was the domino theory, now applied to Central America, with Mexico the largest domino of all. Given this analysis, the United States had no choice but to stand firm.

The Reagan White House interpreted the Kissinger report as an endorsement of its policy. The CIA, in the meantime, was off on a path of its own. In September 1983 CIA-backed planes bombed the airport in Managua—just at the time that U.S. Senators William Cohen (R-Maine) and Gary Hart (D-Colorado) were landing!—an episode that heightened congressional criticism. In early 1984, just after submission of the Kissinger report, CIA-trained operatives planted mines in three of Nicaragua's harbors, and the explosives inflicted damage on a British ship.

The Senate followed up with a resolution denouncing and prohibiting the mining of the harbors by a lopsided vote of 84–12. And in mid-1984 the CIA was revealed to have circulated in Nicaragua a manual on psychological war that included advice on how to hire professional criminals for "selective jobs" that might help "neutralize" officials, especially judges and the police. Congressional support collapsed under the weight of these disclosures.

Undaunted by this turn of events, the White House continued with its policy. William Casey's CIA trained speedboat teams that conducted a predawn raid at the port of Corinto in October 1984, causing the evacuation of 20,000 residents. In May 1985, after his reelection as president, Reagan used his executive authority to impose a trade embargo on Nicaragua in light of a national emergency deriving from "an unusual and extraordinary threat to the national security and foreign policy of the United States." The UN General Assembly condemned this application of economic sanctions on a small, impoverished country by a vote of 91–6, but Washington persisted nonetheless.

The administration's most problematic response to the shutoff of congressional aid was the initiation of a covert war. Under the direction of Lt. Col. Oliver North, the National Security Council (NSC) secretly continued and expanded operations in Central America. Unable to turn to Congress, U.S. officials requested funds in support of the Contras from, among others, Saudi Arabia ($32 million), the Sultan of Brunei ($10 million), Taiwan ($2 million), and possibly Israel. The operation began to unravel in October 1986, when *sandinista* troops captured a CIA agent named Eugene Hasenfus after shooting down his plane over Nicaraguan territory. Under interrogation, Hasenfus revealed that Washington was supporting the Contras with funds diverted from the (equally covert) sale of arms to allegedly moderate groups in fundamentalist Iran. It was only a matter of days before the Iran-Contra scandal was out in the open.

The White House faced withering accusations that it had violated U.S. law and flouted its own policies in order to continue supporting the Contra cause. As the furor mounted, Reagan was forced to accept the resignations of John Poindexter, head of the NSC, and of Oliver North. In an unusually friendly telephone call the president described North as a "national hero" and then issued his ultimate compliment: "Your work," he told North, "will make a great movie one day."

With participants weakened by exhaustion, after eight years of warfare and 43,000 Nicaraguan casualties, the conflict finally wound to a close. In 1987 President Oscar Arias of Costa Rica proposed a new peace plan calling on all sides to agree to an immediate ceasefire, negotiation with the opposition, and termination of outside aid. Implementation of these provisions was to be followed by reductions in armed forces and by free elections. As the world watched in amazement, leaders of all five countries signed the document. Reagan and his advisers could barely contain their fury. The Nobel Peace Prize Committee rubbed salt in Reagan's wound by granting the 1987 award to Arias.

In February 1989 the *sandinista* leadership announced plans to hold an election the following year. The country was in a state of devastation. Because of the

**Nobody's Perfect.** This cartoon neatly captures the contradictions in the Reagan administration's reliance on counterrevolutionary "freedom fighters" in Nicaragua. SOURCE: Courtesy of Western Kentucky University Special Collections Library.

continuous fighting, defense had been soaking up 40 percent of the national budget. Economic production had been sliced in half since the late 1970s. In 1978 Nicaragua had exported $660 million worth of goods; a decade later the figure was around $200 million and still declining. Inflation was running at 14,000 percent in 1988, and at 800 percent in 1989. A compulsory draft plus the imprisonment of political dissidents (a fairly standard wartime measure) further alienated many Nicaraguans. It should have come as no surprise, then, when the opposition movement under Violeta Barrios de Chamorro won the 1990 election with 55 percent of the vote. At last, in roundabout fashion, Reagan thus achieved what he had sought: ouster of the *sandinistas*.

## ON U.S. INTERVENTIONS

As interpreted by Washington, the imperatives of the Cold War led to recurrent U.S. interference in the internal affairs of Latin American states. One of the most telling features of these interventions was political consistency. Under the leadership of both political parties, Democrats and Republicans, the United States attempted the forceful overthrow of *each and every* socialist (or allegedly socialist) government in the Americas. The only conceivable exceptions actually prove the rule: They occurred in Bolivia, where a hybrid government taking power after the revolution of 1952 soon joined the U.S. anticommunist campaign, and Peru, where a nationalist military regime from 1968 to 1975 attempted major reforms but was neither Marxist in dedication nor pro-Soviet in foreign policy. The pattern of U.S. action was impressively consistent.

Washington's perception of "communist" dangers and tendencies rested on exceedingly broad, loose, and often irresponsible criteria. Neither Arbenz in Guatemala nor Bosch in the Dominican Republic nor Allende in Chile nor Bishop in Grenada represented sinister threats to American society or to U.S. national security; they were civilian reformers, more akin to European social democrats than to Soviet KGB operatives. Moreover, even those who declared opposition to the United States and accepted support from the USSR—the *fidelistas* in Cuba and the *sandinistas* in Nicaragua—turned toward the Soviet bloc only after Washington adopted blatantly hostile policies. Much of what happened was the result of exaggeration, misperception, and misunderstanding. History did not always have to be the way it was.

Once decided on a course of action, the United States was usually able to achieve its goals. Only the Cuban invasion of 1961 proved unsuccessful. All the other campaigns, through either covert support for opposition groups or the overt application of military force, from the Dominican action of 1965 to the Contra wars of the 1980s, led to the ouster of allegedly socialist regimes. Of course they engendered political backlash in Latin America. But by the narrowest of Cold War criteria, intervention worked.

## QUESTIONS FOR REVIEW

1. How did the U.S. intervention in Guatemala typify Cold War politics? Why did it seem necessary at the time? What long-term consequences did it have for Guatemala?
2. How did the Bay of Pigs affect triangular relationships between Cuba, the United States, and the Soviet Union?
3. Why did the Allende government in Chile provoke such alarm in the United States?
4. How did the Reagan administration interpret the civil wars in El Salvador and Nicaragua? In what ways could U.S. policies in Central America be termed successful?
5. Generally speaking, did developments in Latin America from the 1940s through the 1980s provide substantial support for U.S. fears of a "domino effect"?

# CHAPTER 8

# Latin America: Fighting the Cold War

We are all Bolsheviks! I don't know what socialism is; but I am a Bolshevik, like all patriotic Mexicans. . . . The Yankees do not like the Bolsheviks; the Yankees are our enemies; therefore the Bolsheviks must be our friends, and we must be their friends. We are all Bolsheviks!

MEXICAN GENERAL (EARLY 1920S)

Before our eyes were these two models—Puerto Rico and Cuba. Surely there was another path, a third path. . . . We were to spend the next years in our periphery exploring that third path.

CARIBBEAN LEADER (LATE 1970S)

The Cold War placed Latin America in a difficult predicament. The United States emerged from World War II as a preeminent superpower, and it was intent, moreover, on asserting its historic claim to hegemony throughout the Western Hemisphere. In the meantime Latin America, as part of the developing world, became a principal battleground in the conflict between East and West. Mindful of protecting its global position, the United States took decisive and extraordinary steps to counter threats of communist intrusion, real and imagined, anywhere in the Americas; from the late 1940s through the late 1980s Washington applied diplomatic pressure, offered economic incentives, engaged in covert operations, and on several conspicuous occasions resorted to military intervention. Leaders from Latin America—intellectuals, politicians, and unionists among them—looked upon these developments with apprehension, alarm, and disdain. They also had to face unpleasant realities of power: The Colossus of the North was stronger than ever before. What could Latin America do?

The Cold War closed off several previously available policy alternatives. It was no longer possible to seek protection from a rival European power, as Bolívar and others had done during the nineteenth century. It was implausible to pursue subregional hegemony, as Brazilians and Argentines had once imagined. It was useless to formulate high-minded doctrines of diplomacy or international law, as Bello and Calvo and Drago had attempted, since the United States simply refused to recognize adverse decisions by the World Court; nor could international organizations impose meaningful restraints on American power, as shown by Washington's domination and emasculation of the OAS.

Essentially, Latin American leaders had three options for confronting the Cold War: (1) They could defy the United States and pursue socialist paths of political change, (2) they could seek support from the United States on the basis of anticommunist solidarity, or (3) they could attempt to forge an intermediate or "third" strategy, hoping to avoid alignment with both East and West and thus to secure economic, political, and cultural independence.

## OPTION 1: THE SOCIALIST PATH

Marxist ideology achieved substantial appeal in Latin America. Its diagnosis of class conflict applied directly to social inequities throughout the region. Its summons to revolutionary action offered hope to downtrodden workers and peasants. Its identification of imperialism as "the highest form of capitalism," in the language of V. I. Lenin, offered both a coherent explanation of big-power politics and a foundation for asserting national sovereignty. Moreover, Marxist internationalists and Latin American nationalists had one enemy in common: the United States, leader of the capitalist world and dominant power in the Western Hemisphere. More important than its doctrinaire principles, however, was an underlying attraction of Marxist-Leninist thought: As an ideology of the oppressed, it struck a deep and resonant chord with the cultures of resistance welling up in Latin America ever since the acquisition of independence. For all these reasons, socialism seemed to offer a promising pathway for Latin America.

### Parties and Elections

Initial efforts in the name of Marxism focused on political parties and electoral competition. In the wake of the Russian Revolution, old-school communist parties appeared in a number of Latin American countries during the 1920s. Usually based in the cities, led by intellectuals and politicians, they tended to espouse "the peaceful road to power" rather than insurrectionary action. During the 1930s and 1940s they developed close, often servile relations to the Soviet Union. As the Cold War erupted, Latin America's communist parties became seriously divided, weakened, or divorced from their traditional or potential constituencies. As recounted earlier, governments of Brazil, Chile, Mexico, and other countries declared them to be illegal in 1947 and 1948; papers were seized, leaders jailed, and followers harassed, repressed, or exiled. During most of the 1950s, parties sought Soviet protection by defending the USSR in the context of the Cold War, thus becoming "tribunal" organizations that were more devoted to the advocacy of Soviet interests than to the struggle for power. Their true "vocation," according to French theoretician Régis Debray, "was not to promote an assault on power, but rather to resist assaults from power." By the 1960s and 1970s communist parties had become passive observers of national politics in most countries of the region.

It was perhaps in Guatemala, during the Arbenz administration in the early 1950s, that local communists (through the Partido Guatemalteco de Trabajadores) exercised their most significant influence on national policy. As coalition partners, communist parties performed only marginal roles in elected governments in Brazil (1961–1964), Chile (1970–1973), and to a lesser degree in Uruguay (1973–1974). Nor were they major factors in revolutionary situations. In Cuba the Partido Socialista Popular achieved an eventual rapprochement with the *fidelista* movement but was never a center of power. In Nicaragua, *sandinista* revolutionaries quickly abandoned their efforts to accommodate the Partido Socialista Nicaraguense. And in other contexts, from El Salvador to Bolivia, communist party apparatchiks stoutly opposed the activities and aspirations of armed guerrilla groups.

Ultimately, communist parties in Latin America were victims of the Cold War. Despite their advocacy of the "peaceful road" and their cautionary policies, their alignment with the Soviet Union opened them to charges of repressiveness and wickedness. "On the one hand," as Mexican commentator Jorge Castañeda has written, the communist party, "no matter how often or vigorously it stressed its moderation and pragmatism, could not shake the image of Communist rule as it existed elsewhere. It was a victim of its own reputation and former policies." Forces of the political right could not trust the party's avowal of moderate positions; but because of its moderation, the party could not reach agreements with the extremist left. "The Communist parties of Latin America never overcame this contradiction, this powerful paradox that haunted them from their conception to their slow and silent passing toward the end of the 1980s." As formal entities, communist parties never posed much of a threat.

Socialist parties, on the other hand, sometimes managed to play a major role in the postwar politics of Latin America. These were groupings that, for the most part, blended Marxist analysis of class struggle with nationalist insistence on the sanctity of sovereignty; while denouncing U.S. "imperialism," they did not, however, follow Soviet dictates in the international arena. More flexible than the communists, more attuned to local realities, socialist parties gave substantial credibility to the political left. Their most conspicuous successes came in Guatemala, under Jacobo Arbenz, and in Chile, under Salvador Allende.

But the fate of those same governments demonstrated the impossibility of the "peaceful road" toward socialism. In collaboration with local allies, the United States worked to overthrow Arbenz in 1954 and Allende in 1973. And for good measure, Washington helped displace the moderately left-of-center administration of Juan Bosch in the Dominican Republic in 1965. No matter how free or fair the ballot, electoral politics could not offer a meaningful route to socialist reform; Washington would always block the path. It did not take long for Latin American leftists to see the handwriting on the wall: Their only alternative was armed revolution.

## Guerrilla Movements

Nearly thirty separate guerrilla movements emerged in Latin America from the early 1950s to the 1980s. Virtually all proclaimed Marxist ideologies, of one sort or another, though they tended to espouse nationalist and populist causes as well. First and foremost among them was the *fidelista* vanguard in Cuba, where Castro's rise to power, as Regis Debray recalled, "descended like a clap of thunder on skepticism and legalism." Universally emboldened by the *fidelista* example and sometimes instigated by Cuban conspiracy, guerrilla movements sprang up in a variety of countries. In Guatemala, reformist military officers challenged the post-Arbenz dictatorship in 1960 by forming the MR-13 guerrilla movement (Movimiento Revolucionario 13 de Noviembre) and later still the Rebel Armed Forces (FAR). In Venezuela, social opposition to the economic austerity program of elected president Rómulo Betancourt erupted in violence and the appearance of guerrilla bands in 1962, followed a year later by the organization of the Armed Forces of National Liberation (FALN), sponsored by the communists, and the Movement of the Revolutionary Left (MIR), led by a splinter group from Betancourt's own party. In Colombia, decades of fratricidal conflict between Liberals and Conservatives (known as *La Violencia*) gave way in the mid-1960s to the formation of multiple guerrilla groups: the Colombian Revolutionary Armed Forces (FARC), allied to the communist party (PCC); the Army of National Liberation (ELN), inspired directly by the Cuban example; and a Maoist group, the Popular Army of Liberation (EPL). Two guerrilla groups made brief, if unsuccessful, appearances in the Peruvian Andes. And in the Bolivian highlands, Ernesto "Che" Guevara organized a Cuban-led *foco* in late 1966. Opposed by local communists and unsupported by the peasantry, Guevara's guerrillas were destroyed in October 1967; Che himself was killed after his capture.

For all practical intents and purposes, Guevara's death marked the beginning of the end to what has been called the "first wave" of guerrilla movements in contemporary Latin America. Despite this ignominious defeat, the Cuban Revolution continued to fire the imagination of the continental left. Through the 1960s and into the 1970s, the *fidelista* triumph showed that it was possible for a radical movement to embrace Marxist-Leninism and to seize power; to oppose the United States but to nonetheless endure; and to promote the cause of social revolution throughout Latin America, partly as an act of solidarity and partly in the interests of self-defense. In emulating Cuba, regional revolutionaries moved away from the ideology and experience of the *fidelista* movement of 1956–1958, when Castro was stressing populist issues and political reform, including restoration of the 1940 constitution, and closer to the radical tactics espoused by Guevara and others in the 1960s.

A second wave of guerrilla movements crested in the 1970s and 1980s. In Guatemala, offshoots of the FAR came to include the Guerrilla Army of the Poor (EGP), the FAR (again), and the Organization of People in Arms (ORPA); by 1982, according to some estimates, the total number of guerrillas came to 6,000 combatants. In Colombia, the 19th of April Movement emerged in protest against allegedly fraudulent elections of 1970; making its first public appearance in 1974, M-19 stole the sword of Simón Bolívar from its hallowed place in a national museum and proclaimed: "Bolívar, your sword returns to the struggle." Pragmatic in its ideology, M-19 cultivated connections with *narcotraficante* chieftains and maintained close communication with the Cubans. In Peru, professors and students at the University of Huamanga organized a Maoist guerrilla group, Sendero Luminoso, or "Shining Path" (originally known as "The Communist Party of Peru—Along the Shining Path of José Carlos Mariátegui," in deference to the country's great Marxist intellectual of the 1920s). Never pro-Castro, its leaders regarded the Cuban Revolution as "revisionist" and unduly pro-Soviet. Launching armed struggle in April 1980, Sendero succeeded in forming a "popular guerrilla army" by 1983. It thereafter expanded operations into urban areas, especially in the shantytowns around Lima, where it posed a major threat to governmental rule.

But the most important movements in this second wave of armed resistance, especially the ones that riveted attention from the United States, erupted in Central America. In El Salvador, a longstanding alliance between the local oligarchy and the military rule showed signs of decay in the early 1970s. A number of guerrilla groups took up irregular warfare: the Popular Forces of Liberation—Farabundo Martí (FPL), born of a 1970 split within the communist party; the Revolutionary Army of the People (ERP), formed of Christians and communists in 1971; and the Armed Forces of National Resistance (FARN), which split from the ERP in 1975. Popular opposition to military rule mounted against patent electoral fraud in 1972 and 1977 and against the undisguised brutality of the General Carlos Humberto Romero regime (1977–1979). Guerrilla groups gradually reached a modus vivendi and merged to form the Farabundo Martí National Liberation Front (FMLN), later establishing an alliance with the civilian-led Democratic Revolutionary Front (FDR). Resistance accelerated after a "reformist" civilian-military junta took power in late 1979 but failed to deliver on its promises of social and political change. A "final offensive" by the guerrillas in early 1981 was unable to oust the government, however, and armed revolutionaries retreated to the countryside. Stalemate continued through the 1980s. Finally, after years of conflict and the loss of more than 80,000 lives, El Salvador reached an uneasy truce under the auspices of the United Nations.

In Nicaragua, resistance to the thirty-year-old dynasty of the Somoza family foundered in the 1960s, despite sporadic efforts by the Sandinista National Liberation Front (FSLN). In the early 1970s the movement broke into three separate factions: One, known as Prolonged Popular War (GPP), gathered strength among peasants in the mountainous north-central region; a second, the Proletarios, splintered from the GPP in 1973 to carry the movement to workers and intellectuals in cities; third were the *terceristas,* a politically moderate and non-Marxist grouping. Throughout the 1970s elements from the middle classes and the business sector began to express dissatisfaction with Somoza, and in 1978 it was widely assumed that he masterminded the assassination of his conservative opponent, newspaper editor Pedro Joaquín Chamorro. Civil and guerrilla opposition to Somoza thereafter coalesced into a semblance of unity. Insurrection continued, pressure mounted, and Somoza left for exile in July 1979. As Castro had done in Cuba twenty years before, the *sandinistas* entered their capital city amidst an atmosphere of popular euphoria.

Of all the guerrilla movements emerging in Latin America during the course of the Cold War, only two managed to seize political power: the *fidelistas* and the *sandinistas*. The reasons are not far to seek: The success of revolutionary movements depended not only on their own resources but also on the social support and military strength of incumbent governments. Especially noticeable is the fact that *fidelistas* and *sandinistas* were both challenging corrupt and patrimonial dictatorships that had lost support from their natural constituencies, landowners and businessmen, and that in the end received only lukewarm backing from the United States. Throughout the Cold War as a whole, El Salvador was more the rule than Nicaragua: Wherever feasible, Washington scurried to the aid of governments under siege from Marxist revolutionists.

## Revolutionary States

As a matter of *realpolitik,* it should have been perfectly possible for revolutionary governments to reach practical accommodations with the United States. The new regimes in Cuba and Nicaragua posed little if any direct threat to the security of the United States; on their own, they were incapable of mounting any significant challenge to U.S. power. They also had much to gain from positive commercial and economic relations with the United States. From Washington's point of view, a modus vivendi with these revolutionary states could reduce the likelihood of Soviet meddling in the hemisphere and, in the bargain, help identify the United States with popular forces for change throughout the world.

---

**BOX 8-1**

### Two, Three, Many Vietnams

One of the most sweeping calls for armed uprising throughout Latin America came from Ernesto "Che" Guevara, hero of the Cuban Revolution who met his death in the Bolivian highlands in 1967. He foresaw the possibility of launching a series of national liberation movements à la Vietnam that would, ironically, confirm the "domino theory" so popular among American cold warriors.

> The fundamental field of imperialist exploitation comprises the three underdeveloped continents: America, Asia, and Africa. Every country also has its own characteristics, but each continent, as a whole, also presents a certain unity. Our America is integrated by a group of more or less homogenous countries, and in most parts of its territory U.S. monopoly capital maintains an absolute supremacy. Puppet governments, or, in the best of cases, weak and fearful local rulers, are incapable of contradicting orders from their Yankee master. The United States has nearly reached the climax of its political and economic domination; it could hardly advance much; any change in the situation could

bring about a setback. Its policy is to maintain that which has already been conquered. The line of action, at the present time, is limited to the brutal use of force with the purpose of thwarting the liberation movements, no matter what type they might happen to be. . . .

But almost every country of this continent is ripe for a type of struggle that, in order to achieve victory, cannot be content with anything less than establishing a government of a socialist nature. . . . There is also such a great similarity among the classes of the different countries that an identification exists among them, as an "international American" type, much more complete than that of other continents. Language, customs, religion, a common foreign master—unite them. The degree and forms of exploitation are similar for both the exploiters and the exploited in many of the countries of Our America. And rebellion is ripening swiftly. . . .

The great lesson of the invincibility of the guerrillas will take root in the dispossessed masses. The galvanizing of national spirit, preparation for harder tasks, for resisting even more violent repressions. Hatred as an element of struggle; relentless hatred of the enemy that impels us over and beyond the natural limitations of man and transforms us into effective, violent, selective, and cold killing machines. Our soldiers must be thus; a people without hatred cannot vanquish a brutal enemy. . . .

What a luminous, near future would be visible to us if two, three, or many Vietnams flourished throughout the world with their share of death and immense tragedies, their everyday heroism and their repeated blows against imperialism obliging it to disperse its forces under the attack and the increasing hatred of all the peoples of the earth! . . .

Our every action is a battle cry against imperialism, and a call for the peoples' unity against the great enemy of mankind: the United States of America. Wherever death may surprise us, it will be welcome, provided that this, our battle cry, reaches some receptive ear, that another hand be extended to take up our weapons and that other men come forward to intone our funeral dirge with its staccato of machine guns and new cries of battle and victory.

Source: Robert H. Holden and Eric Zolov (eds.), *Latin America and the United States: A Documentary History*, 2nd ed. (New York: Oxford University Press, 2011), pp. 251–253.

What seemed possible in principle proved unattainable in practice. To the extent that revolutionary movements in Latin America had a nationalist and anti-imperialist purpose, they were necessarily opposed to the United States; this was especially true in Cuba and Nicaragua, which had suffered long and painful experiences of U.S. domination. (In fact, the *sandinista* party anthem proudly proclaimed its determination to struggle against *"el yanqui, enemigo de la humanidad."*) Opposition to the United States had deep historical roots. And to the extent that revolutionary movements in Latin America followed Marxist ideology, they were bound to seek support and solidarity within the communist bloc. Almost inevitably, anti-Americanism and pro-Marxism translated into approval for the

Nicaragua, 1979: The triumph of guerrilla rebels over the Somoza dictatorship stirred passions throughout the Americas.
SOURCE: Marcelo Montecino/2011.

Soviet Union. Under the pressure of the Cold War, *fidelistas* and *sandinistas* had shared incentives to befriend the enemy of their enemy.

Nor did Washington greet revolutionary governments with open arms. In the case of Cuba, as detailed earlier, the Eisenhower administration first sought to keep Batista in power and then attempted to sustain *batistianismo sin Batista*. And after Fidel's triumph, U.S. officials treated his government with undisguised hostility. In early 1960 Eisenhower authorized the CIA to undertake a series of covert actions, including the arming and training of exiles, and in January 1961 Washington severed diplomatic relations with Cuba. Soon after taking office, President John F. Kennedy approved the fateful Bay of Pigs invasion of April 1961. All this took place before Castro declared his revolution to be "socialist," in April and May 1961, and months before he proclaimed himself to have been a lifelong Marxist-Leninist. In the meantime, U.S. operatives continued to plot assassination attempts. It is little wonder, in retrospect, that Castro turned to the Soviet Union for help: His country and his revolution were under constant siege from the United States.

A similar pattern emerged in Nicaragua. Once in power, the *sandinistas* attempted to create a mixed economy and to pursue an independent foreign policy. Following Cuba's example, the Nicaraguan government achieved prompt and tangible progress through social programs for literacy, public health, and education. In the political realm, however, the FSLN decided to preserve a monopoly on power rather than share it with late-arriving bourgeois supporters. This proved a fateful step. "Once they did," as Castañeda has said, "the die was cast. In particular, the role that Cuba would play was all but predestined: To make a revolution, as opposed to a power-sharing scheme of deep reforms, meant building a new state, without the trusted cadres to do it with; those could only be borrowed, like the funds to reconstruct a nation torn apart by years of civil war." Toward these ends the *sandinistas* welcomed approximately 2,500 Cubans (the count was carefully monitored by the CIA and the State Department)—doctors, nurses, schoolteachers, sanitary engineers—as well as Cuban military, police, and intelligence personnel. And in order to seek allies elsewhere in Central America, the *sandinistas* began distributing arms and aid to FSLN comrades fighting in El Salvador.

In both Cuba and Nicaragua, the United States deliberately pursued courses of action that ended up pushing revolutionary states more and more toward the left and into the arms of the Soviet Union. Of course it is impossible to know what might have happened if the United States had made genuine efforts at accommodation. Yet the basic trend was apparent. By attempting to isolate, intimidate, and harass revolutionary governments in Latin America, Washington succeeded in provoking, promoting, and strengthening their reliance on the Soviet Union. Approaching these regimes within a rigid Cold War framework, the United States thus managed to accomplish precisely what it sought to avoid: revolutionary entanglements with the USSR that could lead to Soviet intrusions in the Americas.

## OPTION 2: THE ANTICOMMUNIST CRUSADE

If the Cold War helped galvanize the radical left in Latin America, it proved to be a godsend for the authoritarian right. In the immediate aftermath of World War II, flushed with triumph over totalitarian forces, the United States embarked on a short-lived effort to promote democracy in the Western Hemisphere. Acknowledging the legacy of FDR's Good Neighbor policy, Harry Truman's secretary of state, James F. Byrnes, insisted in October 1945 that "nonintervention in internal affairs does not mean the approval of local tyranny" and soon endorsed a call from Uruguay for multilateral action against autocratic regimes. Spruille Braden, as U.S. ambassador to Argentina, openly denounced authoritarian and protofascist tendencies in the surging Peronist movement. Also in 1945, a State Department report expressed displeasure over the perpetuation of dictatorship within the region and expressed the view, repeated frequently and publicly in ensuing years, that "the United States cannot but feel a closer friendship and a warmer sympathy for those governments which rest upon the periodically and freely expressed consent of the governed."

Against this background, the outbreak of the Cold War suddenly offered right-wing forces a new lease on life: enlistment in the anticommunist crusade. For elites in Latin America, ideological and political commitment to the anti-Marxist cause could earn goodwill and material benefits from the world's preeminent power. It also had the inestimable benefit of enabling autocrats to denounce domestic opponents as "communists," "socialists," and/or "servants of Soviet imperialism." The dynamics of East-West conflict in the global arena thus led to a redefinition of political struggle within the local arena, a formulation that depicted opposition to pro-U.S. rulers as alien, disloyal, atheistic, unpatriotic, and totalitarian. Given this twist in the terms of the debate, the central issue was no longer dictatorship versus democracy; it was anticommunism versus communism.

## Deliverance for Dictatorship

First to benefit from this fortuitous turn of events was Anastasio Somoza, Sr., of Nicaragua. As World War II came to an end, the U.S. State Department earnestly attempted to persuade the dictator to step down from power. As an "elder states-man," Spruille Braden contended, General Somoza could promote the ideals of democracy "and thus write his name large on the pages of history." Reluctantly, Somoza allowed one of his longtime cronies, Leonardo Argüello, to assume the presidency in May 1947—but when Argüello started acting on his own, Somoza threw him out of office after just twenty-six days. Outraged by this betrayal, the Truman administration decided to withhold diplomatic recognition of the new Somoza regime.

The impasse lasted for nearly a year. Unfazed by Washington's denuncia-tions, the wily Somoza maintained close working relations with the U.S. military mission, thus exploiting a breach between the State Department and the War Department. And once the Cold War erupted in Europe, Somoza took a strident anticommunist stand. Washington retreated to a policy of de facto recognition and soon resumed diplomatic relations. Somoza responded with vigorous efforts to please U.S. officials. By 1950 he confidently explained to an American military attaché that he had successfully met leftist threats to his government and "put his foot firmly on the spark of Communism." On countless occasions he declaimed communism as a great danger to the hemisphere, a result of Soviet infiltration and "a cancerous growth which had to be cut away." Pledging his government's allegiance to the United States, Somoza instructed his diplomats to vote invariably with Washington at the United Nations and the Organization of American States.

The culmination of Somoza's efforts came in 1954, when he actively supported the U.S.-sponsored coup against the Arbenz government in Guatemala. As a dic-tator, Somoza had long regarded the existence of elected governments in Costa Rica and Guatemala as implicit challenges to his authority. (He often claimed that Nicaragua occupied a crucial political position because of its geographical loca-tion between the "leftist" governments of José Figueres and Juan José Arévalo, whom he had attempted to overthrow in 1949.) The U.S. campaign against Arbenz thus came as a heaven-sent opportunity. Somoza eagerly promoted a diplomatic resolution declaring communism as a danger to the region and a proposal for the formation of a Central American military force to eradicate the menace from the isthmus. As the CIA prepared for action against Arbenz, the United States and Nicaragua signed a bilateral military assistance agreement that opened the way for an enlarged military mission and the resumption of arms sales. And once the coup had taken effect, Somoza loudly applauded Eisenhower's decisiveness. Patiently, and cleverly, Somoza had worked his way back into the good graces of Washington.

Others followed the anticommunist tide. Seizing power in Cuba in 1952, Fulgencio Batista immediately gave Washington private assurances that he would respect U.S. interests, especially business interests, and he promised not to renew his old ties to the communists. He depicted his overthrow of Carlos Prío Socorrás as an anticommunist action:

> The Caribbean Legion, composed of Leftists, demagogues, adventurers, and Communist agitators whose mission was to carry out international assignments for the Soviet Union, had the enthusiastic support of President Prío. The Russian Embassy in Havana was the propaganda center for the entire Caribbean region and the Gulf of Mexico. Russian agents came and went carrying printed material from Mexico to Cuba, and vice versa. With the blessings of the President and his Administration, Communist travelers and Havana University students met in the Embassy to conspire against Western democracy.

Once in office, Batista promptly met a longstanding U.S. desire by breaking relations with the USSR—which he had himself established in 1942—and went on to outlaw Cuba's communist party. In 1953 Batista denounced Fidel Castro's July 26 attack on the Moncada barracks as "Communist," "anti-American," and "anti-democratic." In 1954 Batista promulgated a decree stipulating that communist activity of any kind was sufficient cause for dismissal from the civil service, from universities, or from labor unions. At the suggestion of U.S. ambassador Arthur Gardner, Batista established a special office in the Ministry of War to "fight" the communists, the Buró de Represión a las Actividades Comunistas (BRAC). In recognition of these services, Batista earned the gratitude of U.S. leaders: After a visit to the island in 1955, Vice President Nixon reported that Batista was "a remarkable man" who "seems desirous of doing a job more for Cuba than a job of [sic] Batista and is also concerned about the social progress of his country."

Equally audacious was Rafael Leonidas Trujillo Molina, who ruled the Dominican Republic with an iron hand from 1930 to 1961. Like Somoza, Trujillo initially felt U.S. pressure to liberalize his regime at the end of World War II. In 1947 the enterprising Trujillo claimed 92 percent of the popular vote in presidential elections, however, and with the outbreak of the Cold War he quickly suppressed the political opposition. Proclaiming himself to be "the foremost anti-Communist of the hemisphere," he released a *White Book of Communism in the Dominican Republic* that specifically criticized unwitting servants of communism who were falsely working in the name of democracy: Foreign journalists, domestic politicians, a growing number of exiles—all were branded as "communist." One of the first Latin Americans to reach agreement with the United States under the Mutual Security Act of 1951, Trujillo would receive over $6 million in military assistance from 1952 through 1961. In exchange for his loyalty, Trujillo earned extravagant accolades in the United States: Senator Olin D. Johnson (D-South Carolina) proclaimed in 1957 that "the Dominican Republic has rendered a greater force [sic] in deterring the spread of communism in Latin America than any other country in the Caribbean area." And during a visit to the Dominican

Republic in 1959, Representative Gardner R. Withrow (R-Wisconsin) made the astonishing declaration that had Trujillo been born on U.S. soil, he would have become president of the United States!

For these dictators and many others like them, the Cold War provided a transparent political script. To ensure their perpetuation in power, autocrats were encouraged to take several steps:

- Declare fervent opposition to communism in all its forms and expressions.
- Provide support for the United States in international forums, especially the United Nations (where the costs of compliance were virtually zero).
- Endorse the Monroe Doctrine.
- Denounce all domestic opponents as communists, as communist inspired, or as unwitting dupes of communist conspiracies; outlaw the local communist party.
- Subscribe to the domino theory, which meant that domestic subversion presented a threat to neighboring countries as well as to their own governments.
- Open the economy to U.S. investments and commercial interests.
- Express support for U.S. military, paramilitary, and covert actions against "communist threats" throughout the hemisphere.
- Maintain close relations with the U.S. military establishment (Somoza Sr. went so far as to send Somoza Jr. to West Point).
- Curry friendships with members of the U.S. Congress (Somoza Jr. had perhaps the closest friend of all in Representative John Murphy, D-New York).
- Cultivate close personal relations with U.S. ambassadors.

The courting of U.S. ambassadors was routinely facilitated by their intellectual mediocrity. Appointments to small Latin American countries did not receive the highest priority within the U.S. government; in the 1940s and 1950s ambassadorships often went to stalled-out career diplomats or to wealthy businessmen, some of whom could not speak Spanish. Thus Somoza Sr. managed to captivate Thomas Whelan, Somoza Jr. did the same with Turner Shelton, Batista had his Arthur Gardner, and Trujillo had William T. Pheiffer. All were severely afflicted by what diplomats called "clientitis." All were unswerving spokesmen for their autocrats.

Just as the Cuban Revolution came to inspire the left, it hardened the resolve of the political right. After 1959 (or 1961) the threat of a "communist takeover" no longer seemed distant, abstract, or unlikely. If it could happen in Cuba—where the United States had maintained a virtual protectorate until 1933, only ninety miles off the coast of Florida—it could happen anywhere. Moreover, the prorevolutionary activism of the Castro regime allowed the autocrats to identify Cuba as the geographical and political source of their problems. As Anastasio Somoza, Jr., recalled, he had for years "been advising the appropriate people in Washington that my real enemy was Fidel Castro and Cuba." And as late as November 1978 he pointedly insisted to a U.S. diplomat: "The real FSLN is in Cuba. They left from

Havana, and some went from Panama to Cuba." In other words, there was no genuine domestic opposition to the *somocista* dynasty; it was all the result of international conspiracy.

It is ironic, perhaps, that the United States withdrew support from its dictatorial allies at crucial political moments. In Cuba, Washington attempted to persuade Batista to step down from office in the late 1950s and halted military assistance to his regime. In the Dominican Republic, Washington tried to convince Trujillo to leave power (and when he refused, the CIA took active part in plots on his life). And in Nicaragua, twenty years later, U.S. diplomats eased Somoza Jr. into exile. Yet these reversals (or betrayals) did not contradict Cold War ideology. In each and every case, U.S. policymakers reached the conclusion that the perpetuation of dictatorship would increase the chances of a communist takeover, and that removal of the autocrats would keep the communists at bay. Even while abandoning its dictatorial allies, Washington remained faithful to its anticommunist convictions.

## National Security Doctrines

In contrast to the personalistic satrapies of the Somoza-Trujillo category, political developments in South America produced a spate of "bureaucratic authoritarian" regimes from the 1960s to the 1980s. Initiated and usually dominated by professional armed forces, these governments typically represented an alliance of multinational business, local capital, and state interests. With cold-blooded instruments of repression they challenged, intimidated, undermined, and decimated peasant movements and organizations of the working class. To justify such policies they formulated doctrines of "national security" that drew heavily on anticommunist litanies of the Cold War, tailoring the dogma to their own realities and purposes. While American theoreticians of national security stressed total war and nuclear weapons strategy and French analysts focused on limited warfare in response to leftist movements during the Algerian war, their South American counterparts emphasized the threats of internal subversion and revolutionary warfare.

The prototypical version of national security doctrine appeared in Brazil, where the armed forces ousted left-leaning president João Goulart from office in 1964. In collaboration with colleagues at the Escola Superior de Guerra (ESG), a military think tank founded in 1949 with the help of French and U.S. advisers, General Golbery do Couto e Silva began developing ideas that stressed both the possibility of "indirect attack" from the Soviet Union and the dangers of subversion and/or revolution. Under current conditions, he wrote, the concept of war must be expanded to include

> the entire territorial space of the belligerent states, thus involving the whole economic, political, cultural, and military capacity of the nation in the enormity of the struggle. All activities are focused on one single aim: victory and only victory. No distinction is made between soldiers and civilians, men, women, and children; they face the same danger, and identical sacrifices are demanded of them. They must all abdicate the secular liberties, which had been won at such high costs, and place them in the hands of the state, the all-powerful lord of war. . . . Above all

total war has eliminated the time scale, incorporating in itself the time of prewar and postwar, which are in fact now only extensions of one sole and continuing state of war.

The world now faced a situation of "permanent war." As a result, "there is no longer a distinction between where peace ends and war begins."

In this setting, enemies of the Brazilian state would rely primarily on "internal subversion"—particularly "revolutionary warfare," which Golbery defined as "a conflict, normally internal, that is stimulated and aided materially or psychologically from outside the nation, generally inspired by an ideology. It attempts to gain state power by progressive control of the nation." Revolutionary warfare did not necessarily entail the use of armed force. It was essentially a struggle over hearts and minds, a clash of psychological weapons. As Golbery explained,

> A principal characteristic of Communist revolutionary war is the involvement of the population of the target country in a gradual, slow action—both progressive and continuous—which aims at the conquering of minds. It encompasses all aspects, from the exploitation of existing discontent and protest—with the incitement of the population against the constituted authorities—up to the actual organization of dominated and controlled zones or territories.

Tactics of this sort would be especially effective in the developing world, "in countries of weak national power." In the face of such challenges, national security required internal security.

To this general argument, Golbery added innovative features. One focused on geopolitics. Latin America was essential to the West, and Brazil was the most important country in Latin America. This led Golbery to advocate tough bargaining with Washington: "When we see that the United States negotiates, using the weight of dollars, immense amounts of aid in order to gain the support of undecided people or even frankly hostile nations of the Western European region, in the Middle East, or in Asia—it seems to us to be only just that we should learn to bargain at high prices and to use the fact that we, as a nation, hold the trump card." Carried to its logical conclusion, the doctrine furnished the basis for an independent Brazilian foreign policy. ("We may also invoke a 'manifest destiny' theory," he suggested on one occasion, "especially since it does not collide directly with that of our bigger and more powerful brother in the North.") Second, Golbery stressed the significance of economics. Industrialization offered a key to sovereignty and independence, in his view, and economic development could promote the integration and protection of national territory. It was therefore vitally important to develop the country's vast uninhabited expanses, which he categorized as "paths of penetration," and it would be eventually desirable "to flood the Amazon region with civilization." In this conception the purpose of economic development was not so much to raise the standard of living for the populace as to secure national integrity.

Thus imbued by the Cold War, the Brazilian generals seized power in April 1964 with promises to "restore legality" and reinforce the "threatened democratic institutions"—and, above all, to "eliminate the danger of subversion and communism." A series of "institutional acts" then established a putative jurid-ical basis for authoritarian rule. Institutional Act No. 1, right after the coup, cen-tralized political authority, eliminated parliamentary immunity, and, in a revealing phrase, launched inquiries into individuals believed to have "engaged in acts of revolutionary war." Under General Humberto Castello Branco, the government promptly inaugurated "Operation Cleanup" (Operaçao Limpeza). Within a few months the regime arrested perhaps 50,000 persons. A professor of engineering was charged with "being really a Communist, subversive, and agitator, as is well known by public opinion." A public employee was condemned because "his father was always a militant of the Communist party and taught him this as a child." Gratified by such devout expressions of anticommunism, Washington would remain steadfastly loyal to its newfound allies in Brazil.

Nearly ten years later, in Chile, armed forces once again rose to strike down a communist threat. In a radio address on September 11, 1973, General Augusto Pinochet reassured listeners that "this is not a coup d'état, but a military move-ment" aimed at "salvaging the country," while one of his coconspirators, General Bernardo Leigh, vowed to "struggle against Marxism and to extirpate it to the last consequences." An edict the following day proclaimed that anyone displaying a "belligerent attitude" would be "executed on the spot." Like the Brazilians, Chilean military officers were utterly convinced that they were engaged in a permanent war. As Pinochet declared in a press conference: "Marxist resistance is not fin-ished. There are still extremists left. Chile continues in a state of internal war." Leftists in Chile were "masters of subterranean struggle," in Pinochet's words, and communism was "not just another party" but a "system that turned everything upside down, without leaving any belief or faith." Anticommunism thus became a tenet of religious faith. In 1974 the regime established the Dirección de Inteligencia Nacional (DINA), whose mission was nothing less than the "total extermination of Marxism." Years later, Pinochet would look back on the early months of his government with satisfaction: "If the extremists believed the moment of confron-tation was coming, so did I. They wanted triumph to take total power; I wanted it to save Chile from Communism."

Argentina experienced this now-familiar pattern in 1976, when a military coup ousted the government of Isabel Martínez de Perón. Upon seizing power, the generals claimed to have brought back the country from the brink of "dissolution and anarchy" and, like their Brazilian and Chilean counterparts, vowed to combat "subversion." What Argentina required, in their view, was a fundamental reorgani-zation of economic, social, and political life. Hence they christened their regime as the "Proceso de Reorganización Nacional," and they sanctified their fight against subversion as the "Dirty War."

Aside from counterterrorist operations against leftist guerrillas, principally the Ejército Revolucionario del Pueblo (ERP), the Argentine generals unleashed a relentless campaign of repression against unarmed civilians. As explained by Ramón Camps, chief of Buenos Aires police during the height of the Dirty

War: "You always have a latent element which awaits an opportune moment to reappear. . . . This is the thesis of Vo Nguyen Giap and of Mao Tse Tung." Even before taking power, General Jorge Videla had coolly foreseen the use of terror: "As many people will die in Argentina as necessary to restore order." Hundreds and thousands of victims simply vanished, becoming known, in the ungrammatical lexicon of the era, as "the disappeared." A human-rights commission was subsequently able to document more than 9,000 cases of disappearances during the period from 1976 through 1982, acknowledging that "the true figure is much higher." Some observers estimated that there were as many as 15,000 *desaparecidos* and an additional 5,000 people who were murdered but identified. The scope of this official terror was as frightening as its scale: Many of the arrests, detentions, and disappearances appeared to be almost at random, with deliberate disregard for guilt or innocence. Anyone could be a target; there was no sure means for self-protection. The purpose was intimidation of the whole society.

Thus did the Argentines fashion their doctrine of national security. As summarized by Jacobo Timerman, a journalist who was imprisoned in 1977, the creed was both straightforward and bizarre: "World War III has begun; the enemy is left-wing terrorism; and Argentina was the initial battleground chosen by the enemy. . . . World War III is not a confrontation between democracies and communism, but between the entire world and left-wing terrorism." Bringing the domino theory to its apogee, Argentina occupied a vanguard position in a titanic struggle on behalf of Western civilization. A particularly sinister feature of the Argentine ideology was its virulent anti-Semitism. As reported by Timerman:

> It was clear that they hated Karl Marx, Che Guevara, Sigmund Freud, Theodor Herzl. But it was hard to understand why they hated Zionism more than communism, and considered it a more significant enemy; and that they regarded Israel as a more dangerous foe than Russia. . . . Communism was more visible than Zionism, therefore easier to identify, and hence less dangerous, although both ideologies had as their ultimate intention the destruction of nationality.

Anti-Semitism had a long and ugly history in Argentine society, and the generals summoned this legacy of darkness to justify their murderous insistence on national purification.

Throughout Latin America, one long-term effect of the Cold War became readily apparent: the polarization and intensification of political conflict. Applied to the regional context, the East-West conflict provoked and energized both the left and the right. As a consequence of its internal logic, the Cold War tended to encourage extremist forces—at the expense of centrist reform. Over a period of forty years, the Cold War incessantly promoted the radicalization of Latin American politics: Both the revolutionary excesses of Sendero Luminoso and the national-security fantasies of the South American military were consummate, and probably inevitable, expressions of this relentless dialectic. Despite its extrahemispheric origins, the Cold War penetrated deeply, and painfully, into the core of Latin American society.

## Human Rights and the United States

Just as unavoidably, the reactionary zeal of right-wing forces led to disagreements with the United States over the question of human rights. Throughout the Cold War period, U.S. policy pursued two goals that were often in conflict with one another—anticommunism and democracy. It was not until the mid-1970s that human rights became a major political issue. One fundamental reason for this change, in the wake of Vietnam and Watergate, was activism in the U.S. Congress. A 1975 amendment attached to the International Development and Food Assistance Act, sponsored by Representative Thomas Harkin (D-Iowa), called for an immediate halt in economic aid to countries engaged in gross violation of rights; and in 1978, after years of wrangling, Congress finally agreed that "no security assistance may be provided to any country the government of which engages in a consistent pattern of gross violations of internationally recognized human rights."

A second factor was the presidential election of Jimmy Carter. In his inaugural address of January 1977, Carter declared that "our commitment to human rights must be absolute. . . . Because we are free, we can never be indifferent to the fate of freedom elsewhere." And in 1978, on the thirtieth anniversary of the Universal Declaration of Human Rights, Carter went on to pledge: "As long as I am President, the government of the United States will continue throughout the world to enhance human rights. No force on earth can separate us from that commitment. . . . Our human rights policy is not a decoration. It is not something we have adopted to polish up our image abroad, or to put a fresh coat of moral paint on the discredited policies of the past. . . . Human rights is the soul of our foreign policy." Throughout its term, the Carter administration expressed profound unhappiness over human-rights violations in Brazil, Guatemala, Chile, and Argentina—but remained conspicuously silent about abuses in other countries, such as Iran and the Philippines, which were deemed to be of great strategic value in the East-West conflict. Practically speaking, Carter's stance on human rights was a policy for Latin America, not for the world as a whole.

Within this context a crisis arose in September 1976, when the explosion of a car bomb in Washington, D.C., killed Orlando Letelier, an exiled official from the Allende government, and his young American assistant, Ronni Moffitt. There was little doubt that the assassination was the work of the Pinochet regime. The murder drew swift condemnation from the United Nations and from U.S. senator Edward Kennedy; in the House, Harkin redoubled efforts to have aid cut off. Eventually Congress agreed to the ban and approved Harkin's legislation, aimed principally at Chile, prohibiting all nonhumanitarian aid to governments that were violating human rights. The Letelier bombing continued to poison bilateral relations in 1979, when the Chilean Supreme Court refused to extradite three DINA suspects in the murder and authorized their release. Carter's State Department accused Chile of condoning "international terrorism," the U.S. ambassador was twice recalled, private commercial credits were cut, and the navy withdrew from annual exercises with Chile.

Pinochet adopted a defiant stance. Pointing to the Chinese ambassador across the room, Pinochet declared to U.S. ambassador George Landau in June 1978:

"Believe me, Chile can go to China. We are not married to the United States. I could even turn to the Soviet Union. They would help. They would do anything to hurt you." When Landau asked for clarification about the prospect of an alignment with the USSR, Pinochet shot back: "Absolutely! I would do it to protect my country. The Soviet Union would always intervene against American interests. It is unfortunate that you Americans always fail to understand this."

Despite its bluster, Pinochet's response underscored the strength of nationalist sentiment within the South American military establishments. Unlike the satraps of the Caribbean, leaders of these bureaucratic-authoritarian regimes held deep beliefs in the sanctity of state and nation. Challenged by the United States on human rights, they reacted with combinations of annoyance, disdain, and bewilderment—but not submission. Here they were, in their own mindsets, fighting a crusade for the sake of Western civilization and receiving only condemnation for their efforts. Ironically, international ostracism merely heightened their determination to persevere. Protests by human-rights advocates served to further the cause of left-wing subversion, in the generals' eyes, and the only appropriate response was to stand fast. If necessary, right-wing authoritarians would defy the United States in the name of decency, morality, and anticommunism.

## OPTION 3: SEEKING A THIRD WAY

Beyond the strategies of alliance with either the Soviet Union or the United States, of either communism or capitalism, Latin America sought a third alternative: refuge from the Cold War. As illustrated by the fates of Cuba and the Southern Cone, alignment with either the East or the West involved substantial costs. What many leaders were seeking was an independent course of action, one that would maximize the range of policy choice and guarantee national sovereignty. Ultimately, this quest would take two complementary forms: one focusing on economic development, the other on foreign policy. In both endeavors, Latin America relied heavily on—and joined together with—emerging new nations in Africa, Asia, and the Middle East.

### A New International Economic Order?

Decolonization after World War II led to the appearance of new nation-states during the 1950s and 1960s that steadily swelled the ranks of the Third World. With political independence achieved, they faced the challenge of devising effective policies for economic development—an area where Latin America came to play a major role. In 1948 the United Nations established the Economic Commission for Latin America (ECLA, with the Spanish acronym CEPAL), with its seat at Santiago de Chile. Under the leadership of Raúl Prébisch, a brilliant Argentine economist, CEPAL formulated a powerful and compelling interpretation of the world economy. In schematic form, the Prébisch thesis maintained that the international division of labor, under which developing countries exported raw material goods and imported manufactures from abroad, was working to the disadvantage of Latin America. According to *cepalista* analyses, terms of trade were constantly moving against the primary producing countries: The value of their exports was declining, but the cost of their imports was climbing. While increasing productivity in the industrialized "center" of the global economy led to wage and other factor price increases, disguised unemployment and other tendencies resulted in commodity price declines in the "periphery." Meanwhile the income elasticity of demand for raw material imports was relatively low at the center (largely because of Engel's law, holding that proportional expenditures on food are on the average a decreasing function of income) while in the periphery it remained high—especially in view of the high import content of new investments. As income rose in the center, therefore, the percentage expenditure on imports from the periphery declined; but as income rose in the periphery, the percentage of income going for imports from the center was likely to increase.

CEPAL proposed a twofold solution. One was industrialization. As Prébisch sustained in a memorable manifesto of 1949, industrialization is "being forced upon [new countries] by events. Two world wars and a great economic crisis between them have shown the Latin American countries their opportunities, clearly pointing the way to industrial activity." Purposeful state planning and the judicious application of import restrictions could lead to industrial development that would eliminate losses from declining terms of trade, stimulate employment, and enhance the economic sovereignty of developing nations. The second solution was regional integration. Industrialization required large markets. This vision came to fruition in 1960, with the formation of the Latin American Free Trade Area (LAFTA/ALALC). About twenty years later it would be replaced by the Latin American Integration Association (ALADI), headquartered in Montevideo. Neither experiment met with much practical success, though both came to represent Latin America's persisting desire for regional unification. In a significant sense, they served as contemporary formulations of the Bolivarian dream.

The Prébisch analysis provided inspiration for reformist governments of Latin America that were attempting to promote development by strengthening the economic role of the state, encouraging (and protecting) infant industries and local manufacturing, regulating (and restraining) foreign competition, and cultivating support from organized labor. Alternatively described as "nationalist" or "populist," these approaches were producing average annual growth rates around 5–6 percent from the late 1950s to the mid-1970s.

While CEPAL's empirical studies focused only on Latin America, its analytical framework applied to the developing areas as a whole. With the encouragement of Latin American delegates, Third World countries in 1961 pushed a resolution through the UN General Assembly designating the 1960s as the "United Nations Development Decade," a decision that led to the first United Nations Conference on Trade and Development (UNCTAD) in Geneva in 1964. As differences emerged between the perspectives of industrialized and developing nations, representatives of Third World countries issued a "Joint Declaration of the Seventy-Seven," which proclaimed their own "unity" as "the outstanding feature of this Conference. . . . The developing countries have a strong conviction that there is a vital need to maintain, and further strengthen, this unity in the years ahead. It is an indispensable instrument for securing the adoption of new attitudes and new approaches in the international economic field." Thus emerged the Group of 77, whose membership would eventually grow to well over 100, a loose organization of developing nations intent on collective action in the pursuit of social justice and economic development. Operating mainly within the United Nations, the Group of 77 came to be known as a "trade union for the poor." In effect, it represented the economic voice of the Third World.

Fittingly enough, Prébisch became the first secretary general of UNCTAD, a post he held until 1969. All countries of Latin America were among the original signatories of the 1964 declaration of the Group of 77. And because of its institutional capability, rendered through ECLA, Latin America often played a leading role in setting agendas and shaping deliberations at UNCTAD meetings.

Economic tensions between North and South came to a head in the early 1970s. For the Third World, developmental efforts and conventional strategies had yielded disappointing results. The breakdown of the Bretton Woods accords in 1971 (when Nixon took the United States off the gold standard) cast doubt on the viability of the prevailing system. The success of OPEC countries in quadrupling the price of their product during the "oil crisis" of 1973–1974 suggested that it might be time for confrontation, not accommodation. Nations of the South thus reached something of a consensus: Economic fairness could come only through a global redistribution of resources and wealth.

In this spirit, G-77 countries and their supporters called for a special meeting of the General Assembly, which adopted, in May 1974, the "Declaration and Programme of Action on the Establishment of a New International Economic Order." Achievement of NIEO instantly became a key objective for the Third World. NIEO embodied five central demands:

- Increasing the volume and relative value of raw material exports from the Third World.
- Enhancing access to international capital, removing legal constraints on expropriation, and promoting vigilance over multinational corporations.
- Establishing a target of 0.7 percent of GNP for economic assistance from industrialized countries.
- Noting the need for scientific and technological institutions in the developing world and seeking technology transfer from multinational corporations.
- Calling for a greater voice in the management of the international monetary system and for easier access to loans from the International Monetary Fund (IMF).

For G-77 members, the fundamental goal of NIEO was to accelerate the pace of their own development and to shift the pattern of income distribution away from the rich nations of the North and in favor of the impoverished South.

For a brief time NIEO became a rallying cry for the Third World as a whole, but tangible progress proved to be elusive. A central reason for this failure was the heterogeneity of the G-77 itself. The sheer size of the group, with more than 100 members from diverse regions and cultures, made consensus difficult enough. There were structural cleavages as well. The OPEC successes of 1973–1974 and 1979–1981 could not be easily achieved for other commodities, and the resulting price hikes for petroleum imposed serious balance-of-payments difficulties on oil-importing members of the developing world. Moreover, upper-tier countries of the G-77 were closely connected with the industrialized world. As political economist Roger Hansen observed in the late 1970s: "The more the economically advanced members of the South are able to achieve their developmental goals within the present global economic system, the less interest they will have in changing it in the ways desired by other G-77 members." This was especially true for Latin America, whose situation and interests had very little in common with South Asia and sub-Saharan Africa. The final death knell of the NIEO would come with the debt crisis of the 1980s.

## Nonalignment and Foreign Policy

A frequent objective for Latin America and for other countries in the developing world was to avoid diplomatic entanglement in the Cold War. Taking sides implied subordination to one of the rival superpowers. An independent foreign policy, a "third way" of sorts, could expand the range of practical options, maintain flexibility, and assert national sovereignty.

Such was the impetus behind the Non-Aligned Movement, a gathering of Asian and African leaders who held their first major meeting at Bandung in 1955. The conference issued a summons for (1) nonalignment with East or West, (2) the international self-assertion of former colonial countries, and (3) militant anticolonialism. Strongly influenced by Josip Broz Tito of Yugoslavia and Jawaharlal Nehru of India, a subsequent meeting at Belgrade in 1961 emphasized the need for Third World countries to take active steps to prevent war between the United States and the USSR. Denouncing the "two imperialisms" of both East and West, the delegates proclaimed:

> Any attempt at imposing upon peoples one social or political system or another by force and from outside is a direct threat to world peace. The participating countries consider that under such conditions the principles of peaceful coexistence are the only alternative to the "cold war" and to a possible general nuclear catastrophe. Therefore these principles—which include the right of peoples to self-determination, to independence and to the free determination of the forms and methods of economic, social and cultural development—must be the only basis of all international relations.

A 1964 meeting in Cairo brought the theme of anticolonialism to the forefront of the agenda, where it remained for the rest of the decade. Just as the Group of 77 expressed the economic voice of the developing world, the Non-Aligned Movement (NAM) came to represent its political voice.

Latin America's role in NAM expanded over time. The most active participant was Cuba, which sent an official delegation to the Yugoslav meeting in 1961. Democratic governments in Chile and Argentina sent observers to the Cairo meeting in 1964 and became full members in the early 1970s, under Allende and Perón. Peru became an observer in 1970 and a full member in 1973, under the radical military regime of Juan Velasco Alvarado. After the *sandinista* revolution, Nicaragua joined in 1979. Bolivia and Ecuador became full members as well, and Colombia gained admission in the early 1980s. Most of the new Caribbean Commonwealth Countries took out membership after achieving independence. Despite its militantly *tercermundista* policies, Mexico never went beyond observer status. Nor did Brazil, which maintained a scrupulous desire to avoid entangling alignments—even in the name of nonalignment!

Charismatic and ebullient, eager to maintain close ties to both the Third World and the USSR, Fidel Castro became NAM president for a four-year term and hosted a historic summit meeting at Havana in 1979. Under pressure from Moscow, Castro used the occasion to challenge the longstanding thesis of "two imperialisms" by proposing that the Soviet Union should be declared a "natural ally" of the Non-Aligned Movement. Tito of Yugoslavia led the attack on this idea, which found little support from other delegates, and the plan was summarily dropped. After the conference, Cuba's chairmanship suffered an additional blow when a planning session in New York failed to produce any clear priorities or substantive statements in preparation for the upcoming session of the UN General Assembly. Cuba's hope for election to a temporary seat on the UN Security Council was also countered by Colombia, and a deadlock ensued until both countries stood down in favor of Mexico—which was not a NAM member. In the aftermath, Castro was succeeded as NAM president by Indira Gandhi, prime minister of India.

Perhaps NAM's most significant contribution to Latin America was its powerful support of NIEO in the early 1970s. At its Algiers conference of 1973, NAM turned from its traditionally political agenda toward economic matters, adopting an "Action Programme for Economic Cooperation" as a basis for South–South unity and calling for the establishment of "a new international economic order." Anticipating subsequent arguments about a potential "peace dividend," NAM vehemently condemned the East-West arms race and envisioned disarmament as a means to free up resources that could be reallocated for the sake of global development.

By the 1980s the Non-Aligned Movement had more than 100 members. As with the G-77, its membership size was a double-edged sword: It gave NAM enormous potential clout in international arenas, especially the UN General Assembly, but it also led to lowest-common-denominator policy positions. Indeed, its general principles had become high-minded but vague: peace and disarmament, independence and self-determination, economic equality, cultural equality, universalism, and multilateralism. On practical policy issues, however, NAM was unable to act as a unified bloc.

In the meantime several countries in Latin America took deliberate steps to pursue independent foreign policies on their own. Brazil sought to intensify relations with Japan and Western Europe in the 1970s, successfully resisting U.S. pressure to overturn a nuclear agreement with West Germany. The country's reliance on imported petroleum prompted new diplomatic initiatives in the Middle East and Africa. Partly in response to declining military assistance from the United States, Brazil developed a formidable defense industry—and became one of the world's leading exporters of arms. And in frustration over the Carter administration's condemnation of human-rights abuses, the military rulers refused to join the U.S.-sponsored boycott of the 1980 Moscow Olympic Games in protest against the Soviet invasion of Afghanistan.

Mexico played for high stakes as well. In his continuing effort to establish solidarity with Arab and other Third World countries, President Luis Echeverría instructed his representatives in 1975 to support a UN resolution—against Washington's vigorous opposition—denouncing Zionism as a form of racism. The U.S. reaction was swift. Jewish leaders and pro-Israeli groups began a campaign against tourism in Mexico. Bookings were canceled, vacations were changed, and Mexico had over 100,000 fewer visitors in 1976 than in 1975. Echeverría's diplomatic gesture cost his country millions of dollars in foreign exchange. Beginning in 1976 Mexico abstained or voted No on similar anti-Zionist resolutions in UN bodies. Economic pressure took its toll.

It was Echeverría's successor, José López Portillo, who nettled Washington by purporting to play an active role in Central America—the putative "backyard" of the United States. Openly supporting the *sandinista* revolutionaries, López Portillo in May 1979 withdrew diplomatic recognition from the Somoza regime. In 1980 Mexico and Venezuela began shipping petroleum on preferential terms to Nicaragua as well as to other nations of the isthmus. In August 1981 Mexico joined together with France, an extrahemispheric power, to call for recognition of the Salvadoran FMLN as a "legitimate political force." And in February 1982 López Portillo unilaterally issued a three-part plan for peace in Central America—a negotiated settlement in El Salvador, a nonaggression treaty between the United States and Nicaragua, and intensified dialogue between Havana and Washington. Mexico thus offered "to serve as a bridge," the foreign minister explained, "as a communicator, between its friends and neighbors." Intent on imposing military solutions on Central America, the Reagan administration dismissed the Mexican initiative with annoyance and contempt.

## From Contadora to Esquipulas

After taking office in December 1982, Mexican president Miguel de la Madrid embarked on a path of multilateral negotiation. In early 1983 Mexico joined with Colombia, Panama, and Venezuela—the so-called Contadora Group, named for the island where they first met—to begin exploring possibilities for regional mediation of the Central American conflict. Through collective action and joint diplomacy, the Contadora countries strove to fashion a peaceful settlement that would acknowledge the legitimate interests of contending parties. Backing from a four-country *grupo de apoyo* (a "support group" composed of Argentina, Brazil, Uruguay, and Peru) gave additional impetus to the Contadora movement and reflected a new form of political *concertación* among Latin American nations.

The Reagan administration silently resisted these efforts. After the formation of the Contadora group, Washington launched its own Forum for Peace and Democracy under the auspices of Honduras and Costa Rica; the effort failed for lack of regional support. Washington then turned to the OAS, only to discover that the organization strongly supported the Contadora initiative. Also in 1983, President Reagan appointed the National Bipartisan Commission on Central America, the blue-ribbon panel chaired by former Secretary of State Henry A. Kissinger. In January 1984 its much-publicized report endorsed much of Reagan's policy toward the region and dismissed the Contadora effort with a single page of condescending adjectives, asserting that "the United States cannot use the Contadora process as a substitute for its own policies." In other words, Washington would pay no heed.

The Contadora countries nonetheless persisted. In September 1983 the group released a "Document of Objectives"—a list of twenty-one principles that were accepted by all five nations of Central America. A year later, in September 1984, the group presented its "Contadora Act for Peace and Cooperation in Central America," a broad proposal with three key provisions:

- Holding free, fair, and open elections
- Refraining from "all acquisition of military equipment" (and establishing firm schedules for the orderly withdrawal of foreign military advisers)
- Ending assistance of any sort to irregular forces or armed bands "whose aim is the overthrow or destabilization of other governments."

The Contadora treaty meant that Nicaragua would have to repatriate Cuban and other military advisers and allow on-site inspection of its military facilities; Honduras would have to terminate U.S. military maneuvers and encampments; El Salvador would have to remove its U.S. military "trainers." In other words, all extraregional powers—Cuba, the Soviet Union, the United States—would have to withdraw from the isthmus. Under the aegis of the Contadora group, Central America would settle conflicts by itself.

Prospects for the treaty seemed excellent at first. Guatemala, Costa Rica, and El Salvador promptly announced their readiness to sign. Honduras expressed a generally positive view pending "final adjustments." And within days Nicaragua stunned the diplomatic world by endorsing the accord "in its totality, immediately and without modifications," on the sole condition that the United States would have to sign a supplementary protocol (whereby a number of nations, including Cuba and the USSR, would consent to abide by the terms of the treaty). The United Nations, the OAS, and the European Community all expressed strong support.

Taken aback by this development, Washington set out to scuttle the plan. On October 10, 1983, Secretary of State George Shultz made a sudden visit to the region. Honduras, by this time a U.S. client state, was persuaded to harden its insistence on adjustments, and pressure was applied to Costa Rica as well. On October 30 a confidential NSC memorandum exuded smug satisfaction: "We have effectively blocked Contadora group efforts to impose the second draft of the Revised Contadora Act." For public consumption, the Reagan administration contended that its objections to the treaty focused on the question of verifiability. In contrast, most independent analysts thought the true reasons for Washington's intransigence were political: The Contadora accord entailed acceptance of the *sandinista* regime and a curtailment of U.S. hegemony throughout the area. On points of this nature the Reagan White House was not prepared to surrender.

As the Contadora effort stalled, the U.S. government stepped up its activities. Military aid to El Salvador climbed from $33.5 million in 1983 to $176.8 million in 1984. Officer training picked up at the School of the Americas in Panama and at U.S. bases in Honduras. United States operatives planned the mining of Nicaragua's harbors, distributed manuals on the art of guerrilla warfare, and redoubled assistance to the neo-*somocista* "freedom fighters."

Oscar Arias Sánchez, elected to the presidency of Costa Rica in 1986, chose to confront the situation. With skillful diplomacy and dogged determination, he persuaded chief executives from Central America to continue negotiations among themselves. The result was the so-called Esquipulas accords, named after the town where the first meeting took place, that called on war-torn nations of the region to (1) initiate a ceasefire, (2) engage in dialogue with opposition movements, (3) prevent the use of their territory for aggression against other states, and (4) cease and prohibit aid to irregular forces or insurrectionary movements—these last two provisions aimed directly at Nicaragua and the United States. The August 1987 agreement also called for free elections and democratization of all nations in the region. It was an ambitious plan, one that incorporated key provisions from the Contadora documents, and had the additional merit of representing a Central American solution to Central American problems. In fact it helped bring a measure of peace to the region, and it earned for Arias a Nobel Prize.

## LEGACIES OF WAR

The Cold War took a heavy toll on Latin America. It placed the region in the center of a worldwide East-West conflict. It subjected the hemisphere to U.S.–Soviet tension, sometimes real (as in the Cuban missile crisis of October 1962) but more often exaggerated or imaginary (as in Central America throughout the 1980s). It made the region susceptible to heavy-handed vigilance, covert action, and military intervention by the United States. Perhaps even more important, the Cold War deepened political schisms within countries of Latin America and promoted a spiraling process of polarization.

Chief beneficiaries of the Cold War, at least in the short run, were the forces of the political right. From the Caribbean to the Southern Cone, from Guatemala to Brazil, authoritarian governments were able to claim political legitimacy on the ground of anticommunism. With the brief and partial exception of the Carter administration, in the late 1970s, they were able to garner the support of the United States. Devoutly intolerant of political freedom and staunchly resistant to social change, reactionary rulers conducted ruthless campaigns to purge their nations of allegedly subversive, sinister, unpatriotic elements. One result, in some countries, was to deprive entire generations of imaginative, creative, progressive political leadership. Another was to set back the cause of economic development and social justice by incalculable margins.

The socialist alternative had costs and risks as well. Odds were, from the beginning, that revolutionary efforts would end in tragic failure. Only two out of nearly thirty guerrilla movements actually seized power; almost all the others were crushed by military force. And even those that triumphed, in Cuba and Nicaragua, soon encountered implacable hostility from the United States. Their only plausible option was to seek aid and support from the Soviet Union, but this only made them dependent on the USSR and drew them ever more deeply into the Cold War itself. Once the East-West conflict came to an end, they would be left on their own, orphans of a war that no longer existed.

At the outset, the third way, the quest for economic and political independence, appeared to offer the fewest advantages. It meant forgoing all the benefits that would result from firm allegiance in one of the two camps, and it entailed the considerable risk of antagonizing both the superpowers, especially the United States. Association with the Third World offered negligible economic compensation and, outside of such forums as the UN General Assembly, scant political power. But in the long run, the search for an independent stance proved to be the most productive course. It maintained the political integrity of Latin American nations, especially those under civilian and/or democratic governments, it enabled experimentation with a variety of economic policies, and, most important, it avoided the costs of wholehearted alignment with one or the other of the superpowers. Insistence on national sovereignty and Third World solidarity turned out to be more than demagogic appeal. It expanded, preserved, and maximized political room for maneuver.

## QUESTIONS FOR REVIEW

1. What were the principal strategies available to Latin America for confronting the Cold War?
2. What was the appeal of Marxist thought in Latin America?
3. Why were so many different groupings—socialist and communist political parties plus revolutionary movements and regimes—drawn into allegiance with the Soviet Union and opposition to the United States?
4. How did right-wing dictators take advantage of the U.S.–Soviet superpower rivalry? And broadly speaking, how did the Cold War affect political polarization within Latin America?
5. How did economic factors affect the search for a nonaligned "third way" within Latin America and throughout the developing world?

# PART III

# Globalization and War

So, in sum, what do we see? We see five great economic
super powers: the . . . United States, Western Europe, the
Soviet Union, Mainland China, and, of course, Japan . . . .
All nations are important but these are the . . . five
that will determine the economic future and, because
economic power will be the key to other kinds of power,
the future of the world in other ways in the last third of
this century.

RICHARD M. NIXON (1971)

We're an empire now, and when we act, we create our
own reality. And while you're studying that reality—
judiciously as you will—we'll act again, creating other
new realities, which you can study too, and that's how
things will sort out. We're history's actors, and you, all of
you, will be left to just study what we do.

UNNAMED U.S. GOVERNMENT OFFICIAL,
SPEAKING TO A JOURNALIST (2004)

# CHAPTER 9

# The 1990s: Hegemony and Geoeconomics

Out of these troubled times . . . a new world order can emerge:
a new era—freer from the threat of terror, stronger in the
pursuit of justice, and more secure in the quest for peace. An
era in which the nations of the world, East and West, North
and South, can live in harmony.

GEORGE H. W. BUSH (1991)

In the post–Cold War era, no one knows what foreign policy
ought to be.

LESLIE GELB (1994)

Sweeping transformations in the international order during the late 1980s ushered in an era of optimism, hope, and uncertainty. The crumbling of the Berlin
Wall, the reunification of Germany, the liberation of Eastern Europe, the consolidation of superpower détente, and the eventual implosion of the Soviet Union
brought a sudden end to Cold War hostilities. This development had far-reaching implications not only for Europe but also for other parts of the world and,
more generally, for the international system as a whole. Yet the *shape* and *content*
of these ramifications remained far from clear. What kind of international order
would emerge in the 1990s and beyond? How might this affect Latin America and
its relationship with the United States? What forces and factors might determine
U.S. policy toward Latin America?

## AFTERMATH OF THE COLD WAR

The ending of the Cold War brought an unexpected end to relentless and decades-
long hostility between the Soviet Union and the United States. Pundits and politicians in the United States hastened to interpret the end of the Cold War as a final
victory of capitalism over communism. As Francis Fukuyama asserted in 1989, the
world was bearing witness "not to an 'end of ideology' or a convergence between
capitalism and communism, but to an unabashed victory of economic and political liberalism." Communism was as dead as fascism; authoritarian doctrines were

relics of the past. Russia became a sovereign republic, and, in short order, other members of the former USSR soon followed suit: Armenia, Azerbaijan, Georgia, Belarus, Kazakhstan, Kyrgyzstan, Moldova, Tajikistan, Turkmenistan, Ukraine, and Uzbekistan. What Ronald Reagan had once decried as an "evil empire" no longer existed.

Yet the fall of communism was an essentially European affair. It did not extend to Asia. China and North Korea remained resolute communist states, and Russia and the United States both maintained their military presences in the region. Tension continued to prevail along the Asia-Pacific front.

## Rearrangements of Power

Such developments led to fundamental realignments in the international system. One immediate result was the emergence of the United States as the world's sole superpower. The implosion of the Soviet Union meant that the United States would have no serious military rival anywhere: It could enjoy a "unipolar moment" of unchallenged strategic and tactical superiority. Yet many of the challenges of the 1990s did not lend themselves to military solutions. Partly for this reason, the American public expressed repeated and profound apprehension about overseas entanglements that might place U.S. troops in harm's way; and, as a result, the nation's political leaders became extremely hesitant (or at least ambivalent) about the use of force.

A second major transformation, more the result of long-term processes than of short-term events, was the emergence of economic multipolarity. At the end of World War II the United States was utterly dominant: It produced more than half the world's manufactured goods, it produced more than one-third the world's total of all goods and services, and it held almost two-thirds the world's total of gold reserves. Allied nations in Europe made swift strides during the 1950s and 1960s, thanks in part to U.S. assistance under the Marshall Plan, and consolidated their position through a steady process of regional integration. By 1990, after the reunification of Germany, the European Community (as it was then known) contained a joint population of more than 340 million people with a combined gross domestic product (GDP) of nearly $6 trillion, which was larger than that of the United States. By the end of the decade the European Union launched a common currency, the "euro," a development that—in the view of one prominent economist—would signal "the end of the post–World War II American era and the onset of a new economic era."

Asia acquired economic power too. Stimulated first by the Korean War and guided afterward by firm government policy, Japan entered the ranks of advanced industrial nations during the 1960s and 1970s. Such nearby countries as South Korea, Taiwan, Singapore, and Hong Kong—nicknamed the "four little tigers"—made equally impressive strides in the 1970s and 1980s. And the People's Republic of China, prostrate in 1950 after years of Japanese occupation and decades of civil war, adopted a series of economic reforms in the late 1970s that eventually transformed the country into a swiftly emerging world-class economic power.

An additional development was the increasing importance of nongovernmental actors and forces—multinational business firms, international traders, migrant workers, private organizations, and other participants in emerging networks of "transnational interdependence." Large companies forged complex and multinational chains of production and reached consumers in distant parts of the globe. Currency traders could make decisions around the clock, billions of dollars could move at the push of a button. Transnational activities sometimes took illicit form. Arms trafficking, drug smuggling, and clandestine migration took place in explicit violation of state policies and/or multilateral regimes. Criminal organizations and terrorist groups flourished as well. Gangster operations represented a formidable obstacle to the construction of a new international order and, especially, to effective governance by nation-states.

This global panorama was confusing. As political scientist Joseph A. Nye, Jr., wrote in 1992, "No single hierarchy describes adequately a world politics with multiple structures. The distribution of power in world politics has become like a layer cake. The top military layer is largely unipolar, for there is no other military power comparable to the United States. The economic middle layer is tripolar and has been for two decades. The bottom layer of transnational interdependence shows a diffusion of power." While U.S. primacy gave sharp definition to geopolitical dimensions of the new world order, the distribution of economic power was far from clear.

Economic issues thus came to the forefront of the international agenda. Nations focused their attention on "geoeconomics"—their relative position in the global marketplace. The 1990s would reveal creative innovations and abrupt alterations in modes of production and distribution, in alignments and organizations, and in modes of economic governance. The watchword of this era came to be "globalization"—a vague and overarching notion referring to the accelerated movement throughout the world of people, money, and goods.

## Hegemony by Default?

Despite these challenges in the global arena, the United States enjoyed unquestioned supremacy within the Western Hemisphere. By 1990 the population of Latin America was almost 75 percent larger than that of the United States (436 million vs. 250 million), but its economic output was significantly less. United States GDP was more than seven times as large as the Latin American GDP in 1950, seven times as large in 1970, and still over five times as large by 1990. By that same year the GDP of the United States was fifty-eight times that of Argentina, thirteen times that of Brazil, twenty-three times that of Mexico.

A similar picture emerges from patterns of trade. One central fact was that that the United States was by 1990 the largest single trading partner for every country of the region. Another was the presence of the European Community (EC), especially for countries of southern South America (Argentina, Brazil, and Chile), whose trade with the EC as a collective entity was greater than that with the

United States. Third was the virtual disappearance of the Soviet Union, which by this time captured only a miniscule portion of trade with Latin America: Having been Argentina's largest customer in the 1980s, due to its purchase of wheat, the Soviet Union (before and after its collapse) was fading from view. Finally, data reflect the commercial rise of Japan, which would soon become the largest single customer for Chile, though it was elsewhere eclipsed by the United States. The United States thus asserted and affirmed its hemispheric position of economic supremacy; and while Europe and Japan sustained and in some areas strengthened economic relations with Latin America, they did not begin to pose a political challenge to Washington's preeminence in the Americas.

More than half of U.S. trade with Latin America was with Mexico alone. At the start of the 1990s, Mexico was, in fact, the United States' third-largest commercial partner—after Canada and Japan. Second-largest from the region was Brazil, fifteenth among U.S. global partners; Venezuela was eighteenth; Colombia was twenty-eighth. In 1997 Mexico passed Japan to become the number-two trading partner of the United States. Within the Americas, U.S. commercial interests focused mainly on Canada and Mexico.

Further, Latin America's relative importance to the United States was in decline. As a share of total American trade, U.S. commerce with the region dropped from 30 percent in 1950 to just 15 percent by the mid-1990s. Similarly, Latin America in 1950 accounted for well over one-third of U.S. direct investment abroad; by 1990 the figure had slipped to less than 10 percent. Western Europe, Canada, and "other" regions, especially Asia and the Pacific Rim, were all hosting substantially more U.S. investment than was Latin America. Over time, in other words, the United States would have *less* at stake in its economic dealings with Latin America—at a time when Latin America would have *more* at stake with the United States. This growing asymmetry gave Washington great potential leverage over countries of the region.

At the same time, potential rivals were beating a systematic retreat from the region. In this respect the United States came to acquire "hegemony by default." It came about not so much because the United States took bold, innovative, or effective action; it happened, instead, because outside powers withdrew from the Americas and directed their attention elsewhere. The European Community focused on the rehabilitation and reincorporation of Eastern Europe; the Soviet Union withdrew and then collapsed, leaving Russia to cope with enormous domestic challenges; Japan, ever mindful of its relationship with the United States (and beset by its own economic problems), proved reluctant to intensify involvement in the hemisphere; and China, despite its headlong rush toward economic growth, was not yet in a position to pursue an aggressive strategy toward Latin America. For the first time in centuries, there were no strong outside competitors for the United States.

Moreover, the United States was exerting a profound influence on popular culture. At the expense of European and local producers, Hollywood dominated box offices. Among the fifty top-grossing pictures in Argentina in 1993, thirty-six were American, six local, and four British (*Jurassic Park* was at the head of the list). In Chile, leading movie distributors were Warner Brothers (26 percent of the market), Universal (21 percent), and TriStar (17 percent). In Brazil every one of the most popular ten films of 1997 came from the United States, among them *Lost World* and *The English Patient*. In television, too, U.S. companies were capturing the cable market: By 1997 CBS Telenoticias had 10 million subscribers, ESPN had 8 million, and MTV and the Cartoon Network each had 7 million. Especially within the urban middle classes, American fashions and fads set the tone: Teenagers from Mexico City to Santiago wore U.S.-style blue jeans, listened to rock 'n' roll, and followed the antics of Hollywood stars. In an era of rapidly expanding communications, the appeal of American culture brought a significant "soft" dimension to American power.

The objective conditions for U.S. supremacy in the Americas were unusually complete. Never in the history of the hemisphere had there been no extra-hemispheric rivals, never had there been such asymmetry in power resources. Yet a paradox would soon emerge. Because this newfound preponderance did not come about as a result of concerted action by the United States, because hegemony came via default, the American public—and its leadership—would have no clear ideas about whether and how to take advantage of the situation. The question thus became: What would the United States do?

Not surprisingly, this situation provoked considerable apprehension in parts of Latin America. Excessive concentration of power could encourage impunity and irresponsibility. In years past, Latin America had suffered under the heels of American force. What would prevent a recurrence in the future? As one of Lima's prestigious newspapers editorialized in 1994, "The risk remains that the United States may intervene anywhere in the world, especially Latin America."

## TOWARD A NEW ECONOMIC AGENDA

Economic relations between Latin America and the United States were redefined during the 1980s by what came to be known as the "debt crisis." Seeking to increase their profits and exert their political power, members of the Organization of Petroleum Exporting Countries (OPEC) halted production in 1973–1974 and again in 1979–1981. The result on both occasions was a shortage of petroleum throughout the West, long waiting lines at gasoline stations in Europe and the United States, sharp increases in prices, and windfall profits for oil-producing countries. Unable to absorb all the funds, OPEC governments deposited massive amounts of dollars into U.S. and European banks. Obliged to pay interest on these deposits, the banks then had to lend these sums out to borrowers who would pay profitable rates of interest.

The moneylenders turned to Latin America. Since advanced industrial countries were facing recession, the most logical targets for lending were relatively unsophisticated borrowers in the developing world, who were willing to accept higher rates of interest than their industrial country counterparts. This meant especially the so-called upper tier of Third World countries—Argentina, Brazil, Venezuela, and Mexico. Bankers were quite comfortable dealing with public agencies and state enterprises, in the belief that repayment would be guaranteed by governments; countries may not be able to pay, according to a well-known dictum, but neither they nor their debts would disappear. Meanwhile borrowers were encouraged by modest interest rates (at some points in the mid-1970s real interest rates, as measured by the difference between nominal rates and worldwide inflation, were actually negative). Under these circumstances, Latin America's total foreign debt swelled from around $30 billion in 1970 to more than $240 billion in 1980.

Meanwhile the value as well as the volume of traditional Latin American exports, from coffee to nonferrous metals to petroleum, was sharply plummeting. A steady strengthening of the U.S. dollar intensified the trend; as a result, Latin American nations were earning less hard currency from exports. As the cost of debt service was rising, Latin America's capacity to pay was declining.

By the early 1980s both lenders and borrowers were overextended. Indebted countries were caught in a vicious squeeze between declining export prices and rising interest rates, so they began to borrow more and more money just to keep up with payments on debt service. Loans piled upon loans: Between 1975 and 1985 Latin America's external debt spiraled from $99 billion to $384 billion. "You borrowed money like a bunch of drunken sailors," one prominent banker is reported to have said at a meeting with Latin America's finance managers. "Yes," came the tart reply, "but we had a drunken bartender."

These worrisome trends came to a head in August 1982, when Mexico announced that it could no longer meets its obligations on debt. Hurried negotiations reached agreement on two points: a moratorium on the amortization of Mexico's debt to commercial banks, and an international package of emergency loans. The most important point was implicit: Interest payments would continue as scheduled.

Subsequent discussions led to the creation of a mechanism for communication between Mexico and its creditor banks—between 800 and 1,000 institutions in all. Dominated by large-scale "money center" banks, the committee was nominally charged with providing advice to the Mexican government, although it also served to coordinate the negotiating stance of the banks. In effect, the bankers succeeded in forming a cartel.

Negotiations eventually shaped a three-part strategy. The first step was to strengthen Mexico's foreign-exchange reserves in order to enable continued payments on interest, accomplished mainly through agreements with the United States. The second step was to provide long-term financing, and here the International Monetary Fund agreed to provide Mexico a substantial line of credit in exchange for a stringent stabilization program to combat inflation. The third step involved renegotiation of terms and timing of debt repayments. Mexico and its creditors could heave a collective sigh of relief. Seized with self-congratulation, participants in these deliberations regarded their handling of the Mexican crisis as a major success.

Other countries in Latin America thereafter announced imminent default on debt obligations, prompting international authorities to seek a workable response. Bankers and debtors at first attempted to "muddle through" what they saw as problems of "liquidity," with the IMF serving as catalyst and monitor. Once a country proclaimed inability to pay, the IMF would negotiate an austerity package designed to attack inflation and public-sector deficits. Approval of an IMF package would persuade otherwise-reluctant creditor banks to provide fresh loans, which enabled debtor countries to keep up their payments.

Thereafter then-U.S. treasury secretary James A. Baker III stressed the importance of economic growth for indebted countries—thus acknowledging that countries faced crises not just of liquidity (cash squeeze) but also of solvency (basic inability to pay). Recognizing the dearth of commercial lending, Baker assigned a major role to the World Bank, which had thus far stayed on the sidelines of the debt crisis. His proposal led to scant practical results, but it marked an important shift in the definition and conceptualization of the crisis. Baker's successor, Nicholas F. Brady, later proposed a broad portfolio of debt reduction and restructuring alternatives and offered U.S. government support to countries undertaking market-based economic policies. The Brady Plan had two distinct features: One was its flexibility; the other was its explicit recognition of the need for debt reduction. Long anathema to the banks and to the Reagan administration, debt relief was thus legitimized on the ground that it could provide efficiency gains for both the debtors and the banks.

For Latin America the 1980s were an unmitigated nightmare, and those years would come to be remembered as the "lost decade." Economic and social progress was negligible at best, negative at worst. Renegotiations and restructurings led to reliance on continuous lending (and borrowing), which forced the region's external debt up from $242 billion in 1980 to $431 billion by 1990. Meeting their contractual obligations, Latin American countries transferred a net amount of more than $200 billion to advanced industrial countries. They slashed imports—from $98 billion in 1981 to $59 billion in 1984—and doled out one-third to one-half their export earnings in the form of interest payments. Economic growth came to a virtual halt. Growth rates of gross domestic product (GDP) per capita for the region were actually negative for 1981, 1982, 1983, 1988, and 1989, while per capita output declined by 8.3 percent over the course of the decade. Poverty spread, especially in cities, as did inequality. The social reality was painfully clear: For peasants, workers, and downwardly mobile segments of the middle class, the debt crisis had a devastating impact.

## THE WASHINGTON CONSENSUS

While bankers and public officials sought to deal with practical dimensions of the crisis, economists attempted to determine its causes and prescribe long-term solutions. Eventually, the international financial community came to the conclusion that Latin America required fundamental economic reform. A principal source of the region's difficulty was held to be structural distortions resulting from the strategy of "import-substitution industrialization" (ISI), through which Latin American countries sought to manufacture goods formerly imported from abroad. To an extent, ISI grew out of the conviction that secular terms of trade were running against commodity producers: The real price of raw materials was declining while the cost of manufactures was increasing. Domestic industrialization under state protection offered a logical response to these conditions. Through the 1970s, ISI produced high rates of growth, and observers referred glowingly to economic "miracles" in such countries as Mexico and Brazil.

During the 1980s, however, conventional wisdom began to attribute numerous deficiencies to ISI—most notably its emphasis on the state, its reliance on domestic markets, and its protection of the private sector. Of course the debt crisis itself was largely due to factors outside of (and outside the control of) Latin America. Notwithstanding this self-evident truth, economists and policymakers in major international institutions—from the U.S. Treasury to the World Bank and the International Monetary Fund—issued a clarion call for economic restructuring in Latin America.

What came to be known as the "Washington consensus" entailed three sets of prescriptions. First, it called for reduction and revision in the economic role of the state. Latin American governments should exercise fiscal discipline—as commonly preached, but rarely practiced, by Washington itself. They should concentrate their resources not on social subsidies (such as retirement pensions or price controls on foodstuffs) but on such economically productive areas as health, education, and infrastructural investment. They should deregulate their national economies, letting market forces operate without political or bureaucratic constraints.

Second, the Washington consensus advocated support for the private sector. Latin American governments should sell off state-owned enterprises, which could reduce public deficits through proceeds from the sales and through the elimination of wasteful subsidies. The governments should also remove restrictions on foreign capital. Behind the consensus was a doctrinaire belief that private management, driven by profit motivation and market competition, was inherently more efficient than public administration.

Third, Latin American governments should drastically revise policies on trade. They should look outward, not inward, for markets. The reduction of tariffs and other barriers to imports would improve access to intermediate inputs, which was necessary for the ability to export finished products at competitive prices. Excessive protection of domestic industry created costly distortions that penalized exports, punished domestic consumers, and encouraged inefficiencies. (It was assumed that Latin America's recovery required the expansion of nontraditional exports, especially manufactured goods, rather than the expansion of traditional commodities and raw materials.) In this regard, trade policy and the encouragement of private enterprise went hand in hand: Both would stimulate competition, efficiency, and active participation in the international economy.

By either coincidence or design, this policy package fell neatly in line with U.S. national interests. At a time when the United States was seeking new markets abroad, these prescriptions would reduce tariffs and nontariff barriers to trade. And as the United States was searching for ways to improve economic competitiveness, these nostrums would relax conditions for foreign investment and make it easier for American manufacturers to take advantage of inexpensive labor and develop export platforms in Latin America. Generally speaking, the adoption of free-market capitalism by Latin America would be good for the United States. Not for nothing was this doctrine called the Washington consensus.

Yet the neoliberal vision contained a central paradox. Although the program called for reducing the role of the state, the actual implementation of its policies would require a powerful state. Economic reform was bound to encounter resistance from entrenched groups—sheltered entrepreneurs, unionized workers, public-sector employees. Imposition of broad, equitable, and effective tax codes, another of the Washington proposals, would generate opposition from almost everyone. It would take a strong and autonomous state to overcome such pressures. Proponents of the consensus often sought to resolve this paradox by advocating small but efficient government, "lean and mean," but this catchy formulation did little to address the underlying issues.

Eventually, too, the Washington consensus developed political corollaries. Around Wall Street and some academic circles, it came to be argued that free-market policies would establish foundations for political democracy. The liberalization of markets would lead to the liberalization of politics: The dismantling of state monopolies would break up old ruling cliques, the deregulation of business would encourage entrepreneurship, economic competition would foster political competition. Moreover, as newly empowered groups took part in the global economy, they would find it in their practical interest to come from countries with democratic credentials. As these convictions took hold, inconvenient examples from East Asia—open economies with closed polities, such as Singapore and China—were more or less ignored. The early 1990s was an optimistic time, like the early 1960s, and it was imagined once again that all good things could go together.

## NORTH AMERICAN FREE TRADE

In extension of the Washington consensus, a movement in favor of "free trade" swept through the Americas. Attention began to focus on processes of "regional economic integration," which entailed the removal of state-imposed barriers to the mutual exchange of goods, services, capital, or persons. According to standard usage, the removal of barriers to the exchange of goods alone would be sufficient to create a "free-trade area" (FTA). That plus the erection of common external tariffs would constitute a "customs union." Establishment of a "common market" would require the removal of barriers to the free flow of all factors of production, especially services and capital. As later explained in chapter 13, the mutual exchange of persons—that is, the free flow of labor—would constitute one of the most contentious issues in contemporary processes of integration.

The most ambitious scheme of this era was North American Free Trade Agreement between Canada, the United States, and Mexico (NAFTA). Unveiled in August 1992, the pact was signed in the midst of the U.S. presidential campaign. After ratification by legislatures of the three governments, it took effect in January 1994. Building on a bilateral free-trade accord between Canada and the United States (approved in 1988, initiated January 1989), NAFTA created one of the two largest trading blocs in the world—with a population of 370 million and combined economic production of approximately $6 trillion as of 1992, North America could be a worthy rival to the European Union.

NAFTA promoted a free flow of goods between member countries by eliminating duties, tariffs, and trade barriers over a period of fifteen years. Sixty-five percent of U.S. goods gained duty-free status immediately or within five years; half of U.S. farm goods exported to Mexico immediately became duty free. There were special exceptions for certain "highly sensitive" products in agriculture, typically one of the sectors most resistant to economic integration; phase-outs on tariffs for corn and dry beans in Mexico and orange juice and sugar in the United States would extend to the year 2009. Tariffs on all automobiles within North America would be phased out over ten years, but rules of origin stipulated that local content would have to comprise at least 62.5 percent for vehicles to qualify. Not surprisingly, Asian governments regarded this clause as a thinly disguised "protectionist" effort to exclude Japanese industries and products from the North American auto market.

NAFTA opened Mexico to U.S. investments in various ways. Under the treaty, U.S. banks and securities firms could establish branch offices in Mexico, and U.S. citizens could invest in Mexico's banking and insurance industries. While Mexico continued to prohibit foreign ownership of oil fields, in accordance with its constitution, U.S. firms became eligible to compete for contracts with Petróleos Mexicanos (PEMEX) and to operate, in general, under the same provisions as Mexican companies.

One item was most conspicuous by its absence: Beyond a narrowly written provision for movement of corporate executives and selected professionals, the treaty made no reference at all to large-scale migration of labor. The continuing flow of "undocumented workers" from Mexico into the United States—where they were customarily classified as "illegal aliens," in a suggestive turn of phrase—remained a major source of conflict and contention in the bilateral relationship. Apparently sensing that there was no ground for reasonable compromise, NAFTA negotiators decided to avoid the question altogether.

NAFTA precipitated strenuous debate within the United States (and to a somewhat lesser extent in Canada, where organized labor and small business were feeling ill effects from the U.S.-Canadian agreement). In the heat of the 1992 presidential campaign, Democratic candidate Bill Clinton pledged to support NAFTA on condition that there be effective safeguards for environmental protection and worker rights; by September 1993 the governments reached "supplemental" (side) agreements on labor and environment. As the U.S. Congress prepared to vote on ratification, NAFTA moved to the center of the political stage. Texas billionaire (and erstwhile presidential hopeful) Ross Perot led the charge against the treaty, claiming that NAFTA would entice U.S. business to seek low-wage Mexican labor and thus lose jobs for millions of American workers. Proponents insisted that NAFTA would stimulate U.S. exports, achieve economies of scale, and enhance U.S. competitiveness. Disregarding vociferous opposition from unionized labor, a historic bastion of support for Democrats, Clinton lobbied tirelessly on behalf of the treaty. After Perot stumbled badly during a television debate with Vice President Al Gore, the House of Representatives finally approved the NAFTA accord by the surprisingly lopsided margin of 234–200; the Senate followed with a vote of 61–38.

In final form, the NAFTA accord had three outstanding characteristics. One was its implicit commitment to regional economic integration. Despite its title, NAFTA was not primarily concerned with "free trade." By 1990, tariff and even nontariff barriers to U.S.-Mexican commerce were already low. NAFTA was concerned primarily with investment. By obtaining preferential access to U.S. markets and a formal "seal of approval" through NAFTA, Mexico was hoping to attract sizable flows of foreign direct investment—from Japan and Europe as well as from the United States. By obtaining untrammeled access to low-wage (but highly skilled) Mexican labor, the United States was hoping to create an export platform for manufactured goods to improve its competitive position in the global economy. Commerce was only one part of the picture.

Second, NAFTA was essentially an intergovernmental accord. Unlike the European Community (later European Union), which created an elaborate structure for governance with supranational authority, NAFTA relied on negotiations and presumed agreement between national governments. As revealed by its provisions for dispute resolution, which called on contending parties to engage in voluntary deliberations, NAFTA did not entail any "pooling" or "sharing" or "delegation" of political sovereignty along European lines. The result was inconsistency, some thought, between the relatively "deep" degree of economic integration envisioned by NAFTA and its distinctly "shallow" level of political integration.

Third, NAFTA possessed an underlying political rationale, especially for the United States and Mexico. (This was less true for Canada, which eventually decided to join the NAFTA negotiations for defensive reasons.) The United States had four basic goals. One was the preservation of stability along its southern border. This had been the cornerstone of U.S. policy toward Mexico ever since the revolution of 1910. The idea was that NAFTA would stimulate economic growth in Mexico, easing social pressure and sustaining the regime. It was not Washington's primary intent to promote democratic change; it was to uphold political peace.

Second, NAFTA provided the United States with an important bargaining chip in its trade negotiations with Europe, Japan, and the General Agreement on

Tariffs and Trade. In confronting a potential "fortress Europe" or a resistant Japan, in other words, Washington could threaten to form an exclusive economic bloc in North America—or perhaps the Western Hemisphere as a whole—and pursue highly protectionist policies.

Third, the United States sought to assure itself of continuing access to petroleum from Mexico, a leading source of U.S. imports. Mexican shipments in the late 1980s and early 1990s were roughly half as large as those from the topmost source, Saudi Arabia. By 1997 Venezuela had moved into first place, and Mexico—with nearly 14 percent of U.S. imports—was barely behind the Saudis. Petroleum continued to have major geostrategic significance, as the Persian Gulf War eloquently testified, and secure and steady access to sources within the hemisphere could counterbalance the potential costs of political turbulence elsewhere in the world.

And fourth, the United States wanted to consolidate diplomatic support from Mexico on foreign policy in general. As demonstrated by disagreements over Central America during the 1980s, foreign policy had long been a source of bilateral tension. And with NAFTA in place, Mexico became unlikely to express serious disagreement with the United States on major issues of international diplomacy. None other than the U.S. ambassador to Mexico, John D. Negroponte, said as much in a controversial (originally confidential) memorandum to Washington in April 1991. "Mexico is in the process of changing the substance and image of its foreign policy," he wrote to Bernard Aronson, the assistant secretary for inter-American affairs: "It has switched from an ideological, nationalistic and protectionist approach to a pragmatic, outreaching and competitive view of world affairs. . . . The proposal for an FTA is in a way the capstone of these new policy approaches. *From a foreign policy perspective, an FTA would institutionalize acceptance of a North American orientation to Mexico's foreign relations*" (emphasis added). That Negroponte made this statement does not necessarily mean that it was correct, but it does convey a sense of expectations within the U.S. government.

On the other side, Mexico was seeking, first and foremost, preservation of its social peace. The hope was that NAFTA would attract investment, stimulate employment, and provide meaningful opportunity for the 1 million persons entering the job market every year. This would alleviate poverty, reduce social tension, and strengthen the country's political regime. In this sense the goal of the PRI was entirely consistent with Washington's desire to prolong stability in Mexico.

Second, NAFTA offered President Carlos Salinas de Gortari an opportunity to institutionalize and perpetuate his economic reforms. Under his leadership Mexico had taken aggressive steps in accordance with (if not in response to) the Washington consensus—liberalizing trade, privatizing the parastatal sector, encouraging foreign investment, redefining the role of the state. Such policies were threatening to long-established interests in Mexico and caused a good deal of resentment. In order to preserve his innovations, Salinas wanted to insulate them from the historic vagaries of presidential succession, which had permitted each new chief executive to reverse or ignore predecessor policies. Under NAFTA, the *salinista* program of "structural readjustment" now became part of an international treaty—one that was subscribed to by the world's only remaining superpower.

Third, Mexico was seeking international benediction for its not-yet-democratic political regime. Such acceptance was especially important because, in comparison with Argentina, Chile, Brazil, and other countries undergoing processes of democratization, Mexico no longer looked like a paragon of political civility. Prospects for democratization in Mexico became a matter of prominent debate. Skeptics insisted that NAFTA would prolong and consolidate Mexico's authoritarian system. Advocates maintained that NAFTA would promote democracy by unleashing social forces that would ultimately lay the foundation for democratic development in Mexico. According to this logic, the Mexican political regime deserved approbation not because of its authoritarian present but because of its democratic future. Mexico was seeking legitimation through anticipation.

Finally, Mexico believed that NAFTA would provide the country with diplomatic leverage vis-à-vis the rest of Latin America and, by extension, the Third World as a whole. Association with Canada and the United States would link Mexico with advanced industrial democracies and leaders of the "first world." Consequently Mexico could serve as a "bridge" between the developing world and the developed world, as a representative and interlocutor for aspiring peoples of the South. NAFTA prompted some analysts to charge that Mexico was turning its back on Latin America and the Third World. The hope in Mexico City, however, was that NAFTA would strengthen the country's diplomatic and political prestige.

All these calculations were suddenly upset. On January 1, 1994—the day that NAFTA went into effect—a guerrilla movement in the poverty-stricken state of Chiapas rose up to denounce the free-trade accord, the *salinista* economic model, and the undemocratic character of the political regime. With colorful and capable leadership, the Zapatista National Liberation Army (EZLN) captured national and international attention during the course of highly publicized negotiations with governmental authorities.

Political violence would shatter the national image. On March 17 an unknown assassin's bullet struck down Luis Donaldo Colosio, Salinas' handpicked successor and the official *priísta* candidate in the upcoming presidential election. Salinas hastily chose another candidate, the forty-two-year-old Ernesto Zedillo Ponce de León, who scurried to develop a credible campaign. On September 28 another shooting took the life of José Francisco Ruiz Massieu, the number-two leader of the PRI and one of Zedillo's most trusted political allies. These were shocking developments. Mexico could no longer be seen as an up-and-coming country on the brink of joining the first world; it looked, instead, like a Third World society threatening to come apart at the seams.

Under these unsettling circumstances, NAFTA confronted an uncertain future. Some reassurance came from the 1994 presidential elections, in which Zedillo triumphed with 48.8 percent of the vote (compared with 20.6 percent for the rightist PAN and only 16.6 percent for the populist PRD). Most observers

Mexico, 1990s: While the movement addressed age-old grievances in the state of Chiapas, the Zapatista National Liberation Army (EZLN) launched its uprising on January 1, 1994— the date that NAFTA went into effect.
SOURCE: AP Photo/Scott Sady.

interpreted this result as a mandate for continuity rather than change. Only three weeks after taking office in December 1994, however, the Zedillo administration unexpectedly widened the band for trading pesos with dollars from 3.47 to 4.00— in effect, permitting a 15 percent devaluation of the peso. This prompted a speculative run against the peso; within days the government was obliged to abandon its position, letting the peso float freely against the dollar. Unable to persuade foreign investors of Mexico's trustworthiness, the secretary of the treasury submitted his resignation. Investors still failed to respond. The resulting crisis threatened to decimate foreign investments in Mexican securities, derail Mexico's pattern of growth, delegitimize free-market reforms, and destroy the credibility of NAFTA itself.

Faced by such prospects, the U.S. government had no choice but to race to the rescue. In particular, the Clinton administration had invested too much capital in debates over NAFTA ratification to permit disintegration of its neighbor. Chaos in Mexico would vindicate opposition to NAFTA, emphasize the fallibility of the Clinton team, and throw confusion into U.S. relations with trading partners around the world. Washington could not permit "collapse" in Mexico.

Within weeks the United States managed to put together a multilateral package of nearly $50 billion, including $20 billion from the U.S. government, but the peso continued to slide. To combat inflationary pressures (and meet the demands of international creditors), the Mexican government adopted rigorous adjustment programs. Stringent measures eventually stabilized financial and foreign-exchange markets, but at a staggering cost: Output contracted, unemployment increased, and real wages fell. The combination of recession and high interest rates threatened the financial health of numerous companies and jeopardized the solvency of the entire banking system. The Mexican GDP declined by more than 6 percent in 1995, and crime rates rose to record levels.

Zedillo struggled to consolidate his hold on power. His government foundered on numerous fronts. The adjustment measures of 1995 inflicted enormous pain on large sectors of the population. Government investigators failed to solve either the Colosio murder or the Ruiz Massieu assassination. Negotiations with Chiapas guerrillas resulted in stalemate. The economy showed signs of recovery in 1996 and 1997, but the long-term outlook remained uncertain.

## FROM NAFTA TO FTAA?

Also unclear were the prospects for creation of a free-trade zone embracing all of the Americas. Almost from the beginning, NAFTA was envisioned not only as a three-way partnership but also as the steppingstone toward a hemispheric accord (eventually known as FTAA, Free Trade Area of the Americas). As George H. W. Bush proclaimed when launching the Enterprise for the Americas Initiative in June 1990, the ultimate goal was to be a free-trade zone "stretching from the port of Anchorage to the Tierra del Fuego." Eager to gain access to this privileged circle, Latin American leaders came to regard eventual accession to NAFTA as a key part of their development strategy. Expectations were soon running high.

The question was whether they might be fulfilled. The United States had substantial interests in the region, in both investment and trade, and many analysts were predicting that the Latin American market had potential for high rates of expansion. Latin America, for its part, wanted FTAA as a quid pro quo for major transformations in development strategies. In keeping with the Washington consensus, countries of the region were lowering barriers to trade, privatizing state-owned companies, promoting foreign investment, and reshaping the role of the state. It was not clear whether leaders were undertaking these changes on the basis of unilateral and voluntary decisions or in response to pressure from the international community; in either case, they had reason to want something in return. FTAA would enable them to achieve some degree of commercial reciprocity on the part of the United States, thus ensuring access to the North American market, and it could provide new members with an internationally recognized seal of approval as suitable sites for foreign investment.

Creation of FTAA could occur in various ways. One would be for countries of the Americas to enter NAFTA directly through accession: If NAFTA eventually were to include all countries of the hemisphere, it would automatically become an FTAA. A second path would be for the United States (or Mexico) to form a series of "hub-and-spoke" arrangements with Latin American countries that could ultimately lead to integration of the region by "filling in the rims." A third possibility would be for Latin American countries to accelerate their own processes of subregional integration so that these groupings could then negotiate free-trade agreements with NAFTA. There was more than one route to FTAA.

Yet hemispheric integration faced formidable obstacles, economic and political. The commercial rationale was much less compelling than in the case of NAFTA. As shown earlier, trade relations between the United States and Latin America *outside of Mexico* were declining in relative importance over time. Moreover, an FTAA could result in substantial trade diversion, especially for countries of South America (most notably Brazil).

Institutional and political impediments were equally daunting. In final form, NAFTA did not establish criteria for admission. In a deliberately uninformative accession clause, the treaty simply held that new countries may join NAFTA "subject to such terms and conditions as may be agreed" by the member countries and "following approval in accordance with the applicable approval procedures in each country." Such vague language meant that member countries retained the right to establish arbitrary or impossible accession criteria if they so chose—and that it would take considerable time to develop any criteria at all.

Finally, and perhaps most fundamentally, FTAA lacked clear political motivation. NAFTA had the makings of a credible political bargain. FTAA did not. This was a major obstacle. Without strong political motivation, there could be no lasting integration.

## Summitry and Setbacks

As uncertainty and anxiety mounted over prospects for free trade in the Americas, heads of state moved to the center of the hemispheric stage. This was not uncommon for Latin America, but it was most unusual for the United States, which generally relegated decisions on inter-American affairs to middling levels of the governmental bureaucracy. It had been noticed, in capitals around the region, that Bill Clinton made not a single visit to Latin America during his first term as president. And from Washington's perspective, it seemed important to provide assurances that the United States would neither neglect nor abandon Latin American countries outside of Mexico.

The solution came in the form of a dramatic gesture, a high-profile "Summit of the Americas" hosted by Clinton in the Latinized city of Miami in December 1994. Attended by thirty-four heads of state, with the conspicuous exception of Cuba's Fidel Castro, this was the first such gathering since the late 1960s. Once gathered together, the heads of state agreed to the formation of a Free Trade Area of the Americas. Confidently predicting that FTAA "will stretch from Alaska to Argentina," Clinton boasted that the accord marked "a watershed in the history of the hemisphere." With a combination of amnesia and hyperbole, the American president went on to proclaim that "the so-called lost decade of Latin America is a fading memory." With the exception of Cuba, he exulted, the region had "freed itself from dictatorship and debt, and embraced democracy and development."

## BOX 9-1

### Free Trade as Managed Trade

The notion of "free trade" is not as simple as it looks. At face value, it would appear to mean that nations can exchange products and goods "freely"—without any governmental control or interference. What could be more straightforward?

Not so fast. A "free-trade agreement" (FTA) means that participating nations agree to *reduce* tariffs and nontariff barriers to trade, usually according to a carefully designed (and drawn-out) timetable—not to *eliminate* such barriers. Trade will still be managed, but in a different way. For this reason some economists employ the relative adjective "freer" (rather than the absolute "free") to describe such commercial arrangements; others have come to speak of "trade promotion" agreements rather than free trade.

FTAs come in different shapes and sizes. Some refer only to the movement of goods. Others promote the mobility of investment capital as well. Still others are "comprehensive," in that they touch on just about everything that might conceivably be related to trade and the production of exports—governmental subsidies, procurement policies, health benefits, and environmental protection. With its thousands of pages of text, NAFTA qualifies as a highly comprehensive agreement. As an FTA, however, it makes no provision to free up transnational labor migration.

Moreover, FTAs can produce differing configurations. For example, signatories in a single, multilateral FTA presumably have equal access to each other's markets. But if one country has bilateral agreements with several others—which do not have FTAs among themselves—this situation produces what has come to be known as a "hub-and-spoke" arrangement. The central country is the hub, and all the others are spokes. This formation grants enormous leverage to the hub, which is in a position to play off the spokes against each another. What is good for the hub, in other words, is not always so good for the spokes.

---

Despite the president's enthusiasm, the American public was skeptical. In September 1997 Clinton submitted to Congress a proposal for renewal of "fast track" consideration of international trade agreements. Notwithstanding its name, "fast track" referred not to the speed of deliberation but to the stipulation that Congress would have to vote on trade agreements as complete packages, yes or no, rather than amending them. Fast track had become a staple of trade policy since the early 1970s, because it enabled representatives from the United States and other countries to reach agreements with the assurance that they would not be subjected to crippling revisions by special interests in Congress. And for the Western Hemisphere, the fate of the legislation by this time had symbolic as well as practical significance.

As controversy mounted, one expert made the astute observation that "fast track has become a referendum on NAFTA." This meant trouble for the Clinton bill. A *Wall Street Journal*/NBC News poll in early 1997 showed that 43 percent of Americans believed that NAFTA had a negative impact on the United States.

And in September, a *Business Week*/Harris Poll revealed that only 42 percent of the public had a positive opinion of NAFTA; 36 percent had a negative view and 22 percent were undecided or unsure. More to the point, a strong majority—54 percent—did not favor extension of NAFTA to other countries of Latin America, and an identical percentage opposed renewal of fast-track authority. "NAFTA has become a dirty word politically," as one advocate of free trade ruefully acknowledged. Fairly or not, NAFTA seemed to be suffering from a political malady common to integration schemes: Benefits would be long-term and diffuse, whereas costs were short-term and concentrated. It soon became clear that fast track would not pass the House of Representatives, and a frustrated Clinton withdrew the authorizing legislation.

The implications of this stalemate became clear in April 1998 in Santiago, Chile, during a follow-up to the ebullient Miami summit of 1994. Although Clinton

Chile, 1998: Bill Clinton receives a warm welcome from friendly crowds in Santiago.
Source: AP Photo/Greg Gibson.

assured his fellow heads of state that "our commitment to the Free Trade Area of the Americas will be in the fast lane of our concerns," the U.S. delegates were unable to press these issues with force and credibility. To be sure, the Santiago meeting resulted in a unanimous pledge to make "concrete progress" toward creation of an FTAA by the end of the century and to adopt an intensive schedule for negotiating sessions. Participants further decided to set up a multilateral process for evaluating progress against illicit drug trafficking and agreed to hold inter-American summits "periodically"—with the next gathering to be hosted by Canada. Conspicuous, however, was Washington's low-key demeanor on the question of free trade.

## GEOECONOMICS: THE RULES OF THE GAME

All these back-and-forth maneuvers on hemispheric trade came under the purview of "geoeconomics," a generic concept referring to the global dimensions of economic interactions. In contrast to geopolitical standing, which rests largely on military prowess, geoeconomic position stems from financial, technological, and productive capacity. The quest for economic power would naturally give rise to strenuous conflict. Indistinctly, at first, this kind of competition began to forge implicit codes of conduct, or "rules of the game." And by the end of the 1990s, these norms had taken fairly clear shape.

The principal goal for each participating nation was to increase or guarantee its share of global economic benefits. The prize was not control of people or of territory but the augmentation of wealth and/or productive capacity. This implied two related purposes: increasing the size of the economic pie, and increasing your share of the enlarging pie. Competition focused a variety of assets: consumer markets, natural resources (such as petroleum or water), financial transactions, or technological innovation. Ideally, geoeconomic games were supposed to have positive-sum outcomes, instead of zero- or negative-sum. All contestants would end up with more than they had before, but the winners would increase their relative share (that is, they would have more of more).

The game was broadly inclusive. Global markets relied on extensive networks. In an interdependent and globalizing world, everybody needed everyone else. Producers needed workers, sellers needed buyers, lenders needed borrowers, exporters needed importers, and so on. The process of economic interconnection was seen as inevitable and unstoppable. As Bill Clinton said in 1998, "No nation, rich or poor, democratic or authoritarian, can escape the fundamental economic imperatives of the global market." And in a revealing twist of lexicon, opponents were referred to as not as enemies but as "rivals."

The intent was not to destroy or even "defeat" rivals. No right-minded nation would seek to impoverish its neighbors. The United States might quarrel vigorously with Japan (or China) about commercial policies, but such disagreements took place within limits. Isolationist and beggar-thy-neighbor policies had no place in this arena. Losing contestants would not be eliminated from the game.

They would stay to play another round. The game involved an indefinite number of iterations: Once one round was finished, another would begin. There would be no final whistle, no formal declaration of defeat or victory.

For this reason geopolitical competition encouraged long-term calculations. It did not lend itself to surprise attacks or lighting strikes. It resembled a game of chess—one that rewarded deliberation, calculation, and patience. Moreover it was mainly peaceful. Unlike geopolitical competition, it would not usually involve the use or threat of armed force. There might be threatening, bargaining, and blackmail. Nations could resort to brinksmanship, but, under the rules of this game, they would not engage in large-scale military action.[1] War was too expensive.

Global stability was therefore essential. Effective cost–benefit calculations required reliable forecasts and predictable horizons. In keeping with this imperative, economic stability prevailed throughout the 1990s and the early 2000s, though it would be severely tested by global financial crises starting in 2008. Stability was nonetheless a prime desideratum.

Advocates of globalization fostered an ideology that claimed to be nonideological. A core premise was the claim that economic interactions transcended political dogmas. They represented clear-eyed perceptions of forces in the international marketplace. There was nothing political about them. Geoeconomic legitimacy was based on a discourse about the market, not social forces or the state. The underlying forces of the world were economic. States were losing relevance.

Even so, states played crucial roles in the geoeconomic arena. In some countries, such as China, states controlled commanding heights of the national economy. More commonly, they established incentives for economic actors. They had a broad repertoire of policy instruments at their disposal: They could tighten quotas and tariffs (to curtail imports), manipulate foreign-exchange rates (to promote exports), or revise financial regulations (to attract desirable foreign investments). And through diplomatic channels, they defined and reinforced the rules of the game.

For many contestants, one of the most promising strategies appeared to involve regional economic integration. Such schemes resulted directly from political decisions. Prime examples were the European Union, NAFTA, and (to a lesser extent) the project for Asia-Pacific Economic Cooperation (APEC). For the most part these were "open" blocs rather than exclusive clubs or economic fortresses, but they formed core components of the situation. Strong states used integration schemes in order to perpetuate their primacy and to compete with other major blocs or powers. Weaker states joined such agreements in order to avoid exclusion from the global marketplace. These differences created conditions for asymmetrical bargaining, in which large states could exert substantial leverage over smaller partners.

---

[1] Iraq's invasion of Kuwait in 1989 is the exception that proves this rule. Saddam Hussein was seeking to enlarge Iraq's role in the international oil market, and under President George H. W. Bush the United States (and allies) responded with devastating military force.

These rules of this geoeconomic game evolved during the 1990s. After the turn of the twenty-first century, they would coexist with rules for geopolitical conduct deriving from the post–9/11 war against terror. The juxtaposition of these codes will be explored in chapters 11 and 12.

## QUESTIONS FOR REVIEW

1. What factors account for the emergence of the United States as the world's only superpower in the 1990s? What is the meaning of U.S. "hegemony by default" in Latin America?
2. How did the debt crisis come about? Was it anyone's fault? Or was it a logical outcome of inexorable trends?
3. What was (or is) the Washington consensus? How did its principal tenets coincide with U.S. national interests during the 1990s?
4. Why was NAFTA so important? In what ways did it signify a departure from previous practice?
5. Who favored FTAA, and why? Which countries stood to gain the most, and which stood to lose the most?

# CHAPTER 10

# Latin America: Playing the Geoeconomic Game

Latin America's community is the Third World.
COLOMBIAN FOREIGN MINISTER (1974)

We want Mexico to be part of the first world, not the third.
CARLOS SALINAS DE GORTARI (1990)

Passage of the Cold War brought mixed blessings to Latin America. The end of East-West conflict meant that the region would no longer serve as a battleground for superpower rivalry. Within Latin America, this new situation relaxed the terms of ideological contention, weakening forces of left and right and reducing levels of polarization in domestic politics. By strengthening centrist elements, it reinforced processes of liberalization under way and enhanced the prospects for democratic consolidation. Ending of the Cold War prompted the hope, as well, that Washington could come to evaluate and appreciate Latin America on its own terms, respecting regional aspirations and supporting local efforts for social and political development.

It was also anticipated that conclusion of the Cold War would expand the range and quality of policy options for Latin America. Leaders in the region were confronting two imperatives. One was to forge a response to changing patterns in the distribution of international power and, in particular, the intensification of U.S. hegemony within the Western Hemisphere. The other was to find a viable position in the newly emerging global economy, a niche that could provide a foundation for long-term development and growth. How might Latin America address these concerns?

## NARROWING OPTIONS

As major powers wrestled with reconfiguration of the world community and struggled to devise new rules of the game, Latin America found itself at a distinct disadvantage. The continent was not a major power center. It would have only a modest role in determining the shape of the post–Cold War world. Notwithstanding an initial burst of continental optimism, it soon became apparent that the post–Cold

226

War environment provided Latin America with a distressingly slim range of practical options.

In the early 1990s it seemed no longer possible, as Bolívar fervently hoped, to seek protection from an extrahemispheric power. In full enjoyment of its "unipolar moment," the United States held uncontested military supremacy throughout the world. And despite the redistribution of global economic power, major powers were elsewhere predisposed: The Soviet Union had collapsed; Western Europe was promoting the rehabilitation and incorporation of Eastern Europe; Japan was focusing attention on its own economic downturn, the plight of its Asian neighbors, and its bilateral relationship with the United States. There was nowhere for Latin America to turn.

Nor could Third World solidarity provide a plausible substitute. Indeed, the "developing world" was becoming increasingly fragmented into differing strata— between the conventional Third World and what came to be known as the "Fourth World," including countries such as Ethiopia, Burkina Faso, and Bangladesh, an area of bone-crushing poverty and structural underdevelopment. Within Latin America, the World Bank classified only Haiti as a "low-income" country; most countries of the region stood above the international median; Venezuela and Brazil both qualified as "upper-middle-income," in fact, with Mexico and Argentina close behind. And as foreshadowed by struggles over the "new international economic order" in the 1970s, Latin America's strategic and economic interests would not always converge with those of Asia, the Middle East, and Africa. South–South cooperation offered gratifying opportunities for rhetorical expressions of political solidarity; perhaps in search of leverage, too, Argentina, Brazil, Mexico, and Peru joined with other prominent Third World countries to form a so-called "G-15" in 1989. But in the wake of the 1980s debt crisis, Latin America's economic destiny was, for better or worse, inextricably tied to the North. The South could not provide a durable solution.

Moreover, there was no clear-cut formula for attracting support from the United States. During the Cold War, political rulers of all stripes, from centrist reformers to rightist dictators, could invoke the threat of communism in order to obtain moral and material assistance from Washington. This was no longer possible. Leaders of Latin America would have to find some other means of engaging attention from Washington. It was not obvious what this could be.

## Twilight of Revolution?

Finally, the end of the Cold War brought an end to revolutionary ferment in Latin America. With the collapse of communism, Marxism-Leninism lost legitimacy both as a diagnosis of social ills and (especially) as a prescription for their remedy. Without the Soviet Union, there was no external patron for revolutionary movements. And without any fear of retaliation, either in Latin America or some other part of the world, the United States was free to apply unremitting pressure against revolutionary groups and socialist states.

Guerrilla movements throughout the hemisphere quickly lost force. As a rule, only those groups with continuing sources of income—usually obtained through collaboration with *narcotraficantes*, particularly in Peru and Colombia—could keep up operations. And even then, many *comandantes* were able to interpret handwriting on the wall. In Colombia, the M-19 turned in its arms in order to join the electoral arena; its leader, Antonio Navarro Wolf, ran a respectable campaign in the presidential race of 1994. In Peru, Sendero Luminoso lost momentum and popular support after the capture in 1992 of its enigmatic leader, Abimael Guzmán. The only significant new guerrilla movement of the 1990s appeared in Mexico, in the state of Chiapas, with an essentially reformist agenda. Armed revolution no longer offered a path to redemption.

Socialist states faced difficulties too. In Nicaragua, the *sandinista* government fell victim to final vestiges of the Cold War itself. Unceasing campaigns against the U.S.-supported Contras obliged the government to spend half its budget on defense and to alienate its citizens with the imposition of a military draft and other wartime measures. Partly as a result of such factors, the Nicaraguan economy went into a serious tailspin. In 1990, presidential elections pitted Daniel Ortega, the *sandinista* leader, against Violeta Barrios de Chamorro, widow of Pedro Joaquín Chamorro and representative of a fragmented opposition coalition (UNO, from its Spanish initials). In a stunning reversal of fortune, UNO captured 54.7 percent of the vote against 40.8 percent for the *sandinistas*. At the urging of Jimmy Carter, in attendance as an international observer, Ortega made a gracious concession speech. The Nicaraguan revolution came to an end with a whimper.

But it was in Cuba, perhaps, that the end of the Cold War had its most decisive effect. East-West détente and collapse of the Soviet Union sharply curtailed commercial ties and economic subsidies for Cuba. During the Cold War the USSR had consistently overpaid Cuba for sugar, while Cuba underpaid the Soviets for petroleum: The result was a subsidy estimated at between $3.5 billion and $4.5 billion per year. Termination of this arrangement led to economic devastation. Together with the longstanding U.S. boycott, the implosion of Soviet communism imposed the equivalent of a "double embargo" on the beleaguered island. As a result, the estimated gross domestic product dropped by 45 percent between 1989 and 1993—and continued its downward slide in subsequent years. This meant penury for millions of Cuban citizens: In 1992, according to one official source, 65 percent of Cuban families had monthly incomes equivalent to less than $2.00 (U.S.) per capita at prevailing black-market rates of exchange.

Fidel responded to this adversity with an ambiguous stance, alternating between liberalization and crackdown. Seeking to find a new niche in the global economy, the government began attempting to attract foreign capital, technology, and tourism and to stimulate nontraditional exports. Basically, it appeared that Cuba was moving toward hybrid market-Leninism along the lines of post-Mao China. And in the political realm, crackdowns on dissidents coexisted with an uneasy truce between three groups—reformists, centrists, and hard-line *fidelistas*—with Castro retaining the decisive hand.

Without the inspiration of the Cuban model, the revolutionary option tended to evaporate. Disenchanted by politics in general, Latin Americans gravitated toward social movements instead of partisan campaigns. Having endured human-rights abuses by authoritarian regimes and economic deprivation during the debt crisis, citizens became increasingly skeptical about the uses of the state. No longer inclined to seek utopian solutions, they came to rely on local grassroots movements for the sake of pragmatic, practical change. Paradoxically, the gradual emergence of civil society in Latin America coincided with a downsizing of political ambitions, a focus on self-help, and an acceptance of incremental reform.

For Latin America, however, the questions still remained: how to defend and promote national interests, and how to attract the attention and support of the United States.

## FORMS OF ECONOMIC INTEGRATION

Carefully assessing the post–Cold War era, regional leaders turned their attention to economic issues. Their major concern was to avoid isolation and abandonment. Seeking to overcome the painful crisis of the 1980s, policymakers throughout Latin America came to regard "free trade" as an essential component of any long-term solution to the their economic woes. As they focused on strategies for commercial and financial cooperation, they placed economics over politics, opportunity over principle, pragmatism over ideology. They were playing the geoeconomic game.

The Washington consensus furnished the broad framework for strategic designs. (According to a slogan of the time, "There is no alternative" to free-market approaches—a catchphrase abbreviated as the acronym TINA.) Conventional wisdom exerted extraordinary power in the 1990s. Depending on the location, resources, and economic structures of their countries, however, Latin Americans came up with an imaginative array of policy approaches.

### Model 1: Trading Around

One possibility was to undertake unilateral programs of economic liberalization, more or less according to the Washington consensus, and to strengthen commercial and financial ties with major power centers. A "plurilateral" approach toward economic intercourse seemed to comply with multipolar realities of the new global economy, especially the rise of Europe and Japan. Systematic reduction of commercial barriers promised to achieve the anticipated benefits of free trade. Moreover, unilateral action had the advantage of maintaining flexibility. Within a general strategy of export-led development, the corresponding policy prescriptions were relatively straightforward: Diversify products and partners, seek foreign investment from multiple sources, avoid restrictive entanglements; in other words, embark on a unilateral project in the name of free trade.

Among all countries of Latin America, Chile pursued this option with greatest alacrity. Like other nations of the region, Chile adopted an increasingly protectionist trade policy from the 1930s onward. After the 1973 coup, the Pinochet regime imposed a radical change. Most nontariff barriers were eliminated and tariffs were steadily lowered to a flat rate of 10 percent (they were temporarily increased in the early 1980s but then settled back down to 11 percent). The democratic governments of Patricio Aylwin and Eduardo Frei (Jr.) continued the Pinochet emphasis on commercial liberalization. "Free trade has been widely accepted as an integral part of Chile's development model," according to one well-informed analysis, "and there is consensus that a return to protectionism is not a reasonable option."

Results of this outward-looking strategy were dramatic. Exports as a share of Chile's GDP grew from 31 percent in 1974 to 71 percent in 1990. After sharp contractions in the early 1980s, the economy achieved strong and steady rates of economic growth—reaching 10 percent in 1989 and 11.6 percent in 1992, far outperforming the region as a whole. Chile further achieved unusual success in the diversification of its commercial partnerships. By 1991 Japan had replaced the United States as the country's largest customer. Chile also cultivated extensive trade connections with the European Community (EC), especially with Germany, and imported about as many goods from the EC as a whole as from the United States. By the early 1990s, unilateral liberalization could be scored as a success.

In addition, Chilean leaders aggressively scaled back the role of the state. During the 1970s and 1980s, the Pinochet government sold off about 550 state-owned enterprises, about 90 percent of all state companies inherited from the Allende period; after a mild retrenchment in 1982–1983, due to a short-term economic crisis, the regime resumed the program of privatization. One of its most innovative achievements was reform of social security, which was transformed from a traditional "pay-as-you-go" arrangement (as in the United States) to a system based on individual savings funds administered by private investment institutions. Major state firms—telephones, telecommunications, energy, banking—were sold directly to private bidders or first broken up into competitive firms and then privatized. Only two public monopolies—CODELCO, the state-owned copper company, and ENAP, the petroleum enterprise—remained in state hands. And all of Chile's companies, private or public, became subject to uniform rules and regulations. This general policy stayed in place under subsequent democratic governments: The rate of privatization slowed down somewhat, but Christian Democrats granted numerous concessions to the private sector to build and operate public works (roads, tunnels, ports, bridges, parks). The apparent success of Chile's privatization program transformed the country into a poster child for free-market doctrine and the Washington consensus.

## Model 2: Joining with the North

A second strategy was to find a way to join with the North or, more specifically, with the United States. In the early 1990s Washington encouraged this prospect, perhaps more as a means of confronting economic rivals elsewhere in the world (especially Europe and Japan) rather than of proclaiming solidarity with neighbors in the hemisphere, but the resulting opportunity was nonetheless apparent. It therefore became conceivable, under these new conditions, for countries of

Latin America to align themselves with the United States on economic grounds. This alternative looked attractive because it ensured some form of integration with the world economy.

Affiliation with the North would naturally entail costs. Admission to the club would carry a substantial price, usually consisting of multiple elements:

- Acceptance, at least in broad outline, of the economic tenets of the "Washington consensus."
- Liberal opportunities for foreign investment to operate within the local market.
- Substantial concessions for access to raw materials.
- Low-cost labor for foreign investment.
- In the political realm, loyal cooperation on foreign-policy issues.

Bidding could lead to competition and differences among the countries of Latin America rather than to solidarity. As a Central American legislator ruefully predicted: "We will each vie to become the fifth little tiger."

Among all nations of the region, Mexico was in by far the best position to pursue this option. It had a number of built-in advantages—geographical proximity, petroleum deposits, a relatively skilled workforce, and a large and growing market. The complexity of the bilateral agenda, ranging from drugs to migration to foreign-policy questions, added further incentives for Washington.

The negotiation of NAFTA, described in the previous chapter, made it possible for Mexico to affiliate itself with the dynamic core of world capitalism, but as a conspicuously junior partner. (It goes without saying that this was not the same thing as "joining the First World.") In exchange, Mexico would have to abdicate many of its pretensions to independent political leadership in Latin America or the Third World. And within the bilateral arena, in instances of conflict arising from economic integration, Mexico would face a still-enormous asymmetry in power resources. This was perhaps a bitter trade-off, but it was the essence of the bargain.

Precisely for these reasons, NAFTA was not, in fact, Mexico's first choice. Early in his term Carlos Salinas de Gortari attempted to pursue the kind of "plurilateral" strategy pioneered by Chile, reaching out through commerce and investment to multiple centers of world economic power (and, at the same time, carefully tailoring economic relations with the United States through a series of sector-by-sector agreements). But this option proved not to be viable. Financiers in Europe were directing their resources toward the rehabilitation and reincorporation of Eastern Europe, as Salinas learned to his dismay at a memorable meeting in Davos, Switzerland, in February 1990, and Japanese investors were proving reluctant to meddle in what they saw as a U.S. sphere of interest. Anxious to attract investment capital, Salinas then turned toward the United States. NAFTA would guarantee future access to the U.S. market, ensure the continuation of his economic policies, and, most importantly, send a crucial signal to the business community. In one analyst's summation, an FTA with the United States would provide "an excellent chance to advertise to the world the business opportunities available in Mexico."

## Model 3: Subregional Integration

A third alternative entailed regional (or subregional) economic integration. The region had a long history of efforts in this area, of course, dating from formation of the Latin American Free Trade Area (LAFTA) in 1960. Subregional projects also abounded, from the Central American Common Market (successful in the 1960s) to the Andean Pact (1969) to the Caribbean Common Market (1972). Most of these schemes sought to promote industrial development by expanding markets and erecting protectionist barriers against outside competition. Partly because the economies of member countries tended to be more competitive than complementary, however, regional markets never became especially important: Intraregional market shares peaked at 26 percent for the Central American Common Market, 14 percent within LAFTA/ALADI, and merely 4.8 percent for the Andean Group.

In the aftermath of debt crisis and Cold War, Latin American leaders sought to promote new forms of regional integration. The idea was to foster, not growth through market protection, but integration with the global economy. A principal goal of this strategy, as Monica Hirst has observed, was to "reduce [the possibility of] marginalization in the face of global economic processes." By the late 1990s, Latin America had created more than thirty collective or "minilateral" schemes for economic cooperation.

Some projects sought to utilize subregional integration as a pathway toward broader integration. The Central American Common Market was resuscitated, CARICOM reinvigorated, and the Andean Pact reshaped and revitalized. The general goal was to avoid exclusion from the global economy. The more specific goal was to use these schemes as means of gaining access to larger and more important groupings, particularly NAFTA or FTAA. Successful experiments could assist this process in two ways: by demonstrating the capacity of member countries for submitting to the disciplines of international accords, and by consolidating markets and (perhaps) production processes. In tandem, it was thought, these features could enhance the attractiveness of the group (and its members) in the eyes of larger nations and/or blocs. They could also strengthen bargaining positions. As Miguel Rodríguez-Mendoza has written, such subregional groupings "are seen as 'paths' toward larger integration efforts at both the Latin American and hemispheric level."

A second subregional scheme involved the creation of markets for their own sake. The most conspicuous case was the "Common Market of the South," known from its Spanish acronym as MERCOSUR. This effort began with a bilateral agreement between Argentina and Brazil and soon included Uruguay and Paraguay. Under the Treaty of Asunción, created in March 1991, the four member countries committed themselves to construct by December 1994 a customs union, with a common external tariff (CET), and to move toward a full-fledged common market in subsequent years. There were setbacks—partners resisted the CET, and both Argentina and Brazil raised some tariffs in response to the 1995 Mexican "tequila effect" and the 1997 Asian crisis. In view of longstanding rivalries among its members, however, MERCOSUR was a truly remarkable development. Its partner countries comprised nearly one-half of Latin America's gross domestic product, more than 40 percent of its total population, and about one-third of its foreign trade. By 1995 MERCOSUR had a combined GDP of $714 billion, making it the world's fourth-largest integrated market—after NAFTA, the European Union, and Japan.

Moreover, MERCOSUR had clear political goals: the consolidation of democracy and the maintenance of peace throughout the Southern Cone. Argentina and Brazil reached agreement on the uses of nuclear capacity. And at a summit gathering in 1992, all four presidents agreed to stipulate that "an indispensable assumption for the existence and development of MERCOSUR is that democratic institutions are in force." In practical terms MERCOSUR provided civilian democrats with regular opportunities for consultation and mutual support, thus offsetting the long-established conclaves for chieftains of the armed forces.

The project's designers saw it as a dynamic institution, one that would evolve over time and crystallize relations with economies of the North. MERCOSUR thus came to be seen as a powerful instrument for bargaining with both the United States and the European Union. Contradictory tendencies nonetheless emerged: Argentina for some time expressed eagerness to negotiate its own FTA with the United States (and/or NAFTA), an act that would have led to the dismantling of MERCOSUR. Within all such subregional groupings, trade-offs between unilateral initiative and multilateral solidarity posed individual countries with agonizing policy dilemmas.

## Model 4: Hubs and Spokes

Economic integration schemes also promoted geopolitical interests. This was particularly evident in the emergence of "hub-and-spoke" formations. Under this system, a central country, or "hub," enjoys special preference in the market of each "spoke" country under a series of separate bilateral agreements. The spokes, however, do not have preferential access to each other's markets; even worse, they have to compete among themselves for preferences within the hub market. As explained in chapter 9, what is good for the hub is not always good for the spokes.

There were initial fears that the United States was intent on the formation of a hemispheric hub-and-spoke system with itself at the center. It was this concern, in fact, that prompted a reluctant Canadian government to join the U.S.-Mexican negotiations over what would eventually become NAFTA. Rather than become one of two competitive spokes in a North American market, it was preferable for Ottawa to take full part in the creation of a trilateral arrangement.

Efforts to avoid a U.S.-centric system did not, however, prevent Latin American countries from attempting to create their own hub-and-spoke arrangements. By virtue of size and/or strategic location, only three nations had realistic opportunities to pursue this strategy in the post–Cold War era: Chile, Mexico, and Brazil.

Starting in the early 1990s, Chile supplanted its pattern of unilateral liberalization with a selective network of bilateral FTAs. In 1991 the Aylwin administration reached an agreement with Mexico, for the purpose of establishing an FTA by January 1996. In 1993 the government forged compacts with Colombia, for an operational FTA by 1994, and with Venezuela, for the realization of free trade by 1999. Chile also concluded less ambitious agreements with Argentina, Bolivia, Canada, Costa Rica, Ecuador, and Uruguay. The goals of these negotiations were manifold: to open new markets, to ensure supplies of critical products (such as petroleum), and to establish Chile's position as a continental leader. Moreover, the FTAs would provide Chile with a small measure of protection from the vagaries of an uncertain world.

In contrast to Chile's approach, the Mexican strategy was to establish itself as the central interlocutor between the United States and Latin America. This could be welcome to Washington, given its long and troubled history of relations with Latin America; it could also provide considerable leverage for Mexico and compensate for Mexico's loss of independence in other areas of foreign policy. As a founding member of NAFTA, Mexico could exercise a veto over applications for admission. This alone represented a substantial source of hemispheric influence.

Mexico thus began pursuing a series of subregional negotiations: the bilateral pact with Chile (1991), compacts with Central America (1991, 1992), a trilateral arrangement with Venezuela and Colombia (1993) to create the *Grupo de los Tres*, and a bilateral accord with Bolivia (1994). The resulting pattern created a good deal of confusion, but their political meaning was clear: As long as NAFTA expansion remained the chosen path to integration, any road to hemispheric free trade (and the U.S. market) would have to go through Mexico. By the same token, hemisphere-wide negotiations for FTAA would tend to diminish the Mexican role. (In fact, all three members of NAFTA—even the United States—stood to have less bargaining power in FTAA negotiations than they would have on NAFTA accessions.)

Brazil took yet a different tack, attempting to affirm its position as a subregional hegemon rather than as a conduit to the United States. Already the dominant country within MERCOSUR, Brazil officially launched in April 1994 its proposal for a South American Free Trade Area (SAFTA). The stated goal was to create a free trade zone for "substantially all trade" within the continent (in GATT-speak)—that is, on all products except those touching on "sensitive" national interests. This meant about 80 percent of intraregional trade. Public intentions were manifold: to capitalize on the experience of MERCOSUR, to reach out to neighboring countries (and groups), and to accumulate negotiating power for dealing with broader integration schemes in the Americas. Moreover, SAFTA would confirm Brazil's historic claim to be a continental hegemon, its longstanding sense of manifest destiny. By itself, without any formal link to North America or the United States, SAFTA would reflect and ratify regional domination by Brazil. Alternatively, Brazil would become the principal intermediary between the continent and the United States. Either way, SAFTA would strengthen Brazil's international position. It would become the hub of South America.

## THE OUTSIDE WORLD

In the early 1990s it appeared that Latin America would have little chance of striking major deals with extrahemispheric powers and thus offsetting the hegemonic position of the United States. By the middle of the decade, however, regional leaders were making determined efforts to develop economic (and political) ties to outside powers. In differing degrees, they courted two possible allies: the European Union and the Asia-Pacific region, especially Japan. (Both objects of affection, it might be noted, were advanced industrial regions or countries. In a sense this quest for extrahemispheric partnership represented an attempt to extend and consolidate connections with the North.)

### The European Campaign

Efforts to engage European powers in Latin America had a long historical tradition. In 1974, Europe made a modest reappearance in the Americas with the initiation of biennial meetings of parliamentarians. In 1984, Europe discreetly opposed the Reagan administration's policy in Central America through the San José dialogue. Starting in 1990, the European Community (by this time known as the European Union) developed steady interaction with the Rio Group.

There were significant economic ties as well. The European Union was taking in nearly 20 percent of Latin American exports. It was the region's second-leading source of direct foreign investment (during the 1980s, in fact, Latin America received a larger share of net FDI from Europe than from the United States). Europe was also the largest source of economic aid for Latin America: In 1993 the combined total for the EU and member states accounted for 61.5 percent of total assistance to the region, far ahead of Japan and the United States. By 1996 the Union's aid commitment was nearly 50 percent greater than in 1991.

On a rhetorical level, these economic ties were often reinforced by reference to common historic and cultural linkages. In the words of one EU document:

> Latin America's cultural identity is heavily imbued with the values that shaped Europe's character and history. Five centuries of uninterrupted relations between the two regions have caused European ideals to permeate to the core of Latin American societies, which have in turn exercised an irresistible pull on the old continent. Constitutions, legal principles and ideas of liberty and democracy found across Latin America are drawn from the body of philosophical and legal concepts that are Europe's heritage.

This seemed like a generous assessment, given complex legacies of conquest and imperialism, but it served to make the point: Europe and Latin America had much in common, including rivalry with (or resentment of) the United States.

After joining the European Community in 1986, Spain took the lead in promoting strong ties with Latin America. Spanish companies poured billions of dollars into Latin America, purchasing telephone companies, banks, hotels, and airlines in such countries as Argentina, Chile, Mexico, Peru, Venezuela, and Cuba. The government organized state visits by King Juan Carlos to key countries, intensified cultural exchanges, and, since 1991, sponsored an annual Ibero-American Summit. Televisión Española was carried on cable systems almost everywhere, and magazines like *Hola!* and *Interviú* were widely circulated. In Spanish circles, the overall policy came to be known as the creation of "an Ibero-American space." But while Spain wanted to maintain its position as the critical link between the EU and Latin America—as a hub between two large regional spokes—Latin American leaders, for their part, preferred to deal directly with the EU as a whole. They had little desire to leave their commercial links—and access to capital—in the hands of one of the EU's junior members.

In October 1994 the European Council adopted a general policy proposal for a new partnership with Latin America. In December 1995 EU negotiators signed a framework agreement with MERCOSUR. Its immediate purpose was to promote close relations in political, economic, commercial, industrial, scientific, technological, institutional, and cultural fields. It sought to strengthen democracy and respect for human rights and called for regular political dialogue as well as economic cooperation. The eventual goal was "to pave the way for an Interregional Association in the medium term." But beyond all the talk, there was not much material progress. One critical issue would be opening the European market to agricultural goods from Latin America, as Brazilian President Fernando Henrique Cardoso bluntly observed during a visit to London in December 1997.

EU negotiators also undertook discussions with individual Latin American countries. In June 1996 the Union reached a framework agreement with Chile, which was just about to become an associate member of MERCOSUR. Around that same time the EU began talks with Mexico, which had managed to emerge from the 1994–1995 peso crisis as a plausible partner—partly because of its consumer market, partly because of its access to the United States. From the Mexican standpoint, an EU accord offered a way to reduce dependence on the United States (apparently increasing under NAFTA). In turn, NAFTA provided Mexico with a valuable asset for negotiations: "The special treatment that Mexico is receiving from the bosom of the EU is justified by the country's sui generis location. . . . *Geopolitics is destiny,*" as Francisco Gil Villegas wrote, "and for once Mexico does not deserve to be pitied because of its proximity to the United States."

In late 1997, Mexico and the EU announced agreements for economic partnership, political cooperation, and cultural exchange, much along the lines of the MERCOSUR accords. Exulted Mexican foreign minister José Ángel Gurría: "With this agreement we initiate a new and ambitious relationship with the European Union . . . Europe is today a high priority for our foreign policy." This offered the prospect for diversification of international ties and for an alliance, as well, with a "trustworthy partner" in confronting the United States. The allusion, quite clearly, was to the Helms-Burton law, which Mexico and the EU both condemned. United States policy toward Cuba was thus encouraging Mexican ties with Europe.

## The Asia Card

In anticipation of the much-touted "Pacific century," Latin American leaders turned toward Asia as well. This was not only the world's most dynamic region through the early 1990s; with its development model, it also appeared to hold the keys to economic success. The "Asia card" became a potential trump for Latin America.

One way to pursue this avenue was through bilateral ties—principally with Japan, thought to provide a useful counterweight to the United States at this time, and to a lesser extent with China. Conspicuous here were the efforts of Peru, which unleashed "Fujimori fever" throughout Japan with the 1990 election of a president of Japanese descent, and of Brazil, which hosted the world's largest Japanese émigré community. Mexico also sought close links with Japan. President Ernesto Zedillo and Prime Minister Ryutaro Hashimoto exchanged state visits—and in May 1997, after a three-and-a-half-year hiatus (due to political and economic instability in Mexico), the two countries resumed bilateral private-sector talks.

The other mechanism for courting the Asia-Pacific region was APEC, the Asia-Pacific Economic Cooperation forum—which represented 40 percent of the world's population, 55 percent of its wealth, and 46 percent of all world trade. APEC was an unusual institution, preferring to work through consensus rather than traditional diplomatic agreements. Under pressure from the United States, to be sure, the organization agreed to establish an FTA by the year 2020, but in general it evinced a loose form of association that relied on unilateral cooperation rather than political coercion.

In principle, APEC adhered to the high-minded (if oxymoronic) idea of "open regionalism"—a pattern of regional integration that would be outward oriented, not inward looking, designed to achieve integration with the world economy rather than protection from it. As construed in Latin America, open regionalism implied two understandings: average external tariffs (and NTBs) by any member must not be elevated against non-FTA countries, and opportunities for accession by nonmembers should be clearly available. As practiced by APEC, however, open regionalism referred mainly to voluntary agreements by member countries to liberalize trade in concert, according to a common timetable.

Three Latin American countries gained admission to APEC during the 1990s. First was Mexico, largely under the shelter of NAFTA. Second was Chile, which had for some time aspired to establish connections with the Pacific Rim. During the 1980s, in fact, the Pinochet regime began to resuscitate nineteenth-century notions about the country's "manifest destiny" in the Pacific—while also searching for economic partners who would not condemn the regime for human-rights abuse. And soon after its democratic transition, Chile launched a concerted diplomatic initiative toward APEC membership.

Third was Peru, which, like Chile, mounted a persistent diplomatic campaign. At an early stage, Malaysia—the largest importer of Peruvian tin—justified its support for Lima's application on the ground that APEC should not give undue emphasis to human rights and other nontrade issues. Probably more crucial was the role of Japan—which was eager to express gratitude for Peru's support of Tokyo's bid to gain permanent membership in the UN Security Council (and, it is said, for Fujimori's decisive resolution of the Japanese hostage crisis of 1996–1997). So Peru received an invitation to join, along with Vietnam and Russia, in November 1997, just as APEC announced a ten-year moratorium on new memberships.

Although these APEC accessions represented genuine diplomatic triumphs, it was not entirely clear what benefits would result. Precisely because APEC was such a loose organization, Latin Americans did not obtain binding commitments from other members. Nor did it offer an unambiguous means of counteracting U.S. hegemony, since the United States was APEC's most powerful member. Finally, the Asian crisis of 1997–1998 reduced the practical and symbolic value of association with APEC. Asia no longer looked like the answer to Latin America's development problems; indeed, the crisis itself threatened to have negative fallout for countries of Latin America.

### The Problem of Asymmetrical Significance

There was every reason for nations of Latin America—such as Mexico, Chile, and MERCOSUR members—to seek close ties with extrahemispheric powers in Europe and the Asia-Pacific region. Since the mid-1990s, Mexico had been stressing the importance of "diversification" in economic and diplomatic relations. Seeing itself as a "global trader," with commerce all over the world, Brazil also aspired to consolidate links with Europe and the Asia-Pacific region. To emphasize the point, President Fernando Henrique Cardoso insisted that Europe was "central" to Brazil and, by implication, to the rest of South America.

The question was whether Latin America's would-be partners shared this same conviction. How important was Latin America for Europe and Asia?

The sad truth was: not very. This condition of "asymmetrical significance" had serious consequences. It meant that Latin America would give high priority to extrahemispheric negotiations, but the EU and Asia would give them much less time, attention, and energy. Latin America was likely to seek binding and long-term agreements; the EU and Asia would be inclined to settle for vague declarations of principle. Above all, the EU and Japan would not want to undertake any Latin American agreements that might jeopardize larger interests in other parts of the world; in particular, they would not want to antagonize the United States. Under such circumstances, the potential for miscommunication and disenchantment in discussions between Latin America and the EU or Japan became extremely high.

Trade indicators offered one insight into the extent of this asymmetry. As of the mid-1990s, the world's leading economic entities—the United States, the European Union, and Japan—were trading more with advanced industrial countries than with developing areas. The United States conducted 15 percent to 18 percent of its trade with Latin America, but more than half of that was with Mexico alone. The European Union carried on barely 5 percent of its external trade with Latin America, while Japan did only 3 percent to 4 percent. Investments showed a similar picture. Despite expansion in the 1990s, Latin American holdings represented modest proportions of total FDI for prominent investor countries. The major economic centers tended to circulate funds among themselves. To put it more precisely, the United States and Europe were investing in one another, while Japan was investing in both (but twice as much in the United States as in Europe). Despite its efforts and its aspirations, Latin America was not a major economic partner for Japan or the EU.

The outside world might well be important to Latin America, in sum, but Latin America was not so important to the outside world (i.e., to the EU, Japan, or China as of the 1990s). As *The Economist* pithily observed about EU-MERCOSUR relations: "The trouble is that Europe is not, in fact, central to Latin Americans, and still less so—far less so—are they to it. Uncle Sam has not for years been the only, all-powerful outside figure that counted to them, as myth had it. But he is still number one."

## LEGACIES OF NEOLIBERAL REFORM

Faced by international pressures and the threat of economic marginalization, Latin America's leaders hastened to impose reformist policies in the 1980s and 1990s. They lowered tariff and nontariff barriers to trade, opened doors to foreign investment, sold off public enterprises, and reduced the role of the state. Out of necessity or choice, often at the expense of lower-income strata in their own societies, policymakers dutifully obeyed the "neoliberal" prescriptions of the Washington consensus.

Practical consequences of this strategy showed up in data on trade. According to Figure 10-1, Latin American exports (to the rest of the world) increased by nearly 300 percent during the decade of the 1990s. And as protectionist barriers were dismantled, imports increased by almost 400 percent. To this degree, the region was reverting to the export-import patterns of the early twentieth century. This promised to bring substantial benefits. It also entailed considerable risk.

As free-market reforms began taking hold, Latin America finally resumed the path of growth. For 1991–1998 the annual average growth rate for the region as a whole was 3.5 percent, a vast improvement over the dismal record of the 1980s. Chile led the way with an average of 7.4 percent, followed by Argentina (5.8 percent) and Peru (4.8 percent). But there were downsides as well. Some of the largest nations in the region—Brazil, Mexico, Venezuela—posted average growth rates of 3 percent or less. The figure for the Caribbean was just 1.6 percent. Yet year-to-year patterns for most countries tended to be sluggish and uneven. To be sure, economists hailed 1997 as "the best performance in a quarter of a century," with a 5.2 percent growth rate, but there was no guarantee that this would continue. Partly as a result of contagions from Asia and Russia, in fact, the rate for 1998 fell to merely 2.3 percent.

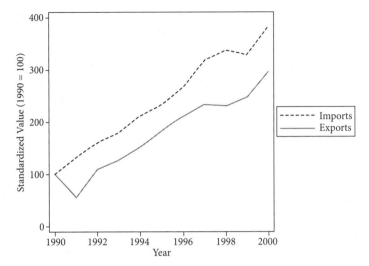

**Figure 10-1** **Latin American Imports and Exports, 1990–2000 (1990 = 100)**
Source: International Monetary Fund, *Direction of Trade Statistics,* 1991–2001.

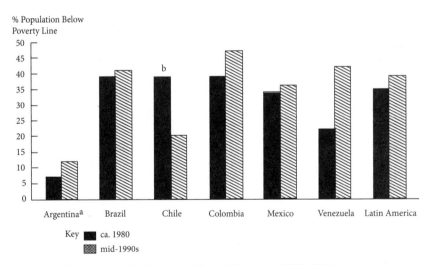

**Figure 10-2** **Poverty in Latin America: Selected Countries, 1980–1990s**
[a] Urban sample only.
[b] Figure for 1987.
Source: Comisión Económica para América Latina y el Caribe, *Panorama social de América Latina 1997* (Santiago de Chile: CEPAL, 1998), pp. 207–208.

Stop-and-go recovery failed to ameliorate one of Latin America's most pervasive and persistent problems: the blight of poverty. According to CEPAL estimates, in fact, the relative incidence of poverty increased, from 35 percent in 1980 to 39 percent in the 1990s. As a result of population growth, this meant that the absolute number of people living under conditions of poverty swelled from 125 million to 186 million, an increase of nearly 50 percent. And as revealed in Figure 10-2, poverty levels held steady or increased in every major nation of the region except Chile. Tangible benefits of economic reform were not yet trickling down.

Indeed, it appeared that the market-led expansion of the 1990s was exacerbating social inequality. Prosperous sectors were doing well, those in the middle faced uncertainty, and those at the bottom—from industrial workers to self-subsistent *campesinos*—were lagging far behind. Working people continued to suffer the brunt of restructuring: In Mexico and Argentina, the average wage in the mid-1990s was 30 percent below 1980 levels; in Peru, the average worker was making just over a third of what he or she made in 1980. The richest quintile in Latin America received nineteen times the income of the poorest 20 percent. In Brazil, the wealthiest 10 percent enjoyed more than half the nation's income; in Chile and Venezuela, the top tenth took in over 40 percent of the total; in Mexico and Colombia, the figure was approaching 40 percent as well. Overall, Latin America displayed the highest rates of income inequality in the entire world.

This situation could have serious political repercussions. "After almost a decade of reform," wrote Sebastian Edwards in 1997, "the region has little to show in improved economic performance and social conditions. Poverty has not been reduced. Growth has been modest at best. In many countries wages have stagnated and job creation has been sluggish. The reining in of inflation has been one of the few commendable accomplishments. . . . " Without visible signs of improvement, Edwards continued, "political support for Latin American reformist governments will erode". Since the United States was so closely identified with the "Washington consensus" that promoted neoliberal economic reform, this could have profoundly negative implications for U.S.–Latin American relations.

## PROTEST AND RESISTANCE

The vagaries and complexities of the post–Cold War world prompted intense intellectual and attitudinal ferment throughout Latin America. The 1990s became a time for rethinking orthodox wisdom, reassessing long-held assumptions, discarding outmoded shibboleths. As leaders and citizens searched for new ideas and solutions, the very meanings of standard political categories—left, right, center—were coming into question. Rearrangements of power in the global and hemispheric arena not only altered the terms of diplomatic and commercial intercourse; they revised perceptions and outlooks as well, altering "cognitive maps" that Latin Americans had constructed about their world, their continent, and themselves.

Perhaps the most conspicuous change was a sharp transformation of other nations' views of the United States. In the wake of the Cold War, peoples of Latin America adopted and expressed increasingly favorable opinions about their northern neighbor. The implosion of the Soviet Union and the collapse of socialist ideology appeared, for many, to confirm the legitimacy (or at least the inevitability) of U.S. leadership throughout the hemisphere. In this new context, the United States was not so much a resented Colossus of the North; it was a triumphant major power. Intimacy with U.S. presidents, rather than anti-imperialist rhetoric, suddenly became a positive commodity in Latin American politics.

Changing views of the United States went hand in hand with relaxation of traditional nationalism. Throughout Latin America, ruling elites were busily engaged in the redefinition (or dismissal) of the classical nationalism that sought to uphold historic principles of sovereignty and self-determination. In pragmatic and flexible fashion, they were tending to define national interests in terms of geoeconomic opportunity, not political principle, and they seemed fully prepared to surrender portions of sovereignty in the interests of regional integration. This transformation was probably more thorough among ruling elites than among the citizenry as a whole. And though it represented a remarkable change, its significance should not be overestimated: Temporarily silenced in the early 1990s, voices of nationalism would make themselves heard once again as the century drew to a close.

Softened sentiments and soothing rhetoric were unlikely to achieve hemispheric harmony. While Latin America was becoming *less* nationalistic in the 1990s, the United States was becoming *more* nationalistic. Within the United States, the end of the Cold War and victory in the 1990 Gulf War set off demonstrations of patriotic triumphalism, just as economic rivalry with Europe and especially Japan prompted expressions of defensive nativism. Indeed, many observers in the United States were interpreting the movement toward orthodox liberalism and free trade within the hemisphere—from NAFTA to the EAI and FTAA—as yet another confirmation of the wisdom and superiority of U.S.-style capitalism. While Latin Americans were seeking a new partnership with the United States, in other words, the United States was anticipating unilateral dominion throughout the Western Hemisphere.

There were subtle signs of restiveness. Even as their strategic options narrowed, Latin American governments refused to comply with Washington's directives on some key policy questions. Throughout the 1990s they voted unanimously for resolutions in the UN General Assembly condemning the U.S. embargo of Cuba. In mid-1994, fourteen presidents of Latin American governments—members of the so-called Rio Group— reiterated this appeal, calling for suspension of the U.S. embargo in exchange for "a peaceful transition toward a democratic and pluralist system in Cuba." Beneath the protestations of harmony, lingering tensions prevailed.

Among the populace at large, the uneven and apparently unfair consequences of economic liberalization gave rise to mounting waves of social protest. In 1989, crowds in Caracas erupted in a riot against the "structural adjustment" program imposed by once-popular president Carlos Andrés Pérez; as a sign of continuing resistance, student protests commemorated the anniversary of the so-called *caracazo* throughout the 1990s. By 1998 the country's soon-to-be president, Hugo

---

**BOX 10-1**

### A Voice from the South

Antiglobalization activists organized the World Social Forum (WSF) as a counterpart to the World Economic Forum, an annual meeting in Davos, Switzerland, that draws together heads of state, finance ministers, CEOs of transnational corporations, business journalists, and major media representatives.

The WSF first took place in 2001 in Porto Alegre, Brazil, and has met every year since then. It is a protest movement on behalf of the developing world, what is sometimes known as "the South." Responding to the claim that economic globalization is "inevitable," participants have adopted the slogan that "Another World Is Possible."

WSF is a space for reflection and debate rather than a policymaking body. According to its Charter of Principles:

- The alternatives proposed at the World Social Forum stand in opposition to a process of globalisation commanded by the large multinational corporations and by the governments and international institutions at the service of those corporations' interests, with the complicity of national governments. They are designed to ensure that globalisation in solidarity will prevail as a new stage in world history. This will respect universal human rights, and those of all citizens—men and women—of all nations and the environment and will rest on democratic international systems and institutions at the service of social justice, equality and the sovereignty of peoples.

- The World Social Forum brings together and interlinks only organisations and movements of civil society from all the countries in the world, but intends neither to be a body representing world civil society....

- The World Social Forum is a plural, diversified, non-confessional, non-governmental and non-party context that, in a decentralised fashion, interrelates organisations and movements engaged in concrete action at levels from the local to the national to build another world.

Essentially, WSF offers an opportunity for people from less developed areas to express grievances, present demands, and generate political support. And although the WSF does not make policy, it is nonetheless significant: There were 155,000 registered participants at the 2005 meeting in Porto Alegre. And because of its geographical origins, the WSF has come to be closely identified with the government of Brazil.

Chávez Frías, a retired army colonel who had led a military coup attempt in 1992, took a populist stance that hinted at a moratorium on debt payments, protectionism against foreign trade, and reconsideration of concessions to foreign oil companies. In January 1994 peasant rebels in the Mexican state of Chiapas denounced NAFTA and its inequities as one of the reasons for their uprising. In 1997 a coalition of social movements seized the cathedral of Quito, in Ecuador, demanding an end to privatization and to a hard-nosed policy package; in 1999 mass movements throughout the country forced the president to soften austerity measures and to cancel a sixty-day state of emergency. In Argentina, as elsewhere, labor unions vigorously denounced structural adjustment programs, especially their impact on employment, with the teachers' union in the vanguard of the charge. Labor manifestations also took place in Brazil, where open unemployment increased sharply, and the presidential candidate of the country's second-largest party—the Workers' Party—vigorously opposed neoliberal economic policies in the 1998 campaign. Political parties in Uruguay and other nations also mounted serious challenges to the neoliberal orthodoxy. Ordinary citizens and social movements were taking fervent issue with free-market dogma and its inequitable outcomes.

## Policy Debates

Within this context of uncertainty and protest, economists and social scientists throughout Latin America were seeking to articulate feasible alternatives to the "Washington consensus." One vital issue concerned the optimal role of the state. Conventional wisdom tended to exalt the omniscience of the market. According to this view, Latin America could find the keys to development merely by "opening" its economies—by enabling external forces to reshape and reinvigorate factors of production through trade and investment. Latin America's principal task was to become a passive recipient of these benevolent influences. States should merely get out of the way and, in the most literal sense, adopt a laissez-faire stance.

A growing corps of analysts came forth to dispute this contention. Market forces were not always efficient or benign. They could lead to unnecessary problems and exacerbate difficult situations, as in Mexico in 1994–1995 and in Brazil in 1998–1999. If it had been necessary for the market to discipline irresponsible states in the early 1990s, it might now be time for states to discipline irresponsible markets. Drawing upon the so-called "Asian model" of development, as typified in Korea and Japan, commentators and policymakers began to stress the need for strong and capable states (which, it will be remembered, were implicitly required by the Washington consensus itself). Instead of "downsizing" the state, the new imperative was "rightsizing"—creating efficient centers of authority that could shape, direct, and channel market forces in productive and equitable directions.

Such concerns crystallized in accelerating debates over a "second generation of reforms"—that is, reforms that would follow upon the initial wave of economic liberalization and neoliberal adjustment. Almost everyone agreed that a new cycle of reform was needed. The question was what they should entail. Die-hard free-marketeers argued that the next step should be to extend and complete the reforms of the 1980s and early 1990s, removing any remaining impediments to market forces and carrying neoliberal prescriptions to their ultimate conclusion. Others claimed that the most urgent task should be to address the problems of poverty and income distribution—which had resulted partly from the first wave of reforms and which were now provoking social protests and rebellions throughout the region. Still others insisted that the next phase should focus on the unfinished tasks of democratization, particularly the creation of institutions that were truly accountable and the empowerment of civil society. These debates were far from merely academic: They defined crucial issues and priorities for public discussion, political resolution, and long-term strategy.

One of the most deliberate and thoughtful analyses of Latin America's predicament emerged from the Economic Commission for Latin America and the Caribbean (ECLAC), the same institution that had so convincingly espoused import-substitution industrialization during the 1950s and 1960s. *Cepalista* policymakers fashioned a series of ideas that stressed the need for national development policies. Analyzing the much-heralded models of East Asia, especially the "four tigers," ECLAC economists argued that Latin America suffered from a relative lack of investment in technology, especially in its exploitation of natural resources. Recognizing the connection between politics and economics, they maintained that the region faced a dual challenge: reinforcing nascent democratic structures in Latin America, and providing effective support for opening national economies within the global system. These imperatives called for substantial investment in human resources, particularly education, which ECLAC regarded as a critical priority.

Economic stimulus could not come merely from outside. On the contrary, according to this view, "Growth is from inside outward and is supply-driven." The key issues confronting Latin America were matters of national policy rather than external commercial arrangements. Free trade alone was not the answer: The challenge was to define Latin America's optimal position in the world economy and to implement policies accordingly. Even in the global economy of the 1990s, with all its uncertainties and ambiguities, Latin America could and should take charge of its future.

## QUESTIONS FOR REVIEW

1. How did the end of the Cold War affect the political atmosphere in Latin America? What happened to Cuba as a result?
2. By the early 1990s, what was the plausible range of policy options available to Latin America?
3. Why did some countries decide to strengthen their links to the United States? What were the results of their efforts?
4. What were the underlying goals of MERCOSUR? Which countries founded it, and why?
5. How did the 1990s affect nationalism and popular culture in Latin America and in the United States?

# CHAPTER 11

# Post 9/11: The War on Terror

I don't have the foggiest idea about what I think about
international, foreign policy.

GEORGE W. BUSH (1997)

We are still living in the 9/11 era. The names and faces are
different, the White House has changed hands, and the country
has turned its gaze from our distant wars to the economic crisis
on the home front. But American foreign policy is still defined
by the choices our leaders made while ground zero smoldered
and the objectives they set. Our approach to the world was
fundamentally altered by 9/11, and nothing that's happened
since has undone that transformation.

NEW YORK TIMES COLUMNIST ROSS DOUTHAT (2011)

The twenty-first century dawned brightly over the Americas. The Cold War
was a fading memory. Central America's frightful civil wars had given way to
peacefully negotiated settlements. Electoral democracy was taking root throughout the hemisphere. The Organization of American States was gaining authority
and respect. A Free Trade Area of the Americas (FTAA) loomed on the horizon.
Citizens of Latin America admired the United States and its popular culture,
including hip-hop music and Hollywood films. These were halcyon days.

During the presidential campaign of 2000, Republican candidate George W.
Bush—the governor of Texas, a major border state—earnestly vowed that he would
"look south, not as an afterthought but as a fundamental commitment." Soon after
taking office he traveled to Mexico for an upbeat, one-on-one meeting with counterpart Vicente Fox and agreed to consider the possibility of immigration reform.
At a Summit of the Americas meeting shortly thereafter in Quebec City, Canada,
Bush expressed his support for FTAA and proclaimed the onset of "the century of
the Americas." Such long-awaited rhetoric gratified political leaders from the Río
Bravo to the Tierra del Fuego. For the first time in decades, a U.S. president was
placing Latin America near the top of his foreign policy agenda.

September 11, 2001, changed all that. In response to the horrendous attacks
of that day, the Bush administration unleashed a "global war on terror" that would

utterly transform the conduct of world politics and of inter-American affairs. The antiterror campaign affected every item on the U.S.–Latin American agenda—migration, trade, and drug trafficking. If the 1990s had been a decade of geoeconomics, this would be a time of geopolitics. Nothing was the same as it had been.

## UNLEASHING WAR

Americans responded to the 9/11 assaults with fear, mourning, and cries for revenge. Suspicions almost immediately focused on Al Qaeda, a terrorist network organized by the mysterious Osama bin Laden. Son of a Saudi billionaire, bin Laden was a fundamentalist Muslim who fought alongside Afghan *mujahadeen* in their successful guerrilla war against the Soviet Union (1979–1989). He thereafter went on to proclaim an Islamic *jihad*—against Israel, against the United States, against modernity in general. Bin Laden's network was thought to be responsible for at least two attacks in previous years—the bombings of U.S. embassies in Nairobi, Kenya, and dar es Salaam, Tanzania, in 1998 and the explosion of the U.S. Navy destroyer *Cole* in 2000. His ultimate intention was the formation of a pan-Islamic theocratic state, one that would uphold religious tradition and assert itself as a world power. Forced to leave his native Saudi Arabia and later Sudan, he had found safe haven in Afghanistan, then under the control of a relentlessly fundamentalist movement known as the Taliban.

It was only a matter of days before the still-untested president declared the U.S. response. In a memorable speech on September 20, Bush vowed to use military force as necessary. Calling for sacrifice and patience from the American people, he set ambitious and far-reaching goals. "Our war on terror begins with Al Qaeda," the president said, "but it does not stop there. It will not end until every terrorist group of global reach has been found, stopped, and defeated." He delivered a stern warning to governments around the world. The United States, he said, "will pursue nations that provide aid or safe haven to terrorism"—not only Afghanistan under the Taliban but other countries as well. As a result, Bush continued, "Every nation in every region now has a decision to make. Either you are with us, or you are with the terrorists. From this day forward, any nation that continues to harbor or support terrorists will be regarded by the United States as a hostile regime." The speech not only issued a general call to arms but also laid the cornerstone for Bush's two-term presidency.

The American public stood firmly behind its newly focused leader, whose approval ratings approached unheard-of levels around 90 percent. Surveys found that between 85 and 92 percent of Americans advocated the use of military force "against groups that are identified as responsible." CBS/*New York Times* polls revealed that two-thirds of Americans would support military action "even if it means that innocent people are killed." Similarly, an *NBC News* poll found 78 percent in agreement with the statement that "combating terrorism is worth risking civilian casualties in Afghanistan." Americans thought the antiterrorist campaign should employ a full arsenal of strategies—not only military force but also diplomatic efforts, financial and economic instruments, enforcement of the law, and secret intelligence. At the same time, they expressed strong support for multilateral cooperation. A Harris poll found 95 percent support for the need to "build a strong international coalition of many countries to support us"—remarkably, "even if this means exercising more restraint than we'd like." An Associated Press poll revealed that 90 percent said that the United Nations, much maligned in U.S. conservative circles, should "play a major role in pulling countries together to fight terrorism."

The Bush administration designed a multifaceted strategy. One element involved formation of a multilateral alliance against terrorism and/or Al Qaeda and/or Afghanistan's Taliban regime. (More than twenty NATO and other countries took part in Operation Enduring Freedom, with most making modest or symbolic contributions; the United Kingdom and Pakistan were the most significant allies.) Bombing sorties in Afghanistan began on October 7, less than a month after the 9/11 attacks. On-the-ground raids by commando units followed soon thereafter.

American firepower took a staggering toll, especially on the ruling Taliban. By December 2001 the U.S.-led coalition was able to patch together an interim government under the moderate leadership of Hamid Karzai, a genial figure and practicing Muslim. That turned out to be the easy part. What the Pentagon called the "long shadow war" was still in its early stages.

September 2001: Cradling in his hand the badge of a fallen police officer, President Bush vows to avenge the loss of American lives on 9/11 through a "global war on terror."
SOURCE: AP Photo/Pool, Win McNamee.

In his January 2002 state of the union address, President Bush vowed to extend the antiterrorist campaign. "What we have found in Afghanistan confirms that, far from ending there, our war against terrorism is only beginning. . . . Thousands of dangerous killers, schooled in the methods of murder, often supported by outlaw regimes, are now spread throughout the world like ticking time bombs, set to go off without warning." Sharply critical of regimes that permitted or supported terrorist action, he denounced three governments—Iraq, Iran, and North Korea—as constituting an "axis of evil." While the United States would seek international support for its policies, it would be willing to act on its own. In the president's words, "Some governments will be timid in the face of terror. And make no mistake about it: If they do not act, America will."

The war on terror led to fundamental revisions in U.S. military doctrine. Strategy during the Cold War was based on the idea of "mutual assured destruction." The United States would employ its nuclear arsenal only in response to nuclear attack; so long as a retaliatory "second strike" could be sufficiently devastating, the threat would serve as an effective deterrent. In a commencement address at West Point in June 2002, President Bush announced that these doctrines were now obsolete. Against terrorists, he said, notions of "containment" and deterrence were irrelevant. The United States must be prepared to strike first. Principal threats to U.S. security came not from rival nation-states but, rather, from terrorist groups with potential access to weapons of mass destruction (WMDs). "If we wait for threats to fully materialize," he said to the uniformed cadets, "we will have waited too long. We must take the battle to the enemy, disrupt his plans and confront the worst threats before they emerge." A corollary of this doctrine was, of course, the need for nearly flawless gathering and analysis of intelligence. As reports of shocking failures in the U.S. intelligence community prior to 9/11 swirled about the capital and country, there was little assurance that this condition could be fulfilled.

It soon became clear that the United States was building a rationale for attacking Iraq, a founding member of the so-called axis of evil. The Bush administration began hinting that Saddam Hussein was working hand in glove with Osama bin Laden. Further, the White House claimed that Iraq was developing WMDs in violation of a United Nations resolution requiring the destruction of all such arsenals in the wake of the 1990–1991 Persian Gulf War.

Early in 2003, U.S. diplomats urged the UN Security Council to authorize military action against Iraq. France, China, and Russia threatened to veto the measure, while other countries—including Chile and Mexico—expressed opposition to the war resolution and urged more time for UN inspection teams to complete their analyses. Impatient and frustrated, the Bush administration decided to bypass the UN. With the support of a handful of nations—a "coalition of the willing," headed once again by the United Kingdom—the United States plunged ahead. In March 2003, U.S. troops spearheaded an invasion of Iraq. Baghdad fell within weeks. Saddam Hussein himself was captured in December. In May 2004 an exultant President Bush proclaimed victory.

This was premature, as things turned out. The United States and its allies soon confronted a determined, ruthless, and violent insurgency—suicide attacks, assassination attempts, and hit-and-run maneuvers against civilians, public figures, and occupation troops. Within Iraq, hatred of foreign authorities merged with hatred among religious groups, especially between Sunni and Shiite Muslims. By the end of 2006, the number of U.S. military deaths surpassed 3,000. Civilian Iraqi deaths were estimated to be in the hundreds of thousands. As Iraq teetered on the edge of civil war, the outlook was grim: The United States had gotten itself into a quagmire.

### Concurrent Developments

As the war on terror took shape, it brought about—and reflected—fundamental alterations in the global arena. Especially unsettling was the controversial idea that the war had unleashed a "clash of civilizations." Essentially, this would be a fundamental conflict between Islam and "the West" (Europe and the United States). At the core of this struggle would be differences between Muslim and Judeo-Christian systems of belief. As defined by Samuel P. Huntington,

> Civilizations are differentiated from each other by history, language, culture, tradition and, most important, religion. The people of different civilizations have different views on the relations between God and man, the individual and the group, the citizen and the state, parents and children, husband and wife, as well as differing views of the relative importance of rights and responsibilities, liberty and authority, equality and hierarchy. These differences are the product of centuries. They will not soon disappear. They are far more fundamental than differences among political ideologies and political regimes. Differences do not necessarily mean conflict, and conflict does not necessarily mean violence. Over the centuries, however, differences among civilizations have generated the most prolonged and the most violent conflicts.

Civilizational clashes were likely to become more frequent and more pervasive. They would be extended, passionate, and brutal. According to one respected Muslim author, the next challenge to the West was "definitely going to come from the Muslim world. It is in the sweep of Islamic nations from the Maghreb to Pakistan that the struggle for a new world order will begin." Such ideas led Huntington to offer the provocative observation that "Islam has bloody borders." Once initiated, wars between civilizations would be extremely difficult—if not impossible—to stop.

At the same time, the enemy proved to be highly elusive. Groups like Al Qaeda formed vast and complex networks across the world. Operating largely out of sight, they maintained communication through informal channels—fax, e-mail, mobile phones. They intermingled with civilian society in order to maintain protective cover and to recruit potential followers. They planted clandestine "sleeper cells" in target countries and established training camps in secluded areas. As a top-ranking member of the U.S. intelligence community observed, "Our enemy

**BOX 11-1**

## Does Islam Promote Violence?

In the aftermath of 9/11, one of the most persistent claims throughout the West has been that Islam promotes violence as a matter of religious doctrine. All faithful Muslims therefore became defined as enemies. The problem was Islamic teaching.

Is there any truth to such accusations? One of the world's greatest authorities on comparative religion, Huston Smith, offers helpful insight on the Muslim conception of just, or "righteous," war:

> The important question is the definition of a righteous war. According to prevailing interpretations of the Koran, a righteous war must either be defensive or to right a wrong. "Defend yourself against your enemies, but do not attack them first: God hates the aggressor." The aggressive and unrelenting hostility of the idolaters forced Muhammad to seize the sword in self-defense, or, together with his entire community and his God-entrusted faith, be wiped from the face of the earth. That other [Christian] teachers succumbed under force and became martyrs was to Muhammad no reason that he should do the same. Having seized the sword in self-defense he held onto it until the end. This much Muslims acknowledge; but they insist that while Islam has at times spread by the sword, it has mostly spread by persuasion and example. . . .
>
> Indeed, if comparisons are what we want, Muslims consider Christianity's record as the darker of the two. Who was it, they ask, who preached the Crusades in the name of the Prince of Peace? Who instituted the Inquisition, invented the rack and the stake as instruments of religion, and plunged Europe into its devastating wars of religion?

And if modern-day Islam indeed has "bloody borders," as Huntington has written, whose fault is that? The Muslims or their bellicose opponents?

SOURCE: Quotes from Huston Smith, *The World's Religions* (San Francisco: HarperCollins, 1991), pp. 255–257.

during the Cold War was easy to find but hard to finish. This new enemy is just the opposite—easy to finish but damnably hard to find."

*Terrorism* is a highly elastic term. By the U.S. government's own definition, the term refers to "premeditated, politically motivated violence perpetrated against noncombatant targets by subnational groups or clandestine agents, usually intended to influence an audience." *International terrorism* means "terrorism involving citizens or the territory of more than one country." It is not an ideology, cause, belief, country, or territory but, rather, a tactic. Anyone can use it. In his first post-9/11 speech, Bush vowed that the U.S. campaign would not end "until every terrorist group of global reach" had been destroyed. Just what did he mean by that?

Moreover, the term could be exploited for political purposes. Government leaders everywhere could now label their opponents as "terrorists" and therefore as threats not only to themselves but also to the United States, the civilized world, and international peace. Thus Vladimir Putin claimed new legitimacy for his campaign to crush anti-Russian rebels in Chechnya, just as Álvaro Uribe asserted that his crackdown on guerrillas in Colombia was part and parcel of the global war on terror. As the U.S.-led campaign intensified, the age-old concept of "state terror"—violence against citizens by agents of a ruling state—lost currency in many circles. Terror came to be seen as something done *against* established states, not by them.

At a broader level of analysis, the war and its consequences revealed and intensified the unipolar structure of global power. Among sovereign states, the United States stood in a class by itself. It had the largest economy, the strongest military, the most advanced technology. No single nation—not Germany, Russia, Japan, or even China—came close to matching America's capabilities. Yet primacy could have a downside. As a thoughtful European analyst would write, "America today has too much power for anyone's good, including its own. . . . [T]he problem with American power is not that it is American. The problem is simply the power. It would be dangerous even for an archangel to wield so much power." Such a domineering position could erode awareness of limits and inculcate a misleading sense of American omnipotence, a feeling that the United States could do whatever it wanted.

Partly as a result, the Bush administration determined to pursue unilateral courses of action. Support from other countries would be welcome, but the United States would not be bound by multilateral obligations, international organizations, or UN conventions. The operative phrase of the day became "multilateralism à la carte," meaning that the United States would make use of multilateral instruments (treaties, alliances, institutions) if and when that seemed appropriate. As just one example, the Bush administration withdrew U.S. support from the International Criminal Court at The Hague, thus "unsigning" a treaty that had been endorsed by the outgoing Clinton administration (though not yet ratified by Congress). Washington would pick and choose; the U.S. government would decide for itself. Multilateralism "à la carte" was unilateralism, pure and simple.

Understandably, this path could lead to resentment around the world—incessant grumbling about American arrogance, shortsightedness, unconcern for others. And there emerged, in this context, a paradox of power: America's supremacy became a source of vulnerability. Terrorists focused their anger and their plots against the United States, not because it was so weak, but precisely because it was so strong. Being the top target was the cost of being Number One. Excess power had become a liability.

Meanwhile, international support for the U.S.-led invasion took a downward turn. Revelations of misconduct by American troops—abuse of detainees at Abu Ghraib prison, for instance, plus a civilian massacre in the town of Haditha—led to worldwide revulsion against the entire operation. Separate investigations further revealed that Saddam was not in league with Al Qaeda and that he did not wield WMDs: The central question became whether U.S. authorities had knowingly misled the world community. The United States began to lose the affection and respect of citizens around the world. As revealed in Figure 11-1, public

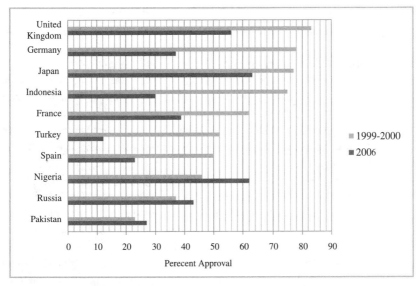

**Figure 11-1** America's Prestige around the World: Selected Countries, 1999–2006
SOURCE: Pew Global Attitudes Project, as reported in *El País* (Madrid), June 21, 2006.

opinion polls showed sharp declines in "favorable perceptions" of the United States between 1999 and 2006, even among traditional allies: down from 83 to 56 percent in the United Kingdom, from 78 to 37 percent in Germany, from 77 to 63 percent in Japan, from 62 to 39 percent in France, and from 50 to 23 percent in Spain. In Muslim countries the drops were precipitous: from 75 to 30 percent in Indonesia, from 52 to 12 percent in Turkey. The figures showed modest improvement only in Russia, Nigeria, and Pakistan. Moreover, many respondents viewed the U.S. campaign in Iraq as a "grave danger" to the world: 60 percent in Turkey, 56 percent in Spain, 45 percent in Russia, and 41 percent in the United Kingdom. (And in many countries, people thought the campaign was more dangerous to the world than the Iranian drive for nuclear capability.) Clearly, the United States was losing substantial degrees of "soft power."

As the war dragged on, it gradually lost the support of citizens in the United States. In the immediate aftermath of the 9/11 attacks, Bush's approval ratings had climbed to astronomical levels. By mid-2002 the ratings were holding in the mid-70s, still very positive levels, but they slipped to the mid-60s by mid-2003, shortly after the invasion of Iraq. By August 2005 only 45 percent of respondents expressed approval of the president's overall job performance; by May 2006 only 33 percent gave him their support. Other factors figured into this stunning decline of Bush's popularity, but Iraq was the principal reason.

Developments followed rapidly. In 2006 congressional elections, the long-beleaguered Democratic Party recaptured majorities in both the Senate and the House of Representatives. *Washington Post* journalist Bob Woodward published a best-selling book entitled *State of Denial*: Respectful in tone, it presented a devastating portrait of decision-making processes about Iraq within the Bush administration. And a blue-ribbon bipartisan commission issued a report stating flatly that "The situation in Iraq is grave and deteriorating." Co-chaired by none other than James Baker, close collaborator of George Bush, Sr. (and mastermind of the Republican Party's successful postelection strategy in 2000), the commission observed that nearly 100 Americans were dying every month, as were 3,000 Iraqi civilians. The United States was spending $2 billion per week for what seemed like a hopeless cause. "Current U.S. policy is not working," the panelists concluded. It was time for a basic change in approach.

Suddenly on the defensive, the Bush Jr. White House reassessed its options. What emerged from these deliberations was the deployment of 30,000 additional troops—a "surge" designed to break through the prevalent stalemate. (It brought the total number of U.S. troops in Iraq to more than 170,000.) Moreover, the increase coincided with the adoption of a "counterinsurgency" doctrine formulated by General David Petraeus. Instead of relying on force, U.S. troops began living among the people, protecting them from danger and meeting their fundamental needs. The goal was to win the hearts and minds of Iraqis. Soft power would supplement hard power and magnify its impact.

Facts on the ground were propitious. In 2006, Prime Minister Nuri Kamal al-Maliki had managed to form a quasi-legitimate government and oversee the execution of Saddam Hussein. That same year an important group of Sunnis, long fearful of domination by the Shiite majority, had abandoned their insurgency and decided to work through the political process. And in 2007, radical anti-American cleric Moktada al-Sadr ordered his Mahdi Army to accept a truce. Violence was declining and security was improving. Although these trends happened to coincide with the U.S. "surge" in troops, they came about largely because of political shifts within Iraq.

The handwriting was on the wall. By November 2008, the al-Maliki government negotiated a timetable for the eventual departure of U.S. troops from Iraq. In so doing, al-Maliki took a strongly nationalist position: "I consider myself a friend of the U.S.," he said at one point, "but I'm not America's man in Iraq." Proponents in the Iraqi parliament referred to the timetable as "the withdrawal agreement." American forces were on the way out.

## OBAMA'S WARS

The election of Barack Obama as president in 2008 heralded prospects for major transformation. It meant a change of party, of administration, and of style. The new chief executive was young, articulate, and well educated. Widespread support for an Afro-American candidate amounted to a victory for tolerance over bigotry and thus marked a historic turning point in American society. At a single stroke, Obama's election restored a great deal of the "soft power" that had been squandered under Bush.

People expected miracles—or, at the least, instantaneous political magic. But reality proved to be harsh. The U.S. economy was in a free fall: Unemployment was rising, industries were tottering, the housing market was shattered. Following the Bush administration's lead, the Obama team developed a multibillion-dollar "stimulus package" designed to rescue the economy. Domestic problems were urgent.

Internationally, Obama inherited a two-front war that was increasingly unpopular at home. By the time he took office, the United States had 161,000 troops in Iraq and 38,000 in Afghanistan. The total cost of the post-9/11 campaigns had amounted to $1 trillion. America could ill afford things as they were.

Obama did not abandon the war on terror. On the contrary, he continued the controversial practice of "renditions," used military commissions for trials, and, contradicting his campaign promise, failed to close the prison at Guantánamo. He authorized preemptive strikes against suspected terrorists, expanded the use of Predator drones, condoned the targeted killing of an American citizen, and deployed Special Forces and other military units in various parts of the world. (According to the *New York Times*, in fact, Obama "turned out to be one of the most militarily aggressive leaders in decades.")

At the same time, President Obama gave the antiterror campaign new focus and direction. He redefined its fundamental purpose. The principal enemy was not a political movement or a religious ideology. It was not Islam. It was to be Al Qaeda, the terrorist organization that had launched the 9/11 attacks. The ultimate goal was not the diffusion of full-fledged democracy, as George Bush had so rashly proclaimed. Nor was it the building of nations. It was U.S. security, the protection of innocent lives, and the promotion of national interests. Obama adopted a realistic and limited sense of America's purpose.

### Exiting Iraq

The first order of business was winding down the war in Iraq, which Obama himself had long opposed. During the run-up to the U.S. invasion he had criticized the Bush administration's policy on the grounds that it would lead to a "U.S. occupation of undetermined length, at undetermined cost, with undetermined consequences." And during his presidential campaign, he had vowed to withdraw American troops from Iraq by the middle of 2010.

It took a bit longer than that. But in December 2011, after nine years of war and 4,500 American fatalities, U.S. troops made their final exit. Speaking in a fortified courtyard in Baghdad, Defense secretary Leon E. Panetta looked ahead to the future: "Let me be clear: Iraq will be tested in the days ahead—by terrorism, and by those who would seek to divide, by social and economic issues, by the demands of democracy itself. Challenges remain, but the U.S. will be there to stand by the Iraqi people as they navigate those challenges to build a stronger and more prosperous nation."

Indeed, Iraq would be facing hard times. Political violence was continuing at high rates, with more than 500 attacks per month. Questions lingered over the allocation of oil revenues, the roles of Sunni and Shiite sects, and religious tolerance in general. "It is the end for the Americans only," wrote one Iraqi columnist. "Nobody knows if the war will end for Iraqis, too."

## Afghanistan

In the meantime Obama ratcheted up America's forces in Afghanistan. After all, this was the country from which Al Qaeda had launched the attacks of 9/11. It occupied a strategic location, at the crossroads of Central Asia, South Asia, and the Middle East. With its hardy population and difficult terrain, Afghanistan had long resisted foreign encroachments—from the nineteenth-century "great game" between the British and Russian empires to the Soviet Union's devastating ten-year occupation of 1979–1989. Indeed, the *mujahadeen's* victory over the Soviets became a beacon to Islamic extremists all over the world.

Obama's concern was that Afghanistan could once again become a refuge for terrorist groups, especially Al Qaeda. The Karzai government was weak, corrupt, and incompetent, with little influence outside the capital city of Kabul. The opium trade was back in full swing. And despite their defeat in 2001, the Taliban was making a comeback, waging guerrilla warfare from the mountains and extending their reach in the countryside. Particularly ominous was the border region with Pakistan—presumably an American ally but also a strongly Islamic society and a potential haven for Al Qaeda.

Eerily enough, U.S. preoccupations with Afghanistan evoked the "domino theory" that had justified intervention in Vietnam during the Cold War. In the words of General James L. Jones (ret.), Obama's first National Security Adviser: "If we're not successful here, you'll have a staging base for global terrorism all over the world. People will say the terrorists won. And you'll see expressions of these kinds of things in Africa, South America, you name it. Any developing country is going to say, that is the way we beat [the United States], and we're going to have a bigger problem." The implication was clear: The United States had to hold the line in Afghanistan.

After intense internal debates, the White House announced in late 2009 that it would mount a short-term military "surge" of 30,000 additional American troops. The goals were limited: to defeat Al Qaeda, the principal enemy, and to disrupt and degrade (but not necessarily "defeat") the Taliban. In fact Obama vowed to start bringing American forces home from Afghanistan in the middle of 2011, saying the United States could not afford an open-ended commitment in that distant country. As the president said to his aides, "I'm not doing 10 years. I'm not doing a long-term nation-building effort. I'm not spending a trillion dollars."

As a sign of his determination, Obama placed General David Petraeus, architect of the 2007 "surge" in Iraq, in command of American forces in Afghanistan. The pace of military operations quickly accelerated, especially in Taliban strongholds. Across the border in Pakistan, a daring raid by Navy SEALs in May 2011 resulted in the death of Osama bin Laden—a source of great satisfaction but one that raised disturbing questions about the reliability of Pakistani allies (some of whom must have known about bin Laden's hideout). The following month Obama declared that "the tide of war is receding," so he could start bringing troops home before the end of the year. Withdrawals would continue thereafter, and American soldiers would be out of the country by late 2014.

Not surprisingly, the timetable reflected political considerations. Obama was facing a strong battle in his bid for reelection in 2012, and the American public was losing patience with the Afghan war—the longest in U.S. history. As of October 2011 a solid majority of respondents (58 percent) said the United States should not be involved in Afghanistan, while just over one-third (35 percent) expressed support for the war. Almost 70 percent said that the war had lasted longer than expected, and 62 percent said that the number of troops should be reduced. Obama's policy was falling in line with public opinion.

Shadows darkened this horizon in early 2012. Tensions with Afghanistan had long been simmering—over "collateral damage" (the military euphemism for accidental civilian deaths) from bombs and Predator drone missiles and over nighttime raids by commando units that harassed and frightened the local population. A crisis erupted in early 2012 when it was learned that NATO personnel had (inadvertently) burned a number of Korans, sparking virulent anti-American demonstrations that led to dozens of deaths. Weeks later a disturbed American soldier went on a murderous rampage, killing sixteen Afghan civilians in cold blood. Meanwhile, growing animosity between NATO and Afghan soldiers had erupted in violent confrontations, including insider killings of dozens of Western troops.

Clearly, the United States (and NATO) was losing soft power in Afghanistan. And this, in turn, fed deepening concerns about the challenges of a troop withdrawal that hinged on the close mentoring and training of Afghan army and police forces. Some voices clamored for an accelerated withdrawal of troops by 2013; others said that the United States should retain its presence into an indefinite future. This was an uneasy time.

## WAR ON TERROR: THE RULES OF THE GAME

As in other eras, the dominant form of global conflict spawned a tacit set of "rules of the game." They were implicit rather than explicit, reflections of actual behavior rather than formal prescriptions for conduct. In the case of the war on terror, the operative rules were imposed on the world by the sole superpower—the United States. Not everyone embraced the rules, and, as we shall see, resistance emerged in conspicuous quarters. Even so, everyone had to face the fact of their existence.

The goal of this game was to eliminate the enemy (whoever that might be). In contrast to the geoeconomic game, where contestants sought to gain material advantage over rivals, this geopolitical game focused on physical survival and national security. It was a life-or-death struggle. The idea was to obliterate the adversary. There could be no quarter given. This game did not assume an indefinite series of subsequent iterations. Once the enemy was gone, that would be the end.

258 PART III • GLOBALIZATION AND WAR

The first rule, perhaps the cardinal one, held that nations possessed the right to respond to attacks in whatever way they chose—including the use of indiscriminate force. Since there was no effective authority above the nation-state, there could be no effective restraint on countries that had endured terrorist assaults. There was no need to document the guilt of alleged perpetrators. There was no need to worry about "collateral damage" as a result of military action. Governments were entitled to defend (and avenge) their citizens. The stronger the state, the stronger the response—that would be a law of both logic and nature.

The second rule stated that preventive action was appropriate. As President Bush explicitly declared and Obama has silently agreed, you could not wait for terrorists to attack. In contrast to the Cold War, military capability (or a nuclear arsenal) no longer deterred the enemy: There could be no form of "mutually assured destruction," especially if opponents were willing to commit suicide during the course of a first strike. By the time you turned the other cheek, you were likely to be dead.

The third rule indicated that it was unnecessary to adhere to international treaties or conventions. They were designed to prevent conventional conflicts or nuclear exchanges between nation-states. They were irrelevant and obsolete. They bore no relevance to wars on terror, where elusive enemies operated through stealth and subversion.

As a reflection of these rules, alliances could (and would) be formed around a single issue—the response to 9/11 and the willingness to join the antiterrorist campaign. This became the sole criterion for alignment with (and gratitude from) the U.S. government. Gone were concerns about human rights, democratic practice, or related issues. The only relevant question was whether governments would enlist in the American-led campaign. To peoples still living under autocratic rule, this deemphasis on democracy might seem like a betrayal. It would strike discordant notes with such movements as the "Arab Spring" that erupted in 2011–2012. In time, popular disappointment could come back to haunt the United States.

Other countries around the world—"spectator nations," as one might think of them—had to tread cautiously on this political minefield. Most of them were, of course, aghast at the cruelty and destruction of the 9/11 attacks. (As a prominent French newspaper headlined the following day, "We are all Americans!") But for one reason or another, many nations were reluctant to join the American crusade: Some feared retaliation, others thought the U.S. response was disproportionate, others wanted to stay out of the fight. Above all, they did not want to become targets themselves—either for U.S. reprisals or for terrorist assaults. This concern became especially clear in the wake of Al Qaeda attacks on two prominent U.S. allies: Spain in March 2004 and the United Kingdom in July 2005. (The war had long been highly unpopular in Spain, where the electorate promptly dismissed the conservative ruling party from power after the terrorist attack on Madrid; Britain would remain a target of continuing terrorist plots.)

Even so, reticence did not often lead to outright critiques of the American campaign. On the contrary, disagreement with the United States was, for the most part, understated or muted. For one thing, many leaders believed—correctly—that antagonizing the Bush administration could result in costly reprisals. Others were more than willing to let the United States assume the major burdens in the war on terror. Further, they saw no point in denouncing the preemptive use of maximum force—in case they ever needed it themselves. Indeed, the aftermath of 9/11 led to widespread relabeling of domestic opponents as "terrorists," an exercise in linguistic acrobatics that could justify violent techniques of repression and, in some instances, attract support from the United States.

One of the most prevalent forms of resistance to American policy became outspoken support for multilateral commitments and international organizations, especially the United Nations. From the standpoint of the developing world, including Latin America, institutions such as the UN deserved and needed the authority to impose constraints on the major powers, including the United States. They offered the only plausible hope for achieving peace, order, and justice in the world. Multilateral organizations thus became, in this sense, a "weapon of the weak"—a means of curtailing the rich and powerful. In diplomatic code, support for the UN signaled disagreement with the U.S. military campaign.

Even as it jettisoned Cold War military doctrines, the antiterrorist struggle came to resemble the former conflict in other, fundamental ways. As in prior eras, the United States had an enemy—a different kind of enemy, to be sure, but an enemy nonetheless. The nation now had an all-consuming mission. And the nation subsumed almost all other interests to the pursuit of this goal. As a leading military analyst observed, "What makes the new crusade so natural to the Bush team is that it looks so much like the old one. It is not conventional terrorism, but the possibility of terrorism with weapons of mass destruction, or WMD, has galvanized the administration. With that possibility comes a renewed appetite for covert action and human agents, a need to root out internal security risks, a rise in Cold War–style government secrecy." Geopolitics returned to the fore.

And though the WMDs and Al Qaeda charges against Saddam Hussein turned out to be fallacious, ends came to justify means. United States authorities held suspects at the military camp in Guantánamo without access to legal counsel, denied that "nonlegal combatants" should be treated as prisoners of war, and organized clandestine prisons in undisclosed locations around the world. Popular anxiety swelled as word leaked out that, in the name of its war on terror, the U.S. government was illegally eavesdropping on telephone conversations of U.S. citizens. Once again, Americans came face to face with a painful dilemma: They supported a legitimate campaign against terrorism, but they became concerned about their own civil liberties.

After the presidential election of 2008, Barack Obama upheld these unwritten rules of the war on terror but in fairly subtle ways. Whereas Bush was abrasive and unilateralist, Obama was gracious and consultative. And whereas Bush sought to transform the Middle East, if not the entire world, Obama defined national interests in crisp and narrow terms. But these were differences of style rather than substance. To paraphrase the dictum made famous by Teddy Roosevelt, Obama spoke softly—but he carried a big stick.

### Two-Level Games

As a result of these developments, international relations in the post-9/11 era obeyed two simultaneous but distinct forms of logic—one focusing on geoeconomics, as explained in chapter 9, and the other dealing with geopolitics, with special reference to the war on terror. These distinct codes of conduct operated alongside one another, sometimes in harmony and sometimes in discord. Their simultaneous interaction thus led to a "two-level game." This dualistic context greatly complicated calculations and cost–benefit analysis by political actors. Gains in one arena could lead to losses in another. What made sense in one game might not make sense in the other.[1]

That is why it has been so difficult to unravel the realities of the post-9/11 era. It has been a time of confusion, contradiction, and uncertainty. The idea of a two-level game provides a conceptual key for unlocking the puzzles of this current era. It is a tool, a means of gaining insight into patterns of political and diplomatic action.

At times when geoeconomic and geopolitical interests contradicted one another, geopolitics generally held the upper hand. The stakes in the war on terror seemed more urgent, immediate, and irreversible than in geoeconomics. You could always revise an exchange rate or amend a free-trade agreement, but you could not undo the loss of life from a terrorist attack. Moreover, geopolitical priorities were being avidly promoted by the strongest country in the world. Superpower status could thus shape the international agenda.

## GEORGE BUSH AND LATIN AMERICA

Seen in this context, the war on terror brought far-reaching changes to inter-American relations. Most fundamental was a shift in Washington's regional priorities under George W. Bush. Central and South Asia and the Middle East—broadly speaking, the Muslim world—vaulted to the top of the ladder. East Asia retained a position of importance, partly because of North Korea's membership in the "axis of evil" and partly because of China's and Japan's roles as major powers. By contrast, Latin America faded far into the background. Briefly privileged by the president's expressions of personal interest, the region fell off the proverbial radar screen—and suffered from inattention as Argentina and the rest of South America plunged into a series of economic and institutional crises. As *New York Times* correspondent Larry Rohter plaintively asked in January 2005, "What will it take to get the United States to pay attention to Latin America? A resurgence

---

[1]See Robert D. Putnam, "Diplomacy and Domestic Politics: The Logic of Two-Level Games," *International Organization* 42, 3 (Summer 1988): 427–460.

of anti-American guerrillas?" Or, one might inquire, the appearance of Al Qaeda cells within the region?

In the immediate aftermath of 9/11, Latin American leaders expressed great sympathy with the United States; indeed, scores of Latin American citizens lost their lives at the World Trade Center in New York. And as events unfolded, they took sides with the United States—but cautiously. The Organization of American States unanimously approved a resolution denouncing the September 11 assaults, pledging to combat terrorism and to take action "as appropriate" (whatever that might mean). Watching from the sidelines, countries of the region cautiously urged the Bush administration to craft a "proportionate" response to the attacks. Indeed, it seemed that many observers shared the opinion expressed so succinctly by Cuba's Fidel Castro—against terrorism and also against war.

Tensions came to a head in early 2003, as the U.S. government pressed the UN Security Council to authorize a military attack on Iraq. Mindful of popular opinion at home, most democratic leaders throughout Latin America proclaimed reservations about the drive to war. A few, such as Hugo Chávez of Venezuela, announced outright opposition; only Álvaro Uribe of Colombia expressed avid support. It so happened that two Latin countries, Chile and Mexico, held temporary seats on the Security Council, and Mexico was slated to preside over the council during these particular debates. Both resisted U.S. pressure to vote in favor of the war resolution (parenthetically, Chile hinted that it might support a subsequent resolution authorizing action against Iraq if UN inspection teams found hard evidence of WMDs). As the council debates locked in stalemate, the United States gave up its quest for UN authorization and went ahead with an invasion. Anti-U.S. demonstrations promptly broke out in major cities of the hemisphere— La Paz, Lima, Bogotá, Santiago, São Paulo, Rio de Janeiro, and Mexico City. Angry crowds denounced U.S. leadership, U.S. policy, and U.S. arrogance. George Bush would never regain popularity within the region.

Washington's reaction was to ignore Latin America. In a fit of pique, Bush refused to accept telephone calls from his erstwhile friend Vicente Fox. And in a deliberate diplomatic snub, the ceremonial signing of a free-trade agreement with Chile was downgraded from a gala White House event (which Singapore had received) to a ministerial conclave in Miami. The region was effectively put on hold. It was neither a source of political support nor a clear and present danger. It could be safely dismissed.

Institutionalized neglect was reflected in high-level appointments in the Bush administration. Seasoned Latin American experts were most conspicuous by their absence. Not one of the topmost officials in the foreign-policy team (at State, Defense, or the National Security Council) had extensive experience within the region; indeed, it was half-jokingly observed that the only "Latin Americanist" in the administration was the president himself. Furthermore, many of the midlevel administrative posts were occupied by hard-line representatives of the Cuban American community, perhaps as payback for its fervent support of the Republican cause during Florida's contested presidential election in 2000. It was not until Bush's second term, with the appointment of Thomas Shannon as assistant secretary of state for hemispheric affairs, that Latin America finally found a thoughtful and responsible advocate within the U.S. government.

Generally speaking, Latin America recoiled against the Bush administration. A 2004 poll of elites throughout the region revealed that 87 percent held a negative opinion of Bush's foreign-policy performance, while only 12 percent felt that he was making good or excellent efforts in dealing with the hemisphere. In a follow-up survey in 2006, 50 percent of regional leaders judged that Bush's policies toward Latin America were worse than those of preceding presidents, while just 6 percent said they were better. Four out of five of these elite respondents (81 percent) gave Bush an unfavorable overall job rating. They did not like what they were seeing.

## Regime Change and Democracy

Latin Americans get nervous when the United States proclaims its intention to spread the gospel of democracy. They imagine that trouble is coming. Such was the response to President Bush's second inaugural speech and his proclamation of a grand Wilsonian crusade around the world. As though to justify the military invasion of Iraq after the failure to locate WMDs, Bush asserted that the best defense against terrorism was the expansion of democracy: "It is the policy of the United States," he went on to proclaim, "to seek and support the growth of democratic movements and institutions in every nation and culture, with the ultimate goal of ending tyranny in the world." This was an immodest and capacious claim, one that struck raw nerves in much of the developing world. Did this portend a new wave of U.S. intervention? Was it an ultimatum of some sort? In response to these intimations, one respected consulting firm (in Mexico City) expressed the judgment that, "for the rest of the world, George W. Bush offers little reason for reassurance" (*dista de ser motivo de tranquilidad*).

Ironically, too, democracy in Latin America could become a Trojan horse for the United States. A cardinal presumption of U.S. policy had long held that democratic leaders would, by definition, become American allies. (Thus the conception of the "free world" during the Cold War.) But what if free and fair elections gave victory to nationalist, populist, or otherwise anti-American candidates? It has been said before and will here be repeated: The more that dispossessed and disenchanted sectors of Latin American society are able to express themselves through elections, the more likely it is that triumphant candidates will take issue with U.S. policy and power. Or, in starker terms: The more that Latin American politics resembles American democracy, the more strident and frequent will be disagreements with the United States. This hypothesis was finding strong support in the wave of left-wing presidential leaders that was surging throughout the region. Such developments brought considerable discomfort to Bush administration policymakers: They didn't like the leftist politicians, but they had to acknowledge their democratic legitimacy.

Cuba was a special matter. Since first taking office, the Bush administration had expressed unrelenting opposition to the *fidelista* regime. In part, this opposition reflected a cold-blooded political calculation: As solid bastions of anti-Castro sentiment, Miami and surrounding areas had played a crucial role in the president's electoral victory in 2000, and he wanted to reward their efforts. In part it reflected deep-seated belief: As a conservative Republican, George W. Bush was unalterably opposed to any kind of socialist regime. Finally, he and his associates shared the frustration that had bedeviled American presidents since the early 1960s: They wanted to remove Fidel Castro from power, but they couldn't find a means of doing so. Everything had failed—invasion, attempted assassination, economic asphyxiation, political isolation, mobilization of dissidents. What next?

Bush's policy took shape in the wake of 9/11. In September 2002 he offered to ease bans on travel and trade (that is, the embargo) only if Cuba would hold free and fair elections, allow citizens the right to free speech and assembly, and "ease the stranglehold on private enterprise." This offer came across as an ultimatum: The United States would relax its stance only if Cuba agreed to scuttle its political regime. A year later Bush announced additional steps. Because the Castro regime refused to change by itself, he said, the United States would undertake initiatives "intended to hasten the arrival of a new, free, democratic Cuba." These initiatives included:

- Tighter enforcement of travel restrictions
- Expanding immigration for political refugees, by "improving our ability to identify and protect those who face persecution in Cuba and provide them the opportunity to come to the United States safely"
- Formation of a Commission for Assistance to a Free Cuba, whose purpose would be to "consider the elements of a comprehensive program to assist the Cuban people to establish democracy and the rule of law, create the core institutions of free enterprise, modernize infrastructure, and provide health, housing, and human services"—that is, to dismantle or replace the Castro regime.

Constantly referring to Fidel Castro as a "tyrant" or a "dictator," Bush fervently declared his intention to bring democracy to Cuba. Practically speaking, this meant pushing Castro out of power.

September 11 and the war on terror presented the Bush administration with a paradox. Castro and most Cubans were truly horrified by the terrorist attacks on the Twin Towers in New York. In a humanitarian gesture, the Cuban government offered air space and landing facilities for stranded American airliners and, in a political gesture, the sharing of intelligence about terrorists. And as the United States rounded up suspects, Cuba acceded to the use of the Guantánamo Naval Base as a prison facility. But as the Bush administration ignored the United Nations and launched the invasion of Iraq, Fidel drew a line. As Castro had said at the beginning, he was opposed to the use of military force.

Eventually, Havana's objections to the war on terror evoked furious condemnation from Washington. An official U.S. statement in 2003 complained that Cuban functionaries had ridiculed the U.S.-led antiterror campaign as a "war for terrorism." In a speech to the UN General Assembly, according to the declaration,

Cuba's foreign minister made "deeply offensive and patently false" remarks, accusing American troops of targeting "children, the civilian population, and the International Red Cross as enemies." Other officials had denounced the war on terror as "militaristic and fascist." Generally speaking, the American statement concluded, "Cuba's reaction to the global war on terrorism *was little different from that of Iraq*" [emphasis added]. Thus associating Fidel with Saddam, the statement implicitly presented Cuba as a prime enemy in the fight against terror.

Tensions returned to a high point in mid-2006. Approaching his eightieth birthday, Fidel Castro fell seriously ill and underwent a delicate operation for gastrointestinal hemorrhaging. Festivities broke out in the streets of Miami, as Cuban Americans gathered to celebrate the prospect of Fidel's imminent demise. A weakened Castro urged his people to be prepared for bad news in the future and announced that his brother Raúl would assume the reins of government. This was, many said, the autumn of the patriarch. It was only a matter of time.

The Bush administration took a cautious stance. As Cuban officials proclaimed their insistence on continuity—categorizing the change in leadership as a "succession" rather than a "transition"—the U.S. president announced his intention to "take note" of the behavior of new leaders. Secretary of State Condoleezza Rice ruled out any thought of outright U.S. intervention and declared that the political future of the island was a challenge for "the Cuban people" to determine—although it was not clear if she meant to include Miami exiles in this statement. Thoughtful experts warned of the dangers in rash action and pointed out that the United States might soon be able to affect the course of events through deft use (or dismantlement) of the embargo. As reports trickled out about Fidel's health, the world—and Washington—waited expectantly. What would the future bring?

## OBAMA AND LATIN AMERICA

Barack Obama continued to emphasize the geopolitical focus passed on by George W. Bush. Latin America was never a top priority for the new president. Taking office in January 2009, he was moreover obliged to deal with urgent matters—financial crisis in the United States and the wars on terror in Iraq and Afghanistan. These issues would define his legacy and, ultimately, his prospects for reelection. First things would have to come first.

Even so, Obama signed a presidential order on the day of his inauguration to close the prison facility in the U.S. naval base at Guantánamo (see box on page 37), a task begun but not yet accomplished. At the urging of Hillary Clinton, the secretary of state, he made a lightning visit to Mexico in March to express support for that government's war on drugs, as drug-related violence threatened to spill over into the United States. And the following month, as a matter of diplomatic obligation, he attended the fifth Summit of the Americas, this time in the tiny Caribbean nation of Trinidad and Tobago. In formal remarks,

Obama proclaimed his commitment to hemispheric cooperation: "There is no senior partner and junior partner in our relations; there is simply engagement based upon mutual respect, common interests, and shared values. So I am here to launch a new chapter of engagement that will be sustained throughout my Administration." As possibilities for partnership, he cited microfinance, energy, and the fight against drugs.

## Cuba (Again)

Since the summit took place in the Caribbean, Obama made specific reference to Cuba. "The United States seeks a new beginning with Cuba," he said.

> I know there is a longer journey that must be traveled in overcoming decades of mistrust, but there are critical steps we can take toward a new day. I have already changed a Cuba policy that has failed to advance liberty or opportunity for the Cuban people. We will now allow Cuban Americans to visit the island whenever they choose and to provide resources for their families—the same way that so many people in my country send money back to their families in your countries to help them pay for their everyday needs.

Indeed, Obama had not only lifted restrictions on remittances to Cuba. His administration had also begun regular back-channel talks about migration issues. "Let me be clear," the president said at the summit: "I am not interested in talking for the sake of talking. But I do believe that we can move U.S.-Cuban relations in a new direction." The overall tone was cautious but optimistic, and leaders throughout the hemisphere generally voiced positive approval.

Good feelings would not last for long. At a June 2009 meeting of the Organization of American States, foreign ministers considered a proposal to readmit Cuba to the OAS. In 1962 Cuba had been expelled from the OAS because of its "incompatible" embrace of Marxist-Leninist ideology and its alignment with the Soviet Union. Most countries regarded the continuing ostracism of Cuba as an obsolete relic of the Cold War and believed that much could be gained by engagement with the country's leadership. Indeed, the United States was the only country in the Western Hemisphere not to have restored full diplomatic relations with Cuba.

Despite widespread support for the resolution, Secretary of State Hillary Clinton vigorously insisted that Cuba take steps toward democratization before being allowed to reenter to the OAS. Delegates clearly saw this as a demand for capitulation by the Castro regime. After hasty negotiations, a compromise came forth: The expulsion of Cuba was declared to be "without effect," but Cuba would have to formally seek reinstatement as a member. Moreover, consideration of the request would depend on a "process of dialogue" in line with OAS pro-democracy "practices, proposals, and principles." Secretary Clinton claimed victory and left the meeting in haste: "I am pleased that everyone came to agree that Cuba cannot simply take its seat and that we must put Cuba's participation to a determination down the road—if it ever chooses to seek reentry."

Almost everyone else thought otherwise. Foreign ministers applauded the rescinding of the decades-long suspension. "What we have done here is to fix a historic error," said the foreign minister of Ecuador. Echoed the meeting's host, President Manuel Zelaya of Honduras: "The Cold War has ended." Quietly, too, attending diplomats drew considerable satisfaction from their near-unanimous disagreement with the U.S. position. Leaders of the region were asserting their independence. And despite early feelings of good will, the Obama administration found itself way out of step.

As of mid-2012, Cuba had steadfastly refused to seek reinstatement in the OAS. It has for decades derided the organization as the "Ministry of Colonies" of the United States. Moreover, it regards the process of "dialogue" about its application as a violation of national sovereignty. For the time being, stalemate has prevailed.

## Coup in Honduras

A major crisis soon developed in Honduras—involving, ironically, the president who had hosted the OAS meeting. The son of a wealthy businessman, Manuel Zelaya was involved in ranching, logging, and the timber trade. He had worked long years within the Liberal Party and served three terms in the national congress. There was every reason to expect that he would preside over a pragmatic, moderate, middle-of-the-road administration.

The Honduran political climate changed markedly in 2008. Early in the year Zelaya called on the United States to legalize drugs, partly as a means of reducing gang-related violence in his country. In July he announced his decision to join the leftist Bolivarian Alliance for the Americas (ALBA), formed and promoted by Venezuela's Hugo Chávez. In November he called for a nonbinding poll to determine whether to convene a constituent assembly to write a new constitution. This provoked widespread fears that Zelaya wanted to rescind the country's historic no-reelection rule and perpetuate his hold on power. On the morning that the referendum was slated to take place (June 28, 2009), uniformed soldiers roused Zelaya out of bed and whisked him off to Costa Rica.

The coup took most observers by surprise. The United Nations General Assembly promptly condemned Zelaya's ouster. The Organization of American States suspended Honduras's right to participation in that institution while reinforcing "diplomatic initiatives to restore democracy and the rule of law . . . and the reinstatement of President José Manuel Zelaya Rosales." The European Union backed the OAS's position and halted aid to Honduras. As Roberto Micheletti assumed power, no country officially recognized the new regime.

The United States offered an ambiguous response. President Obama initially said that "the coup was not legal and that President Zelaya remains the president of Honduras, the democratically elected president there. . . . It would be a terrible precedent if we start moving backwards into the era in which we are seeing military coups as a means of political transition, rather than democratic elections." Secretary Clinton took a more moderate stance. The State Department briefly suspended economic aid, but it soon resumed development and military assistance.

For a while Washington policymakers let the OAS take the lead and endorsed negotiations brokered by the Costa Rican president, Oscar Arias. Talks dragged on for months. One potential deal unraveled when the Honduras Congress announced that it would postpone a vote on Zelaya's return to power until the completion of elections scheduled for November 2009. Zelaya urged his backers to boycott those elections. Breaking ranks with most countries of Latin America, the Obama administration announced that it would recognize the results of the vote, with or without Zelaya's reinstatement. Zelaya sent an impassioned letter to Barack Obama criticizing his endorsement of the elections.

In September 2009 Zelaya carried out a fifteen-hour trek through mountainous back roads, slipped back into Tegucigalpa, and sought political asylum in the Brazilian embassy. The hard-line government of Roberto Micheletti proceeded to disrupt utility services to the embassy and to close off the surrounding area. Partly in response, Brazil then took the lead in denouncing the November elections as a backhanded means of legitimizing the military's power grab.

---

## BOX 11-2

### In Honduras, a Mess Made in the United States

In the aftermath of the crisis, most Americans turned their attention from Honduras to other parts of the world. In early 2012, however, one observer offered a sobering picture of that country's plight:

> It's time to acknowledge the foreign policy disaster that American support for the Porfirio Lobo administration in Honduras has become. Ever since the June 28, 2009, coup . . . the country has been descending deeper into a human rights and security abyss. That abyss is in good part the State Department's making.
>
> The headlines have been full of horror stories about Honduras. According to the United Nations, it now has the world's highest murder rate. . . . Much of the press in the United States has attributed this violence solely to drug trafficking and gangs. But the coup was what threw open the doors to a huge increase in drug trafficking and violence, and it unleashed a continuing wave of state-sponsored terrorism. . . .
>
> President Obama quickly recognized Mr. Lobo's victory, even when most of Latin America would not. Mr. Lobo's government is, in fact, a child of the coup. It retains most of the military figures who perpetrated the coup, and no one has gone to jail for starting it.
>
> This chain of events—a coup that the United States didn't stop, a fraudulent election that it accepted—has now allowed corruption to mushroom. The judicial system hardly functions. Impunity reigns. At least thirty-four members of the opposition have disappeared or been killed, and more than 300 people have been killed by state security forces since the coup.

SOURCE: Dana Frank, "In Honduras, a Mess Made in the U.S.," *New York Times*, January 27, 2012.

With Zelaya's supporters boycotting the race, the presidential winner was Porfirio Lobo, a wealthy landowner who claimed to receive 55 percent of the recorded votes. The Obama administration proclaimed that the post-coup election was "a significant step forward" in solving the Honduran political crisis. Panama and Colombia went on to congratulate Lobo. Oscar Arias said Costa Rica would recognize the outcome if there was no evidence of fraud. Peru also followed suit. Under pressure from Micheletti, the Honduran Congress then voted against restoring the ousted president to serve out the last two months of his term. Thereupon Brazil and twenty other Latin American and Caribbean countries refused to recognize the election results, calling into question the legitimacy of the post-coup regime.

After continuing pressure from the United States, Honduras was readmitted to the OAS by a vote of 32–1 in June 2011. A key condition for the vote was permission for Zelaya to return to his country after nearly two years of exile. The lone dissent came from Ecuador, whose representative said that her country could not support the move because of human-rights violations in Honduras. Thus the crisis seemed to pass.

It was to be noted, however, that the United States had once again found itself out of touch with most nations of the region. It had displayed logical inconsistency: insistence on democracy in Cuba, lack of support for democracy in Honduras. Moreover, some observers detected a difference in viewpoints between President Obama and Secretary Clinton. Even so, apparent inconsistencies in U.S. policy underlined an element of underlying logic: Geopolitics was paramount.

## QUESTIONS FOR REVIEW

1. At least for now, the war on terror targets mainly South and Central Asia. How does it relate to Latin America? What have been its effects on the region?
2. What role might Latin America play in a so-called clash of civilizations?
3. Why did President Bush's second inaugural address provoke such discomfort in Latin America? Why should anyone be nervous about a campaign to spread democracy?
4. Obama redefined, but did not abandon, the war on terror. What implications might this have for Latin America?
5. What are the rules of the game in the war on terror? What has been their effect on U.S.–Latin American relations?

# CHAPTER 12

# Latin America: Seizing Opportunities

Fortunately, Latin America is no longer a priority for the United States, where priority often signifies crisis.

JOSÉ MIGUEL INSULZA (2006)

Go to hell, gringos! Go home!

HUGO CHÁVEZ (2007)

The war on terror presented Latin America with potential threats, substantial dangers—and unanticipated opportunities. Initially, the 9/11 attacks on the United States provoked widespread outpourings of heartfelt sympathy from the peoples of the Americas. As the George W. Bush administration focused its attention and energy on its military campaigns in Afghanistan and Iraq, many Latin American leaders became annoyed and perplexed. Why the sudden lack of interest in the region? But in time they discovered, perhaps to their surprise, that inattention from the United States enabled them to explore a broad variety of policy alternatives.

As explained in previous chapters, inter-American relations would unfold within the context of two simultaneous "games." One set of rules pertained to geoeconomic alignments and pursuits; the other prescribed codes of geopolitical conduct. The interaction between these two regimes would prove to be complex. Free-trade agreements might initially respond to geoeconomic logic, but they could also be interpreted within the framework of the antiterror campaign. From the standpoint of the United States, the guiding question was clear: Were you on the U.S. side or not? In this sense, as in many others, this troublesome new era would bear an unsettling resemblance to the Cold War.

Latin Americans evinced clear preferences about these issues. Generally speaking, they adhered to the post-9/11 geopolitical game by adopting a "spectator" role: While responding to the antiwar sentiments of their citizens, they did not want to antagonize unduly the United States (or Islamic terrorist groups, for that matter). One effect of this stance was to bow out of the global war on terror. An additional effect was to enable countries of the region to focus on the geoeconomic arena instead. This was a much more appealing alternative.

Tectonic changes in the international order provided powerful incentives for this strategy. As a result of its excessive application of hard power, the United States was losing considerable amounts of "soft" power around the world; it would also plunge into an extended recession by the year 2008. The European Union would also confront deep-seated economic difficulties. In the meantime, large and leading countries of the developing world—India, Brazil, and especially China— emerged as potential world powers. Four of these nations—Brazil, Russia, India, and China—joined together in an informal association known from its initials as "BRIC." Such rapidly shifting arrangements led to confusion and uncertainty; they also offered unprecedented opportunities.

## THE POLITICAL CONTEXT

Democratization was becoming a central feature of Latin American politics. By the early twenty-first century, all but two or three countries were holding free and fair elections. To be sure, citizens remained skeptical about the quality of these contests. As of 2006, the highest levels of confidence in "clean" elections appeared in Uruguay and Chile (83 percent and 69 percent, respectively); then Venezuela (56 percent), Costa Rica (55 percent), Argentina (47 percent), Brazil (44 percent), and Mexico (40 percent); other countries followed at much lower levels. While democracy was omnipresent, it had not yet taken root within the civic culture of the region.

Even so, electoral competition meant that established governments could lay claim to popular legitimacy. It also provided leaders with a protective shield against the United States. However strenuously the United States might object to policy stances or public statements, it could not easily overthrow a freely elected government. There were many steps that the U.S. government still could take to demonstrate dissatisfaction. But now, as a result of the spreading of democracy, Washington would have to respect and recognize constraints. It was one thing to denounce a well-known tyrant; it was something else to overthrow a democratic leader. Elections became a line of defense.

These realities became all the more apparent in light of widespread opposition to the U.S.-led antiterror campaign. Most Latin Americans accepted the rationale for action in Afghanistan; by the same token, they rejected the invasion of Iraq. It was not their intention to defend, protect, or support Saddam Hussein and his regime. The concern was that the doctrine of preemptive war amounted to a repudiation of efforts to uphold international law and institutions as means to promote the peaceful resolution of conflicts. Such commitments had long been cherished in Latin America.

Only seven out of thirty-four nations of Latin America supported the U.S. action in Iraq. Among these countries, six—Central American nations plus the Dominican Republic—were involved in FTA negotiations with the United States; the seventh, Colombia, was receiving more than $600 million per year in U.S. military aid. Generally, however, citizens of the region expressed increasing

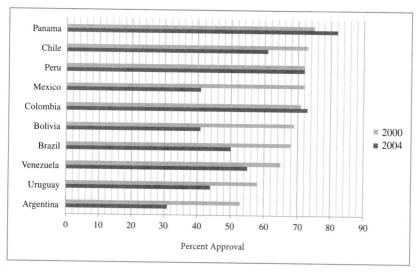

**Figure 12-1  America's Prestige in Latin America: Selected Countries, 2000–2004**
*Note:* Percentage of respondents expressing "good" or "very good" opinion of the United States.
*Source:* Latinobarómetro.

disapproval of American society. According to Figure 12-1, surveys for 2000 and 2004 revealed that the shares of respondents with "favorable" views of the United States dropped from 73 to 61 percent in Chile, from 72 to 41 percent in Mexico, from 68 to 50 percent in Brazil, and from 53 to 31 percent in Argentina. (The figures held steady for Peru and Colombia and showed a discernible increase only in Panama, where FTA negotiations began in 2004.) According to a separate study, 78 percent of Mexicans reported in 2004 that U.S. foreign policy had led them to view the United States unfavorably, while only 18 percent said their view had improved; among Brazilians, the result was 66 percent negative and 17 percent positive; for Argentines, the result was 65 percent negative and just 5 percent positive!

It was only a matter of time before this combination of elements—frustration over economic conditions, repudiation of the Washington consensus, apprehension about the entire process of globalization, and resentment of U.S. domination—would generate substantial popular protest. People were angry and upset. Under the banner of social justice, they were demanding political change. This welling-up led to a resurgence of left-wing and populist movements. And because the vote was mostly free and fair, it was becoming possible for the political left to win presidential elections.

## The New Left

What came to be known as the "pink tide" did not sweep ashore as an organized movement. It was a spontaneous upsurge of popular will. Its leaders did not always get along with one another. It lacked a clear-cut ideology. Some observers regarded the tide as a swelling of the political "left" (but in diluted form, hence the label "pink" instead of the more radical "red"). Others disparaged it as a form of "populism." Hardly anyone bothered to define terms with care.

The seas began to part in the late 1990s, when Hugo Chávez won the Venezuelan election with 56 percent of the vote. A military figure who had taken part in an unsuccessful coup in 1992, he denounced the country's institutions as "corrupt" instruments of a "rancid oligarchy." As oil revenues increased (due to rising prices), he launched social programs designed to meet the needs of the poor—and asserted increasingly authoritarian control over the nation's political apparatus. With the passage of time, his discourse became more and more radical—antiestablishment, antiglobalization, and anti-American. Chávez announced his intention to create "socialism for the twenty-first century" and forged a close alliance with Fidel Castro.

Soon afterward the tide gained strength. Brazilians in 2002 elected as president Luiz Inácio Lula da Silva ("Lula"), founder of the Workers' Party and undisputed leader of the nation's political left. The following year saw the triumph in Argentina of Néstor Kirchner, a renegade member of the Peronist party who resisted economic pressures from the International Monetary Fund. In late 2005 Bolivia elected as president Evo Morales, an indigenous leader of rural *cocaleros* (coca leaf farmers) and a radical firebrand. With chief executives firmly ensconced in Venezuela, Brazil, Argentina, and Bolivia, the new left appeared to be on a roll. Elections in subsequent years gave rise to like-minded presidents in such diverse countries as Ecuador, Nicaragua, Paraguay, Peru, and Uruguay. A near-miss took place in 2006 in Mexico, where a strident left-wing candidate squandered a double-digit lead in the polls to finish a hair's breadth behind the conservative Felipe Calderón.

The pink tide bore ominous messages for the Bush administration. First, the depth and range of anti-American feeling showed that the United States had lost virtually all of its "soft power" in Latin America. Since time immemorial it had been true that Latin Americans, especially intellectuals and members of the "scribbling class," had staunchly opposed American policies but had firmly embraced American society. This was no longer the case. Atrocities at Abu Ghraib and elsewhere provoked widespread disgust, surprise, and disapproval of American society at large. This reaction led to boycotts of such trademark American establishments as McDonald's, the Gap, and Banana Republic.

Second, the trend made it abundantly clear that democratically elected leaders would not necessarily become allies of the United States. It thus demolished one of the most cherished myths of American policymaking, the idea that democratization would produce automatic support for U.S. policies. On the contrary, the surge of the new left meant that the United States would have to face vigorous and persistent criticism—opposition to the war in Iraq, resentment of Washington's arrogance, rejection of pro-U.S. economic policies—from democratic leaders representing popular opinion in their countries. And because they were elected, Washington's hands were tied.

**BOX 12-1**

## What's Left of the Left?

With the ending of the Cold War, many anticipated that the "left" would disappear from the face of the earth. In Latin America, however, electoral triumphs by left-of-center candidates suggested that something else was happening. Was it a resurgence of the left? The question begs for careful definition.

What defines the "left," at its core, is a structure of ideological beliefs that corresponds to fundamental social values. The same is true of the "right." Crucial to this understanding is the ideological spectrum extending from left to right. The watchword for the left is *justice*; for the right it is *freedom*. Both positions invoke noble principles, but they take opposing views:

- The left holds that the well-being of society as a whole supersedes the interests of self-centered individuals; the right insists on the inalienable right of individuals to seek property, status, and self-satisfaction.

- The left stresses the importance of collective responsibility; the right upholds the autonomy of the individual.

- The left calls for the extension of equal opportunity to all sectors of society; the right insists that the social order reflects the "survival of the fittest" and is therefore not in need of change.

- The left argues for the necessity of a strong state, one that has the capacity to rectify social injustice; the right deplores governmental interference and places ultimate faith in the "invisible hand" of the market.

- The left advocates the state-sponsored redistribution of material goods, usually invoking the ideal of fairness; the right justifies the prevailing distribution of goods, usually making the claim that investments by the rich will "trickle down" to benefit the poor.

- The left promotes fundamental change in the structures of social and political power; the right seeks to preserve the status quo.

This framework yields a simple insight: You don't need to be a Marxist in order to be on the left. You do not need to have digested *Das Kapital*. Nor do you need to have lamented the demise of the Soviet Union or the collapse of the East German state. You are not even required to belong to a political party that labels itself as "socialist" or "communist." You simply need to embrace the values of the left and policy prescriptions deriving from those values.

---

Such trends threatened to undermine America's position in the broader international arena. The United States was increasingly perceived as unable to control its own "backyard." Relationships with the United States became hot-button issues in electoral campaigns. Most chief executives carefully distanced themselves from Washington, while a few, the pink wave populists, openly challenged U.S. policies. The United States could no longer count on its closest neighbors for automatic support in the global arena. What kind of superpower was that?

## The Burial of FTAA

Tensions came to a head in November 2005 at a Summit of the Americas in the Argentine resort city of Mar del Plata. With Bush scheduled to be in attendance, the occasion offered a golden opportunity for anti-U.S. declarations—and for Hugo Chávez. The day before the opening of the conference, demonstrators held a massive "People's Summit," or "American Anti-Summit," that featured appearances by Bolivian presidential candidate Evo Morales, Argentine soccer legend Diego Maradona, and Cuban singer-composer Silvio Rodríguez. At a World Cup soccer stadium, Chávez rallied the rambunctious crowd and joined in a "people's march" to repudiate the presence of the American president. "Every one of us brought a gravedigger's shovel," Chávez proclaimed, "because here in Mar del Plata is FTAA's tomb. Let us repeat together: FTAA, FTAA, FTAA to hell" (*ALCA, ALCA, ALCA al carajo*).

Apparently unfazed by this publicity, the Bush delegation stubbornly promoted its plan for a Free Trade Area of the Americas. The discussion soon dissolved into disagreement over U.S. intentions to continue protectionist measures in favor of American farmers. As major agricultural producers, Brazil and Argentina angrily refused. Neither side budged. Negotiations ground to a halt. A jubilant Chávez pronounced that FTAA had effectively been "buried."

## LATIN AMERICA DIVIDED

The fate of FTAA revealed sharp divisions within Latin America. Democratization brought new leaders to the fore—and with them, a broad range of views on how to deal with the United States. One thing was clear: Latin America would no longer follow U.S. leadership in unanimous lockstep. And in divergent ways, leaders of Mexico, Brazil, and Venezuela would aspire to positions of regional leadership.

### Mexico: Fox and Calderón

After his stunning electoral triumph in 2000, Vicente Fox presented himself as a responsible interlocutor between Latin America and the United States. As noted in chapter 9, he committed himself and Mexico to the idea of a "special relationship" with the United States. The unspoken idea was that, by cajoling the United States into immigration reform, he would demonstrate a unique capability for dealing with the Colossus of the North. He would show how things could be done—not by shrill antics but, rather, by mature diplomacy, judicious lobbying, and tactical alliances with selected pressure groups. This approach would certify leadership capacity not only within the hemisphere but also in the world arena. As his foreign minister said in a pugilistic analogy, such a display of political skills would enable Mexico to "punch above its weight."

The collapse of Fox's hopes for comprehensive immigration reform in the wake of 9/11 led to considerable disappointment, and Bush's cool attitude in subsequent months must have caused considerable personal anguish for the Mexican president. Yet he recovered his balance and persisted.

Actually Fox had no choice in the matter. The fact was that NAFTA inextricably bound Mexico to its northern neighbors. It was unthinkable for Mexico to engage in high-profile conflict with the United States. From the 1950s through the 1980s, Mexico had espoused a nationalist stance of resistance to U.S. hegemony: Claiming to be the institutional heir of the Revolution of 1910, the PRI often defied the will of Washington (within carefully circumscribed limits), jealously protected national sovereignty, and spoke up for the region as a whole. That ended with NAFTA. The conviction quickly spread forth that Mexico had turned its back on Latin America.

Mexico's changing identity left Fox with only one plausible role: to serve as a bridge between the United States and Latin America, especially those countries seeking institutional links with the United States. As interlocutor, Mexico could acquire and exert considerable leverage over these negotiations and the resulting shape of hemispheric relations. Throughout the 1990s, in fact, it had been hoped that Mexico could assume this role by controlling country-by-country accessions to NAFTA. By the time Fox had taken office, however, the idea of NAFTA expansion had faded out of view. The remaining opportunity was FTAA, which would at least have given Mexico some say in the process—whereas it was totally locked out of minilateral and bilateral negotiations, which the United States was pursuing in unilateral fashion. And that option disappeared in the aftermath of Mar del Plata.

Fox's successor as president, Felipe Calderón, placed a high priority on a close relationship with the United States, especially in support of his battle with

Mexico, 2005: Vicente Fox sharply denounces American plans to construct a wall along the U.S.–Mexican border.
Source: AP Photo/Mario Armas.

drug-trafficking organizations. At the same time he publicly criticized America's role in the drug trade—most notably its growing appetite for illicit substances and its sale of high-power weapons to agents of criminal gangs.

Further, Calderón made deliberate efforts to strengthen Mexico's ties with Latin America. He promoted engagement with Cuba. He proclaimed support for multinational organizations as distinct from bilateral ties with Washington. He hosted and helped found CELAC, the Community of Latin American and Caribbean States, an organization that pointedly excluded both the United States and Canada. In such ways, Calderón operated as a traditional Mexican nationalist.

## Brazil: Lula and Dilma

Lula seemed so different from Vicente Fox. It was expected, in many quarters, that this self-made labor leader would mount an all-out campaign against the hegemonic position of the United States. After all, Lula had valiantly opposed the military generals who had seized power with U.S. support, he had been the founder of a left-wing party, and he had launched numerous barbs over the years against prominent American officials. Under his leadership, it was thought, Brazil would lead a hemispheric uprising against the overweening arrogance of the United States.

Such expectations fell wide of the mark. First, it was to be remembered that Lula won the election of 2002 on his fourth attempt. On previous occasions he had done well in the first round, only to suffer defeat by centrist coalitions in the second round. In order to win the presidency, he would have to trim his sails and move toward the center of the political spectrum. That he did. According to some disenchanted supporters, Lula was not Lula anymore.

Second, Lula had never been an ideologue. He shaped his political views not through extensive exegesis of Marxist treatises and Hegelian dialectics but, rather, as a metalworker in the foundries of São Paulo. He was a pragmatic politician, accustomed to give-and-take bargaining as a labor union leader. Lula never lost sight of his goals, but he was willing to make concessions in order to achieve them.

Third, Lula subscribed to the longstanding idea—a key component in the concept of *grandeza brasileira*—that his country should co-govern the Americas as a co-equal partner with the United States. This aspiration had been the lodestar of Brazilian diplomacy since the late nineteenth century. It continued to shape foreign policy during the period of military rule, during the uncertain years of democratic transition, and during the enlightened leadership of Fernando Henrique Cardoso. It prevailed under Lula as well. He was, at heart, a Brazilian nationalist.

This posture led to ambivalent relations with the United States. On the one hand, there was a clear-cut rivalry: Brazil was out to become the equal of the United States. Doing so would not only strengthen the hand of Brazil but also, in a zero-sum game, reduce the influence of the United States. Brazil was therefore in the business of accumulating power at U.S. expense. On the other hand, there was to be a partnership: In consultation with each other, the two countries would govern the Western Hemisphere as a joint enterprise. The United States would take care of North America, Brazil would take care of South America, and the two regional powers would collaborate on ways to promote the well-being of their dominions and to maintain their mutual preeminence. Lula walked a very fine line.

The complexities of Brazilian foreign policy found clear expression in the decision to accept the command of a UN peacekeeping force in Haiti. In early 2004 the Bush administration had acquiesced in the ouster by paramilitary thugs of the elected president, Jean-Bertrand Aristide. American and French forces thereafter imposed partial law and order but were eager to leave the area. When the UN agreed to dispatch a peacekeeping force, the Brazilian decision to contribute 1,200 soldiers and to accept overall command of blue-helmeted units came as a godsend to the White House. By the same token, the decision helped reinforce the Brazilian claim to regional leadership. As Celso Amorim, Lula's foreign minister, declared, "You can't be a supporter of multilateralism and when it comes to act say it's [too] dangerous." Preeminence entailed responsibility.

It was on international trade that Lula led the anti-U.S. charge. As a major agricultural producer, Brazil suffered mightily from America's protectionist policies—especially for textiles, sugar, and frozen orange juice. Steel was another key item. It was estimated, in fact, that U.S. subsidies and nontariff barriers cost Brazil as much as $10 billion per year. Particularly onerous was the Bush administration's lavish farm bill of 2002. Ultimately, this was the bill that determined Brazil's firm opposition to FTAA.

Lula aggressively challenged U.S. trade policy in multilateral forums, particularly the World Trade Organization. Repeatedly, and thoughtfully, he demanded reduction or elimination of agricultural subsidies in the world's richest nations—the United States, the European Union, and Japan. This posture raised Brazil's profile not only in the Americas but also within the global arena.

- In 2003, Brazil emerged as a leading voice in the Group of 20-plus (a.k.a. the Group of 21), a coalition of developing nations demanding reduction of farm subsidies in the United States and Europe as part of international trade negotiations. (Note: This organization was different from the Group of Twenty "major economies" established in 1999 with membership including Argentina, Brazil, and Mexico as well as the EU and the United States.)
- Also in 2003, Brazil created the Group of Three (G3) along with India and South Africa—with the intention of later including China and Russia in a Group of Five (G5) that would mobilize the global influence of top-tier developing nations.
- In early 2004, Brazil forged a "strategic alliance" with India and signed a preferential customs accord. With a combined population of 1.2 billion, Lula proclaimed, "India and Brazil together can build a strong political force that is capable of making a contribution, so that the trade geography of the world can change for the better."

On this particular front, Brazil's national interest coincided neatly with the needs of developing nations. Lula's defense of farmers in Brazil became a defense of poor people everywhere around the world. In this particular arena, geoeconomics merged with geopolitics.

Not so in other arenas. In 2010, Brazil attempted to raise its international profile by joining together with Turkey to sponsor negotiations over the Iranian nuclear program, regarded by many as a threat to stability in the Middle East and throughout the world. This was an especially hot-button issue for the United States and its longtime ally, Israel. So the Brazil-Turkey initiative drew a stern rebuke from Secretary of State Hillary Clinton, who had in the meantime been promoting a punitive resolution against Iran in the United Nations. The two countries were forced to back down but ultimately voted against the U.S.-sponsored resolution. The episode seriously damaged U.S.-Brazilian relations, at least for a while, and it underscored a basic lesson: It was acceptable for emerging nations to play the geoeconomic game aggressively but not the geopolitical game. That was still the ultimate preserve of the United States.

Such tensions also affected Brazil's longstanding quest for a permanent seat on the UN Security Council. With urging from Lula, the foreign office intensified its diplomatic campaign. At one time or another Brazil gained the support of four of the five permanent members—Great Britain, France, China, and Russia—but not of the United States. This oversight would be a continuing thorn in the side of Brazil.

Lula's hand-picked successor as president, Dilma Rousseff, concentrated largely on domestic issues. She also continued to follow his foreign policy agenda.

Beijing, 2011: President Hu Jintao greets Dilma Rousseff in the Great Hall of the People.
SOURCE: Photo By Sheng Jiapeng/Color China Photo/AP Images.

She promoted Brazilian claims to continental leadership through UNASUR/ UNASUL, the Union of South American nations, and through the expansion of MERCOSUR in 2012 to include Venezuela.[1] In concert with other candidate nations, she pressed the campaign for permanent Brazilian membership on the UN Security Council. She emphasized the importance of BRIC (the gatherings of Brazil, Russia, India, and China), and she expanded Brazil's relationships with countries throughout the developing world.

## Venezuela: The One and Only Hugo

By far the most vociferous challenge to U.S. power and preeminence came from Venezuela and its mercurial leader, Hugo Chávez. His foreign policy ambitions took shape over time. Two factors proved critical. One was an attempted coup against him in April 2002: It was an unsuccessful and ill-managed affair, but it led Chávez to conclude that the United States had actively taken part in the plot against his rule. (Subsequent evidence suggested that the Bush administration supported the coup and probably gave plotters a green light to proceed but that American officials did not participate directly in the planning or operations.) The second factor was a rise in the price of crude oil, largely as a result of surging demand in Asia and especially in China. The average price per barrel soared from around $12 (USD) in 1998 to more than $60 by 2005 and then to $140 in early 2008. Windfall earnings provided funding for extensive social programs within Venezuela and presented Chávez with an invaluable resource for international wheeling and dealing.

To bolster his standing, Chávez launched the *Alternativa Bolivariana para las Américas* (ALBA, or Bolivarian Alternative for the Americas), an initiative designed to provide an "alternative" to FTAA and, by extension, to American supremacy. Presenting himself as the political heir of Simón Bolívar, Chávez proffered a series of petrodollar-funded programs to needy countries and prospective allies: oil on preferential terms, low-cost loans, and a left-leaning television outlet. The *Alternativa* thus combined material rewards with ideological propaganda. Initially dismissed as the grandiose fantasy of an uncivilized loudmouth, ALBA gradually acquired supporters throughout Latin America. Bolivia joined the program in 2006, as would Nicaragua in 2007 and Ecuador in 2009, together with Honduras (from 2008 to 2010) plus some other, smaller states.

A linchpin for the *Alternativa* was a close alliance with Cuba. Although Chávez was more populist than Marxist, he revered Castro as a mentor and model—in particular, because of Fidel's survival in the face of U.S. hostility. In fact the partnership had plausible foundations: Venezuela could offer social funding (from expanding petroleum revenues), while Cuba could offer medical assistance (with highly trained doctors). The collaboration became so intimate that some anxious observers even began to contemplate a formal Cuban–Venezuelan federation. "A couple of years ago we would have said that such an idea just reflected right-wing

---

[1] The stated goal was to establish MERCOSUR as "a new pole of power" by extending its influence into the Caribbean and Central America; an additional motive was to offset the newly created Alliance of the Pacific (Chile, Colombia, Mexico, and Peru).

hysteria," noted a European ambassador in Caracas. "Not any more. The Cuban view is that Venezuela is too important to be left to the Venezuelans."

From time to time, Washington aroused itself to issue a warning or denunciation. Secretary of State Condoleezza Rice declared that Venezuela was "a negative force in the region" and announced her intent to "inoculate" the Chávez regime with the support of a "united front" of hemispheric nations. It was unclear who might join such a front. As speculation mounted, Ricardo Lagos of Chile punctured the balloon: "We have signaled that we have a good level of relations with Venezuela, that there are certain positions of the Venezuelan president that we do not share, but that it is better to have a political relationship of exchange and fluid dialogue." In fact, Lagos said, the new left was not a threat to the United States but, rather, a positive sign of deepening democracy throughout the region. So much for the inoculation strategy.

At the global level, Chávez pursued instrumental goals. One was to become the undisputed leader of the developing world—in particular, of the Conference of Non-Aligned Nations, which held its fourteenth meeting in Havana in September 2006. As explained earlier, this organization began in the mid-1950s as an effort by Third World nations to find a neutral path through the Cold War. In a similar vein, its members were by this time hoping to find safe passage through the war on terror. Although he was too ill to attend, Fidel Castro used the meeting as an opportunity to establish his brother Raúl as the authentic head of Cuba's government and to designate Hugo Chávez as the leader of an anti-American, anti-imperialist coalition of developing nations. The principal achievement of the gathering was institutional: reinvigoration of the G-77 as a forum for the developing world.

In addition, Chávez was actively seeking a two-year, nonpermanent seat for his country on the United Nations Security Council. By far the most decisive forum within the UN, the Security Council has fifteen members—five permanent members, each with a veto, and ten temporary members. The permanent members are the victorious allies from World War II: China, France, Great Britain, Russia, and the United States. It would have been a great political and publicity coup for the Venezuelan regime to occupy one of the other ten seats.

Chávez delivered a speech to the UN General Assembly about a month before the voting. He absolutely stunned the multitude. Referring to a prior appearance by President Bush, he declared that "the devil came here yesterday. Yesterday the devil came here. Right here. . . . And it smells of sulphur still today." To make himself completely clear, he went on: "The President of the United States, the gentleman to whom I refer as the devil, came here, talking as if he owned the world. Truly. As the owner of the world." He denounced American arrogance, its use of force, and its effort to impose a "hegemonic system of domination." Throughout the remainder of his statement, Chávez went on to offer a thoughtful and articulate analysis of the UN system. Hardly anyone remembered that. This became the "devil" speech.

It would cost him dearly. Chávez had broken the rules of civilized diplomacy. He had insulted a U.S. president by name. He had publicly accused the

New York, 2006: Hugo Chávez recommends a book by American scholar Noam Chomsky at the outset of his "devil" speech.
Source: AP Photo/Ed Betz.

world's only superpower of immoral behavior. He thus furnished his enemies with powerful ammunition, apparently confirming the charge that Venezuela could not be trusted with a prestigious seat on the Security Council. After intense behind-the-scene negotiations, the seat on the Council finally went to Panama.

In retrospect, this episode marked the pinnacle of Chavez's international campaign—and the beginning of its decline. Leading a "moderate" wing within the new left, Lula began to distance himself from Chávez. Brazil developed a cool but cooperative stance toward the United States. Lula hosted George Bush on part of a multination tour of the region, signing a joint accord to promote the production of ethanol as an alternative source of energy. A sudden drop in the price of oil in mid-2008 imposed limits on Venezuela's largesse; it would climb upward in 2009 and 2010, but not to previous highs. ALBA was losing momentum.

As Chávez began campaigning for reelection in 2012, it became apparent that he was seriously ill with cancer. He underwent intensive medical treatment in Cuba. As he struggled to keep up with public duties, details on his condition were closely guarded state secrets. The fate of Venezuela seemed to be hanging in the balance.

## THE REST OF THE WORLD

As in previous eras, Latin American leaders were scanning the post-9/11 world in search of potential partners. The hope was to establish economic and political relationships that would help improve social welfare, to broaden the range of international connections, and to navigate the narrow path between contending parties in the global war on terror. The perennial question arose: How much interest would nations outside the hemisphere have in Latin America?

### Europe
One place to look was the European Union. The story had a familiar ring: Europe held benevolent views of Latin America but was too absorbed in its own problems to pay much attention. Serious issues divided the union. One issue was the war on terror itself, especially the U.S.-led invasion of Iraq. The United Kingdom and Spain supported the action, at least at the outset, while France and Germany did not. Throughout the continent, public opinion was strongly opposed to the Iraqi operation.

Second, Europe was uncertain about its own future. Objections were rising against the continuing expansion of membership. Having begun as a cohesive group of twelve nations, the union now comprised more than twenty-five states—including Bulgaria, Romania, Estonia, Latvia, Lithuania, Poland, the Czech Republic, Slovakia, Cyprus, and Malta. Future additions were likely to include Serbia, Montenegro, Bosnia, Macedonia, Slovenia, Croatia (the former Yugoslavia), and such ex-Soviet states as Ukraine, Moldavia, and Georgia. In the meantime the most intense controversy was swirling around the potential admittance of Turkey, a largely Muslim state with a dubious human-rights record.

Europe was in no position to grant much time or attention to Latin America. In May 2006 a summit meeting of European and Latin American heads of state produced elegant declarations that were utterly devoid of meaningful content. Participants solemnly affirmed that "we reiterate our commitment to continue promoting and strengthening our strategic bi-regional association as agreed in previous summits." As summarized by the Spanish newspaper *El País*, "A paralyzed Europe collides with a divided Latin America." In the meantime, the much-publicized idea of an FTA between the EU and MERCOSUR languished for lack of attention—and for lack of commitment on both sides. And as the international community was reeling from the effects of global financial crises after 2008, the EU was facing internal divisions over debt crises in Greece, Portugal, and Spain that threatened to unravel its entire fabric. Europe was struggling to get its own house in order, much less reach out to emerging areas.

## Japan

As it became apparent that Europe would be unable (and unwilling) to solve Latin America's problems, leaders turned their attention toward Asia. After all, the two regions had substantial cultural and social connections, they were both seeking new partners, they belonged to common organizations (such as APEC), and they were anxious to forge a countervailing mechanism to offset the hegemony of the United States.

Early in the 1990s the most avidly sought partner was Japan. Its economic prowess, its bureaucratic efficiency, and its rising international position imbued Japan with substantial prestige. In the years that followed, however, Tokyo became increasingly concerned with its own economic situation and with worrisome developments in China and North Korea. Japan's overseas development assistance to Latin America dropped by more than half between 1995 and 2004. Trade and investment steadily slipped. By the turn of the century, Japan's banks and businesses were pulling back from Latin America. The principal exception was Mexico, which entered into an FTA with Japan in 2004.

In the meantime, Japanese diplomacy assumed an ever-lower profile in the Americas. By tradition Japan tended to take a cautious stance toward Latin America, mainly in order to avoid counterproductive quarrels with the United States. After 9/11, Japan was not about to risk disapproval or reprisal from the world's only superpower.

## China

China was an altogether-different story. Just as Japan was disengaging from Latin America, nothing less than "China fever" gripped the leaders of the region. Presidents, ministers, entrepreneurs, and journalists suddenly "discovered" China and its growing impact on the world.

The fundamental reality was economic. China's rapidly expanding consumer market displayed a boundless appetite for agricultural goods. Similarly, the country's surging industrial sector needed voluminous supplies of raw materials, especially minerals and petroleum.

Latin America could provide these things in abundance. Starting at $3.6 billion in 2000, regional exports to China grew to $18.6 billion in 2005 and then swelled to $72.8 billion by 2010. By that year China was absorbing nearly 25 percent of Chile's exports, over 15 percent of Brazil's, and nearly 10 percent of Argentina's. China also accounted for 14 percent of Latin American imports. Within a single decade or so, it had become a major trading partner.

PRC leadership had long been paving the way for this burgeoning relationship. Jiang Zemin paid goodwill visits to the region in 1993, 1997, and 2001. Stepping up the pace, President Hu Jintao took advantage of an APEC meeting to visit Argentina, Brazil, Chile, and Cuba in 2004; he also toured the region before and after a BRIC gathering in Brasília in 2010. China's vice president and high-level officials made visits to Mexico, Ecuador, Colombia, and other countries. The message was everywhere the same: It was time to open a new era in trans-Pacific relations. Hu spoke not only of trade but also of production, declaring that China would raise its investments in the region to $100 billion within the next decade. As one of Beijing's leading experts observed, the twenty-first century was becoming "the best period in history in China–Latin American ties."

China's official priorities for Latin America found expression in the government's carefully calibrated scale of relations with individual countries. Brazil gained the maximum recognition as a "strategic partner" as early as 1994, followed by Venezuela in 2001 and Argentina and Mexico in 2004. Chile held the more modest status of a "cooperative partner." At a still lower level was Cuba, with which China held "friendly and cooperative relations." (Political relations with Cuba had often been very tense.) As the rankings suggest, the PRC's principal concerns were economic rather than ideological or political.

Brazil occupied the topmost rung in China's priorities because of its importance as a source of key materials, such as soybeans and iron ore. For its part, Brazil was seeking China's support for its campaign to gain a permanent seat on the UN Security Council. Venezuela's status derived mainly from its petroleum, while Argentina relied on its exports of soybeans and wheat. Chile was valued largely because of its copper—and, seeking to improve its standing, signed a free-trade agreement with China in August 2006. In contrast, Mexico acquired "strategic" status because of its membership in NAFTA and, in consequence, its singular importance as a site for Chinese overseas investment. All these relationships were positive in orientation, pragmatic in tone, and low in ideological content.

This atmosphere led to complications in the geopolitical arena. Most governments in Latin America were hoping that China would provide a counterweight to U.S. hegemony in the region, yet these expectations took divergent forms. Cuba and Venezuela wanted harsh and heavy-duty balancing; Argentina, Brazil, Chile, and Mexico wanted soft balancing instead. From its own standpoint, the PRC was determined to follow its own path in dealing with the U.S. government. Whether this path coincided with Latin American wishes was a relatively minor matter.

Geopolitical interests included the question of Taiwan. After the Chinese communists seized power in 1949, a conservative opposition (so-called nationalists) set up an alternative government on the island of Taiwan. During the early years of the Cold War, the United States and other Western allies recognized the nationalist movement in Taipei as the sole and legitimate government of China. As the PRC gained more and more stability, the contradictions of this stance became increasingly apparent. After brief experimentation with a "two-China" policy, Washington finally extended diplomatic recognition solely to Beijing during the 1970s. Most Latin American governments thereafter followed suit by the 1990s. Yet largely because of substantial levels of economic assistance from Taipei, twelve nations—small countries in Central America and the Caribbean, plus Paraguay—still recognized Taiwan as the legitimate government of China. In mid-2007 Costa Rica suddenly broke ranks and extended recognition to the PRC. Clearly, Beijing would prefer to achieve recognition from all countries of the region, and that was one goal of its diplomatic offensive. But just as clearly, Beijing was willing to tolerate this anomaly and patiently await the moment for change.

Not everyone took a roseate view of the rapprochement with China. There was concern in some quarters that China might attract foreign investment that might otherwise go to Latin America. But the greatest worry, especially prevalent in Mexico, was that China would take over sizable shares of the U.S. market. Low costs of labor plus state-led investments offered unbeatable (if not unfair) advantages for the PRC. Moreover, the composition of Chinese exports showed considerable overlap with Mexican products. Having worked so hard to reap the benefits of NAFTA, Mexico was now in danger of losing its place of privilege.

Conservatives in the United States voiced disapproval over China's continuing support for Fidel Castro, over its growing interest in Venezuela, and over the deployment of Chinese peacekeepers in Haiti. Skeptics dismissed such disapproval as, at bottom, resentment that an extrahemispheric power was daring to intrude on America's backyard. Why shouldn't China take an interest in the affairs of the region? And why shouldn't regional leaders welcome China's presence? As a senior aide to the Foreign Relations Committee of the U.S. Senate said, speaking on condition of anonymity: "For years and years, the hemisphere has been a low priority for the U.S., and the Chinese are taking advantage of it. They're taking advantage of the fact that we don't care as much as we should about Latin America."

## Iran?

As the wars on terror continued, an unlikely controversy fastened on a novel theme—the growing presence in Latin America of the Islamic Republic of Iran. There is no question that the fundamentalist theocratic regime launched a deliberate diplomatic offensive. After the presidential election of Mahmoud Ahmadinejad in 2005, the country opened six new embassies in the region (in Bolivia, Chile, Colombia, Ecuador, Nicaragua, and Uruguay) in addition to five preexisting ones (Argentina, Brazil, Cuba, Mexico, and Venezuela). Ahmadinejad became a frequent visitor to the region, especially to Venezuela. In 2009 he made a state visit to Brazil, during which Lula defended Iran's right to the peaceful development of nuclear capabilities. As Ahmadinejad himself declared: "When the Western countries were trying to isolate Iran, we went to the U.S. backyard."

The question was what this all meant. Did Iranian influence pose a genuine threat to U.S. interests? Or did it merely mark Iran as part of an "axis of annoyance"?

Right-wing analysts came up with ready answers. In 2009, Norman Bailey surmised that Iranian activities in Venezuela were "designed to facilitate and provide cover for illegal and subversive endeavors that not only involve the Iranian government but also terrorist organizations such as Hamas, Hezbollah, Islamic Jihad, the Colombian FARC and drug cartels from Colombia, Mexico and Venezuela." And in 2012, José Azel testified to the U.S. Congress that "Iran is an increasingly important politico-economic player in Latin America." In concert with Cuba and Venezuela, Iran expressed "a virulent hostility towards the United States, liberal democracy and market economies, as well as opposition to Israel." Azel declared that this was "fundamentally an anti-American political alignment" that was extending its reach to Bolivia, Ecuador, and Nicaragua. Or, in Ahmadinejad's own words, the partnership was based upon "a large anti-imperialist movement that has emerged in the region."

Both sides in this exchange were seeking support from the other. Leaders of ALBA countries would welcome political and, especially, economic support. And for its part, Iran wanted to show that it was not isolated and wanted to challenge Washington's influence. More specifically, it wanted approval for its nuclear program. Indeed, the nature of this bargain was captured at a ceremony for a new factory in Venezuela that was designed to produce three things: "tractors, influence, and angst" (tractors for Venezuela, influence for Iran, and angst for the United States). Rising to the bait, U.S. Speaker of the House John Boehner denounced Iran as a threat to democracy in the Americas.

**Table 12-1   Economic Growth: Latin America and the Caribbean, 2001–2010**

| | GDP GROWTH RATES, AS % | | | |
|---|---|---|---|---|
| COUNTRY | AVERAGE 2001–2003 | 2004 | 2005 | 2010 |
| **FTAs with United States** | | | | |
| Chile | 3.2 | 6.2 | 6.3 | 5.2 |
| Costa Rica | 3.5 | 4.1 | 5.9 | 4.2 |
| Dominican Republic | 2.3 | 2.7 | 9.2 | 7.8 |
| El Salvador | 2.1 | 1.8 | 2.8 | 1.4 |
| Guatemala | 2.2 | 2.7 | 3.2 | 2.8 |
| Honduras | 2.9 | 5.0 | 4.1 | 2.8 |
| Mexico | 0.7 | 4.2 | 3.0 | 5.6 |
| Nicaragua | 2.1 | 5.1 | 4.0 | 4.5 |
| **No FTAs with United States** | | | | |
| Argentina | − 2.2 | 9.0 | 9.2 | 9.2 |
| Bolivia | 2.3 | 3.6 | 4.1 | 4.1 |
| Brazil | 1.2 | 4.9 | 2.3 | 7.5 |
| Colombia* | 2.4 | 4.8 | 5.2 | 4.3 |
| Cuba | 2.5 | 5.4 | 11.8 | 2.1 |
| Ecuador | 4.4 | 7.9 | 4.7 | 3.6 |
| Haiti | − 0.3 | − 3.5 | 1.8 | −5.1 |
| Panama* | 2.3 | 7.5 | 6.9 | 7.6 |
| Paraguay | 2.0 | 4.1 | 2.9 | 15.0 |
| Peru* | 3.1 | 5.2 | 6.4 | 8.8 |
| Uruguay | − 4.1 | 11.8 | 6.6 | 8.5 |
| Venezuela | − 4.4 | 17.9 | 9.3 | −1.5 |
| Latin America and Caribbean | 0.5 | 5.9 | 4.5 | 5.9 |

*FTA negotiated but not ratified as of 2010.

SOURCE: Economic Commission for Latin America and the Caribbean.

## ECONOMIC GROWTH AND CHANGE

One of the most important achievements of Latin America during the war on terror has been a resurgence of economic growth. To demonstrate the point, Table 12-1 presents growth rates from 2001 through 2010 for the twenty countries of the region, separated according to whether or not they had free-trade agreements with the United States. As the data show, the overall situation was miserable in 2001, 2002, and 2003—with overall growth hovering around zero. Things improved markedly in 2004, when the region achieved a growth rate of 5.9 percent; the positive trend continued through 2005 and 2006, with estimated growth of 4.5 and 5.3 percent, respectively. After declines in 2008 and 2009, due largely to global financial crises, the region recovered with an overall growth rate of nearly 6 percent in 2010.

Warnings still lingered on the horizon. First, this spurt of growth came after many years of growing popular disenchantment—disenchantment with the Washington consensus, with the democratic leaders who promoted neoliberal reforms, with the whole process of globalization, and with economic linkages to the United States. Second, the turnaround of 2004–2005 was due not so much to ingenious policymaking by Latin America—it resulted from growing demand for raw materials and agricultural goods, especially in Asia. It merely perpetuated the region's traditional role as a source of petroleum, minerals, and foodstuffs; it meant, in effect, "growth without development." Third, the levels of growth were still inadequate—to meet its social challenges, according to many experts, Latin America required sustained growth rates of 6 or 7 percent.

Even so, the resumption of growth helped raise levels of popular satisfaction. According to a survey in 2006, 31 percent of respondents in Latin America believed that the overall situation in their country was "better" or "much better" than the year before, compared with only 14 percent in 2001. Also in 2006, 18 percent judged the economic situation to be "good" or "very good," compared with just 7 percent as late as 2003. The *trends over time* showed considerable improvement. At the same time, it was painfully clear that the *overall levels* of satisfaction were still pretty low.

Finally, some of the most notable performances appeared in countries that did not have (or were not preparing for) free-trade agreements with the United States. During 2004, no fewer than four non-FTA countries—Argentina, Ecuador, Uruguay, and Venezuela—had growth rates higher than the best-performing FTA country (Chile, as usual). During 2005 and 2006, Argentina and Venezuela held rankings at or near the top, now alongside Cuba, while other non-FTA countries performed relatively well. In 2010 the highest growth rates appeared in Paraguay, Argentina, Peru, Uruguay, and Brazil (exceeded only by the Dominican Republic among FTA countries). To be sure, FTA countries displayed steadier rates of growth, with somewhat less oscillation. Growth rates provide only one indication of overall economic performance, of course, but in the minds of many Latin Americans they posed a basic question: If growth could occur without close links with the U.S. economy, why seek FTAs with the United States?

The most beneficial effect of this surge in regional growth was a sharp reduction in poverty, a deep-seated condition that had plagued the region from time immemorial. According to recent statistics, overall *rates* of poverty declined from 48.3 percent in 1990 to 44.0 percent in 2002 and then plunged, rather suddenly, to 31.4 percent in 2010. In less than a decade the rate thus dropped from nearly one-half to less than one-third. Meanwhile the absolute *number* of people in poverty fell from 221 million in 2002, the year with the highest levels, to an estimated 177 million—a decline of 44 million. It appeared, indeed, that this rising tide was lifting a very large number of boats. Equally encouraging were preliminary signs that levels of economic inequality might have begun to decline in the early 2000s.

## Pulling Away from the United States?

All this time, the United States was losing geoeconomic leverage in the region. As shown by Table 12-2, the U.S. share of exports declined sharply between 2000 and 2010, especially in South America—from 24 percent to 12 percent in Bolivia, from 22 percent to less than 10 percent in Brazil, from 28 percent to 16 percent in Peru. Overall percentages remained higher in Middle America and the Caribbean, but changes were apparent even there: U.S. export shares dropped from 55 percent to 34 percent in Costa Rica, from 87 to 52 percent in the Dominican Republic,

**Table 12-2  U.S. Shares of Latin American Trade, 2000–2010, in %**

|  | EXPORTS | | IMPORTS | |
|---|---|---|---|---|
|  | 2000 | 2010 | 2000 | 2010 |
| **Middle America & Caribbean** | | | | |
| Costa Rica | 55.0 | 33.6 | 23.6 | 40.0 |
| Dominican Republic | 87.3 | 52.0 | 60.6 | 44.0 |
| El Salvador | 65.4 | 43.5 | 50.0 | 32.1 |
| Guatemala | 36.1 | 36.9 | 40.1 | 34.6 |
| Honduras | 53.8 | 65.0 | 47.6 | 50.7 |
| Mexico | 88.7 | 73.5 | 72.0 | 60.6 |
| Nicaragua | 39.7 | 58.2 | 25.0 | 23.4 |
| Panama | 45.4 | 5.3 | 32.9 | 10.0 |
| **South America** | | | | |
| Argentina | 12.0 | 5.4 | 19.1 | 13.8 |
| Bolivia | 24.0 | 12.3 | 22.5 | 11.9 |
| Brazil | 22.4 | 9.6 | 23.1 | 15.0 |
| Chile | 16.8 | 10.4 | 17.8 | 17.0 |
| Colombia | 50.4 | 37.4 | 35.5 | 32.4 |
| Ecuador | 38.0 | 37.3 | 25.0 | 29.6 |
| Paraguay | 3.9 | 1.3 | 7.2 | 16.6 |
| Peru | 28.1 | 16.1 | 24.7 | 24.7 |
| Uruguay | 8.4 | 2.9 | 9.8 | 8.8 |
| Venezuela | 51.9 | 38.7 | 33.5 | 26.6 |

Source: International Monetary Fund, *Direction of Trade Statistics*.

and from 89 percent to 74 percent in Mexico (notwithstanding its membership in NAFTA). Some countries were sending hardly any exports directly to the U.S. market. (Uruguay and Paraguay were trading mainly with their partners in MERCOSUR, Argentina and Brazil, while Panama was serving as a clearing house for international trade.)

United States shares of Latin America's imports revealed similar patterns. In Mexico the proportion slipped from 72 percent to 61 percent, in Argentina it dropped from 19 to 14 percent, and for Brazil it faded from 23 to 15 percent. Data are ambiguous for several other cases, but an indelible impression emerges nonetheless: Diversification in Latin America's commercial relations meant less economic leverage for the United States.

Such developments prompted considerable anxiety in conservative circles, where the loss of U.S. power has often been exaggerated and lamented. The emergence of China as the largest single trading partner for both Chile and Brazil has prompted especially widespread concern. In contrast, progressive analysts have applauded the resulting surge in economic growth as well as autonomy for Latin America. And, predictably enough, centrist observers have embraced contradictions: It's good for Latin America to acquire more independence but bad for the United States to have less influence. (You really can't have it both ways.)

## THE BENEFITS OF INATTENTION

One of the most conspicuous features of U.S. diplomacy toward Latin America during the post-9/11 era was inattention. Initially a champion of inter-American harmony, George W. Bush turned his back on the region once the war on terror was begun. Despite proclamations to the contrary, Barack Obama has done much the same. In a nutshell, Latin America was simply not important—or dangerous— enough to attract the interest of the White House.

Diplomats and commentators repeatedly lamented this turn of events. Washington's neglect of the region was not constructive or benign. It revealed shortsightedness, ignorance of history, and lack of imagination. There was nothing good about it—except for the fact that, for Latin America, inattention from the United States opened up surprising possibilities. While the White House was distracted, leaders of the region could explore a broad range of alternatives. Consider what happened in the wake of 9/11:

- A pink tide of anti-American sentiment swept a cadre of leftist/populist politicians into power in a number of key countries and registered significant vote shares in others.
- A populist president of Venezuela helped reestablish the political significance of Fidel Castro, long thought to be an irrelevant figure.
- Brazil led developing countries in a successful effort to stymie U.S. proposals on agricultural subsidies in major meetings on international trade.

- A coalition of South American nations defeated a U.S. initiative to promote a Free Trade Area of the Americas.
- A Latin American leader forged close alliances with nations at odds with the United States—including Cuba, Russia, and Iran.[2]
- Prominent countries, among them Argentina and Brazil, forged "strategic alliances" with the People's Republic of China, still under communist leadership.
- As a whole, the region achieved substantial rates of economic growth—while the relative importance of trade with the United States was in sharp decline.

How was Latin America able to get away with all the things it did? There could be only one answer: The United States wasn't paying attention (at least, not enough attention at the highest levels). As a vacuum developed, Latin America was able to seize new opportunities. Neglect could have its benefits. Who would have expected that?

## QUESTIONS FOR REVIEW

1. How would you explain Latin America's ambivalence toward the United States—that is, its dismay over 9/11 and its opposition to the war in Iraq?
2. What accounts for the recent surge of the "pink tide" in Latin American politics? Does it pose a serious threat to U.S. national interests?
3. Why did FTAA become such a contentious issue in Latin America? Why did it arouse such opposition?
4. Which broad diplomatic strategy has proven to be most effective for Latin America—that of Fox, Lula, or Chávez?
5. What areas outside the Western Hemisphere offer the most promising relationships for Latin America? To what extent? How and why?

---

[2]This led to the assertion in 2012 by Roger Noriega, former assistant secretary of state for inter-American affairs, that Venezuela posed genuine threats to American security and should be counted as an "enemy" of the United States.

# CHAPTER 13

# Dilemmas of Immigration

> International migration is ultimately driven by economic
> realities. Whether "pushed" by untenable conditions in Mexico
> or "pulled" by opportunities in the United States, workers face
> an essentially economic decision.
>
> BILATERAL COMMISSION ON THE FUTURE OF UNITED
> STATES–MEXICAN RELATIONS (1988)

> In this land of opportunity, it is unacceptable that immigrant
> workers labor in unsafe conditions for wages insufficient to
> support their families. It is unacceptable that immigrants,
> including children, are shackled and detained in deplorable
> conditions. And it is unacceptable that already this year
> immigrants have died by the dozens in the California desert or
> other parts of the Southwest.
>
> ARCHBISHOP ROGER MAHONEY (2005)

Increasing interdependence between the United States and Latin America greatly broadened the inter-American agenda in the closing decades of the twentieth century. Human interaction on a routine, day-to-day basis penetrated deeply into both societies. These connections resulted not from governmental initiatives or diplomatic negotiations but from decisions and actions on the part of private citizens. Such transnational linkages arose apart from the state and, in some cases, in spite of the state. In the post–Cold War environment, the resolute persistence of these ties betrayed the continuing inability of governments to exert control over social dimensions of the inter-American relationship.

## IMMIGRATION IN LONG-TERM PERSPECTIVE

International migration has occurred throughout history in nearly all parts of the world. During the nineteenth century vast waves of people left Europe in search of a better life in the Americas, settling in the United States and, in the Southern Hemisphere, in Argentina and Brazil. Migration continued into the twentieth century and spread to all corners of the globe: Turkish workers moved to Germany, Algerians to France, Commonwealth citizens to England, Salvadorans to Honduras,

Colombians to Venezuela. Out of a world population of 6.9 billion in 2011, there were approximately 214 million migrants, refugees, and legal and illegal workers living outside their country of citizenship.

The United States developed as a nation on the basis of migration. Between 1900 and 1910 the United States accepted 8.8 million additional immigrants, mostly from Europe, and over the following two decades the country granted legal access to nearly 10 million more new arrivals. This influx came to a near-halt in the 1930s, under pressure from the Great Depression, and resumed after the close of World War II.

Figure 13-1 displays trends in the magnitude and composition of legal immigration from the 1960s to 2010, a period during which the United States attempted to set strict limits on migratory flows. Several patterns stand out. One is a steady increase in the volume of legal migration, from 3.2 million in the 1960s to 6.2 million in the 1980s and over 10 million from 2000–2009—the highest figure in the world, it might be said, but well below the levels of the early 1900s. Another is the precipitous decline in the proportion of immigrants from Europe and Canada (mostly Europe), from nearly 50 percent in the 1960s to 13–15 percent from the 1980s through the turn of the century, and the concomitant rise in Asian immigration from 11 percent in the 1960s to 38 percent in the 1980s and 34 percent in the early 2000s. Legal immigration from Mexico held steady, 12 percent to 15 percent of the total, while flows from elsewhere in Latin America hovered around 25 percent of the total.

These trends underline important points. First, there was, and continues to be, a significant volume of legal migration from Mexico and Latin America to the

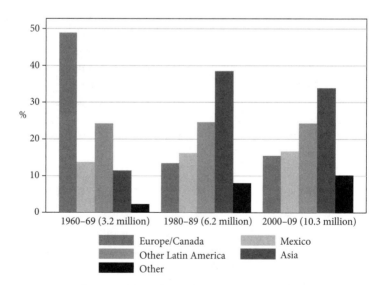

**Figure 13-1** Regional Origins of Legal Immigrants in the United States, 1960–2009
Source: U.S. Department of Homeland Security.

United States. Indeed, the inflow of Mexicans in the 1920s was just about as large as during the 1960s, and legal admissions increased markedly in the 1970s and 1980s. Even in the absence of illegal immigration, these flows would have a considerable impact on American society.

Second, alterations in the composition of the immigrant stream— especially the relative decline of the component from Europe—prompted xenophobic, nativistic reactions among the U.S. public. Often this response took overtly racist form. As conservative presidential candidate Patrick J. Buchanan opined in 1992, "I think God made all people good, but if we had to take a million immigrants in, say Zulus, next year, or Englishmen, and put them in Virginia, what group would be easier to assimilate and would cause less problems for the people of Virginia?" In some parts of the country, particularly California, racist feelings erupted in virulent denunciation of Mexicans, condemned as "illegal aliens" in a land that once was theirs.

Third, the establishment of numerical quotas proved to be an illusory exercise. Even the increase in legal entries—which nearly doubled between the 1960s and the 1980s—could not accommodate growing pressures for migration to the United States. As a result many people chose to enter the United States without official authorization, in violation of the law. It is by definition impossible to gauge the magnitude of this population with much precision, but responsible demographers have settled on estimates around 2 million for 1980, 3.5 million for 1990, and 8+ million by 2000. And as shown by Figure 13-2, the total number of "illegal aliens" from all parts of the world had risen to approximately 11 million by 2010. Particularly conspicuous was illegal migration from Mexico, estimated to account

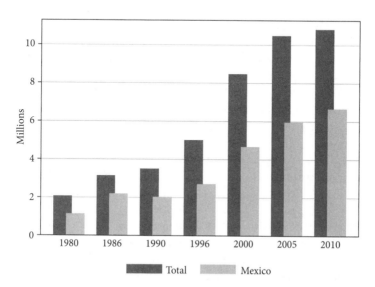

**Figure 13-2** Undocumented Immigrants in the United States, 1980–2010
Source: U. S. Department of Homeland Security.

for 55 percent to 60 percent of unauthorized residents in the United States. Other migrants came from all points of the globe, from Haiti to Ireland to China, frequently entering the country legally and then overstaying their visas.

## TRENDS IN U.S. POLICY

Within the Americas, U.S. policy on migration devoted special attention to Mexico. From the turn of the century until the 1930s, an informal "open border" policy toward Mexico provided U.S. employers with an immense pool of unskilled workers to accommodate seasonal and cyclical variations in labor demand, primarily in agriculture, mining, and construction. Mexican workers met special needs for temporary labor during World War I and, more generally, played a valuable role in the development of the American Southwest. Restrictions during the 1930s came as a direct consequence of the Great Depression. Not only did Mexican migration come to a screeching halt; amidst anti-Mexican sentiment, the forcible deportation of a half million Mexicans led to a reversal of the flow.

World War II began a second cycle of Mexican immigration. In response to labor shortages in agriculture, the U.S. government in 1942 proposed a formal agreement to utilize Mexican workers. Popularly known as the *bracero* program, this temporary-worker agreement between Mexico and the United States began as an emergency measure to replenish labor lost to military service. The accord continued without significant interruption until 1964, when Washington allowed the agreement to lapse.

The Walter-McCarran Immigration Act of 1952 continued and tightened the quota system first established in the 1920s. By creating a preference system that gave priority to prospective immigrants with special skills in short supply in the United States, Walter-McCarran explicitly acknowledged the principle that immigration should be coordinated with labor demand in the United States. But the statute also revealed internal contradictions. Most glaring was the Texas Proviso, which enabled growers in that state to hire undocumented field hands from Mexico; as a result, Walter-McCarran made it illegal to *be* an undocumented alien but not to *hire* one. In actual practice, Mexicans were largely exempted from these regulations.

Next came the immigration reforms of 1965. Passed in the midst of the Civil Rights movement, this legislation set the stage for dramatic changes in the size and composition of migrant streams. To abolish the discriminatory quota system, the 1965 amendments nearly doubled the worldwide number of annual U.S. visas, from 158,000 to 290,000; established a more equitable distribution of visas by region; and reordered priorities for visa preference categories, giving relatively greater emphasis to family reunification over labor-market considerations. The original legislation set a maximum of 20,000 visas per nation from the Eastern Hemisphere but placed no ceiling on individual countries in the Western Hemisphere, a provision that allowed Mexico to acquire a disproportionate share. In 1976, however, supplementary legislation applied the 20,000 limit to nations of the Western Hemisphere—to the direct detriment of Mexico.

Against this backdrop, the Immigration Reform and Control Act of 1986 (IRCA) culminated a succession of attempts to curtail undocumented immigration. Passage came amidst a national clamor to "take control of our borders," in President Ronald Reagan's telling phrase, and as persistent unemployment fueled public resentment against workers from Mexico and other countries. Sponsored by Senator Alan Simpson (R-Wyoming) and Representative Peter Rodino (D-New Jersey), the bill contained three principal provisions:

- Economic sanctions against U.S. employers who "knowingly employ, recruit, or refer for a fee" undocumented workers
- Permanent amnesty for undocumented workers who could prove continuous residence in the United States since any time before January 1, 1982
- Partial amnesty for undocumented workers in the agricultural sector.

Ultimately, the law represented a compromise between those political forces opposing unauthorized migration (from organized labor to racist reactionaries), those who benefited from its existence (mostly employers), and Hispanic leaders expressing concern about the potential aggravation of ethnic prejudice.

IRCA achieved mixed results. The employer-sanctions provision proved to be toothless. It remained possible for employers to comply with the law and still hire undocumented workers. For instance, Simpson-Rodino obliged employers to request official papers from job applicants but did not require them to verify the authenticity of the documents: Merely by inspecting any one of twenty-plus possible documents, widely available in counterfeit form, employers could technically satisfy their legal requirements. As a consequence, employer sanctions had only marginal impact on illegal migration.

Support for this point comes from data on annual apprehensions of illegal aliens (most apprehensions took place along or near the U.S.–Mexican border, so 90 percent or more of the detainees were Mexican). The figures suggest that IRCA posed only a temporary deterrent to illegal migration. Unauthorized inflows increased in 1985–1986, as anxious migrants sought to gain access before implementation of the much-discussed law; and second, it led to a temporary reduction in illicit crossings in 1987–1989, but this almost certainly resulted from the extension of amnesty to formerly illegal migrants rather than to the effect of employer sanctions.

In contrast to employer sanctions, the amnesty portion of IRCA turned out to be highly successful. Seeking to improve its public image, the Immigration and Naturalization Service (INS) gave high priority to the program. Nearly 3 million people acquired legal status in the United States as a result of Simpson-Rodino.

In the meantime there continued a historic shift in the nature and composition Mexican *indocumentados*, away from the temporary or seasonal migration of single working-age males and toward the longer-term settlement of families, women, and children. But as one expert concluded, "There is no evidence that IRCA has reduced the total pool of Mexican migrants employed or seeking work in U.S. labor markets." While sharpening the distinction between migrant workers with and without legal status, in fact, IRCA might even have served to increase the size of the overall pool, and in so doing it may have exacerbated social and political tensions within American society.

During the 1990s the United States redoubled efforts to deter illegal immigration. Seeking to take a tough line on this issue, the Clinton administration increased the INS budget from $1.4 billion in fiscal year 1992 to $2.6 billion for fiscal year 1996. It sharply expanded the size of the Border Patrol. And it intensified enforcement efforts at key crossing points: In 1993 the administration proclaimed Operation Hold-the-Line in El Paso, Texas (formerly known as Operation Blockade), in 1994 it launched Operation Gatekeeper in San Diego, and in 1997 it initiated Operation Rio Grande in McAllen, Texas. An INS strategic plan called for a long-term, phased effort to extend such concentrated enforcement operations across the entire southwestern border. As Attorney General Janet Reno declared at the inauguration of Gatekeeper: "We *are* securing our nation's borders, we are aggressively enforcing our nation's borders, and we are doing it *now*. We will not rest until the flow of illegal immigrants across our nation's border has abated."

It remained unclear whether such efforts could ever be effective—or whether they would simply encourage would-be entrants to seek new modes of access. Indeed, detention statistics suggest that concentrated enforcement operations had more effect on *redirecting* migrant streams than on deterring them. As a share of the total, Border Patrol apprehensions in California (East and West regions, the latter including San Diego) dropped sharply during the 1990s; Texas showed a moderate downward trend; and arrests in Arizona shot up from under 10 percent in 1990 to roughly one-half the total during the 2000s. Clearly, migrants were seeking new routes for entry into the United States. And according to recent research, more than 90 percent were succeeding.

The inland corridors through California and Arizona were exceedingly dangerous. Migrants had to traverse barren deserts and climb mountains. Water was scarce and dangers were abundant, including poisonous snakes. Unscrupulous *coyotes* would sometimes abandon groups that they were smuggling across the border. The result was a grisly increase in loss of life, as hundreds of migrants—about 500 in some years—lost their lives in the crossing. This was more than one person per day.

Migration would continue to generate friction and misunderstanding. Labor-exporting countries were likely to tolerate, if not favor, these outward flows: Annual dollar remittances to Mexico alone amounted to nearly $23 billion in 2005, while the northward flow of workers provided the country with a social safety valve. At the same time, governments of sending countries expressed outrage when their citizens were subjected to abuse, mistreatment, harassment, and violence within the United States. Undocumented migration tended to create bad feelings on all sides. Stepped-up measures to deter the flows exacerbated inherent tensions.

There was a special complication in regard to Mexico: The United States was embracing economic integration through NAFTA on the one hand and constructing walls along the border on the other. (Some would even assert that Washington was taking steps to militarize the border, a claim that was dramatized by the shooting of a Texas teenager in May 1997.) The resulting policy contradiction emerged on three levels. One was symbolic and political: The construction of a wall along the U.S.–Mexican border seemed utterly inconsistent with the spirit of economic partnership. A second was procedural and institutional: Although NAFTA made no provision for labor migration, the U.S. emphasis on unilateral assertion undermined the principles of cooperation and consultation enshrined in the free-trade agreement. The third level was substantive: Experience around the world showed that economic integration fostered social integration. Freer trade encouraged transnational investment, which generally stimulated cultural interaction and, ultimately, labor migration.

By taking anti-immigration measures, the Clinton administration was tacitly attempting to restrict and curtail the social consequences of the economic policy that it so strongly endorsed. This stance thus contravened the logic of geoeconomic integration, which would in principle endorse a free flow of labor. As one expert would later write: "In summary, the U.S. decision to fortify its borders has reduced trade, investment, tourism, and jobs while irritating or angering its neighbors. The investment in border security was substantial, but there is no evidence that it has provided more security. The problem is not just the thickening of the border; it is the way the United States has redefined itself."

## CRISIS IN HAITI

A substantial number of foreigners came to the United States as political refugees, seeking to escape persecution and repression in their native lands. As a matter of U.S. law, individuals were entitled to asylum in the United States if they could demonstrate a "well-founded fear of persecution on account of race, religion, nationality, membership in a particular social group or political opinion." And as a matter of U.S. tradition, acceptance of refugees reinforced the nation's self-image as a bastion of political freedom. Unlike economic migrants, refugees were coming to this country not merely for wages or employment; like America's forefathers, they were seeking the full expression of their fundamental human rights.

By its nature, the granting of asylum was an explicitly political decision—and it was inevitable, perhaps, that it would be used (and abused) for political purposes. Since there was no scientific means for discerning whether someone had a "well-founded fear of persecution," judgments tended to be arbitrary. In general, the U.S. government was quick to grant asylum to people fleeing from hostile regimes and loath to give asylum to people fleeing from its allies. During the Cold War, this meant that Washington was happy to embrace refugees from the Soviet Union, the People's Republic of China, or *fidelista* Cuba and *sandinista* Nicaragua but notoriously inhospitable to applicants from Guatemala, El Salvador, or Chile under Pinochet. The actual hazard to human rights had little bearing on such cases. What mattered was the U.S. desire to embarrass its enemies, support its friends, and reap propaganda value on behalf of the "free world."

Especially perplexing was the prospect of massive waves of refugees from nearby countries of Latin America. At the outset, policymakers had imagined that actual numbers of refugees would be modest enough to avoid entanglement in questions about assimilation into American society. Indeed, the preference was for high-profile individuals whose defection from enemy states would endorse the superiority of Western capitalism and the wisdom of U.S. policy. In 1980 the Mariel boatlift challenged that happy assumption by suddenly unloading 125,000 Cubans in the United States, creating numerous episodes of social turbulence and turmoil. Refugees en masse posed questions not only about respect for human rights in foreign countries but also about U.S. attitudes toward foreigners. Arriving in large numbers, political refugees from Latin America encountered the same kind of rancor, resistance, and reaction as did economic migrants.

Haiti would represent a problematic case. One of the most cynical acts of the Cold War was a 1981 compact between the Reagan administration and the right-wing regime of Jean-Claude ("Baby Doc") Duvalier, an agreement under which the U.S. Coast Guard would repatriate Haitian citizens after perfunctory onboard hearings. Over the next ten years the United States picked up 22,716 Haitians on the high seas, most attempting to flee their country in small boats or makeshift rafts—and admitted only 28 (0.12 percent!) for political asylum. The purpose of this accord, in the name of anticommunism, was to spare embarrassment for the murderous Duvalier regime, to intimidate its political opponents, and to minimize the number of unwanted arrivals on Florida shores. In the eyes of American society, Haitians were uniquely undesirable: They were poor, they were black, and they were rumored to be carriers of AIDS.

After Duvalier's fall in 1986, Haiti finally held a free and fair election in December 1990. The undisputed winner, with two-thirds of the vote, was Jean-Bertrand Aristide, a 37-year-old Catholic priest who curried support from the popular masses. In September 1991, less than nine months into his term, he was forced into exile by a military coup. The overthrow drew sharp condemnation from the Organization of American States, which promptly imposed an embargo on trade. United States Secretary of State James A. Baker III proclaimed that Haiti's illegal regime had "no future." An already-poor populace suffered from the embargo while illicit commerce flourished.

As repression mounted, Haitians embarked for the United States. By January 1992, the U.S. Coast Guard had taken at least 12,600 Haitians into custody at sea, providing "safe haven" for thousands at Camp Guantánamo (in Cuba). By May 1992, U.S. authorities had processed 34,000 requests for asylum, granting about one-third, while Guantánamo was bursting at the seams. Citing a "dangerous and unmanageable situation," President George H. W. Bush that same month ordered the Coast Guard to pick up all Haitians on the seas and return them to their homeland without any screening. Democratic presidential candidate Bill Clinton denounced the policy as immoral, "a callous response to a terrible human tragedy." Yet the Coast Guard held the line.

Emboldened by Clinton's campaign rhetoric, Haitians began taking to the sea after his election. Coast Guard analysts estimated that 200,000 Haitians were preparing to set sail for the United States. Notified of this development prior to his own inauguration, Clinton ruefully announced that the Bush policy of forced repatriation would stay in place. An aide to Aristide bitterly denounced the "floating Berlin Wall" and Aristide himself expressed impatience with the OAS: "History will never forgive thirty-four countries if they continue to just talk instead of doing what they have to do."

The initiative then moved from the OAS to the United Nations, which made extensive but unsuccessful efforts to negotiate a settlement. The Clinton administration then sought to find a compromise solution that would resolve the crisis without restoring Aristide to power. Under pressure from black leaders in America, Clinton reverted to a hard line against the military regime. Washington pressed for a resolution by the UN Security Council to impose new economic sanctions and condemn the usurpation of authority from Aristide.

News of this shift led to yet another wave of rafters in search of asylum. The U.S. Coast Guard was suddenly picking up 2,000 Haitians per day. Hundreds drowned. Guantánamo was reopened, and the administration began looking for other countries to provide "safe haven" until Aristide could be restored.

Clinton was running out of options. The only choice was to remove Cédras and reinstate Aristide, and to use force if necessary. The UN Security Council approved a new resolution authorizing the United States "to use all necessary means to facilitate the departure from Haiti of the military leadership." As the countdown continued, U.S. politicians began to express reservations. Republicans called for a congressional vote on any possible invasion. Senator Bob Dole put it bluntly: "Is there any real national interest in Haiti?" An ABC News poll showed that 73 percent of Americans opposed the idea of invading Haiti.

Clinton finally explained his position in a nationally televised speech. Denouncing the Haiti's military government as "the most violent regime in our hemisphere," the president cited several reasons for concern: "to stop the brutal atrocities that threaten tens of thousands of Haitians, to secure our borders, to preserve stability and promote democracy in our hemisphere, and to uphold the reliability of the commitments we make and the commitments others make to us." But beneath the presidential rhetoric, it was the refugee issue that defined the fundamental interest of the United States.

> Thousands of Haitians have already fled toward the United States, risking their lives to escape the reign of terror. As long as Cédras rules, Haitians will continue to seek sanctuary in our nation. This year, in less than two months, more than 21,000 Haitians were rescued at sea by our Coast Guard and Navy. Today, more than 14,000 refugees are living at our naval base in Guantánamo. The American people have already expended almost $200 million to support them, to maintain the economic embargo, and the prospect of millions and millions being spent every month for an indefinite period of time looms ahead unless we act. Three

hundred thousand more Haitians, 5 percent of their entire population, are in hiding in their own country. If we don't act, they could be the next wave of refugees at our door. We will continue to face the threat of a mass exodus of refugees and its constant threat to stability in our region and control of our borders.

No American should be surprised that the recent tide of migrants seeking refuge on our shores comes from Haiti and from Cuba. After all, they are the only nations left in the Western Hemisphere where democratic government is denied, the only countries where dictators have managed to hold back the waves of democracy and progress that have swept over our entire region.

As Doyle McManus of the *Los Angeles Times* would remark, "Never before has the United States gone to war to stop refugees from coming to our shores." Haitian journalist Anne-Christine d'Adesky concurred, arguing that Clinton's stance reflected "less his concern about human rights or democracy, than his belated assessment that the only way to keep refugees away from Miami is to stop the murders in Haiti."

As Haitian leaders countered Clinton's warning with expressions of defiance, an invasion seemed imminent. Then the president dispatched a high-level delegation, led by Jimmy Carter, for a last-ditch effort at negotiation. When talks reached an impasse, U.S. commanders launched sixty-one planes toward Haiti with troops aboard. Negotiators paid a final call on President Émile Jonaissant. "We'll have peace, not war," said the octogenarian executive. Though Haiti's military chieftains refused to sign the document, the deal was nonetheless done. A relieved Clinton recalled the planes and canceled the invasion.

The next day U.S. troops would occupy the country without any organized resistance. In less than a week there were more than 15,000 American troops on the ground. The nature of this operation, called by some an "intervasion" (a cross between an intervention and an invasion), was elusive and shifting. It began as a limited military occupation but evolved into a takeover of the governmental apparatus. By the end of March 1995, a contented President Clinton celebrated the replacement of U.S. troops by a UN peacekeeping force of 6,000 troops—with 2,400 American soldiers and a U.S. commander in charge. In mid-1996 this "UN Mission in Haiti" was scaled back to 600 troops and placed under Canadian leadership. A year later this force was replaced by a "UN Transition Mission in Haiti," which began training thousands of recruits for a Haitian National Police.

## THE POST-9/11 ENVIRONMENT

After winning the presidency of Mexico in 2000, Vicente Fox undertook a high-stakes gamble. As the country's first democratically elected president in decades, he set about improving his country's relationship with the United States. Conservative himself, he was more than willing to abandon the special links to Fidel Castro's Cuba that had so long annoyed the U.S. policy establishment. A former business executive, he ardently supported NAFTA and the long-term plans for an FTAA. Early in 2001 he hosted newly elected George Bush at his ranch in Guanajuato, where they appeared to get on famously (posing for photos in cowboy hats and boots). Challenging one of the sacred shibboleths of Mexican politics, Fox was hitching his star to the American wagon.

What he wanted was U.S. immigration reform. In the year 2000 there were approximately 25 million people of Mexican origin residing in the United States. About 10 million were immigrants. Of these, an estimated 4.7 million were "undocumented"—they had arrived in the United States without legal visas. These *indocumentados* were living and working under extremely difficult conditions—sleeping in makeshift camps, accepting low-wage jobs, hiding out from law enforcement officers, doing their best to stay out of trouble. Their principal goal was to send hard-earned savings back to families in Mexico. Usually in the form of money orders, remittances were climbing dramatically—from an estimated $3.6 billion in 1995 to $6.5 billion in 2000 to $23 billion in 2005. This was a lot of money.

Fox was seeking U.S. immigration reform for a variety of reasons. First, he wanted to protect the fundamental human rights of Mexican citizens. (By the time he took office, an average of one Mexican per day was dying while attempting to cross the U.S. border.) Second, he wanted to protect what he regarded as the "right" of Mexicans to seek work in the United States—and, presumably, to keep sending home those handsome remittances. He even suggested that NAFTA should follow the example of the European Union and make explicit provision for labor mobility. Third, he was hoping to ensure his popularity. Almost everyone in Mexico had a relative somewhere in the United States. People would appreciate his efforts to protect family members, and, more broadly, they would admire his ability to extract something important from the Colossus of the North. Moreover, the Mexican American community was showing the potential to become a significant pressure group within the U.S. political system. In addition, Mexican citizens living abroad were acquiring the right to vote in Mexican elections, and they could eventually become a crucial electoral bloc.

Achieving U.S. immigration reform thus became a top priority. At a lunch gathering in Los Angeles, Mexico's foreign secretary, Jorge Castañeda, was asked to name the top three issues on his department's agenda. "That's easy," he replied. "Immigration, immigration, and immigration."

For some time it appeared that the gamble would pay off. Fox exerted his considerable personal charm on U.S. politicians. Describing his hopes for reform, Castañeda declared that Mexico wanted both an amnesty for *indocumentados* who had been living for years in the United States plus a generous guest-worker program—"the whole enchilada," in his memorable phrase. At a press conference in the White House Rose Garden at the beginning of September 2001, less than a week before 9/11, Fox expressed the belief that it should be possible to wrap up an agreement before the end of the calendar year. Bush responded with the stunning declaration that the partnership with Mexico was the United States' most important bilateral relationship anywhere in the world. Mexican policymakers were confident, even buoyant.

September 11 brought those good feelings to a sudden end. One of the U.S. government's first responses to the attacks was to seal the country's borders as tightly as possible. The terrorists who seized those airplanes had somehow gained entry to United States; that could not be permitted to happen again. Law enforcement personnel fanned out along the U.S. borders. Would-be entrants were scrutinized with unprecedented care. Lines at busy crossing points stretched for miles, especially along the Southwest border.

Immigration reform was put on indefinite hold. There could not even be any discussion of the subject. To be sure, Mexico's negotiating position had always contained two visible weaknesses: (1) It was seeking a change in U.S. laws, over which it had no control, and (2) there was never a clear quid pro quo—what would Mexico give to the United States in exchange for immigration reform?

Yet the collapse of the Mexican strategy came as a devastating blow. The idea of a special partnership with President Bush went down along with those airliners, and there was nothing to put in its place. "In these difficult times," said a disappointed Vicente Fox in May 2002, "Latin America seems to have been abandoned to its fate."

### Immigration and National Security

As a component of the "global war on terror," the United States devoted special attention to the Mexican border. Security became the preeminent issue, while generalized anxiety after 9/11 nourished widespread xenophobia. In response to such concerns, the Bush administration doubled the size of the Border Patrol—from 8,500 agents in 2000 to more than 17,000 by 2008. The budget for border protection climbed at a comparable rate. Fortification was under way.

Even so, the flow of undocumented migrants showed a surprising increase in the wake of 9/11. Between 2000 and 2005, the annual influx of undocumented workers rose to 850,000 per year—five times the level of the 1980s. It thereafter declined to around 300,000 per year, largely as a result of the U.S. economic recession (and the downturn in jobs). By 2010 it even appeared that the net inflow of *indocumentados* from Mexico (incoming minus outgoing) might be approaching zero. But as shown earlier in Figure 13-2, the total number of undocumented people in the United States nonetheless swelled from 8.3 million in 2000 to 11 million in 2010. Thickening of the border was not achieving its presumptive goals.

With presidential elections looming in 2004, Bush unveiled a proposal for a guest-worker program plus a form of amnesty. This may well have been a good-faith effort to redeem a promise to Vicente Fox. But Democrats viewed the plan as a cynical attempt to curry support among Hispanic voters, while right-wing Republicans denounced it as in immoral reward to migrants for breaking U.S. laws. The bill consequently languished in the halls of Congress. In 2005 the House of Representatives voted to discourage the issuance of driver's licenses to undocumented migrants, to criminalize illegal migration, and to authorize the extension of walls and fences along the U.S.–Mexican border. President Fox angrily denounced the scheme as "a violation of the immigrants' rights to liberty."

Enlightened leaders proclaimed respect for the rights and roles of immigrants, but their pleas fell mostly on deaf ears.

Pressure mounted throughout 2006. As the U.S. Senate prepared to take up the issue, the Latino community erupted in protest. Demanding legal protections for illegal immigrants and clear pathways to citizenship, demonstrators streamed past the White House in Washington DC, jammed streets near City Hall in New York, marched in Atlanta, and held a candlelight vigil in Los Angeles. They rallied in front of the Arizona statehouse and sang "We Shall Overcome" (in Spanish) in Mississippi. It was an awesome and, to many, surprising display of organizational capacity and potential political power. As the head of a Latino organization pointedly observed, "Today we march, tomorrow we vote." And as another spokesperson proclaimed, "We decided not to be invisible anymore."

Bush attempted to straddle the fence. He expressed cautious support for a compromise bill providing a path to legal status but declined to pressure Republicans to act on it. He unveiled plans to increase the size of the Border Patrol; to deploy 6,000 troops from the National Guard as a transitional measure ("The United States is not going to militarize the southern border"); to create a temporary-worker program; to apply sanctions against conniving American employers (and issue an identity card for every legal foreign worker); and to grant the possibility of citizenship to longtime migrants with roots in the United States. "They should not be given an automatic path to citizenship," he warned. "This is amnesty, and I oppose it. Amnesty would be unfair to those who are here lawfully, and it would invite further waves of illegal immigration."

There followed a classic legislative minuet. After prolonged debate, the Senate approved a guest-worker program, a potential path to citizenship, and a shortened border wall. Angrily objecting to what they saw as "general amnesty," Republicans in the House refused to compromise with the Senate—thus ending all hopes for comprehensive immigration reform. Conservatives resuscitated the proposal for a full-length wall along the border. Michael Chertoff, the head of national security, declared that it would help to keep the nation safe. Congresspersons calculated that it would improve prospects for reelection. And by a stunning margin of 80–19, the Senate approved construction of a barrier 1,200 kilometers in length—about one-third the entire length of the border—at a projected cost of $1.2 billion. Even Hillary Rodham Clinton, a leading contender for the Democratic presidential nomination in 2008, cast her lot with the majority.

President Bush made a last-gasp effort in 2007, convening a bipartisan group of lawmakers who produced a broad-based bill including a path to citizenship, a guest-worker program, and a shift in focus from family reunification toward labor needs. Once again, conservatives denounced it as amnesty in disguise. It never reached the Senate floor. So much for comprehensive immigration reform.

For Mexico this was the worst of all possible outcomes. Once again, the United States took unilateral action. There were no friendly consultations. Having once proclaimed "the whole enchilada" of immigration reform as a plausible goal, Mexican authorities would have to cope with ruination of their once-high expectations.

**Walls and Ladders.** Cartoonist John Trever reveals the futility of building fences along the U.S.-Mexican border and tacitly salutes the ingenuity of would-be migrants.

All these back-and-forth maneuvers took place within the context of two-level games described in previous chapters. As formalized by NAFTA, the logic of geoeconomic integration would lead to support in favor of freer flows of labor. But in the wake of 9/11, geopolitical concerns called for tighter controls on the border—and they ultimately won the day. Geopolitics trumped geoeconomics. Security was more important than prosperity.

## IMMIGRATION UNDER OBAMA

During his 2008 presidential campaign, Barack Obama promised to fix the immigration situation. And after his inauguration, he repeated the pledge to offer a comprehensive bill before the end of 2009. As though to emphasize the point, he brought well-known proponents of immigration reform into his cabinet—Janet Napolitano (Department of Homeland Security, DHS) and Hilda Solis (Labor). Hope then foundered on the shoals of harsh reality. As the U.S. economy fell into recession and millions of Americans lost jobs, the prospects for immigration reform turned negative. The whole idea would have to wait.

In actual fact, Obama extended some of Bush's basic policies. He expanded the Border Patrol to more than 20,000 agents and increased its budget to $3.6 billion. Border security became a litmus test for public officials. Public support for hard-working *indocumentados* became exceedingly scarce. In an atmosphere of acrimonious polarization, hardly anyone dared stir the wrath of a confident and determined right-wing movement. The Tea Party was making major strides.

The operative question became what to do about undocumented migrants already in the United States. Given paralysis at the national level, states began to enter the fray—and passed anti-immigration laws of their own. The most conspicuous case occurred in Arizona, where a 2010 statute charged police with detaining people on grounds of "a reasonable suspicion" that they *might be* illegal. Officers were ordered to check a person's immigration status while enforcing other laws, and immigrants were required to carry their papers at all times. The Arizona rule had serious problems: It would institutionalize racial profiling, place Latinos at the mercy of untrained police, and raise dubious claims about the constitutional rights of state authorities.

Even so, anti-immigrant measures garnered significant levels of popular support. A poll in 2011 showed that 61 percent of Americans favored the Arizona law, while 56 percent said they would like to have a similar law in their state. Arizona-like measures were passed into law in Alabama, South Carolina, Georgia, Utah, Indiana, Missouri, and Oklahoma.

Obama's Department of Justice eventually challenged these laws on the grounds that only the federal government has the authority to make laws about immigration (and citizenship). More specifically, it aimed to strike down statutes in Arizona, Alabama, and South Carolina—states that Democrats could not expect to carry in national elections. Pro-immigrant activists heaved a collective sigh of relief. In June 2012, in the heat of the U.S. presidential campaign, the U.S. Supreme Court rendered a split decision on rhe Arizona case—striking down most of the statute's provisions but upholding the stipulation that state and local police could check the immigration status of people whom they lawfully detain. Both sides claimed victory, but the basic verdict was clear: states cannot preempt federal immigration law.

In the meantime, the Obama administration had gone ahead with an accelerated expulsion of undocumented immigrants. To the dismay of Latino supporters, Obama's enforcement strategies led to the deportation of more than 1 million people by the end of 2011, at a record-setting pace of nearly 400,000 per year.

Modes of deportation gradually evolved. Ad hoc expulsion of allegedly undesirable immigrants began in the early 1980s. Official authorization came in 1996 through clause 287(g) of the Illegal Immigration Reform and Immigrant Responsibility Act, which permitted state and local law enforcement officials to enforce federal immigration laws after receiving appropriate training. In 2003 the U.S. Immigration and Customs Enforcement Agency (ICE) was created within DHS. In 2007 a program known as "Secure Communities" was established within ICE to "identify" criminal aliens, "prioritize" them according to the severity of their crimes, and facilitate their removal from the country.

Secure Communities relied heavily on electronic data sharing. In participating states and communities, fingerprints of all arrestees were checked against DHS immigration records as well as FBI criminal history records; when matches occurred, ICE could place detainers on individuals in order to conduct interviews or take them into custody—and decide on deportation. John Morton, the head of ICE, called Secure Communities "the future of immigration enforcement" because it "focuses our resources on identifying and removing the most serious criminal offenders first and foremost." Secretary Napolitano and President Obama also endorsed the program.

Secure Communities provoked intense opposition. An independent study revealed that its workings were deeply flawed. In actual practice, the program had:

- Led to the unlawful detention of thousands of U.S. citizens
- Focused disproportionately on Latinos, who accounted for 93 percent of all detainees (while representing only 77 percent of the undocumented population in the United States)
- Denied due process to a large majority of detainees
- Deported arrestees with low-level offenses, such as traffic violations, as well as individuals who had no criminal histories.

The removal process itself was also unduly heartless, providing no opportunity for arrestees to gather their belongings, get their affairs in order, or bid farewell to family members.

Further, Secure Communities placed a substantial strain on local resources. In effect, local police were acting as ICE agents—often arbitrarily. Latino groups protested vigorously against what they saw as racial and ethnic profiling. For all these reasons, the governors of three major states—New York, Illinois, and California—refused to cooperate with ICE.

In August 2011, the Obama administration declared that DHS would thenceforth render decisions on a case-by-case basis. Deportation proceedings would no longer affect individuals who posed no public safety threat. This approach would require a profound change in the mentality of ICE agents, who operated on the basic principle that any violation of the law was cause for deportation. Conservatives denounced the shift as a backdoor form of the so-called Dream Act—a bill, blocked by Republicans in Congress, that would provide relief to illegal immigrants who were brought to the United States as children and who attended college or joined the armed forces. And in June 2012, Obama issued an executive order allowing work permits and preventing deportation for as many as 1.4 million undocumented immigrants under the age of 30 who were brought to the United States as children.

As his first term came to a close, Obama's record on immigration was mixed. He had forsaken the cause of far-reaching immigration reform, he had continued to fortify the U.S.–Mexican border, and he had overseen a draconian program of deportations that imposed enormous hardship on Latinos. Needing Hispanic support for his 2012 reelection bid, however, he took kinder and gentler stances in some areas. His administration:

- Challenged the constitutionality of anti-immigrant laws in Arizona, Alabama, and South Carolina

- Softened the application of deportation policies, especially with regard to children of undocumented migrants,
- Eased green-card application procedures for especially qualified candidates.

Under an administrative ruling in early 2012, undocumented parents of U.S. citizen children and unauthorized persons with American spouses would be able to file for adjustment of their status within the United States rather than being forced to return to their countries of origin. This would remove a massive burden for such families. As one Latino activist proclaimed, the decision offered a "welcome rational solution to a simple problem" that would mean that "thousand upon thousands of families would remain together."

The picture was ambiguous. One view was that the Obama team was making incremental but earnest gains in an inhospitable climate, waiting for an opportunity to introduce comprehensive immigration reform during his second term. Another was that the president was making a cynical effort to bolster Hispanic support for his reelection. Either way, political concerns were paramount. Was there anything new about that?

## QUESTIONS FOR REVIEW

1. How did changes in the composition of migratory flows affect U.S. public opinion? How were popular attitudes toward migrants reflected in immigration policy? How did changes in policy affect Latin America?
2. What were the goals of IRCA? Was the reform successful?
3. What has been the effect of increased border security on migratory flows? How might building walls pose a policy contradiction?
4. How did U.S. immigration policy change after 9/11? What were the implications for U.S.–Mexican relations?
5. How would you explain Obama's stance toward immigration in light of his campaign pledge for comprehensive reform? How have U.S. states responded?

# CHAPTER 14

# Drug Trafficking, Drug Wars

The only law the narcoterrorists do not break is the law of
supply and demand.

VIRGILIO BARCO (1990)


They figure out a way to do it, we figure out a way to stop them.
They figure out a way to do it again. It's like a big chess game.

ANONYMOUS DEA AGENT (ca. 2000)


International drug trafficking resembles undocumented migration in fundamental ways. Both situations result from the interplay of economic forces: The
drug trade responds to consumer demand, whereas migration reflects the search
for employment. Both have exerted impacts on social orders in Latin America
and the United States. Both have been unwelcome to the U.S. government, which
has declared them to be illegal. And, as in the case of Haiti, frustration over the
drug trade led to calls for forceful action—and to the military invasion of a hapless nation.


## PRODUCTION AND SUPPLY

There are drugs and there are drugs. They are not all the same. They are produced
in various places and in various ways, they have distinctive supply chains, and they
have different pharmacological consequences. For present purposes, they fall into
four broad categories.

*Cocaine* is a stimulant derived from the leaves of the coca bush, which is cultivated in the South American Andes. It is commonly ingested intranasally (by
"snorting") or by injection. In recent years Colombia has produced about two-
thirds of the worldwide crop, followed by Peru and Bolivia. Almost all coca for
export is transformed into powder (cocaine hydrochloride) in clandestine laboratories in Colombia and then transshipped to foreign markets—principally Europe
and the United States. Over the last decade or so, Mexico has become by far the
leading transit point for smuggling cocaine into the U.S. market.

*Heroin* is a semisynthetic derivative of morphine, which comes from the opium
poppy. It is most frequently taken by injection (or, like opium, by smoking). During
the 1990s the most important center of production was the "Golden Triangle" in

Southeast Asia (Burma/Myanmar, Laos, Thailand). In recent years Afghanistan has become the world's primary source, which is now estimated to produce over 90 percent of the global supply. Latin America produces only 1 percent of global opium, most of which is refined into heroin for distribution in the U.S. market.

*Marijuana* is the dried leaf of the cannabis (or hemp) plant, which has a narcotic effect. It can be cultivated almost anywhere—in open fields, greenhouses, or mountain lands. It is typically ingested through smoking. Latin America has long been a major source of this drug. It has been estimated that approximately one-third of the marijuana consumed in the United States is actually produced in the United States.

A fourth category might be called "designer drugs," also known as amphetamine-type stimulants (ATS). These are synthetic substances that are concocted in pharmaceutical laboratories, often in or near advanced industrial countries. They are usually consumed orally as tablets or pills. Examples include MDMA (ecstasy), LSD (lysergic acid diethylamide, a.k.a. "acid"), and mathaqualone (a.k.a. "Quaaludes"). An increasingly worrisome trend relates to prescription drugs, usually painkillers, that are used and abused by young adults in the United States; OxyContin ("hillbilly heroin") provides an especially lethal example.

What all these drugs have in common is their "illicit" status. Under U.S. law and a succession of international conventions, the production, transportation, sale, and consumption of these substances have been declared illegal. (Medical prescriptions for painkillers are legal, of course, but their abuse by nonpatients is not.) It must be noted that the legal status of specific drugs has derived from social convention, not scientific deduction or concern for public health. While the sale and use of tobacco and alcohol have been permitted under U.S. law, for instance, these other drugs have been prohibited. The U.S. legal structure has thus determined that two of the world's most harmful and widely used drugs are acceptable while other drugs of varying potency are not. The logic has been inconsistent.

## Sources of Supply

Since the early 1970s the United States has attempted to suppress the production of illicit drugs throughout the Western Hemisphere. In pursuit of this goal the U.S. government pursued two approaches: first, elimination of the sources of supply, by destroying crops and laboratory facilities; second, interdiction of shipments bound for the U.S. market, by conducting surveillance at the border and on the high seas. The idea has been to reduce the flow of illicit drugs into the United States, drive prices upward, harass the traffickers, discourage consumption, and push the users out of the market.

By official U.S. estimates, coca leaf production nonetheless remained at high levels. During the 1990s, around 200,000 hectares of land were devoted to coca cultivation, mainly in Peru and Bolivia. Near the end of the decade, production moved toward Colombia, as the area under cultivation climbed to 232,500 hectares in 2007. With significant year-to-year oscillations, the potential for pure-cocaine production hovered between 750 and 900 metric tons from the late 1980s to the early 2000s. Production has been steady and strong.

Partly because of competition from U.S. growers, marijuana cultivation in Latin America has undergone a cyclical pattern, rising sharply in the 1990s, easing off around the year 2000, and then surging again by 2008. Mexico has been by far the leading source, followed by Colombia and Jamaica (and Belize to a much lesser extent). Boutique-style cultivation of cannabis has also flourished in Canada.

Eradication campaigns had intermittent effects on marijuana but only minor impacts on cocaine. During 1992 an estimated 217,808 hectares of land were devoted to coca leaf production; only 6,108 hectares—less than 3 percent of the total—were actually eradicated. A decade later, aerial fumigation led to substantially reduced cultivation in Colombia, while Peru and Bolivia picked up much of the slack.

Nor did seizures of shipments make much difference in availability. Through the 1990s, foreign and U.S. governments together captured about one-quarter of all the cocaine destined for the American market. This meant that three-quarters came through. By 2010, intensified efforts raised the interdiction rate to approximately 30 percent (with an eventual target of 40 percent by 2015). Traffickers eventually came to anticipate seizures and incorporated quantitative estimates into marketing strategies, shipping extra quantities as insurance against the likelihood of interdiction.

Variation in drug prices basically responded to variations in levels of production, not to rhythms of eradication or interdiction. The most telling evidence came from trends in retail prices, displayed in Figure 14-1. Prices for cocaine and heroin declined steadily from the 1980s through the 1990s and flattened out thereafter. Contrary to expectations, supply control was not constricting the market or pushing retail prices out of reach. In contrast, prices for marijuana surged from the mid-1980s to the mid-1990s before leveling off around 2000.

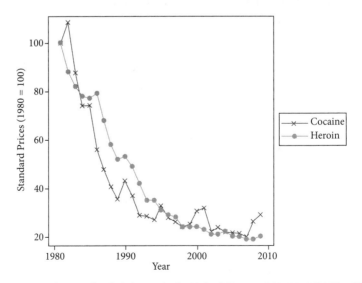

**Figure 14-1** Retail Prices for Illicit Drugs in the United States, 1980–2010 (1980 = 100)
Source: U.S. Office of National Drug Control Strategy.

The allocation of profits varied according to distribution channels for each illicit product. Earnings from cocaine and heroin tended to be concentrated in the hands of drug-trafficking organizations (DTOs), often referred to as "cartels." Profits from marijuana and designer drugs were more dispersed. Such patterns underscored key features of the trafficking phenomenon. First, economic values of drug shipments correlated with perceived levels of risk, which in turn responded to the likelihood of law enforcement. Second, most of the profits stayed in the hands of distributors, of middlemen, rather than producers. Third, the largest share of profits accrued not in Latin America but at the retail end of the market, suggesting that a great deal of drug money stayed in the United States. For this reason, money laundering has become a issue.

Table 14-1 illustrates the phenomenon. When sold by *campesinos*, or small farmers, a quantity of coca leaf sufficient to produce one kilogram of cocaine in the year 2000 had a market value of approximately $300; if transformed into coca base, it was worth about $900. After being processed into cocaine hydrochloride in Colombia, its value climbed to $1,500. Then the upward trend accelerated. Once the shipment reached the United States successfully, the value climbed by a factor of 10—to $15,000. Distributed at the wholesale level, the value rose to $40,000; at the retail level, it could fetch as much as $150,000!

The figures are breathtaking at face value. They also reveal important points. One is that the *campesinos* have not been not getting rich. Another is that interdiction and eradication policies have had only modest and short-term effects on the market, since DTOs could replace lost shipments at very little cost. Still another is that money laundering was essential to the profits of cartels.

Over time, trafficking and distribution routes became extremely flexible. In response to new obstacles or opportunities, traffickers switched routes from one country to another or from one form of transportation to another. Increased risk of apprehension in the Caribbean led Colombian cartels to move transit routes from the Caribbean to Mexico. Joint ventures between Colombian lords and Mexican traffickers thoroughly transformed the drug scene in Mexico, as the profits and power of local organizations multiplied. Around 1990, U.S. officials believed that more than half of South American cocaine shipments were entering the United States through Mexico. Thereafter the Colombians curtailed shipments through Mexico and turned back to the Caribbean, especially to the Bahamas and

**Table 14-1  Cocaine Prices Through the Distribution System, ca. 2000 (price per kilo)**

| | | |
|---|---|---|
| Coca leaves | Farmgate | $ 300 |
| Coca base | Farmgate | 900 |
| Cocaine hydrochloride | Export/Colombia | 1,500 |
| Cocaine hydrochloride | Import/U.S. | 15,000 |
| Cocaine (67% pure) | Dealer/U.S. | 40,000 |
| Cocaine (67% pure) | Retail/U.S. | 150,000 |

SOURCE: Latin American Commission on Drugs and Democracy, *Drugs and Democracy: Toward a Paradigm Shift* (2009), p. 23.

the Dominican Republic, where states were weak and enforcement lax. In the late 1990s they went back to Mexico once more. Antidrug authorities chased after them and scrambled to catch up with changing realities.

## DIMENSIONS OF DEMAND

The drug trade is really big business. As of 2009, the United Nations estimated that the number of people who had used drugs at least once in the previous year ranged from 149 million to 272 million. About half were "current" drug users—that is, they had imbibed within the past month. And among all consumers, between 15 million and 39 million were classified as addicts or "problem users." Around the world in general, cannabis was by far the most popular drug.

Estimates of the economic size of the global drug market have varied widely. Around 2002–2003, a UN agency calculated the total drug market at $322 billion per year. Subsequent studies have produced lower figures, in part because of the continuing decline in prices (shown earlier in Figure 14-1). Even so, the basic fact remains: The global market runs into hundreds of billions of dollars.

And it reaches all parts of the world. As early as 1994, a U.S. government report painted a somber picture: "Multi-ton shipments of cocaine, which once flowed mainly to the United States and Canada, now reach every corner of the globe. All major European capitals report a growing influx of the drug, with Russian authorities seizing over a metric ton of Colombian cocaine in St. Petersburg alone. No place seems exempt. The heroin situation is no more reassuring. The drug which cocaine displaced in the 1980s is making a comeback everywhere." Ironically, the ending of the Cold War opened markets for drugs throughout the former Soviet Union. And within Latin America, consumption was expanding, especially in transit-point countries, most notably Brazil.

For decades, the United States has been the world's largest market for illicit drugs. Official reports have estimated the number of users through a periodic survey conducted by government agencies—initially the National Institute on Drug Abuse (NIDA) and then the Substance Abuse and Mental Health Services Administration—whose representatives administer a questionnaire to willing respondents about drug use by household members. Resulting data showed a substantial decline in the number of current users (those who had taken drugs within the past thirty days) from more than 25 million in 1979 to 13.5 million in 1990 and to 13.0 million in 1996. This implied a drop of nearly 50 percent in overall drug usage. Current users of marijuana, by far the most popular of the illicit drugs, declined from nearly 19 million in 1985 to 10 million or so in the 1990s. Past-month users of cocaine followed a similar trend, dropping from 5.7 million in 1985 to an estimated level near 1.5 million. Casual drug usage was declining within the American middle class, especially the white suburban middle class. Judged by these standards, the "war on drugs" could claim some partial success.

Suddenly the trend reversed itself. Between 2000 and 2010, the estimated number of current drug users rose steadily from 14.0 million to 22.6 million, an

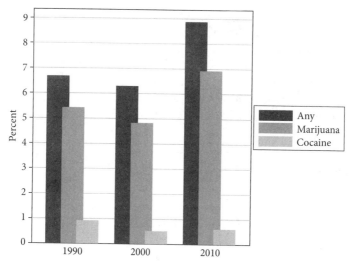

**Figure 14-2** Current Drug Users in the United States, 1990–2010 (% of population age twelve and older)

Sources: National Household Survey on Drug Abuse/Substance Abuse and Mental Health Services Administration, various years.

increase of more than 60 percent. Figure 14-2 depicts the pattern in relative terms. According to the data, the estimated share of adult Americans consuming illicit drugs dropped from 6.7 percent in 1990 to 6.3 percent in 2000—and began climbing upward again. By 2010 approximately 8.9 percent of adult Americans were past-month users of drugs.

Most of the increase during this period appears to have involved marijuana, as the number of past-month consumers rose from 10.7 million to 16 million (6.9 percent of the adult population). By 2010, in other words, nearly three-quarters of the drug-using population was smoking marijuana. As in earlier eras and in other parts of the world, pot was the preeminent drug of choice.

Levels of hard-core addiction were in the meantime holding steady. Cocaine consumption hovered around its historic levels of 1.5 million to 2.0 million users (for 2010, roughly 0.6 percent of the adult population). The consumption of heroin has shown greater fluctuation, peaking in the 1990s and subsiding slightly in recent years.

All in all, the demand for illicit drugs has created a huge consumer market in the United States. One analysis pegged the total volume of retail U.S. sales in 2000 at $64 billion. Approximately $36 billion was spent on cocaine, by far the most expensive drug, well over half of the total. Around $10 billion went for heroin, $5.4 billion for methamphetamines, and $11 billion for marijuana. However imperfect the estimates, there could be no lingering doubts: This was real money. And all these transactions took place in violation of the law.

Drug usage inflicted significant costs on American society. Overconsumption posed threats to public health, especially to "crack babies" born to drug-dependent mothers. Jobs were lost and productivity reduced. Conflicts between rival drug gangs led to rising violence in major cities—in Miami, New York, Chicago, Los Angeles, and Washington, D.C. Costs of law enforcement were steadily mounting. According to one U.S. government analysis, the annual costs to society were amounting to $120 billion in lost productivity, $61 billion for the criminal justice system, and $11 billion for health care. It is not entirely clear how these numbers were generated. Nor is it clear how much of the overall cost stemmed, not from the use of drugs, but from the legal prohibition against them. Even so, these were large-scale losses.

## POLICIES AND WARS

The United States has devoted massive resources to its war on drugs. In the international arena, as mentioned before, U.S. policy stressed the control of supply, especially through (1) suppression of production, including crop eradication, (2) interdiction of shipments, especially at the U.S. border, and (3) encouragement of other nations to join in these efforts, usually through bilateral arrangements but also through multilateral treaties.

On the domestic front, U.S. efforts have emphasized law enforcement, especially the incarceration of drug users. As of 2006, the United States had over 2 million people locked in jail—by far the highest per capita rate in the world, followed by Russia, Cuba, and Ukraine. Large numbers of U.S. inmates had committed drug-related offenses, most commonly possession of marijuana (in contrast, arrests for the sale of heroin and cocaine were relatively rare). According to official statistics, the cost of incarcerating drug offenders was approaching $40 billion per year.

During the 1980s, public concern over drug abuse and drug-related violence mounted steadily until, characteristically enough, the Reagan/ Bush administrations chose to declare a "war" on drugs. At stake was not only the health of U.S. citizens. According to William J. Bennett, first head of the Office of National Drug Control Policy, it was a matter of national sovereignty:

> The source of the most dangerous drugs threatening our nation is principally international. Few foreign threats are more costly to the U.S. economy. None does more damage to our national values and institutions and destroys more American lives. While most international threats are potential, the damage and violence caused by the drug trade are actual and pervasive. Drugs are a major threat to our national security.

Thus draped in the banner of "national security," U.S. international policy on drugs justified its longstanding emphasis on supply control.

Almost by definition, this strategy focused mainly on Latin America. Countries of the region produced or transshipped more than 80 percent of the cocaine and 90 percent of the marijuana that entered the United States. In particular, the concern with cocaine prompted U.S. authorities to devote special attention to nations of the Andes—especially Bolivia, Peru, and Colombia—and toward the processing and trafficking DTOs in Colombia.

The preoccupation with national security led to one of the most remarkable events of the era—a military invasion of Panama. A quasi-colony of the United States, this tiny country had been under the sway of authoritarian rule for nearly 20 years. Moreover, the then-current strongman, Manuel Noriega, had close links with Washington, allowing the Reagan administration to use Panama as a staging area for military operations in Nicaragua and assisting the CIA in its efforts to destabilize the *sandinista* regime. Ever the opportunist, Noriega opened Panama to money laundering for profits from illicit drug trafficking and established working relations with cocaine cartels in Colombia. He also made the mistake of rigging presidential elections and unleashing thuggish "Dignity Battalions" that administered a public bloody beating to an opposition candidate.

Yet it was drugs that caused the trouble. In September 1989 President George H. W. Bush denounced illegal drugs as the country's "gravest threat." In

---

**BOX 14-1**

## Overwhelming Force—Was It Really Necessary?

Shortly after midnight on December 20, 1989, U.S. armed forces launched "Operation Just Cause" against the tiny republic of Panama. Its central goal was to capture General Manuel Antonio Noriega and remove him from power. Instead of using a SWAT team or a squad of commandos, the George H.W. Bush administration chose to apply the doctrine of "overwhelming force," which in this case included thousands of troops, scores of jet planes, teams of Navy SEALs, and two Stealth fighter-bombers, each armed with a 2,000-pound bomb. The assault on Noriega's headquarters (the Comandancia) inflicted widespread devastation on the nearby El Chorrillo section of Panama City, as described in this report:

> Exploding shells and tracer bullets set fires that were clearly visible from the other side of the city within just a few minutes. U.S. loudspeakers told residents to stay in their houses, but U.S. gunships fired directly into one building after another as crews tried to kill the snipers scattered throughout the neighborhood. Wooden structures blazed and collapsed, and when people ran into the streets many fell under the torrent of firepower from the sky. The assault continued until approximately 6:00 a.m., when U.S. troops moved up to the pockmarked, scorched, but still standing Comandancia. It was 10:00 a.m. before they entered the structure and counted the bodies, many of which were clad only in underwear.
>
> In densely packed El Chorrillo, fires razed nearly 2,000 dwellings, making some 15,000 residents homeless. Many of them crowded into an open field in front of Balboa High School. Hospitals, such as Santo Tomás, filled up. The counting of the civilian dead began, and it continued for a long time.

SOURCE: Kevin Buckley, *Panama: The Whole Story* (New York: Simon & Schuster, 1991), p. 240.

mid-December Panama's pro-Noriega government proclaimed that a "state of war" existed with the United States and installed the military leader for the first time as chief of state. The next day members of the Panama Defense Force opened fire on a group of U.S. military officers. Professing "enormous outrage," Bush authorized a military strike. Employing overwhelming firepower, U.S. forces secured control of the country within five days. Noriega surrendered shortly after that. Intoned Republican Senate leader Bob Dole: "Noriega's bad news is good news for our war on drugs. It proves America won't cave in to anyone, no matter how powerful or corrupt."

## The Clinton Years

Bill Clinton's administration announced its antidrug policy in early 1994. Drug policy director Lee Brown proposed a record-high budget of $13.2 billion, with a slight revision in spending priorities—targeting 59 percent for supply control and law enforcement and 41 percent for demand reduction. Domestically, Brown expressed special concern for hard-core users in the inner cities and pledged to provide more education and treatment. Internationally, the Clinton program placed less emphasis on interdiction of drugs, except along the U.S.– Mexican border, and planned instead to move directly against the DTOs (without indicating how this would be done). One of the most significant changes came at the rhetorical level: Instead of depicting drug abuse as the result of moral failure or criminal conspiracy, Brown and his associates interpreted inner-city drug addiction as a response to poverty and hopelessness.

For political reasons this line looked too soft (it is to be remembered that Clinton himself was vulnerable on the drug issue, having uttered the unbelievable claim that as a youth he had tried marijuana but did not inhale). So in 1995 Clinton replaced Brown, the African American former police commissioner of New York City, with retired General Barry R. McCaffrey, a career military officer and former head of the U.S. Southern Command in Panama. With symbolism back in place, the federal antidrug budget continued its inexorable climb, reaching $17.1 billion for fiscal year 1999. Priorities also resumed their customary positions: Demand reduction accounted for just one-third of expenditures, as in the Reagan/Bush years, while law enforcement went back up to two-thirds of the total.

Throughout these shifts in emphasis, the Clinton policies provoked persistent tension with Latin American governments. Washington expressed initial frustration with the government of Alberto Fujimori in Peru, which refused to conduct eradication campaigns against peasant growers in the Andes; occasional frustration with the government of César Gaviria in Colombia, which negotiated terms of amnesty with leading drug entrepreneurs; intermittent frustration with the government of Ernesto Zedillo in Mexico, which seemed incapable of stanching corruption within its own ranks; and unrelenting hostility toward the government of Ernesto Samper in Colombia, who had allegedly gained office by accepting drug money during a hotly contested presidential campaign. In May 1998, American customs agents climaxed a three-year investigation by luring scores of mid-level Mexican bankers into the United States through a "sting" operation and arresting them on money-laundering charges. Notified only at the last minute, Mexican authorities were outraged by the deception and the lack of trust: "There are a lot of things that we have not accepted and that we are not going to accept," declared foreign minister Rosario Green. "We Mexicans are very jealous of our national sovereignty."

With the ending of the Cold War, the "war on drugs" became the signature conflict of its time. A fitting symbol came to be known as "Plan Colombia." As initially proposed by Colombian authorities in 1998, the multi-billion-dollar program envisioned the promotion of alternative development in coca-producing areas; as later revised and supported by the United States, it relied largely on military campaigns (against drug traffickers and rebel groups) and the large-scale use of aerial fumigation. As these efforts intensified, Colombia became the world's third-largest recipient of U.S. foreign aid. More than 80 percent of this assistance was dedicated to police and military forces. Overall, Plan Colombia reduced the country's coca production, weakened rebel movements (most notably the FARC), and strengthened state authority. It had little effect on the cocaine market, however, as production rebounded in Bolivia and Peru. Critics also noted the widespread abuse of human rights.

## The Bush Era

Throughout the 1990s, illicit drug trafficking became the most contentious and prominent issue on the inter-American agenda. Despite overwhelming evidence about the importance of consumer demand, Washington continued to focus largely on the reduction of supply. Following the disputed election of 2000, the Republican administration of George W. Bush showed every sign of following suit.

After 9/11 the war on terror superseded, and enveloped, the war on drugs. International antidrug efforts derived their ultimate rationale from their contribution to the war on terror. According to the 2006 National Drug Control Strategy, the disruption of production and transportation of illicit substances "contributes to the Global War on Terrorism, severing the links between drug traffickers and terrorist organizations in countries such as Afghanistan and Colombia, among others." (One has to wonder what "others" the authors had in mind.) Moreover, continued the report, market disruption "renders support to allies such as the courageous administration of President Álvaro Uribe in Colombia." (That is, the policy offered help to those who have requested it.) No longer would eradication of poppy fields and seizures of cocaine be celebrated in and of themselves; their ultimate purpose was advancing the war on terror.

The logic here was tenuous. Afghanistan was a traditional source of the opium poppies used for the production of heroin. According to official U.S. government data, poppy cultivation dropped to near-zero levels under the rule of the Taliban; it began to rebound only after the U.S.-led invasion of 2001. Fulminations by U.S. officials often bordered on the ludicrous. One case in point was a Super Bowl commercial in January 2002 that accused American drug users of providing tacit support to terrorists—which meant, by implication, that pot smoking was subversive and antipatriotic. Never mind the fact that the heroin consumed in the United States came mostly from Latin America rather than Afghanistan.

With the passage of time, the Bush policy concentrated on three major countries—Colombia, Mexico, and Venezuela. Bolstered by "Plan Colombia," this nation became the hemispheric poster child for American efforts. Indeed, the country's leaders initially expressed hope that the U.S. war on terror would extend to their own territory. After all, the FARC and ELN and the paramilitary organizations all qualified as "terrorist" groups; President Bush had declared war on terror in general—so why not U.S. military action in Colombia? (The answers, apparently, had to do with the fact that those terrorist groups had not committed major acts of violence on American soil—nor were they likely to do so—and they therefore did not demonstrate sufficient "global reach.") In any event, Álvaro Uribe's administration took an implacable stance toward guerrillas and drug traffickers and offered full cooperation with the United States. One key indication came through the extradition of alleged drug traffickers, always a delicate issue in U.S.–Latin American relations. Under Uribe, the number of extraditions climbed from 13 in 2000 to 134 in 2005.

Mexico presented a more complicated case. A declared friend of the Bush administration, Vicente Fox took high-profile actions against corruption and drug trafficking. In particular, law enforcement authorities managed to place well-known cartel leaders under arrest. Even so, Mexico continued to supply 30 to 40 percent of the U.S. market for heroin; it served as the transit zone for 70 to 90 percent of the cocaine entering the United States; and it had become the largest foreign source of methamphetamines. Conflicts with, within, and between DTOs spawned unprecedented levels of violence, especially in border cities. And the criminal organizations wielded vast amounts of economic power. According to U.S. government estimates for 2005, "Mexican traffickers receive more than $13.8 billion in revenue from illicit-drug sales to the United States." (Subsequent estimates of cartels' annual earnings ranged from $6 billion to $39 billion.) Needless to say, funds of such magnitudes furnished exceptional resources for large-scale bribes of Mexican officials.

Ultimately, the Bush administration gave Fox credit for his efforts. There were still some problems (because Mexican law prohibited capital punishment, for instance, Mexico was reluctant to extradite traffickers to the United States). "To help overcome these challenges," the U.S. government declared, "the United States and Mexico will continue to work to address our shared problem with drug production and trafficking." Fox received a passing grade.

Venezuela ran afoul of Washington for entirely different reasons. The country was accused by the U.S. government of serving as "a key transit point for drugs leaving Colombia"—without, it should be said, any quantitative estimate of the proportions involved. Contributing factors were alleged to be official corruption and a weak judicial system. At the same time, U.S. drug officials conceded that Venezuela produced only minimal quantities of cocaine, that the Chávez government seized a fair number of shipments, that it passed laws against corruption, and that it established a program to reduce local demand.

The problem was political. As noted earlier, President Hugo Chávez had embarked on a stridently anti-American foreign policy. He virulently denounced what he regarded as U.S. complicity in an attempt to overthrow his government in April 2002. The Bush administration made no attempt to disguise its distaste for his bombast, his accusations, his personality, and his policies. In July 2005, as rhetoric heated up on both sides, Chávez accused agents of the U.S. Drug Enforcement Administration of spying on his government and plotting yet another coup—so he asked DEA personnel to leave the country. Outraged at this reaction, President Bush subsequently decertified Venezuela (along with Myanmar) "as countries that have failed demonstrably during the previous 12 months to adhere to their obligations under international narcotics agreements." Yet Bush also determined that economic assistance to "selected" development and institutional projects was "vital to the national interests of the United States." Thus Washington would have

---

### BOX 14-2

### Frustration in the War on Drugs

A quarter-century after it was proclaimed by President Ronald Reagan, the "war on drugs" was losing momentum. Crops were destroyed, shipments were seized, cartels were disrupted—but the trafficking continued, and the number of American drug users was back on the rise. A clear-cut expression of weariness appeared in, of all places, an official report of the U.S. State Department in 2006:

> Fighting the drug trade is a dominant element in a broader struggle against corruption. Drug organizations possess and wield the ultimate instrument of corruption: money. The drug trade has access to almost unimaginable quantities of it. No commodity is so widely available, so cheap to produce, and as easily renewable as illegal drugs. They offer dazzling profit margins that allow criminals to generate illicit revenues on a scale without historical precedent. For example, assuming an average U.S. retail street price of one hundred dollars a gram, a metric ton of pure cocaine is worth $100 million on the streets of the United States—twice as much if the drug is cut with additives. That same metric ton would typically have cost around $3,000,000 ($3,000 per kilogram) when it left Colombia. Few legitimate businesses can boast of a 30-fold return. At $100 per gram, the 329 metric tons of cocaine seized in Mexico and Latin America in 2005 could in theory be worth as much as $30 billion to the drug trade, more than the gross domestic product of many of the countries of Central America. If only a portion of these profits flow back to the drug syndicates, we are still speaking of hundreds of millions, if not billions, of dollars.
>
> To put these sums into perspective, in FY 2005 the State Department's budget for international drug control operations was approximately $1.2 billion. That equates to roughly 12 metric tons of cocaine. *The drug syndicates have lost that amount in a single shipment, with no serious consequences, except to the unfortunate subordinate responsible for the loss* .

SOURCE: U.S. Department of State, Bureau for International Narcotics and Law Enforcement Affairs, *International Narcotics Control Strategy Report* (March 2006), pp. 18–19.

it both ways: The government of Venezuela would be ostracized, while domestic political opposition to Chávez would continue to receive American support under the guise of civil society programs.

What is so glaringly apparent is that the decertification of Venezuela bore no direct connection to its role in the drug trade. This was a wholly political maneuver, defined within the context of the war on terror. Officials in charge of U.S. antidrug policy tacitly acknowledged as much on more than one occasion. In full-length congressional testimony in March 2006, Assistant Secretary of State for International Narcotics and Law Enforcement Affairs Anne Patterson reported, "The Venezuelan government's willingness to cooperate with its neighbors and with the U.S. is obviously critical to the regional strategy." She characterized Venezuela's recent counternarcotics performance as, "at best, mixed"—a statement falling far short of wholesale condemnation. "With the recent surge in production in the region," Patterson added, "Venezuela constitutes a hole in our counternarcotics strategy in Latin America. Given Venezuela's excellent record for cooperation in the past, we hope to see a return of that cooperative spirit in the coming year." (In later years, elements of the Venezuelan military would be accused of cooperation with drug trafficking, but that was a subsequent story.)

Over the years, U.S. antidrug campaigns thus became linked to larger geopolitical goals. Yet the consumption of drugs increased steadily under the Bush administration, as the number of past-month users climbed from 14 million in 2000 to 20 million in 2008. It comes as no surprise to discover that the drug control policy had become part and parcel of the antiterrorist campaign. What is surprising is the extent to which this drew public attention so far away from the increase in American drug usage. In effect, the war on terror provided cover for the failure of the war on drugs.

### Obama: Rhetoric or Reality?

As in other areas, the election of Barack Obama raised widespread hopes for substantive policy change. In March 2009 President Obama designated Gil Kerlikowske, the highly regarded police chief of Seattle, as the new director of the ONDCP. Within a week of taking office, Kerlikowske proclaimed that the Obama team would discard all reference to the "war on drugs." Instead of demonizing villains or amorphous enemies, the new administration would pursue "enduring national interests" on the basis of scientific analysis, consultation with experts, and the identification of plausible policy goals.

So the Obama team forged a "balanced" approach to drug policy, with increasing emphasis on reducing consumer demand and drug abuse. In its 2010 report the ONDCP defined its central goal as a 15 percent reduction by 2015 of drug use and its consequences, including drug deaths and drugged driving. Treatment and prevention would come to the forefront of these efforts. And in the international arena, the United States would openly acknowledge "co-responsibility" for drug trafficking and make determined efforts to intercept southbound flows of money and of lethal weapons. "Shared responsibility for the origin of a problem implies shared responsibility to solve it." This would entail joint law enforcement operations, training and technical assistance, and the pooling of intelligence with partner countries.

Yet reforms could go only so far. Kerlikowske took a hard line on the prospect of "legalization" of marijuana, which he denounced as "waving the white flag." The whole idea was "off the charts when it comes to discussion, from my viewpoint, . . . legalization vocabulary doesn't exist for me and it was made clear that it doesn't exist in President Obama's vocabulary." (In fairness, it should be noted that his office is legally prohibited from even thinking about legalization. According to a 1998 law, no federal funding for the ONDCP "shall be expended for any study or contract relating to the legalization [for a medical use or any other use] of a substance" on the illegal list, and it was the ONDCP's duty to "take such actions as necessary to oppose any attempt to legalize the use of a substance (in any form)" without approval by the FDA. Those are pretty serious constraints!)

In keeping with his stance against legalization, Kerlikowske went on to criticize marijuana as "a dangerous drug." He strongly opposed state-level efforts to legalize the medical use of marijuana, proclaiming in the face of scientific research that "we will wait for evidence on whether smoked marijuana has any medicinal benefits—those aren't in." In November 2010 he expressed relief that California voters rejected Proposition 19, which would have legalized marijuana for personal use (not only consumption but also cultivation and sale). "Californians recognized that legalizing marijuana will not make our citizens healthier, solve California's budget crisis, or reduce drug-related violence in Mexico," he said. He did not acknowledge that the vote was very close.

Indications of actual policy priorities emerged from budgetary plans. For FY 2012, Obama's ONDCP proposed a total budget of $26.2 billion, as displayed in Table 14-2. The data point to several realities. First, the combined proportion for prevention and treatment came to just over 40 percent—well within the range of pre-Obama budgets. Second, domestic law enforcement—including incarceration—remained the largest single item. (Part of the "interdiction" activity would also involve domestic law enforcement.) Finally, the "international" component came in at less than 10 percent, with the winding down of Plan Colombia and the increasing transfer of responsibilities to such partner nations as Afghanistan. On balance, this budget did not represent a major break with prior practices.

**Table 14-2  U.S. Drug Control Budget for FY 2012**

|  | $ (MILLIONS) | % |
|---|---|---|
| Prevention | 1,682.8 | 6.4% |
| Treatment | 8,982.1 | 34.3 |
| Domestic law enforcement | 9,505.4 | 36.3 |
| Interdiction | 3,901.0 | 14.9 |
| International | 2,138.4 | 8.2 |
| Total | 26,209.7 | 100.1% |

Source: U.S. Office of National Drug Control Policy.

Mexico still posed a special problem. From the Bush administration, the Obama team had inherited the "Mérida Initiative," a multi-billion-dollar plan to support efforts against drug trafficking, transnational organized crime, and money laundering in Mexico (and Central America). Rather like Plan Colombia, the initiative focused on military-related strategies; funds would be used for training, equipment, and intelligence. After the initial phase came to an end in 2010, the Obama administration decided to renew and expand the commitment. With eyes wide open, the United States was stepping directly into Mexico's drug wars.

## Crisis in Mexico

Mexico had been for generations a major site for the production and transit of illicit drugs, especially marijuana and heroin. The country's role began to shift in the 1980s, when Colombian cartels decided to transship U.S.-bound cocaine through Mexico. The partnership proved to be effective and profitable. Eventually acquiring shares of drug shipments (rather than fees for service), Mexican DTOs

**Poor Ol' Mexico.** This cartoon vividly illustrates the principle of "shared responsibility" for international drug trafficking—and the hypocrisy of U.S. finger-pointing against Mexico. Source: ©2011 Matt Wuerker. Used with the permission of Matt Wuerker and the Cartoonist Group. All rights reserved.

expanded operations and moved into wholesale and retail marketing. As their profits and power increased, the U.S.-Mexican border area became something of a no-man's land.

By the early 2000s the Mexican drug trade was dominated by seven key organizations. Strongest among them was the Sinaloa cartel, followed by groups dispersed along the U.S.–Mexican border (in Tijuana, Ciudad Juarez, and the Gulf) plus several others (Los Zetas, the Beltrán Leyva organization, and La Familia Michoacana). From production through marketing, the Mexican drug industry employed hundreds of thousands of people. The DTOs were thought to have more than 1,000 retail outlets in the United States; with billions of dollar in collective earnings, they accumulated enormous amounts of economic power. The DTOs were on a roll.

In 2007 it was estimated that Mexican cartels smuggled nearly 90 percent of the cocaine consumed in the United States as well as 80 percent of the methamphetamines. They also increased production of marijuana and heroin. As shown in Figure 14-3, cannabis production was less than 5,000 hectares in 2000 but then began a steady climb—to approximately 17,500 hectares by 2009, a record high, while the cultivation of opium poppy rose from 3,000 hectares in 2000 to 19,500 hectares in 2009. (A "hectare" is 10,000 square meters, roughly equivalent to 2.5 acres.) Output was climbing to unprecedented levels.

Given the dispersion of power and resources, however, the Mexican DTOs did not cooperate among themselves. Instead they fought each other mercilessly. The economic motive was to protect and maintain market share. The psychological

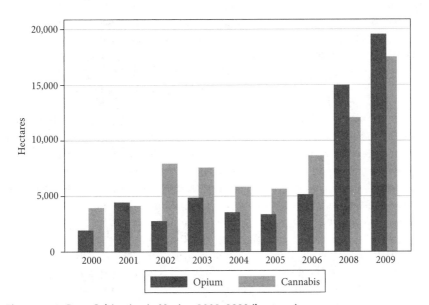

**Figure 14-3  Drug Cultivation in Mexico, 2000–2009 (hectares)**
Source: U. S. Department of State, International Narcotics Control Strategy Reports, 2001–2011.

motive was to instill fear and loyalty. Acts of betrayal were avenged with shocking cruelty. And as the DTOs asserted their brutal authority, they openly challenged the forces of law and order. They were operating with impunity.

After his election in 2006, President Felipe Calderón determined to challenge the cartels and enlisted the military in a head-to-head "war" against the traffickers. The result was a grisly spiral of violence. The military, the police, and the DTOs engaged in mortal combat. Abuse of human rights became widespread. By the end of 2011 the death toll had taken the lives of 50,000 people. Much of the carnage resulted from struggles among the DTOs, but thousands of innocent civilians were caught in the deadly crossfire. Mexico was facing a crisis of public security. To the acute discomfiture of government officials, some observers began musing about the potential "failure" of the Mexican state.

This predicament posed serious challenges for the United States. One involved security along the 2,000-mile border: the less effective the Mexican authority, the less controlled the area. Spillover violence presented grave dangers, as gang activity intensified in such border cities as Phoenix and San Diego. And in 2010, gunmen believed to be linked to drug traffickers shot a pregnant American consulate worker to death in the violence-racked town of Ciudad Juárez. At a time when American politicians were insisting that U.S. authorities must take control of the border, this was an unacceptable threat.

Mexico was crucial in other ways. As a founding member of NAFTA, it was by this time America's third-largest trade partner—and a reliable source of energy. It was host to nearly $100 billion in foreign direct investment from the United States. Further, Mexico represented a geopolitical anchor for stability throughout the surrounding region, especially Central America. And if the notion of "co-responsibility" had any meaning, it had to be acknowledged that the United States had helped fuel the crisis by its appetite for drugs and by its unregulated sale of firearms. Failure for Mexico would constitute a major setback for U.S. national interests.

Responding to a growing sense that Calderón's military-led fight against DTOs had stalled, the United States and Mexico set their counternarcotics strategy on a new course in 2010 by refocusing efforts on strengthening civilian law enforcement and rebuilding communities crippled by poverty and crime. Building on programs already undertaken through the Mérida Initiative, this revised strategy would emphasize American support for training Mexican police officers, judges, prosecutors and public defenders. Agencies in both countries would work to develop screening systems to facilitate legitimate cross-border flows of people and goods. Most striking was the shift away from military assistance. Instead of providing hardware, equipment, and technology to the Mexican military and police, subsequent efforts would stress training for the civilian police.

To many Mexicans, the rising count of gruesome drug-related murders was firm evidence that the government's strategy had failed. In the words of a report by the independent Council on Foreign Relations, "Mexico is in the midst of a worsening security crisis. . . . [F]ew Mexican citizens feel safer today than they did ten years ago, and most believe that their government is losing the fight." And according to an official report of the U.S. government, "Major Mexican-based [DTOs] and their associates are solidifying their dominance of the U.S. whole-sale drug trade and will maintain their reign for the foreseeable future." Generally speaking, the document concluded, "The threat posed by the trafficking and abuse of illicit drugs will not abate in the near term and may increase." The outlook was at best unclear. In Mexico's presidential election of mid-2012, popular disenchant-ment with Calderón's hard-line policy (and its consequent levels of violence) helped lead to a crushing defeat for his party and to the restoration in power of the for-merly reviled PRI.

## RETROSPECT: IMPACTS ON LATIN AMERICA

Antidrug policies produced complex and contradictory results. In the United States, repeated public declaration of a "war" on drugs led to demands for "total victory" (whatever that might mean), encouraged calls for enlistment of the mili-tary in antidrug efforts, and often led to ostracism of those who disagreed with the government—as though their patriotism and/or sanity were in question. In Latin America, campaigns of repression erupted in organized violence between armed groups, including the military and the police.

To provide a sense of this complexity, Table 14-3 outlines seven simultane-ous kinds of drug wars waged throughout the region from the 1980s through the 2000s. In the first, the United States took on drug suppliers in one way or another, most conspicuously through agents of the Drug Enforcement Administration. In the second, Latin American governments responded to challenges by "narcoter-rorists," agents of drug cartels who used terror, violence, and intimidation to assert raw political power. (In this battle the government of Colombia achieved a major political victory by killing Medellín kingpin Pablo Escobar in December 1993.) In the third drug war, Latin American governments engaged in struggles with armed guerrilla movements that formed unholy alliances with traffickers. In the fourth, Latin American governments waged armed campaigns against narcotraffickers—those who produced and exported illicit drugs but did not engage in systematic political terrorism. In the fifth war, drug cartels fought among themselves, usually over market share. This explained much of the violence in both Colombia and Mexico and also in the cities of America, where rival distributors waged cam-paigns of attrition against one another. In the sixth confrontation, drug traffickers engaged in conflict with their sometime allies, armed guerrilla groups; this often occurred once the *traficantes* began to use their profits to purchase land and join the socioeconomic establishment, against which the guerrillas had taken arms in the first place. In the seventh and last kind of war, unique to Colombia in the 1980s, *narcotraficantes* declared war against political opponents, in this case left-wing parties. For the most part, however, drug operations obeyed no single ideol-ogy and sought to maintain low political profiles.

The diversity in drug wars underlined the range and variability of inter-ests involved in public policy. The "drug problem" in Colombia was markedly

**Table 14-3  Drug Wars in Latin America**

| CONFLICT | COMBATANTS |
|---|---|
| War No. 1 | United States versus suppliers |
| War No. 2 | Latin American governments versus narcoterrorists |
| War No. 3 | Latin American governments versus guerrillas |
| War No. 4 | Latin American governments versus narcotraffickers |
| War No. 5 | Narcotraffickers versus narcotraffickers |
| War No. 6 | Narcotraffickers versus guerrillas |
| War No. 7 | Narcotraffickers versus political left |

SOURCE: Reprinted from *Drug Policy in the Americas*, Peter H. Smith (ed.), 1992, by permission of Westview Press, Boulder, Colorado.

different from the "drug problem" in Peru, Bolivia, or Mexico (not to mention the United States). Also striking was the ubiquity of unintended consequences. Colombia's crackdown on the Medellín cartel produced a temporary decline in the price of coca leaf in Peru and Bolivia; instead of enticing coca producers to turn to cultivation of licit crops, however, it encouraged them to process their products (thus increasing value added) and to export coca base instead of coca leaves. In this fashion, a "success" in the Colombian drug war could exacerbate the problem in Bolivia or in other neighboring countries. Indeed, it appears that the Colombian crackdown accelerated the dispersion of drug-trafficking activities throughout the continent, from Chile and Argentina to Costa Rica and Belize, especially as transit routes and as sites for money laundering. "Latin America as a whole is sliding into the drug war," said one well-informed observer in the 1990s. "Argentina and Brazil can see their future in Bolivia. Bolivia sees its own [future] in Peru, Peru in Colombia, and Colombia in Lebanon. It's an endless cycle."

While the U.S.-sponsored drug wars failed to achieve the goals of reducing supply and raising prices for illicit drugs in the American market, they had serious effects on Latin American society and politics. First, they subjected the countries and peoples of the region to staggering levels of violence and intimidation—not only in Colombia and Mexico but also in Peru and other countries, where antidrug campaigns produced large-scale violations of human rights.

Second, the drug wars exposed national institutions to corruption. One of the lessons of antidrug campaigns, around the world, was that law enforcement agencies risked corruption by drug traffickers and lords; increased contact with *traficantes*, even in an adversarial manner, increased the possibility of compromise and subversion.

Third, prosecution of the drug wars placed increasing autonomy and authority in the hands of the Latin American armed forces. Drug wars encouraged militarization. This could pose a substantial threat to still-fragile democracies throughout the region.

Finally, the drug wars created major complications for U.S.–Latin American relations. One specific source of aggravation was the annual process of "certification," mandated by congressional amendment to the Foreign Assistance Act of

1986. According to the statute, governments failing to cooperate with U.S. anti-drug strategy would lose economic assistance and face U.S. opposition in multilateral lending organizations. The world's largest consumer market thus took it upon itself to judge the efforts of countries engaged in production or transit. In 1996 and 1997 Colombia was denied certification; in 1998 it received a national-interest waiver. Every year the evaluation of Mexico led to high drama. As criticism of the process mounted, the U.S. State Department decided to publish only the names of decertified countries rather than assess each and every nation under evaluation. Rancor nonetheless ran deep. After Bolivia was decertified once again in 2011, President Evo Morales proclaimed that it was time for Latin America to "decertify" the United States.

Debates over drugs became dialogues of the deaf. United States politicians regularly succumbed to the temptation to charge Latin American countries (usually Mexico, Bolivia, or Peru) with responsibility for drug-related problems in American society; in reply, Latins pointed their fingers at U.S. demand. Moreover, Latin American countries faced different challenges from those in the United States. Rising consumption was a growing concern but it remained well below U.S. levels. Instead their most urgent problems stemmed from the power of DTOs, from waves of narcoviolence, and from the subversion of state authority (through corruption and other means). As described by María Celia Toro for the case of Mexico, the most pressing concerns were fundamentally political. One was "to prevent drug traffickers from directly confronting state authority," to obstruct the formation of "states within the state," and to diminish the threat of narcoterrorism. A second goal, "equally important," was "to prevent U.S. policy and judicial authorities from acting as a surrogate justice system in Mexico." In other words, U.S. policy itself posed a significant danger to Mexican national interests.

For reasons of its own, the United States strongly encouraged Latin American governments to enlist in the antidrug wars. In this way, suggested critics, the United States succeeded in exporting its own drug war to Latin America.

Leaders throughout the region responded, but for differing reasons. Sometimes, as in the case of Bolivia, they were reluctant to precipitate what they regarded as all-out wars against the peasantry. Other times, as in the case of Colombia, they reacted to challenges from drug cartels with considerable force—but even then, *they were not waging the same war that the United States was advocating.* The U.S. government was asking Latin American governments to join ranks in a war against the narcotraffickers and thus to forge an alliance with the United States. (In terms of Table 14-3, this would mean a combination of War No. 1, waged by the United States, with War No. 4, to be waged by Latin America.) But as successive Colombian presidents have shown, the concern in Colombia was not so much with narcotraffic as with narcoterror (War No. 2 in Table 14-3). This meant different purposes, strategies, and policies. Such incongruity in antidrug campaigns led not only to confusion but also to missed opportunities; and, in one conspicuous instance, it helped provoke armed conflict between governments.

## PROSPECT: DEBATES OVER POLICY

Ambivalent consequences of the wars on drugs raised questions about the prospects for wholesale change in U.S. policy. Predictably enough, Washington's stance was negative. What was needed, officials said, was a continuation and acceleration of the present policy. Victory lay just around the corner. With a little more money and a little more effort, consumption would decline, the DTOs would be dismantled, and violence would disappear—or at least be reduced to acceptable levels. Make minor adjustments here and there, but do not surrender. Give no quarter to law breakers, pushers, or users. Stand fast.

A chorus of criticism nonetheless swelled. A Latin American Commission on Drugs and Democracy, co-chaired by three ex-presidents (Cesar Gaviria of Colombia, Ernesto Zedillo of Mexico, and Fernando Henrique Cardoso of Brazil), called for a fundamental "paradigm shift." The war on drugs had "failed," in their view, spawning violence and crime and corruption. It was "imperative to rectify the 'war on drugs' strategy pursued in the region over the past 30 years," according to their 2009 report. "The long-term solution for the drug problem is to reduce drastically the demand for drugs in the main consumer countries." That meant the United States.

Two years later this analysis found support from the Global Commission on Drug Policy, a blue-ribbon group including former presidents or prime ministers of five countries, a former secretary general of the UN, and business and government leaders—including George P. Shultz and Paul A. Volcker. The commission recommended treatment rather than incarceration for people who use drugs but do not harm others, plus targeting international law enforcement efforts against violent criminal organizations rather than nonviolent, low-level offenders.

A central issue revolved around "legalization." Many saw this as a magic bullet. Abolish all laws against sale, possession, or consumption. Subject the market to laissez-faire competition. This would drive the DTOs out of business or at least force them to go into other activities. Sales taxes could fund programs for education and prevention. There would be no need for police dragnets, paramilitary action, or extensive incarceration. Curiously enough, this kind of initiative drew support from both the American right, including such prominent conservatives as William Buckley and Ron Paul, and the left, including a host of onetime celebrities from the antiwar 1960s. This strange alliance—of "pinstripes and ponytails," as one wag described it—showed the breadth and depth of public concern with longstanding U.S. policies.

Yet the issue was not as simple as that. As experts observed, the devil was in the details. At least four main questions arose:

1. Which drugs? Marijuana, heroin, cocaine, or ATS-type designer drugs? Would they all be legal?
2. What consumers? Would there be an age limit? Or no limit at all?

3. What means of distribution? Would there be licensed retail outlets? Or government stores, as for liquor in some U.S. states?
4. What kind of prices and taxes? It would be necessary to minimize black-market sales; at the same time, hefty taxes might help cover the costs of (a) educational campaigns and (b) medical treatment and rehabilitation for serious addicts. How could this be accomplished?

Upon inspection, it became clear that most responsible proposals envisioned not legalization of the status quo but some form of "regulation." Many thoughtful analysts supported one or another variation on these themes. Given the political need for U.S. legislators to remain "tough" on drug traffickers, however, the prospects for such reform seemed minimal.

As debates intensified, they came to focus largely on one specific possibility—legalization of marijuana. Essentially, it would fall under the same set of rules applying to alcohol: a legal age limit together with warnings against overuse. In supporting the report of the Global Commission, former president Jimmy Carter reminded readers that he had proposed legalization of marijuana for personal use in 1977. A handful of congressional leaders advocated the removal of federal prohibitions on marijuana, leaving ultimate authority up to the states. California voters came close to approving legalization in 2010. And in direct repudiation of U.S. intransigence, a number of Latin American countries decriminalized and/or depenalized the possession of marijuana for personal use: Argentina, Brazil, Colombia, Costa Rica, Mexico, Peru, Uruguay, and Venezuela. The United States was losing control of the international debate.

Still another option—perhaps in combination with legalization of marijuana—called for a major shift in U.S. policy priorities. Such an alternative would devote well over half the federal drug budget to prevention and treatment; elimination of incarceration for possession (of marijuana at least, perhaps of other drugs); and intensification of law enforcement efforts against money laundering and illicit sales of firearms. For Latin America, the United States would devote substantial resources to strengthening state capacities and the rule of law.

One extension of this view advocated the initiation by the United States and Mexico (plus possibly Colombia) of a hemispheric initiative against the consumption of dangerous drugs. The principal means would be education and rehabilitation. A project of this kind would go far beyond the prohibitionist tone of the international discourse on drugs. It could focus on the source of the problem. It could save lives and protect public health. It might save money. And it would set inter-American cooperation on a wholly new course.

## QUESTIONS FOR REVIEW

1. What have been the consequences of eradication and interdiction campaigns? How have drug producers responded to these efforts?

2. How did 9/11 impact the war on drugs? What were the implications for Colombia, Venezuela, and Mexico?
3. The Obama administration has acknowledged "co-responsibility" for drug trafficking. In what ways has the United States been responsible? Did this declaration lead to a major change in policy?
4. In what ways did U.S.-sponsored drug wars affect Latin American society and politics? What are the implications for U.S.–Latin American relations?
5. Prominent Latin American leaders have called for a "paradigm shift" in the U.S. war on drugs. What might this shift look like? Why might it be politically problematic for the United States?

# PART IV

## Reflections

# CHAPTER 15

# Debating U.S. Policy

The United States can manage by itself. It does not require an
imaginary international community.
>
> Condoleezza Rice (U.S. Secretary of State, ca. 2008)

If the United States realizes that its long-run strategic interests
lie not in Afghanistan or Pakistan, but in Latin America, we
can do great things.
>
> Juan Manuel Santos (President of Colombia, 2012)

Power brings responsibility. Within the Western Hemisphere, the primacy of the United States means that American foreign policy has pervasive effects throughout Latin America. Can U.S. policy change? Are there plausible alternatives? Scholarly analysis often conveys the impression that the current situation is inevitable, that long-term forces and factors leave no room for innovation or reform. Even political activists sometimes surrender in the face of daunting obstacles—the effectiveness of the presidential "bully pulpit," the pursuit of partisan advantage, the bias of the media, the strength of patriotic appeals. Yet the query persists: Do things have to be the way they are? Could there be another policy?

As one example, U.S. policy could focus mainly on humanitarian concerns. In this perspective, too many Latin Americans still live in abject poverty. They cannot provide basic care for their families; their children are condemned to deprivation. They are poor, and we are rich: It is our duty to help. The United States should therefore use its wealth and power to alleviate poverty and improve life chances for citizens throughout the Americas. Moreover, some would add, we have a historical debt to repay. Over the past two centuries, the United States has ruthlessly exploited the region and its peoples. We have seized their territories, plundered their natural resources, imposed ungenerous terms of trade, demanded profits for investors, required compliance with our foreign policies, and, when all else has failed, sent in the marines. History has been unjust: It is time to make amends.

Despite such noble generosity, sentiments of this kind are unlikely to provide enduring foundations for real-world policies. International relations do not reflect high-minded emotions; they reflect the interplay of national interests, usually construed in self-centered fashion. A key question then becomes: What long-term interest does the United States have in Latin America, especially in the aftermath of 9/11?

A reshaping of U.S. policy toward Latin America would require two kinds of change: one involving goals and strategies, the other involving the process of policymaking. Effective policy requires effective process. Top officials might hatch all sorts of innovative ideas for inter-American diplomacy; without efficient implementation, however, those ideas have no practical meaning. The obstacles to policy reform can be imposing: large and sprawling bureaucracies, conflict between government agencies, opposition from congressional representatives, lack of popular support (as shown in all-important opinion polls), concern about upcoming elections, hesitation in the White House, and so on. The status quo always offers the path of least resistance. Policy reformers thus confront two separate but related tasks: rethinking key issues in U.S.–Latin American relations and streamlining institutional arrangements so as to facilitate meaningful policy change.

## VARIETIES OF REALISM: CONSERVATIVE AND PROGRESSIVE

How can we best understand global politics and foreign policy? Current debates revolve around two divergent paradigms, both based on the conception of international relations known as *realism*. As a school of thought, realism in international relations can trace its origins to such hard-nosed analysts as Thucydides (*History of the Peloponnesian War*), Niccolò Machiavelli (*The Prince*), and Thomas Hobbes (*Leviathan*). Temporarily challenged by the "idealism" of Woodrow Wilson and others in the wake of World War I, realism regained prominence after World War II under the label of "neorealism." Its central goal has been to comprehend the world as it is, not as it should be, and to derive "realistic" policy frameworks from empirical observation.

In its classical form, realism relies upon five basic premises:

1. The international system is anarchical. In other words, there exists no higher authority to regulate relations among nation-states.
2. Sovereign states are the principal actors in the international system.
3. States are rational actors, pursuing their national interests, and they are in competition with each other.
4. The overriding goal of every state is its own survival and security, which are most effectively guaranteed through the expression of power— especially military power.
5. States are inherently aggressive and/or preoccupied with security. Territorial or political expansion is constrained not through friendship or self-control but through the resistance of opposing powers.

For present purposes this worldview will come under the label of *conservative realism*. It is inherently "conservative" in the sense that it does not seek to improve the world; rather, it seeks to maximize advantage within the system as it stands. It focuses mainly on competition between major powers rather than on the weak and disadvantaged. And within an American perspective, the realist approach has been most clearly and effectively implemented by conservative administrations. Most memorable is the Republican team of Richard M. Nixon and Henry Kissinger, who opened relationships with communist China and pursued a strategy of détente with the archenemy Soviet Union.

A modification of this outlook has come to be known as *neoconservatism*. Like realism, the neoconservative outlook expresses deep suspicion of international institutions and of high-minded efforts to improve the world (through, for instance, economic assistance programs). It also espouses the deliberate application of military power. Unlike classical realism, though, the neoconservative approach insists that America must consider the internal character of political regimes, not just their foreign policy; that American policy must reflect the philosophical values of democratic societies, not just narrow practical interests; and that American power should be used for moral purposes, not merely for tactical advantage. It is assumed, if not always stated, that the United States is inherently superior to other nations—in politics, war, and way of life. Assertions of American "exceptionalism" provide a foundation for this framework. Throughout the Cold War, neoconservatives expressed unrelenting hostility toward communism in general and toward the Soviet Union in particular. Their views were implemented most clearly by President Ronald Reagan, who during the 1980s openly denounced the USSR as an "evil empire."

Among neoconservatives as well as conservative realists there has been little concern with the plight of the developing world. And after the Cold War, the neoconservative outlook came to exhibit moralizing, self-righteous, and pretentious qualities. It was one thing to challenge a great power like the Soviet Union; it was something else to overwhelm poor countries like Grenada and Nicaragua. Were these interventions truly "moral" causes? Was it our purpose to establish democracy or to oust leaders who disagreed with us? Or was it merely part of a big-power contest?

After 9/11 the foreign-policy team of George W. Bush applied neoconservative principles—with a vengeance. A turning point was the invasion of Iraq. The initial justification was concern that Saddam Hussein possessed WMDs: This was a foreign-policy issue. When the evidence failed to appear, the subsequent justification focused on Saddam's repressive rule: This was about the internal character of the regime. That shift launched a crusade to bring democracy to Iraq, the Middle East, and, later on, the rest of the world. Bush policymakers assumed that bold applications of American power could accomplish virtually anything, they expressed contempt for dissident views of other nations, and they conducted themselves with arrogance. They developed a doctrine of preemptive war and subjected prisoners to inhumane treatment.

Significantly enough, there emerged considerable disagreement between conservatives and neoconservatives with regard to Iraq. As former Republican

President Gerald R. Ford proclaimed, "I just don't think we should go hellfire damnation around the globe freeing people, unless it is directly related to our national security." Former NSC Director Brent Scowcroft expressed repeated concerns about Iraq. And, reading between the lines, one can only conclude that George Bush, Sr., had his reservations, too—after all, he was the president who chose not to overthrow Saddam during the course of the 1990–1991 Persian Gulf War.

An alternative approach to foreign policy might be called *progressive realism*. The progressive school accepts the fundamental tenets of classical realism—that we must deal with the world as it is, that we should rely on facts instead of norms, and that America's foreign policy must serve American interests. At the same time, progressive realism offers a substantially different view of the world. In this vision:

1. Instead of being anarchical, the international system possesses structures that set implicit boundaries on the actions of nation-states. (This is essentially the notion of "international regimes," as set forth in the introduction to this book.)
2. States are key actors in the international arena, but they are not the only ones; nonstate actors and international organizations play significant roles.
3. State preferences, not capabilities, are the prime determinant of international behavior; all states do not always seek the same thing. Preferences vary from place to place and from time to time—according to culture, society, economics, regime types, and other variables.
4. States do not necessarily compete with each other, and they are not inherently aggressive—they act within the constraints of the prevailing international system, and they can change their preferences.
5. Cooperation can yield mutual gains for participating states—the application of power, even military power, is not always the most effective means to guarantee survival and security.

Progressive principles lead to practical disagreement with conservative positions. One key issue concerns the nature of power. Conservative realists hold that authentic power is military—the capacity to apply more force than anyone else, usually as a result of economic and technological superiority. In contrast, progressives believe that power has two distinct dimensions—the "hard" power represented by military force and the "soft" form that emerges when citizens around the world admire and appreciate a country's creative energy and social order—its educational system, race relations, athletic achievements, artistic expressions, and so on. As shown in chapter 11, the United States lost a great deal of "soft power" as a result of the war in Iraq. Acknowledging these trends, conservatives insist that military might is still the more important: In the long run, hard power trumps soft power.

A second issue relates to sovereignty, interdependence, and the developing world. Autonomy of the nation-state is central to the conservative view. States do whatever they want, and what happens within a state is nobody else's business. In contrast, progressives claim that the growing interdependence of nations has demolished the notion of unfettered sovereignty. Disease, pollution, droughts, and ideologies (and terrorists) cross borders and enter bodies politic without regard to national boundaries. States are not billiard balls: They do not bounce harmlessly off one another. As a result, the progressive approach devotes considerable attention to issues of economic poverty, societal well-being, and national development. The conservative indifference to the interiors of nations is "intolerable," as one critic has written, while the neoconservative notion of political "morality" seems fundamentally wrongheaded.

Third are questions of war and peace. The conservative view explains war. States compete with each other, they are inherently aggressive, and they fight as a result. Two world wars furnish ample evidence to this effect. But what about peace? Progressives take note of the fact that, according to a well-established theorem in political science, established democracies do not go to war with each other. Progressives argue that this benevolent coexistence results directly *from the internal properties of government*—from the fact that these are political democracies. Because conservative realism ignores the domestic structure of political regimes, it cannot account for the "democratic peace."

For progressives, the spread of democracy should clearly serve America's interests. It fosters peace among nations and reduces violence around the world. The question is how to promote democratization. In Iraq and Afghanistan, the neoconservative Bush administration chose to do so by conquest—assaulting nations, overthrowing governments, imposing military rule, and proclaiming the existence of democracy by decree. Progressives maintain that such approaches are costly, ineffective, and counterproductive. As Joseph Nye, Jr., has written, "Democratic promotion is better accomplished by attraction than coercion, and it takes time and patience. The US would be wise to encourage the gradual evolution of democracy, but in a manner than accepts the reality of cultural diversity." Adds Robert Wright: Peaceful and above-board forms of influence will lead to "more indigenous, more culturally authentic paths to democracy than flow from invasion or American-backed *coups d'état*—and [are] more conducive to America's security than, say, the [then-current] situation in Iraq."

Another source of disagreement relates to international cooperation. Conservatives (and neoconservatives) are unilateralists; progressives are multilateralists. This is a defining difference. Conservatives claim that states must act by themselves to protect their own interests; no one else will do it for them. International relations amount to a zero-sum game: One state's gain is another state's loss. Alliances and institutions represent tactics of convenience, to be discarded or ignored according to the dictates of necessity. Progressives insist, to the contrary, that creative diplomacy can result in jointly profitable arrangements and compromises: Win-win outcomes are entirely possible. (For this reason they have also been called "liberal internationalists.") The virtue of strong international institutions is that they can place meaningful constraints on rogue nations—such as North Korea and Saddam's Iraq. (Take weapons of mass destruction: With nothing to hide, the United States has nothing to lose from accepting intrusive inspections—and much to gain from supporting effective inspections elsewhere.) Quoting Robert Wright again: "We need multilateral structures capable of decisively forceful intervention and nation building—ideally under the auspices of the United Nations, which has more global legitimacy than other candidates. America should lead in building these structures and thereafter contribute its share, but only its share."

A belief in institutions goes hand in hand with a preference for international engagement. Conservatives tend to isolate rogue nations until they change their ways—essentially, until they capitulate to pressure. Progressives believe that it would be more effective to promote gradual processes of engagement (for example, through increased trade, scholarly exchange, and other confidence-building measures). The anticipation is that, as a result, formerly ostracized states will change their ways voluntarily. Prominent examples include Vietnam and the People's Republic of China, which have opened their economies and softened their political regimes. In the progressive view, enticements work better than threats.

Finally, there is a practical disagreement about the contemporary extent of American power. Notwithstanding recent alterations in the global order, the United States remains by far the strongest nation on earth. It stands alone as a superpower. It produces one-quarter of the world's economic output. It accounts for nearly one-half of all military expenditures. Its command of hard power is unrivaled. As a result, the neoconservative position claims, in effect, that the United States can do whatever it wants. In contrast, progressives warn that preeminence does not mean omnipotence. (Many conservative realists would agree with this assessment.) As Nye has observed, "A progressive foreign policy would start with an understanding of the strengths and limits of American power . . . preponderance is not empire or hegemony. America can influence but not control other parts of the world." Insurgent movements in Afghanistan and elsewhere clearly confirm this assertion. Moreover, the steady erosion of America's soft power until 2008 greatly diminished the moral authority and political leverage that the nation once enjoyed.

## THE RELEVANCE OF LATIN AMERICA

How does Latin America fit into this picture? As earlier explained, George W. Bush devoted unusual attention to the region after his inauguration, making an early state visit to Mexico and striking up an apparently warm friendship with Vicente Fox. This situation changed abruptly after 9/11. Latin America slipped out of view. Avidly applying neoconservative principles to the conduct of international affairs, the Bush administration shifted its focus to South and Central Asia.

Most foreign leaders accepted the legitimacy of military strikes against Al Qaeda and its state sponsor, the Taliban regime in Afghanistan. (Some analysts criticized the occasionally indiscriminate use of American firepower and resultant "collateral damage," in the euphemism of the day, but that is another matter.)

Similarly, most observers understood that regional priorities would have to change, that Latin America could no longer command special attention from the White House. That was just the way of the world.

But as Latin America plunged through economic and institutional crises in the years immediately following 9/11, critics argued that inattention to the region had gone too far. A former member of the Clinton team asserted that indifference under Bush had moved "beyond benign neglect." To assuage hurt feelings in the hemisphere, he went on to say, "the president and his administration need to signal that they really do care." In an article disarmingly entitled "Is Washington Losing Latin America?" (one has to ask: Was it ours to lose in the first place?), the president of a prominent D.C.-based think tank declared that "After 9/11, Washington effectively lost interest in Latin America. Since then, the attention the United States has paid to the region has been sporadic and narrowly targeted at particularly troubling or urgent situations." From elsewhere on the ideological spectrum, an analyst from the archconservative Heritage Foundation argued that the United States "must re-engage in Latin America." A voluble right-wing expert on the region sarcastically diagnosed the Bush approach as suffering from "attention deficit disorder."

Why should Latin America matter in the post-9/11 environment? Geography provides one answer: The region is right next to the United States. We share a 2,000-mile land border with Mexico and maritime boundaries with Central America, northern South America, and islands of the Caribbean. Airplanes can reach U.S. destinations within a few hours. To state the obvious: Latin America offers a primary route to the United States. Terrorists from any part of the world might try to enter U.S. territory from Latin America. One might therefore imagine that the region would command a good deal of interest.

Moreover, Latin America presents many of the conditions that are widely believed to be underlying causes of terrorist movements—poverty, oppression, and inequality. Over one-third of people in the region live on less than $2 per day. At the same time, Latin America boasts a growing number of new billionaires— members of the mega-rich international elite. Such glaring degrees of inequality are likely to spawn popular resentments. If everyone is poor, that can be construed as common fate; but if many are poor and few are rich, that constitutes social injustice. Viewed in this light, Latin America would appear to be a potential hotbed for terrorist recruits.

What are missing, so far, are the Al Qaeda–type terrorists themselves. It is not self-evident why this is so. It is not as though the region has been immune to political violence. Authoritarian regimes imposed brutal forms of "state terror" on thousands of citizens, and, in retrospect, many daring deeds of revolutionary guerrillas would now qualify as terrorist acts. Why has there been no Latin American *jihad* against the United States?

Analysts offer two interpretations. One points to the strength of cultural values. This view stresses the centuries-old influence of the Catholic Church, which has preached doctrines of humility, acceptance, and tolerance (except when converting indigenous peoples to the one and only faith). This idea also invokes the philosophical impact of the Enlightenment, with its emphasis on reason and learning and its doctrines of human dignity and individual rights. In other words, Latin America and the United States share Judeo-Christian traditions of religion and spiritual belief; they both belong to "the West." In a global clash of civilizations, Latin America would surely end up on our side.

The other interpretation, more convincing and more important, relates to long-held aspirations for political democracy. Since the independence era, democracy has been a fundamental goal for Latin America. It has been a beacon for the region—an elusive one, to be sure, but a beacon nonetheless. Even authoritarian leaders have justified their rule on the tenuous ground that they were laying authentic foundations for durable democracy. And in recent decades, the extension of electoral democracy throughout the region has rekindled flickering embers of popular hope. Contemporary democracy in Latin America is far from perfect, but it represents a vast improvement over dictatorship—and the direction of change at long last seems positive. The better the prospects for democracy, the less the likelihood of terrorist conspiracy.

So Latin America has not yet produced home-grown terrorist movements aimed at the United States (none that we know of, anyway). Nor has any government offered logistical support or safe haven to Al Qaeda or any comparable movements. Evidence suggests that Hamas and Hezbollah might be maintaining sleeper cells in the tri-border area shared by Paraguay, Argentina, and Brazil—but such cells exist in spite of official policy, not because of it. And while Hugo Chávez consorts with anti-U.S. regimes on the world stage, he is far from offering hospitality to terrorist groups. Latin America has no *imam* urging the faithful to seek martyrdom in an anti-American crusade.

In yet another sense, relative tranquility throughout the Western Hemisphere has proven to be a major benefit to the United States. *It has enabled Washington to project its military and economic power around the globe without fear of deadly retaliation on the southern flank.* Imagine otherwise: What if we had Lebanon or Iraq as a near neighbor instead of Mexico? What if Venezuela were Iran? What if Latin America were Africa or Central Asia? By being as peaceful and as quiet as it has been, Latin America has provided a very substantial (and largely invisible) subsidy for America's foreign policy in other parts of the world. It should therefore serve the U.S. national interest to keep things as they are.

From all perspectives, conservative and progressive, the way to preserve this status quo is not to ignore the region. Neglect is not benign, nor is it intelligent. Seen through the prism of the war on terror, Latin America deserves high-level attention from Washington for at least three reasons:

- Because hostile forces could use the region as a launching pad for terrorist assaults.
- Because radical terrorist movements could eventually emerge within the region itself.

- Because upheaval within the region could require a diversion of U.S. resources away from other parts of the world.

No matter how you look at it, the security of Latin America is essential to the security of the United States.

Two corollaries follow from these observations. First, the conduct of America's relations with Latin America should be treated as a matter of authentic foreign policy. It should not be a plaything of domestic interests. High governmental appointments should not be granted as rewards for partisan political support. Nor should they be allocated to lobbies and pressure groups. The inter-American relationship deserves and needs effective attention, and it should be managed by the brightest and the best.

Second, the White House must be prepared to resist demands from interest groups, even the most influential ones. In recent years, scholars have come to the near-unanimous conclusion that issues on the U.S.–Latin American agenda tend to be "intermestic"—they are international problems that generate responses, inputs, and demands from important domestic constituencies. (Immigration, trade, and drugs offer telling examples.) One unforeseen implication of this insight is the sense that Latin American policies are beholden to powerful interests and therefore cannot change. Illogical and counterproductive outcomes simply result from money politics. A serious policy toward Latin America would have to override such concerns.

## CONFRONTING THE POLICY PROCESS

A meaningful transformation of U.S. relations with Latin America involves not only change in policy *goals* but also reform of the policy *process*. Effective implementation is essential for the success of any policy. Policy should be clear in its purpose, coherent in its application, and consistent over time.

More easily said than done. The U.S. government is a massive and unwieldy bureaucracy. The noble principle of "checks and balances"—among the executive, legislative, and judicial branches—often produces disorganization, confusion, and paralysis. The federal bureaucracy contains thousands of agencies, commissions, and entities; task forces and committees multiply at will. As a sheer exercise in logistics, interagency communication requires Herculean efforts.

Within this context, U.S. policy toward Latin America has been shaped by three central factors: (a) the level or priority accorded to the region, (b) the breadth of the policy agenda, and (c) the number and diversity of participating agencies. The net result has been that, in implementation as well as design, inter-American policy has suffered from undue complexity and inconsistency.

### Presidential Prerogatives

The presidency stands at the apex of governmental authority and, in theory, wields the instruments of central command and control. The White House is the pinnacle of power. The presidency bears constitutional responsibility for the conduct of international relations, and the president—alone or with advisers—sets priorities for foreign policy. Governmental agencies take their cues from the White House.

Within the executive branch, institutional responsibility for foreign relations belongs to the Department of State (DOS). It is the designated lead agency with regard to key questions: the public articulation of U.S. policy, the forging of alliances, the pursuit of negotiations, the uses of persuasion and threats. The secretary of state has one of the most demanding and sensitive positions within the federal government. Almost invariably, the secretary is a high-profile figure.

Within DOS, the day-to-day management of Latin American policy usually falls to the assistant secretary of state for Western Hemisphere affairs. (Neither the president nor the secretary of state can devote sufficient time to inter-American issues.) This situation means, in effect, that U.S. policy toward Latin America is directed and managed at middling and upper-middling levels of the federal bureaucracy. The position provides only modest opportunity for policy innovation: Broad outlines come from the White House and the secretary of state, and the assistant secretary has to work within those boundaries. Frequently, but not always, the post goes to a career foreign service officer.

Ambassadors serve in high-visibility, low-wattage posts. They report not to the White House but to the secretary of state. They do not create much policy in the conventional sense of the term. They are messengers: Their principal role is to explain U.S. policy to foreign governments. They are reporters: They keep Washington apprised of relevant developments, events, and personalities. They are whistle-blowers: They can warn their superiors about potentially counterproductive consequences of policy proposals. Through a mind-numbing series of social rituals, they send political signals: What receptions does the ambassador attend? With whom does he or she carry on conversations? Who appears in the photo ops? Does the ambassador discuss human rights as well as free trade, meet with opposition leaders as well as government officials, consult with labor organizers as well as business impresarios? And ambassadors can provide ideas; with luck and skill, they can improve the content and presentation of prevailing U.S. policies. Above all, they try to make sure that their host country gets appropriate attention from Washington when it needs and deserves it.

Emphasizing the importance of the White House, diplomacy reaches a peak of activity during the course of presidential travel. When the president of the United States decides to visit a country, the trip becomes a statement about the host nation's importance. Things have to happen: Agreements have to be reached, treaties signed, announcements made (these are known as "deliverables"). And all these have to be arranged in advance. As former Ambassador Jeffrey Davidow recalls, the inevitable search for deliverables is useful "because nothing better concentrates the mind of bureaucrats than a presidential trip. Tasks that should have been accomplished the year before finally get done. Programs that have been dwindling get reinvigorated. And the funds promised elsewhere get hijacked. A bureaucracy aroused to meet a president's expectations is a thing to behold."

**BOX 15-1**

## The Politics of Presidential Travel

Jeffrey Davidow, an experienced member of the U.S. diplomatic corps, served as ambassador to Venezuela and to Mexico and as assistant secretary of state for Western Hemisphere affairs. Here he offers amusing and telling insight into the complexities of White House politics:

> It is precisely to avoid confusion that presidential trips are minutely choreographed. Every meeting, every speech, every movement from point A to point B is the subject of long memos, charts, and stage directions. It is far easier to put on a production of *Macbeth* than to organize one afternoon of a presidential trip. The president himself becomes a hostage to his staff and to the program they have devised for him.
>
> On occasion, presidents rebel, but rarely for long and hardly ever successfully. When I was assistant secretary of state, Joan and I attended a state dinner at the White House for President Frei of Chile. As we passed through the receiving line, I had a brief conversation with President Clinton about a trip we were planning to Latin America to take place a few months later.
>
> "I'm really looking forward to it, Jeff."
>
> "Yes, sir, the planning is going well," I said while moving slowly along the line. But the president did not let go of my hand and stopped my movement.
>
> "Convince them that I want to stay longer."
>
> "Sure," I said, and took another step. But then I stopped and turned back. I was confused. Certainly, his Latin American hosts would be thrilled to have him stay longer. They needed no persuasion. "Convince whom?" I asked. He must have thought I was as thick as three bricks.
>
> "My staff. Tell my staff to let me stay longer."
>
> "Sure," I repeated. Another step. Another turnaround. "Wouldn't it make more sense for you to tell them?"
>
> "Oh, they never listen to me," he laughed.
>
> President Clinton was not a meek prisoner of his staff. But White House schedulers are engaged in a constant battle over the president's time. It is sliced thinner than prosciutto. The president can and does express his preferences, but he has neither the time nor the energy to fight the continuing battle over his schedule. Planning foreign visits is left to others. Generally, the president spends little time thinking about the visit until he boards Air Force One.

SOURCE: Jeffrey Davidow, *The U.S. and Mexico: The Bear and the Porcupine* (Princeton, NJ: Markus Wiener, 2004), pp. 199–200.

Summit meetings complicate planning and logistics in geometric proportions. Not only must there be deliverables; they should be consensus items—acceptable not only to the U.S. president and to the host leader but also, if possible, to all the other chief executives in attendance. Such conditions cannot always be met. According to these criteria, the Miami summit of 1994—which launched negotiations for the Free Trade Area of the Americas—constituted a resounding success.

By the same token, the successor summits—in Chile, Canada, Argentina, Trinidad and Tobago, and Colombia—have not always produced such positive results, at least from the official U.S. point of view. Summits can be effective, but they are high-risk operations. Whatever happens, they are subject to intense scrutiny from all over the world.

## Complicating Factors I: Bureaucratic Wrangling

The concentration of decision-making power in the White House leads directly to a corollary: The greater the level of presidential attention to any foreign-policy issue, the greater the level of bureaucratic coordination and consistency. Over the years, the White House has adopted a utilitarian calculus: How can Latin America help bolster America's position in the global arena? How can it contribute to the U.S. quest for primacy? And the answer has tended to be—some, but not that much. In the eyes of most U.S. presidents, Latin America has been a midlevel priority; since 9/11, it has slipped down several rungs on the ladder of importance.

As a result, U.S. policy toward Latin America has often suffered from "balkanization." Different agencies and units have tended to forge their own initiatives with little if any regard for what other agencies might be doing. With relatively little coordination from higher levels, the net result has been inconsistency.

A contributing factor has been the breadth and diversity of issues involving Latin America. This is not a single-issue agenda. Political questions concern governmental stability, democratization, human rights, military cooperation, and alignment with (or against) the United States in multilateral forums; economic questions concern trade, investment, immigration, and access to (and protection of) natural resources; social questions relate to immigration (again), gender policies, educational exchanges, and so on. It is a remarkably capacious agenda. At the same time, it rarely involves the "high politics" questions of peace, war, and international security. Inter-American issues tend to be nitty-gritty matters of "low politics."

Partly as a consequence, the shaping of everyday policy toward Latin America has come to involve a large—and ever-growing—number of governmental agencies. As already noted, issues on the inter-American agenda tend to be "intermestic"—they are international in nature, but they affect domestic interests as well. During the imperial era and the Cold War, the Department of State was the principal center of decision making in relation to Latin America. In recent times, however, DOS has had to compete with myriad other cabinet-level agencies, all seeking the presidential ear. These include the departments of the Treasury, Defense, Justice—and the National Security Council, which has the inestimable advantage of being located within the White House itself. Policy discussions frequently produce fierce intrabureaucratic squabbles, which, in turn, tend toward paralysis.

Bureaucratic influence depends on the issues at hand. With regard to the debt crisis of the 1980s and early 1990s, for instance, the most important agency was the Department of the Treasury, which exercised control of lending policy, along with the U.S. Federal Reserve Board, which could determine interest rates.

(In fact, these agencies worked in tandem with the International Monetary Fund, a multilateral financial organization.) During the war on drugs, numerous agencies have taken part: within State, the Bureau of International Narcotics Affairs; within Justice, the FBI and the Drug Enforcement Administration; within Treasury, the U.S. Customs Office; and within Defense, a host of less-visible entities. In the late 1980s the White House created the Office of National Drug Control Policy in order to bring overall coherence to these efforts. The results have been less than impressive.

Due to the intermestic content of the inter-American agenda, the U.S. Congress has also come to play a central role in policy toward Latin America. This fact has been especially conspicuous with regard to drugs and immigration, areas that can be greatly affected by U.S. federal law, and by policy toward Cuba, which has been such a hot-button political issue. Rather than evaluating foreign-policy issues on their merits, however, legislators seek to enhance prospects for their own reelection. Frequently, they engage in "logrolling" deals on issues that bear no substantive connection to each other. And to the extent that Washington exhibits a "divided government"—with the legislative and executive branches held by opposing parties—there is bound to be discord and confusion. This situation plagued the Clinton presidency, after the Republican Party captured majorities in both houses of Congress; it would afflict the Bush presidency, after Democrats won both chambers in 2006; and it would paralyze the Obama administration, after Republicans regained control of both houses in 2010. Generally speaking, Congress has become a loose cannon in shaping U.S. policy toward the hemisphere.

State-level politicians throughout the American Southwest have become significant actors with regard to immigration and cross-border questions. Reflecting Anglo backlash in the 1990s, for instance, voters in California decisively approved one ballot measure designed to prevent illegal migrants and their children from receiving social benefits (Proposition 187) and another intended to eliminate racial and ethnic preferences under "affirmative action" (Proposition 209). In 2010 Arizona passed a controversial law designed to detain (and ultimately deport) illegal immigrants. And, in effect, governors of major states like Texas and California develop their own "foreign policies" with regard to Mexico and Central America.

In the aftermath of 9/11, the White House has vigorously and assertively shaped overall policy at the global level. The Bush administration's most decisive innovation was the creation of the Department of Homeland Security (DHS) "to develop and coordinate the implementation of a comprehensive national strategy to secure the United States from terrorist threats or attacks." With approximately 184,000 employees, Homeland Security immediately became the third-largest department in the U.S. federal government. To promote consolidation and coordination, it brought together units formerly dispersed among diverse federal agencies, including Immigration and Naturalization (formerly in the Department of Justice), the Coast Guard (formerly under Defense), and Customs (formerly under Treasury). All in all, DHS has represented the largest U.S. governmental reorganization in the last half-century. At the same time, it has stirred considerable confusion: As an ambassador-designate to Washington once proclaimed in frustration, "Now we don't know whom we're supposed to talk to. What doors are we supposed to knock on?"

## Complicating Factors II: Engaging the Public

Additional sources of influence—and uncertainty—stem from public attitudes toward Latin America. Americans do not know much about the region. As a rule, they receive shallow pictures of the region in grade-school texts, erratic exposure in college curricula, and superficial coverage on television nightly news. Popular media aggravate the problem. Such Hollywood films as *Butch Cassidy and the Sundance Kid* (1969) depicted Latins as inept and ridiculous, unable to cope with the derring-do of characters played by Robert Redford and Paul Newman. Woody Allen's *Bananas* (1971) presented political dictatorship and instability as a form of comic opera. *Bring Me the Head of Alfredo García* (1974) revived the image of Latin Americans as violent and bloodthirsty "greasers." *Clear and Present Danger* (1994), from the novel by Tom Clancy, stressed the greed and ruthlessness of Colombian drug lords. There were exceptions to this pattern: As books and as films, *House of the Spirits* by Chilean Isabel Allende and *Like Water for Chocolate* by Mexican Laura Esquivel offered subtle and compelling views of Latin American life through the lens of "magical realism." But for the most part, stereotypes have continued to prevail.

Such images have helped form U.S. public opinion toward the region. A series of polls by the Chicago Council on Foreign Relations has shown that Americans take an ambivalent view of Latin America. One full year after 9/11, 72 percent of respondents agreed that Mexico represented a "vital interest" for the United States. Because of its own wars on terror and drugs, Colombia constituted a vital national interest for 62 percent in 2002; for wholly different reasons, Cuba was a vital interest for 60 percent. Argentina, in contrast, was viewed as a vital U.S. interest by just 39 percent of Americans, and Brazil—the largest and most powerful country in South America—was seen as a vital interest by merely 36 percent. These numbers represented a substantial decline; twenty years before, in 1982, Brazil was considered a vital interest by 80 percent of respondents. Public opinion thus confirmed a historic dichotomy in U.S. perceptions of Latin America: intense concern about nearby countries (especially Mexico) and much less concern about nations farther south.

One of the most vexing calculations for American politicians concerns the weight of the "Hispanic" population, the fastest-growing demographic segment in the United States. With over 50 million members in 2010, the Latino community seems poised to exert enormous influence over the nation's political destiny. Resident Cubans and Cuban Americans in Florida and (to a lesser degree) in New Jersey have formed effective and visible lobbying groups with major impact on U.S. policy toward Cuba; less obviously but perhaps inexorably, Mexican Americans were acquiring influence on U.S. policy toward Mexico. To some, the accumulation of Hispanic power has resembled a growing tidal wave, the result of inexorable natural forces.

Confusion has nonetheless prevailed. As of 2010, Hispanics accounted for 13 percent of the total population—and cast about 7.4 percent of votes in the 2008 presidential election. There were two main reasons for this shortfall: Many Latinos were too young to vote, while others were noncitizens and therefore ineligible to vote. And despite recent voter registration drives, many Latinos have shown reluctance to take part in the electoral process. In 2008 just under half (49.9 percent) of eligible Hispanics cast their vote, compared with 65 percent of blacks and 66 percent of whites. In actual practice, the Hispanic bloc is not as big as it looks.

Nor are Latinos a unified group. Mexican Americans in California have different concerns from Cuban Americans in Florida and Puerto Ricans in New York. And because they belong to varying occupational strata and racial categories, Latinos seem unlikely to form a cohesive bloc. In the 2004 presidential election, over 40 percent of Latinos voted for George W. Bush; in 2008, about two-thirds voted for Barack Obama. While Republican and Democratic parties both have solid bases of Hispanic electoral support, there also exists a volatile "swing" vote that can go either way.

Generally speaking, the determinants of Hispanic power in American politics reveal contradictory tendencies. (1) Because of their sheer demographic weight, especially in such major states as California, Florida, and Texas, Latinos are becoming a significant political factor. In highly competitive areas especially, they can tip the electoral balance. (2) The more assimilated Latinos become in U.S. society—through education, occupation, intermarriage, and so on—the more they will react, respond, and vote like other Americans. They will disappear into the melting pot. The long-term result defies clear-cut prediction.

## Complicating Factors III: Partisan Polarization

U.S. politics has taken a hard turn rightward in recent years. Galvanized by the grassroots Tea Party, energized by electoral success in 2010, and led by a voluble chorus of media pundits, the Republican Party has come to embrace far-right positions on political, social, and economic issues. The result has been to recast the ideological spectrum. What used to be the "center" of national debate has now become the "left"; ideas previously regarded as "extremist" now define the "right." Compromise and moderation, once admired as the heart of politics, have been jettisoned in favor of purity and principle. These trends became conspicuously apparent during the campaign for 2012 national elections, when Republicans declared that their central goal was to make Barack Obama "a one-term president." Partisanship has triumphed over policy.

Latin America per se has not held center stage in these debates. Even so, conservative and progressive policy mavens take divergent stands on Western Hemisphere matters. (In contrast, conservatives and neoconservatives tend to be in agreement.) Here follows a brief inventory.

**Immigration:** Because of its complexity, this issue has not produced a consistent split along the conservative/progressive divide—until the last several years. Many conservatives have called for the use of military force along the U.S.–Mexico border. They see border security as an urgent matter for national security: It is, in their view, the only way to prevent international terrorists from sneaking into the United States. Moreover, they add, this approach offers the only conceivable way of stanching the inexorable flow of Mexicans into the United States—where they take away jobs, drive wages down, and, worst of all, contaminate true-blue American culture. At the same time, many rightward-leaning employers have welcomed the presence of a labor force that is low-cost, hard-working, nonunion, and trouble-free. Migrant workers harvest crops, wash dishes, tend gardens, clean bathrooms, muck out stables, and perform hundreds of other unpleasant tasks. (To get a sense of their invisible importance one has only to remember the 2004 Hollywood film *A Day without a Mexican,* which depicts the chaos and confusion resulting from the sudden disappearance of California's Latino population). It is because of this contradiction that President Bush, former governor of Texas, adopted an equivocal stance on this issue.

Nor have progressives put forth a clear solution. They argue that Americans should understand and appreciate the myriad contributions made by immigrants. They express horror over the fact that hundreds of Mexicans die every year while seeking to cross the U.S. border; as a practical matter, this statistic tends to diminish America's "soft power" throughout the world. Invoking humanitarian principles, progressives might order the U.S. Border Patrol to respect the fundamental rights of would-be migrants, even as they seek illegal entry. Ultimately, progressives would want to have the best of both worlds—increasing quotas for migration to the United States, providing amnesty for those who have already been here for several years, and tightening restrictions on illegal crossings. Immigration would become open, aboveboard, and subject to legal regulation. In keeping with these views, Barack Obama called for comprehensive immigration reform during his 2008 presidential campaign.

Republicans after 2010 would have none of this. In October 2011, would-be presidential candidate Herman Cain proposed an electrified fence along the U.S.–Mexico border that would be strong enough to kill on contact; he would also dispatch military troops "with real guns and real bullets." Rick Santorum, himself the child of immigrants, expressed support for construction of a more conventional (nonlethal) fence. So did Mitt Romney, whose plan would be to make life so treacherous and difficult for illegal migrants that they would engage in voluntary self-deportation (that is, they would just go home). "I love immigration," the ex-governor said at one point, but "I don't like illegal immigration." He pronounced strong opposition to "any form of citizenship amnesty" and promised as president to veto the Dream Act, which would establish a path toward U.S. citizenship for children of migrants who attend college or serve in the armed forces. As anti-immigrant rhetoric was climbing to new heights, ironically enough, demographic research was showing that the net flow of undocumented migrants from Mexico (inflow minus outflow) had fallen to just about zero.

**Cuba:** Questions about "the pearl of the Antilles" have long produced some of the sharpest differences between conservative/neoconservative and progressive approaches to Latin America. Conservatives have wanted to bring down the Castro regime for decades—by force, stealth, or economic suffocation. They regard the Cuban revolution as a genuine threat to American interests and security, as shown by the missile crisis of October 1962. Cuba must be contained, controlled, and defeated. The principal strategy now is to isolate the regime, keep the embargo in place, encourage domestic opposition—and wait for Fidel's death. Conservatives further advocate threats of military force and, depending on the circumstances, the potential use of force as well. Neoconservatives stress the moral importance of bringing about regime change in Cuba.

In contrast, Barack Obama and progressives have looked for opportunities to engage with Cuban leadership—and, in particular, with the younger reformers serving in the successor regime of Raúl Castro (regardless of his brother Fidel's personal health). Instead of isolating Cuba, progressives seek to bring the country more openly into the international community. In specific terms, they would eventually lift the U.S. embargo on trade and investment. They would thus follow the example of previous (and successful) U.S. diplomacy toward Vietnam and China. For the sake of American security, they would say, it is unhelpful to have a besieged and angry neighbor so close to our doorstep. And as Cuba's leadership prepares for change, under the label of either "succession" or "transition," it is time for the United States to reconsider its outlook toward the island.

As the U.S. presidential race picked up steam in 2012, Republicans took an implacable stand. Mitt Romney's camp announced "a clear policy toward the Cuban regime: no accommodation, no appeasement. The United States should not relent until the day when the Castros' regime meets its end and their history is written among the world's most reviled despots, tyrants, and frauds." The irrepressible Newt Gingrich adopted a similar line: "I don't think it occurs to a single person in the White House to look south and propose a Cuban spring," he said to a group of college Republicans. Obama's policy of engagement was "almost exactly the opposite" of what it should be. "More than 50 years of dictatorship is more than enough," he proclaimed as the audience cheered. In deference to Florida's importance in the upcoming election, Obama himself began to equivocate on the issue.

**Drugs and Drug Wars:** As a matter of principle, conservatives fight the war on drugs with vigor and intensity. They regard trafficking from Latin America as the principal source of the problem: The way to protect American society would be to eradicate crops, interdict shipments, and punish *narcotraficantes*. This approach requires massive amounts of lethal force. And this force, in turn, leads to the deployment of Latin American armed forces in the antidrug campaign (plus U.S. military units in some operations). Within the United States, the conservative stance would punish drug offenders—including consumers—with substantial prison sentences. Strict penalties should act as a deterrent and send a message as well: As the police chief of Los Angeles once said, drug users are committing "treason" in the war on drugs and they therefore deserve to be shot! Consumers of illicit drugs are accused of giving moral and material aid to anti-American terrorists.

**The Partisan Divide.** This caricature deftly illustrates the paralyzing impact of excess partisanship on prospects for cooperation between the United States and Latin America.
SOURCE: © Copyright 2011 PareshNath - All Rights Reserved.

Progressives oppose the use of harmful drugs, but they would focus more on demand than on supply. They note that the principal force underlying the drug trade is the size and strength of the U.S. market. They would devote substantial resources to reduce demand—through persuasive education programs, through the rehabilitation of drug users, and through the use of "drug courts" rather than outright incarceration. They might broaden international antidrug treaties to include programs for reduction of demand as well as interdiction of supply. They might persuade the U.S. Congress to abandon completely the requirement for annual certification of countries thought to be involved in drug trafficking; at the very least, they would desist from the practice of decertifying hostile or recalcitrant countries on purely political grounds, as was the case with Venezuela in 2005.

The Obama administration parts company with most progressives on the legalization of marijuana. The president and his top advisers are staunchly opposed to change in the legal regime, even for medical uses. On this point Republicans tend to be in agreement. As Newt Gingrich declared, "Every place where drugs are legalized the net effect is more people on welfare, more people who are dependent, more people with bad health care outcomes, fewer people who are able workers able to pay attention on the job and a drain of money into illegality, because immediately behind legalized marijuana comes cocaine and heroin." Instead of reducing incarceration, Gingrich would actually increase the penalties for drug use and distribution. For his part, Mitt Romney dismissed the legalization movement as resulting from "the passion and zeal of those members of the pleasure-seeking generation that never grew up." (Farther to the right, however, libertarian Ron Paul actually expressed support for legalization.)

**Hemispheric Institutions:** International organizations have provoked additional disagreement. Conservatives tend not to like them. John Bolton, George W. Bush's flame-throwing ambassador to the United Nations, openly expressed his disdain for the UN itself. Hardheaded conservatives generally believe that international organizations frustrate U.S. interests. We would do better to go it alone—and save the money we provide.

Conservatives and neoconservatives alike regard the Organization of American States (OAS) as a nuisance. Its membership includes all countries of Latin America and the Caribbean, except Cuba, and it tends to rely on agreement by consensus. This procedure makes it a cumbersome instrument. From time to time the United States has exploited the OAS in order to justify foreign-policy actions, as in the case of the Dominican intervention of 1965. Similarly, the Bush administration attempted to pressure the OAS into endorsing the U.S.-led war on terror, including the invasion of Iraq. But these have been matters of convenience rather than conviction, expressions of "multilateralism à la carte." As a frustrated U.S. President Lyndon Johnson is reported to have quipped, "The OAS couldn't pour piss out of a boot even if the instructions were written on the heel." It was derided either as a tool of American interests or, if not that, as harmless and ineffective.

The political equation changed with the surge of the "pink tide" in recent years. In response to this new trend, far-right Republican leadership in the House Foreign Affairs Committee voted in 2011 to terminate U.S. funding for the OAS (a paltry sum of $48.5 million). Declared Connie Mack of Florida, sponsor of the amendment: "Let's not continue to fund an organization that's bent on destroying democracy in Latin America." Chimed in Rep. David Rivera, another Florida Republican: "The OAS is an enemy of the U.S. and an enemy to the interests of freedom and security." An astounded Gary Ackerman (D-NY) replied: "This is folly. It's more than folly, it's dangerous. . . . We should be looking at opportunities to reach out to the world." Added Howard Berman (D-CA): "The OAS is an enemy? We are really living in two different worlds." Funding was eventually restored, but the Tea Party types had made their point.

Progressives, given their belief in international organizations, would prefer to strengthen or rebuild the OAS. At the very least they would hope to make it a respected forum for the exchange of information and ideas, a venue for multilateral consultations and diplomatic understandings. As proposed by Arturo Valenzuela, a high-level official in the Clinton and Obama administrations: "Multilateralism does not mean turning over vexing problems . . . to the OAS Secretariat. It means genuine engagement with leading countries to strengthen collective solutions to the region's problems that can be implemented with the organization's institutional help. Washington needs to view the leadership of the OAS as a tool to promote effective dialogue, not as a reward for loyalty to U.S. foreign-policy objectives elsewhere in the world." The OAS could become more useful than it has been, in other words, but there are limits to what it can do.

Organizations that exclude the United States pose another kind of challenge. UNASUR, the South American Union sponsored by Brazil, has a clear geographic definition and does not appear to contradict U.S. interests. Somewhat different is CELAC, the Congress of Latin American and Caribbean States, which pointedly excludes the United States and Canada. It is off to an uncertain start, although joint leadership under conservative Sebastian Piñera of Chile and radical Hugo Chávez of Venezuela suggests an effort to bridge ideological differences and promote cooperation among countries of the region. Many progressives regard this as a hopeful sign; others might be dismissive or apprehensive.

In any event, this collection of issues—immigration, drugs, Cuba, hemispheric institutions—demonstrates how partisan politics have affected U.S. policymaking with regard to the Americas. The bottom line is clear: Polarization has paralyzed the government. Under these circumstances it has become virtually impossible for the Obama administration—or probably any other administration—to implement major policy reforms. One might imagine all sorts of constructive reforms. But with knee-jerk and rock-ribbed opposition, they have no realistic chance of implementation.

---

## BOX 15-2

### The Cartagena Summit

The sixth Summit of the Americas took place in Cartagena, Colombia, in April 2012, with delegates from thirty-three countries. Not being an OAS member, Cuba was absent from the gathering. Also missing were outspoken leaders of the new left: Hugo Chávez (Venezuela), due to ill health, and Rafael Correa (Ecuador) and Daniel Ortega (Nicaragua), both in protest against the exclusion of Cuba.

Media coverage of the summit focused on a tasteless and salacious scandal involving agents of the U.S. Secret Service and local prostitutes. But beneath the sensational headlines, suggestive developments took place.

Almost all Latin American delegates lamented the absence of Cuba and called for its inclusion in the next summit. President Obama repeated the timeworn litany that Cuba could not participate until it became more democratic. Argentina, Brazil, and other countries promised to boycott the next meeting (Panama, 2015) unless Cuba is included.

Formal discussions focused on the feasibility of legalizing marijuana, presumably to reduce drug-related violence and promote harm reduction. Prominent leaders of Latin America have openly called for major policy reform, while the United States has been firmly opposed. In a face-saving gesture, delegates agreed to have the OAS study the issue and propose recommendations in the future.

Contention also surrounded a resolution supporting Argentina's historic claim to sovereignty over the Falkland/Malvinas islands (which had provoked a war with Britain in 1982). Latin Americans tended to support Argentina, while the United States and Canada did not. An angry Cristina Fernández de Kirchner went back to Buenos Aires in a huff.

Lacking consensus, the summit concluded without a joint declaration. Even so, the meeting underlined important points:

- Isolation of the United States—supported only by Canada on the most divisive issues (thus pitting what used to be known as "Anglo" America against Latin America)
- Solidarity of Latin America—and its willingness to stand up to the United States
- Institutional uncertainty—unless Cuba is included in the 2015 summit. As one analysis says, "There is a distinct possibility that the OAS could lose all legitimacy as well as its influence as exasperated Latin American countries refuse to participate."

Who knows, maybe this could be a wake-up call for the United States.

## GETTING FROM HERE TO THERE

The United States has not given high priority to Latin America since the end of the Cold War. Under Bill Clinton, George W. Bush, and Barack Obama, Washington has paid slight attention to the region. Why might this have been the case? Several explanations come to mind:

- Human error, resulting from ignorance and/or poor information—a conceptual misinterpretation of global and regional realities
- Involvement in other parts of the world—i.e., Iraq and Afghanistan—leading to a situation that historian Paul Kennedy has called "imperial overstretch"
- A calculation that the benefits of greater U.S. attention to the region would not be worth the costs (since, paradoxically, power entails responsibility).

So a basic question arises: Has this indifference threatened American national interests? Not really. Disagreements occur within the boundaries of diplomacy. Trade and investment have not been causing much friction. Oil-exporting countries in the region (including Mexico and Venezuela) continue to supply the U.S. market. Governments under siege from drug-trafficking organizations have been waging dangerous and violent wars against drugs. And no leader in the hemisphere, not even the most virulently anti-American, has expressed open support for Al Qaeda or its allies. Under these circumstances, there has been little need for

Cartagena, 2012: President Obama makes a statement at the Summit of the Americas.
Source: SAUL LOEB/AFP/Getty Images.

the United States to devote huge resources to inter-American affairs. The region presents no serious challenge to U.S. national interests. Costs of inattention seem to be low and bearable for the time being.

### Back to the Future

How can a major change in U.S. policy toward Latin America be brought about? Once again, the question is twofold: How can more attention be paid to Latin America? How can a more enlightened policy be promoted?

One key lies in the White House. But it is not just a matter of electing (or reelecting) a Democrat instead of a Republican. Democrats can be just as conservative as Republicans about foreign policy. And, like Republicans, they are likely to be more concerned about global politics than hemispheric issues. Needed would be the election of an enlightened president with a personal commitment to the progressive paradigm and a strong personal interest in Latin America. This development would be promising but not necessarily sufficient because it could easily be overridden by unforeseen events. (Remember, George W. Bush expressed great personal interest in Latin America prior to the 9/11 attacks.)

Change in Congress is essential too. Compromise is necessary for policy innovation. Partisan polarization serves no positive national interest. On the part of both political parties, moderation is a must. Paralysis simply perpetuates the status quo. This will depend on the voters. American citizens should cast their ballots on the basis of the issues, on substance and accomplishment rather than on anger and emotion. They should punish representatives who indulge in mindless polarization. They should reward positive policy instead of irresponsible rhetoric.

In the long run, demographic and political change could seriously affect the outcome of future U.S. national elections. Continued expansion of the Latino population might lead to the creation of a more or less unified electoral bloc that might be able to extract effective campaign promises from presidential candidates. (This scenario might become more likely in the aftermath of change in Cuba, which might enable contending Latino groups to reach a political consensus. In the meantime, generational changes in the Cuban American population of Florida hold out prospects for increasing political moderation.)

What about trends within Latin America? One ominous scenario might stem from the launching of a terrorist attack against the continental United States from somewhere, almost anywhere, in Latin America—a scenario that would be more likely to precipitate a conservative, neoconservative, or militaristic response than a progressive policy. Other potential developments might well be negative: a wave of terrorist activity, disintegration of institutional authority, or a governmental takeover by drug cartels. Such misfortunes might occur as cause or consequence of a sudden radicalization of popular and political opinion.

Ultimately, the hope is that the United States can "rebalance" its regional interests in the aftermath of the war on terror. A fundamental purpose must be to avert any possibility of a worldwide "clash of civilizations." Cast in this light, Latin America becomes a crucial U.S. partner in a changing and unsettled world arena. The first step, of course, is to initiate debate. It is essential to broaden the scope of discourse, to amplify the national agenda. That will not guarantee success. The only certain thing is that silence will guarantee perpetuation of the status quo.

## QUESTIONS FOR REVIEW

1. What are the basic points of philosophical disagreement between "conservative" and "progressive" forms of realism in international relations? How has the neoconservative approach of the Bush administration differed from a traditional conservative approach?
2. What are the most important sources of disagreement between conservative and progressive realists with regard to Latin America?

3. What factors shape U.S. policy toward Latin America?
4. What implications do bureaucratic complexity and partisan polarization have for U.S. policy toward Latin America? What role does the White House play?
5. What impact do public attitudes have on U.S. policy toward Latin America? How would you describe the current situation? Might it change in future years?

CHAPTER 16

# Conclusion: Structure and Change in U.S.–Latin American Relations

The evolution of U.S.–Latin American relations reveals patterns of continuity, consistency, and change over the last two hundred years. Long-term historical trends can provide a basis for looking ahead to the future. The purpose of this chapter is not to prescribe policy nostrums, however, but to reexamine fundamental questions: What have been the driving forces behind U.S. policy toward Latin America? What have been the key determinants of Latin America's response? What has been the nature of the interaction? And, by extension, what are likely to be major factors in shaping U.S.–Latin American relations in years to come?

## LOOKING BACK: SUMMATION

As postulated at the outset, the dynamics of U.S.–Latin American relations complied closely with what I have interpreted as prevailing rules of conduct in the global arena. Transformation of these rules reflected changing global realities and gave sharp definition to three distinct chronological periods: the imperial era, stretching from the 1790s through the 1930s; the Cold War, lasting from the late 1940s through the late 1980s; and the post–Cold War era, stretching from 1990 to the present.[1] Each of these epochs contained its particular rules of the game—codes that informed not only U.S. behavior toward Latin America but also the Latin American response. This conceptual framework shapes and supports the fundamental contentions of this book: that U.S.–Latin American interactions revealed structural regularities, that these regularities followed principles of logic, and that these regularities changed over time in understandable ways. Inter-American relations have responded not to cultural whimsy or psychological caprice but to objective realities and governing norms in the international scene.

During the imperial era, major powers promulgated an operative code of conduct that sought to maintain a balance of power among themselves and to preserve their sovereignty. Each of these powers acquired colonial possessions that ultimately figured in the calculus of power, and each therefore controlled a clearly defined and widely recognized sphere of influence. The United States entered this

---

[1]One might also think of four distinct periods, if the "war on terror" is considered a separate era.

contest in the early 1800s as an aspiring challenger and soon began to advance its claims by acquiring territory, mostly from Spain (Florida) or from ex-Spanish colonies (Mexico). American politicians, publicists, and theologians justified this expansionist policy on the grounds of "manifest destiny," with its presumptive mission to extend the reach of political democracy throughout the hemisphere. The Monroe Doctrine and its subsequent corollaries established rationales for restricting Europe's presence in the New World and securing the area for U.S. domination. Since curtailment of European power in the Caribbean area was of paramount importance, the island of Cuba became an object of special imperial desire. At the end of the nineteenth century, Washington shifted its overall strategy from territorial expansion toward the promotion of economic and commercial interests, adjusting its political tactics toward the installation of protectorates and the periodic use of military intervention. In contrast to most European powers, the United States rarely created formal colonies, with the conspicuous exceptions of Puerto Rico and the Philippines, while continuing to proclaim its dedication to democratic principles. Franklin Roosevelt's Good Neighbor policy represented a culmination of U.S. imperial strategy, not a departure from it, as Washington managed to consolidate its sphere of influence through commercial exchange, hemispheric diplomacy, inculcations of Pan-American solidarity, and the cultivation of goodwill.

Confronted by this steady rise of U.S. power, Latin America had several plausible responses at its disposal. One enshrined the Bolivarian dream of continental unification, a theme that would appear and reappear in varying guise over time; another sought extrahemispheric protection; still others included aspirations for subregional hegemony, entertained mainly by Argentina and Brazil, and reliance on legalistic codes of international behavior. Expressions of cultures of resistance, with special emphases on national self-determination and the rejection of American society and values, were not quixotic manifestations of collective envy; they offered meaningful counterinterpretations to North American claims of manifest destiny and cultural superiority, exposing ideological tensions that would persist in decades to come. As cultivated by the weak against the strong, doctrines of resistance constituted a substantial resource for Latin America and its leadership.

Beginning in the late 1940s, the Cold War led to major rearrangements of the global arena. The United States and the Soviet Union emerged from the ashes of victory in World War II to dominate a bipolar world. Locked in a nuclear standoff, these leading powers would engage in a geopolitical and ideological rivalry that interpreted the Third World as a global battleground. Reflecting the intensity of this struggle, the rules of this international game acquired remarkable transparency and clarity. Within Latin America, by now established as a U.S. sphere of influence, Washington pursued relentless but coherent policies—banishing or outlawing what it regarded as suspect forces, supporting friendly governments, and overthrowing allegedly dangerous regimes. The anticommunist crusade pervaded virtually every facet of U.S. policy toward the region, from the cultivation of moderate labor movements in the 1960s to the promotion of counterrevolutionary guerrilla movements in the 1980s. For Washington, the Cold War was an obsession.

These circumstances left Latin America with a limited range of strategic alternatives. The most daring and ambitious was the quest for socialist revolution, an effort that could succeed only with the protection of an extrahemispheric superpower—meaning, in practice, the Soviet Union. The fate of revolution thus became hostage to big-power politics. A second alternative, pursued with energy and verve by an unseemly assortment of dictators, was to join the anticommunist crusade. This tactic offered the great advantage of defining one's rivals as enemies of capitalism, democracy, and, therefore, the United States, whose power could then be brought into play. A third option was to seek an independent path, a "third way," often through political affiliation with the Non-Aligned Movement or economic membership in the G-77. While such alternatives made some significant strides, as in the Contadora Group's efforts to mediate the Central American conflict of the 1980s, it usually drew expressions of wrath or disdain from the United States. In a bipolar world, there was not much room for maneuver.

In the late 1980s the end of the Cold War brought another transformation to the international arena. The distribution of global power became multilayered and complex—unipolar in the military sense, where the United States remained supreme, and multipolar in the economic sense, where Europe and Japan (and other burgeoning regions) vied for global preeminence. Globalization laid the foundation for worldwide geoeconomic competition, a perpetual contest in which participants vied to improve their long-term economic fortunes by strengthening their control of capital, labor, markets, natural resources, and technology. One of the most common tactics was "regional economic integration" schemes that privileged their members but were at the same time open to interaction with nonmembers. Rules of this contest were subtle but clear: Seek advantage over rivals but do not destroy them, focus on incremental gains, uphold the principle of global stability. This was a nonelimination game.

Within the Western Hemisphere, by contrast, U.S. geopolitical hegemony was uncontested and complete: There were no significant extrahemispheric rivals, and the power differential between the United States and Latin America reached unprecedented heights. As U.S. interests shifted from military security toward economic and social concerns, domestic constituencies came to have conspicuous impacts on American foreign policy: The business community promoted free trade, environmentalists pushed for biological diversity, a disparate coalition supported a sometimes-hysterical crusade against illicit drugs, nativists joined an equally hysterical crusade against undocumented immigration. Largely in response to such domestic political pressures but always in the name of democracy, the United States took military action against Panama in 1989 and Haiti in 1994.

In the immediate post–Cold War context, Latin America had even fewer options than before. There was no way to avoid or evade the fact of U.S. power. There were no extrahemispheric patrons immediately at hand. Revolution was out of the question. International law and multilateral organizations would have little serious impact. Essentially, the alternative for countries of Latin America was to play the geoeconomic game—to adopt the growing emphasis on liberalization and "free trade." They could seek to implement this strategy in one (or more) of several ways: by expanding commercial ties with Europe and Japan as well as the United States, as Chile did; by seeking an institutionalized relationship with the United States, as Mexico did; or by resuscitating dreams of subregional unification, as Brazil attempted to do through MERCOSUR and SAFTA. There still lingered traces of popular resistance to U.S. power, as shown by the Chiapas uprising in January 1994 and street demonstrations at other times, but these were relatively few and far between. This signaled not the end of history, as some analysts surmised, but the triumph of neoliberal ideology.

The terrorist attacks of September 11, 2001, inaugurated yet another phase of post–Cold War politics. Under the neoconservative leadership of George W. Bush, the United States launched a far-reaching military campaign. Seeking revenge against Al Qaeda, the Bush administration dispatched troops to Afghanistan, overturned the Taliban regime, and scoured the hillsides in search of the mercurial Osama bin Laden. Early in 2003 the United States followed up with a massive invasion of Iraq, initially on the grounds that the tyrannical Saddam Hussein was harboring weapons of mass destruction. After WMDs failed to materialize, Bush asserted that the U.S. goal was to bring democracy to Iraq and to the Middle East. In 2007 a "surge" of additional U.S. forces helped bring a semblance of order to Iraq, but uncertainty prevailed. After taking office in early 2009, Barack Obama revised the focus of the war on terror—withdrawing troops from Iraq, turning attention to Afghanistan, and concentrating on Al Qaeda and its allies.

The war on terror imposed clear-cut rules for international conduct, a geopolitical code that coexisted with—and usually overshadowed —the rules for geoeconomic competition. Nations subject to terrorist attack were entitled to retaliate in any way they chose—including the preemptive use of military force. Captured or suspected terrorists were not protected by the Geneva accords or by due process of law. International treaties and agreements were of little relevance. Terrorists posed a new kind of enemy, it was often said, and this was a new kind of war. It was a world where might made right. The juxtaposition of these geopolitical and geoeconomic codes created a complex two-layered game that required judicious calculations of costs and benefits on the part of all nation-states, the weak as well as the strong.

While the United States focused its energy and resources on Iraq, the Bush administration paid only lip service to inter-American affairs. Generally speaking, leaders and peoples of Latin America adopted low-profile "spectator" roles and discovered, somewhat to their surprise, that U.S. neglect gave them substantial room for maneuver. Partly out of distaste for America's foreign policy, voters cast their ballots for antiestablishment "pink tide" candidates in presidential elections. While Mexico stressed its close relations with the United States, other nations emphasized their autonomy and independence from Washington. Brazil became a leader of developing-nation blocs in the World Trade Organization, and

Venezuela sought (albeit unsuccessfully) to raise its profile in the United Nations. Several countries of the region curried favor from—and trade with—Asia's rising giant, the People's Republic of China. So long as they kept a fairly modest profile, Latin American leaders managed to explore an expansive menu of strategic options and geoeconomic opportunities.

## LOOKING BACK: ANALYSIS

The central thesis of this book is that the dynamics of U.S.–Latin American relations reflected prevailing rules of the international game within each historical period and that these dynamics underwent change in accordance with alterations in the rules of the game. Transformations in these operative rules, or codes, came about in response to change in three factors: the number of major powers, the nature of power resources, and the goals of international policy (Table 16-1). The number of powers determined whether global contests would be multipolar, as in the imperial era; bipolar, as in the Cold War; multilayered in an economic sense, as in the 1990s; or unipolar in a geopolitical sense, as in the early 2000s. The nature of power resources varied in complex ways: Military capacity ranged from conventional forces to thermonuclear capability to a combination of the two; economic capacity ranged from commercial penetration to direct investment to financial linkages, all employed in varying degrees over the time spans in question. The principal goals of international rivalry evolved from the acquisition of territory (either as colonies or possessions) to the cultivation of political affinity (especially during the Cold War) to the pursuit of geoeconomic advantage (in the post–Cold War era) to demands for acquiescence and support (in the war on terror).

Throughout these transformations the invocation of ideology played an important but essentially subordinate role in these contests. The United States proclaimed its "manifest destiny" as the diffusion of political democracy, European powers embarked on civilizing missions, the Soviet Union insisted that its goal was the socialist liberation of downtrodden peoples. During the early twentieth century, racist doctrine helped legitimize the U.S. tendency to impose protectorates

**Table 16-1  Global Contexts for U.S.–Latin American Relations**

| FACTOR | IMPERIAL ERA 1790s–1930s | COLD WAR 1940s–1980s | GEOECONOMICS 1990– | WAR ON TERROR 2001– |
|---|---|---|---|---|
| Distribution of power | Multipolar | Bipolar | Multipolar | Unipolar |
| Policy goals | Territorial, commercial | Geopolitical, ideological | Economic gain | Geopolitical, military |
| Rules of the game | Balance of power | Global containment | Peaceful competition | U.S. primacy |

(or military governments) on countries in Central America and the Caribbean. After other claims failed for lack of evidence, promoting democracy became the key rationalization for the war on Iraq. Ideological proclamations provided essential and significant justifications for big-power actions, though they rarely determined the course of such policies.

In its broad international contexts, the conduct of U.S.–Latin America relations was essentially derivative. Notwithstanding the Monroe Doctrine, the Western Hemisphere was not an isolated arena; on the contrary, the doctrine itself can best be understood as a challenge to European powers. The United States sought to impose a sphere of influence in the Americas not so much for its own sake but as a power resource for dealing with extrahemispheric rivals. The evolving drama of inter-American relations played out on a broad international stage.

## Explaining U.S. Policies

Within these global schemes, there were significant sources of variation in U.S. conduct toward Latin America. Four factors, or variables, helped determine patterns and changes in U.S. behavior over time: (1) the relative importance of Latin America vis-à-vis other world regions, (2) perceptions of extrahemispheric rivalry, (3) definitions of U.S. national interest, and (4) the relationship between state actors and social groups in policy formation. These factors were closely interrelated.

The historical record demonstrates that Latin America commanded considerable attention from the United States throughout the nineteenth and twentieth centuries, although there was significant variation in the relative degree of importance ascribed to the region. During the imperial era, Latin America was a central policy concern for Washington: It was the area where the United States expressed its own imperial ambitions and sought to eradicate all vestiges of European power. By the late 1920s and throughout the 1930s, when the United States appeared isolationist with respect to Europe and the rest of the world, Latin America came to occupy "first place" in the nation's diplomacy. During the Cold War, the dynamics of East–West competition transformed Latin America into an arena for struggle, a prize in the superpower contest, a status it shared with the Third World as a whole: Latin America commanded special attention from Washington because of geographical propinquity and alleged "security" interests, but it was less unique or privileged in this sense than at previous times. Once the Cold War ended, Latin America occupied an ambiguous position in the eyes of Washington. In ways that were reminiscent of the imperial contest, the region came to constitute a sphere of U.S. influence, uncontested at last, a place where the United States could exercise its hemispheric hegemony for the purpose of confronting a complex and multipolar world; but attention to Latin America became selective as well, more focused on Mexico and the Caribbean than on South America, more attuned to social and economic interactions than to broad geopolitical concerns. After September 2001, the U.S. government turned its attention to South and Central Asia and the Middle East, while Latin America slipped far down the ladder of official priorities. In summary, Latin America was always important to the United States, but its relative degree of importance varied across these historical periods—roughly speaking, from very high to high to ambivalent to very low.

Washington's view of Latin America depended on its rivalry with extrahemispheric powers. The basic rule was straightforward: The greater the perception of extrahemispheric threat, the greater the attention to Latin America. During the imperial era, the United States was explicitly and consciously engaged in an effort to banish European influence from the Western Hemisphere: In a multipolar world, Britain and Germany were the most powerful rivals, though other continental powers—Italy, Holland, France—also played meaningful roles. During the Cold War, the United States steadfastly pursued its policy of "containment," seeking to prevent the Soviet Union—and/or its allies or puppets—from gaining influence in the Americas. The perception of danger was greatly exaggerated, as a result of anticommunist hysteria, but it had profound political meaning: Washington saw itself as the leader of a worldwide crusade, and it formed policies in accordance with this sense of purpose. With the end of the Cold War, extrahemispheric influence in the Americas temporarily vanished. For the first time in history Washington had no rivals (real or imagined) in the hemisphere, though it confronted a multipolar challenge in the geoeconomic arena. By the 1990s the United States had finally realized its ambition of the 1790s: to create a zone of uncontested influence within the Western Hemisphere. Geopolitical hegemony persisted well beyond the turn of the century.

A third key factor behind U.S. policy concerned prevalent definitions of national interests. At the most general level, these interests were constant: the accumulation and expression of international power. Yet the specific content of U.S. national interests varied over time. During the imperial era, the United States pursued two goals: territorial expansion and commercial influence. The overall purpose was to achieve rank as a major power. During the Cold War, as one of two rival superpowers, the United States sought geopolitical and ideological advantage in a worldwide struggle. And in the 1990s, the United States attempted to consolidate geoeconomic hegemony in the Americas, partly as a tool for bargaining with other powers in a multipolar world. In light of increasing interdependence, Washington was also attempting to protect the United States from unwelcome social influences, such as illicit drugs and undocumented migration. In long-term perspective, the primary impetus behind U.S. policy thus shifted from territorial and commercial motivations from the 1800s to the 1930s, to ideological and geopolitical purposes from the 1940s through the 1980s, to economic and social concerns during the 1990s, and to geopolitical and military issues in the antiterrorist campaign that started in 2001.

Throughout this sweep of history the United States steadfastly professed its intention of fostering democracy throughout the Americas, often invoking notions of hemispheric solidarity and the existence of a "Western Hemisphere idea." The promotion of democracy supplied a useful, sometimes crucial, rationalization for the application of American power. In this particular respect, the post–Cold War era came to bear a strong resemblance to the pre–Cold War period. No longer able to appeal to anticommunism for ideological orientation, Washington now proclaimed the extension of democracy as its guidepost in foreign affairs. Bill Clinton's earnest pronouncements about democracy had more in common with the lofty declarations of Woodrow Wilson than with the Machiavellian calculations of Cold Warriors. American efforts to promote democracy had been conspicuously unsuccessful in the imperial era, however, and there was not much sign that Washington had learned its lessons by the 1990s—or in time to prevent the invasion of Iraq. In this respect Barack Obama provided a notable contrast, for he explicitly discarded nation-building and deemphasized democratization as central policy goals.

A fourth factor shaping U.S. policy concerned the relative roles of state elites and social actors. During the early nineteenth century, when the United States embarked on territorial expansion, the government apparatus defined and implemented American foreign policy. It was statesmen of the time—Jefferson, Adams, Polk, and others—who steadfastly pursued the acquisition of land; and while they enjoyed considerable popular support in this enterprise they did so largely on their own initiative. Later in this era, from the 1890s through the 1930s, state elites operated in close collaboration with the business community, especially banking interests. Intent upon the extension and consolidation of economic influence rather than the expansion of physical boundaries, governmental elites and financial representatives developed joint strategies that ranged from diplomatic pressure to military intervention. This partnership was especially evident in Central America and the Caribbean, where private bankers assumed control of outstanding national debts, thus eliminating the primary motivation for European powers to meddle in the hemisphere, while the U.S. government backed up the bankers with American military force. Though its goals may seem nefarious in retrospect, "dollar diplomacy" provided the basis for a smooth and effective public–private alliance.

The Cold War brought governmental elites to a supreme and unchallenged position in policymaking. In light of the bipolar U.S.–Soviet rivalry, international strategy derived from a geopolitical and ideological calculus stressing the containment and curtailment of communist influence. Application of this doctrine was the preserve par excellence of professional bureaucrats, career diplomats, and seasoned politicians. Business interests (and organized labor) occasionally played a strong supporting role: United Fruit promoted U.S. intervention in Guatemala, ITT clamored for action in Chile, the AFL-CIO trained and supported anticommunist labor leaders. Yet investors and financiers tended to have subordinate parts in policy formation during this period: U.S. interventions in Cuba, the Dominican Republic, and Grenada came about as a result of ideological and geopolitical considerations, not for economic reasons. State elites dominated the policy arena throughout the East–West conflict. For better or worse, one consequence of this monopoly was a clear, even rigid, consistency in U.S. policy.

Termination of the Cold War brought a sudden end to this bureaucratic stranglehold. Now governed by a geoeconomic (not geopolitical) calculus, foreign policy in the 1990s became susceptible to the interplay of domestic interests. Ethnic groups with growing importance in the electoral arena—Cuban Americans, Mexican Americans, African Americans—came to have a crucial impact on America's policies toward Castro's Cuba, the NAFTA agreement with Mexico, and the Cédras regime in Haiti. Popular condemnation of drug trafficking and undocumented migration helped stiffen governmental resolve to halt these flows, while business interests avidly supported promotion of the Washington consensus on free trade and on economic policy. Such influence was not so much a deliberate and voluntary partnership, as in the 1910s and 1920s, as the result of grass-roots mobilization and electoral blackmail. By the 1990s, pressure groups were able to penetrate (if not to capture) specific issue areas in foreign policy. Washington fell into a decidedly reactive mode, responding not only to the outbreak of international crises but also to the clamor of domestic interests.

With the outbreak of the war on terror, the White House regained control of foreign policy. At least at the outset, decisions were made by a handful of individuals within the executive branch: the president, the vice president, the secretary of defense, the national security adviser, and, to a lesser extent, the director of the CIA. Preoccupied by events in Afghanistan and Iraq, this group paid little attention to inter-American affairs. From the standpoint of the Bush administration, the most pressing concern was whether countries of Latin America supported the U.S. military campaign: Nothing else really mattered. As a result of presidential indifference, decision making on hemispheric issues—such as it was—moved down to middling levels of the federal bureaucracy. There was little control, coordination, or centralizing leadership.

Table 16-2 summarizes the determinants of U.S. policy toward Latin America for each time period and demonstrates that a combination of factors—the relative importance of Latin America, the presence (or perception) of extrahemispheric rivals, the definition of national interests, and the composition of policy actors—had a determining influence on the resultant set of strategies and policies. Even in schematic form, the table serves to emphasize two central points: first, that there was an underlying logic behind the construction of U.S. policy *within* each historical period, and, second, that there was an underlying logic to the transformation of U.S. policies *between* these periods as well.

Within these broad parameters, policymakers still had meaningful room to maneuver. To explore this point, Table 16-3 presents a fourfold display of various policy configurations or "packages" from the 1960s to the present. One dimension refers to the level of priority accorded by the United States to Latin America—low or high. A second dimension reflects "policy style"—as depicted here, unilateral or multilateral. A unilateral style entails a narrow focus on short-term U.S. interests, a lack of serious consultation with Latin American leaders, a disregard for hemispheric institutions, and, on occasion, an intransigent stance; a multilateral style reflects a broad concern with shared interests, meaningful consultation with Latin American leaders, respect for inter-American institutions, and tactful diplomacy.

Abstract as it might seem, the resulting schema bears a close connection to real-world trends and events. The combination of high priority and

**Table 16-2  Principal Determinants of U.S. Policy**

| DETERMINANT | IMPERIAL ERA 1790s–1930s | COLD WAR 1940s–1980s | GEOECONOMICS 1990– | WAR ON TERROR 2001– |
|---|---|---|---|---|
| Importance of Latin America | Growing to very high | High | Ambiguous | Low |
| Extrahemispheric rivals | European powers | Soviet Union | — | Al Qaeda, terrorist movements |
| Primary goals | Spheres of influence | Anticommunism | Economic gain, social exclusion | National security |
| Policy actors | Government + business | Government alone | Government + interest groups | Government alone |
| General strategy | Territorial, commercial incorporation | Political penetration | Economic integration | Military action |

**Table 16-3  U.S. Policies Toward Latin America, 1960s–Present**

| U.S. POLICY STYLE | LATIN AMERICA AS PRIORITY | |
|---|---|---|
| | LOW | HIGH |
| Unilateral | Ad hoc imposition (Bush 2001–2009) | Systematic intervention (Reagan 1981–1989) |
| Multilateral | Intermittent, low-level diplomacy (Clinton 1993–2001, Obama 2009– ) | Consistent, high-level engagement (Kennedy 1961–1963) |

multilateralism—consistent, high-level engagement—characterized the Good Neighbor diplomacy of Franklin Delano Roosevelt as well as the Alliance for Progress under John F. Kennedy. During the 1980s, the neoconservative Reagan administration resorted to systematic interventionism, employing unilateral means for the purpose of a high-priority agenda. During the 1990s, the Clinton administration relied on multilateral instruments but accorded a low priority to inter-American affairs, thus resulting in intermittent and low-level diplomacy, a mode also adopted by the Barack Obama team.

It is the remaining configuration—low priority plus unilateralism, or ad hoc imposition—that most accurately describes U.S. policy during the George W. Bush administration. Absorbed in military campaigns in distant lands, Washington ignored key developments in the Americas. And when it focused on the region—usually too little and too late—it relied on unilateral tactics and declarations. The Bush administration paid scant heed to institutional crises in Argentina and Bolivia, gave tacit approval to a (failed) military coup in Venezuela, issued veiled threats to voters in El Salvador, assisted in the ouster of an elected president in Haiti, and, of course, refused to engage with Cuba and the Castro regime.

This analysis demonstrates, among other things, the importance of presidential leadership. Chief executives can make a difference. The White House has command of foreign policy. Whenever that power is focused on relations with Latin America—or other world regions, for that matter—it can exert a considerable impact. As shown here, developments at the global level establish basic incentives and constraints for U.S. policies. But within those boundaries, there are choices to be made; and more often than not, it is the president who makes those key decisions.

## Understanding Latin American Responses

As U.S. strategies underwent long-term change over time, so did Latin America's capacity to respond. There were continuities as well. A central premise of this analysis has stressed the presence and significance of power inequalities. From the mid-nineteenth century onward the United States was stronger than all countries of Latin America—economically, militarily, and politically—and by the early twentieth century the United States had become more powerful than the region as a whole. The conduct of inter-American relations reflected and reasserted this fundamental asymmetry in myriad ways. Interaction took place not between equal partners but between the strong and the relatively weak. Individually and collectively, Latin American countries were constantly confronting a more powerful and better-endowed adversary, a sometime-ally engaged in a quest for constant advantage, a hemispheric neighbor smitten by global ambitions, an expansive power proclaiming the virtues of democracy: the Colossus of the North.

To counter the United States and to pursue its own destiny, Latin America over time developed a cumulative total of six distinct strategic alternatives. One was the Bolivarian notion of collective unification. Though it never took full institutional form, the idea persisted over time and could claim some notable success—in the insistence on principles of self-determination and nonintervention from the 1890s to the 1930s, in the formulation of economic doctrines in the 1940s and 1950s, and in the settlement of Central American conflicts in the 1980s. A second broad strategy consisted of a search for support, protection, and patronage from extrahemispheric powers—especially the United Kingdom in the nineteenth century and the Soviet Union during the Cold War (and, to a more modest extent, Europe and the Asia-Pacific region in the current era). A third strategy entailed a quest for subregional hegemony, visions entertained by Argentina and Brazil in the nineteenth century and by Brazil in the contemporary era. A fourth stressed the uses of international law and/or international organization, the principles of which could protect weaker countries from predatory or arbitrary actions by the strong; relatively successful during the imperial era, these efforts foundered during the Cold War and show little prospect for realization during the contemporary age. A fifth strategic alternative, especially plausible during the Cold War, sought South–South solidarity with other nations of the so-called Third World. Sixth was the quest for social revolution, especially socialist revolution, an effort that also reached its peak during the period of East–West confrontation.

Beyond these assertions of defiance and autonomy there remained, of course, another kind of option—alignment with the United States, either in deference to Washington's power or in pursuit of tactical advantage. During the imperial era, Brazil sought an alliance with the United States as a matter of grand geopolitical strategy, while client rulers in Central America and the Caribbean accepted Washington's tutelage as a matter of political survival (and personal profit). The Cold War offered association with the United States as a strategic opportunity for the authoritarian right, which, with notable success, invoked the cause of anticommunism to justify its claims on power. During the 1990s, Mexico most categorically threw itself into the arms of the United States; other countries of the region, from Costa Rica to Argentina, seemed prepared to follow this same course. It should be noted, however, that leaders and peoples of Latin American have not always chosen affiliation with the United States out of admiration, loyalty, or affection—but because it has appeared to suit their purposes. This implies a portent for the future: If reliance on the United States does not produce the anticipated results for Latin America or if other plausible options emerge, public displays of inter-American harmony will not endure forever.

Strategic alternatives became available to differing degrees and in differing combinations at different periods of time (Table 16-4). During the imperial era, leaders of Latin America could entertain a fairly broad array of choices, achieving a substantial measure of success in the area of international law (partly as a result of diplomatic unity). The Cold War narrowed the range of maneuver, pressuring Latin American countries into alignments with either the United States or the USSR, though courageous and enterprising leaders pursued an independent path, often in collaboration with other Third World countries, and were able to help mediate conflicts in Central America and elsewhere. During the 1990s, ironically, the inventory of options appeared even more restricted: Whether they wanted to or not, most Latin American leaders had little choice other than to implement policy prescriptions of the Washington consensus and to seek economic accommodation with the United States and the advanced industrial nations of the North, including the European Union and Japan. More recently, during the war on terror, most Latin American leaders have attempted to tread a fine line—avoiding high-profile engagement in the war on terror, preferring to play the geoeconomic game rather than the geopolitical game, discreetly asserting autonomy from the United States while avoiding risks of U.S. retaliation. Only a few, like Chávez, threw down the gauntlet. In contrast, Mexico sought to forge a close alliance with the United States in order to wage its war against drug trafficking.

In summary, the display in Table 16-4 demonstrates yet another basic thesis of this book: Latin America's reactions to the United States reflected just as much logic and regularity as did U.S. policies. Both the United States and Latin America were forging reasonable responses to their prevailing environments. The dynamics of their interaction as well as of their policy initiatives have revealed regularity and structure.

**Table 16-4  Strategic Options for Latin America**

| STRATEGY | IMPERIAL ERA 1790s–1930s | COLD WAR 1940s–1980s | GEOECONOMICS 1990– | WAR ON TERROR 2001– |
|---|---|---|---|---|
| Collective unity | Attempted (political integration) | Attempted (economic integration) | Unlikely | Extremely unlikely |
| Extrahemispheric protection | Attempted (Europe) | Attempted (USSR) | Attempted (Asia, Europe) | Unlikely |
| Subregional hegemony | Attempted (Brazil, Argentina) | — — | Possible (Brazil) | Attempted (Brazil, Venezuela) |
| International law/ organization | Successful | Attempted | — | — |
| Social revolution: | | | | |
| Nonsocialist | Mexico | Bolivia[a] | — | Bolivia? |
| Socialist | — | Cuba, Nicaragua | — | Venezuela? |
| Third World solidarity | — | Attempted (NAM, G-77) | — | Attempted (NAM) |
| Alignment with United States | Attempted (Brazil + client rulers) | Successful (authoritarian right) | Attempted (Mexico + others?) | Attempted (Mexico, Colombia) |

—: Not available or not feasible

[a]The Bolivian Revolution of 1952 had socialist tendencies, among others, but soon gave way to close cooperation with the United States.

Yet another essential component of Latin America's response to the United States took the form not of practical policy measures but of cultural interpretations of reality. Latin American politicians, pundits, and intellectuals developed a series of ideological and attitudinal outlooks. During the imperial era, leaders and representatives of Latin America forged cultures of "resistance." During the Cold War, many expressed resentment of the United States by subscribing to Marxist beliefs. In the post–Cold War period, an era most notable for its absence of ideological contentiousness, many Latin Americans took part in inchoate protests against the conventional wisdom; others forged cultures of "accommodation" that recognized realities of U.S. power but also sustained the value and integrity of Latin America's social identity. It has been only with the appearance of the "pink tide," during the war on terror, that anti-American sentiment in Latin America has found its full voice once again.

## Differentiating Latin America

Some countries of Latin America, in some situations, were better prepared than others to confront the United States. Variations in capability reflected the impact of five related factors: (1) size and strength, (2) export capacity, (3) geographical proximity, (4) links to extrahemispheric powers, and (5) intellectual and cultural resources.

In terms of population size, economic output, and military capability, some nations of Latin America were stronger than others. Argentina and Brazil possessed resources that Honduras, Haiti, and Cuba did not. Such capacities enabled these countries not only to avert outright U.S. interventionism but also, at times, to entertain visions of continental grandeur and subregional hegemony. In the nineteenth century, Argentina and Brazil each nurtured notions of challenging, or at least offsetting, the rise of U.S. power; in the twentieth century, Brazil has continued to see itself as the natural leader of South America. The resulting proposition borders on the circular: Differential levels of power meant differential capacity to resist pressures from the United States. Size and power also exercised a deterrent effect: While the United States displayed recurring willingness to launch military invasions of small countries, Washington never considered sending troops into Brazil.

A related source of differentiation came from economic structure and, more specifically, from export capacity. Endowment with highly valued natural resources enabled countries to engage in profitable commerce, accumulate foreign exchange, sustain strong levels of economic growth, develop ties to world power centers, and acquire political influence. Until the Great Depression of the 1930s, exports of beef and wheat nurtured Argentina's aspirations of balancing U.S. power within the hemisphere. Beginning with coffee, Brazil's diversified exports helped underwrite the perennial quest for national *grandeza*. The sale of copper has bolstered Chile's position as a poster child for neoliberal reform. And in recent years, of course, petroleum has become the power source par excellence. As oil prices have risen, so have the prospects for the *Alternativa Bolivariana* of Hugo Chávez in Venezuela. Countries that export can claim success and influence; those that cannot, cannot.

Geography supplied a third determinant. Countries surrounding the Caribbean Rim—Mexico, Central America, the islands of the Caribbean—were much more likely to feel the weight of U.S. power than were South American nations. From the 1790s onward and especially from the 1890s through the 1990s, policymakers in Washington ascribed particular importance to the greater Caribbean Basin—because of maritime routes, commercial ties, financial investments, natural resources, geographical propinquity, and (for all these reasons) national security. From the start, Washington was more predisposed to project its power in this area than in South America. Exceptions to this rule occurred mainly during the Cold War, when all countries of Latin America became squares on a global checkerboard; hence U.S. support for the Brazilian coup of 1964 and, even more conspicuously, for the Allende overthrow of 1973. With the ending of the anticommunist crusade, the United States reduced its interest in South America and refocused its attention on the Caribbean Basin. Geographical location did much to shape the tenor and tone of bilateral and continental relations: The closer to the United States, the greater the degree of attention from Washington—and the greater the potential for conflict.

A fourth factor concerned linkages with extrahemispheric powers. For historic and economic reasons, some countries, such as the ABC nations of South America, enjoyed close and significant ties to Europe, especially in the late nineteenth and early twentieth centuries. As Simón Bolívar anticipated in the 1820s, these connections furnished a significant amount of diplomatic and political leverage in dealing with the United States. During the Cold War, Cuba and (to a lesser degree) Nicaragua turned toward the Soviet Union in search of protection. This was a high-risk strategy, however, since it ran directly counter to anticommunist ideology and to Washington's persisting quest for undisputed hegemony within the hemisphere. (Latin American nations did not have the luxury enjoyed by other Third World countries, such as Egypt, that were able to play the superpowers off against each other: Located within the putative "backyard" of the United States, Latin American countries would generally have to follow Washington's lead—or move into the rival camp.) And with the end of the Cold War and the virtual withdrawal of extrahemispheric powers, this alternative collapsed. By the late 1990s, Latin America was making earnest efforts to develop ties with Europe and Asia, and several countries of the region formed strong ties with China after the turn of the century. Even so, Latin America would still have to confront the United States.

Yet another differentiating factor among Latin American countries was cultural tradition. This was an amorphous concept, to be sure, one that embraced intellectual resources, educational institutions, and historical legacies. Yet in actual practice it was a factor that provided some countries, such as Mexico and Cuba and Nicaragua, with the capacity to construct powerful cultures of resistance that ultimately laid the ideological foundations for social revolution. In different form, it was a factor that shaped the cosmopolitan and European outlook of such distinguished jurists as Chile's Andrés Bello and Argentina's Carlos Calvo, who devised legal doctrines of national sovereignty and nonintervention. And it was a factor that, still more recently, permitted the rise of subtle and complex cultures of accommodation in the wake of the Cold War.

In this respect there was a countervailing factor at work. Because of traditions of continental solidarity, dating back to Bolivarian dreams of unification, intellectual and cultural achievements in any one part of Latin America quickly became assets for the region as a whole. José Martí spoke not only for Cuba but for what he called "*nuestra América*"; Víctor Raúl Haya de la Torre sought reform not only in Peru but across the entire continent; César Augusto Sandino became a martyr not only for Nicaragua but for all revolutionary activists; Fidel Castro and Salvador Allende fired political imaginations not only in their own countries but throughout the region; in different ways, Raúl Prébisch and Fernando Henrique Cardoso charted paths of economic development for all of Latin America; and writers of the left and right, from Gabriel García Márquez and Carlos Fuentes to Jorge Luis Borges and Mario Vargas Llosa, gained renown as interpreters and representatives for Latin America as a whole. Each national struggle had regional dimensions, each voice became the clamor of a continent at large. A defining paradox of Latin American nationalism was its ability to transcend national borders, especially insofar as it focused on the paramount challenge of common concern: the overweening power of the United States.

In retrospect, the determinants of U.S. policies and of Latin America's options combined to establish the dynamic structure of interactions between the United States and Latin America. During the imperial era, the United States was attempting to *incorporate* all or parts of Latin America into its own sphere of interest, through either conquest or commerce, while Latin American leaders engaged in various forms of resistance. During the Cold War, the United States attempted to *penetrate* into Latin American societies and governments, to purge them of undesirable political and ideological elements and thus rid the hemisphere of putative threats to national security; right-wing Latin Americans responded by exploiting the resultant opportunities, leftists reacted with calls for revolution, reformists attempted to identify intermediate paths. And from the 1990s onward, the United States has been seeking to *integrate* Latin America into its geoeconomic community and at the same time to repel unwanted social interactions. Confronted by this ambivalent message, Latin American leaders have responded by seeking selective cooperation with the United States—choosing to cooperate on economic matters, in other words, while retaining freedom of action in other areas.

## LOOKING AHEAD: WHAT NEXT?

The principal outlook for the future of U.S.–Latin American relations flows directly from this book's central argument: It will be conditioned in large part by the nature, form, and implicit rules of global politics. As the post–Cold War world continues its search for a "new international order," if one is ever to appear, it is the worldwide pattern and conduct of international relations that will determine the shape and substance of inter-American relations. As in previous eras, hemispheric affairs throughout the foreseeable future are likely to be cast within a global framework. As from the beginning to the present, U.S.–Latin American relations will be intimately linked to trends and developments in the global arena. More to the point, the underlying codes for hemispheric interaction will be essentially derivative from the international rules of the game.

In many senses the 1990s bore more resemblance to the imperial era than to the Cold War. Like the late nineteenth century, the end of the twentieth century displayed a complex and multipolar distribution of power, at least in the economic arena. In the context of geoeconomic globalization, the prevailing environment placed fewer constraints on big-power action than did the Cold War. And the countries of the South, or Third World, had little power and few strategic options. Their major concern was not so much that they would be colonized, however, as the fear that they would be neglected and abandoned. During the Cold War, especially in Asia and Africa, developing countries at least could entertain hopes of taking advantage of the superpower rivalry, of playing off the United States and the Soviet Union against one another. Such leverage no longer existed.

A principal difference between the imperial age and the 1990s was the fact of uncontested U.S. hegemony within the hemisphere. During the earlier period, as shown in Part I, the presence of European nations established a multipolar distribution of power within the Americas. It was a complex contest, a long-term struggle in which the United States sought consistently to banish or reduce extrahemispheric influence in order to assert its own preeminence. That struggle took new form during the Cold War. But with the implosion of the Soviet Union, the withdrawal of extrahemispheric powers, and the triumph of neoliberal ideology, the United States stood supreme within the hemisphere. In the post-Cold War world, there were few constraints on Washington. The United States could intervene at will.

It is pointless to hazard specific prognostications about the future of U.S.–Latin American relations. Given the complexity of the global environment, almost anything could happen. To anticipate possible trends in the twenty-first century, however, it should be useful to identify key factors at both the global and hemispheric levels that seem most likely to affect the shape of future developments.

The most critical variable in the worldwide arena concerns the eventual distribution of power and associated forms of alignment and conflict. As world events followed inconclusive paths toward the future, there were six distinct scenarios in play:

1. **Global Hegemony for the United States.** A reassertion of U.S. primacy in geoeconomic and/or geopolitical arenas gained plausibility as Europe and Asia faced unwelcome problems, since these developments enhanced America's relative standing. As a sole superpower, the United States would be in a position to lay down and enforce international rules of the game.
2. **Intensification of Multipolarity.** The international system would come to contain a half-dozen major powers—as Henry Kissinger once predicted, "the United States, Europe, China, Japan, Russia, and probably India—as well as a multiplicity of medium-sized and smaller countries." The United States would be important but not dominant, and codes of behavior would result from agreement, cooperation, and balancing among the power centers.
3. **Rival Regional Blocs.** This idea envisioned a small number of powerful economic and political blocs, each headed by a major power. A common version portrayed three regional units: a "European" bloc, dominated by Germany and the EU, with a sphere of influence stretching through Eastern Europe to parts of the Middle East and much of Africa; an "Asian" bloc, led by China or Japan (or both), extending throughout the Asia-Pacific area to the borders of South Asia; and an "American" bloc under the United States, embracing the entire Western Hemisphere.
4. **North-South Separation.** In this perspective there could develop a "North–North" axis of economic and political cooperation encircling

the upper half of the globe—from the United States to the European Union through Russia to Japan. Capital and investment would flow freely around this circuit; with few exceptions (such as Brazil, China, and India), the developing world would be left out. An abandoned South would become ever more dispirited, desperate, and reckless. Moderate leaders would lose credibility. Radicals of one stripe or another—nationalists, populists, *ayatollahs*, if not leftists—would rise to power. With little to lose, they would be tempted to pursue high-risk strategies of confrontation.

5. **Clash of Civilizations.** Broad cultural groupings would transcend nation-states and shape the outlooks, associations, and interests of key actors in the world. Conflicts between them would be frequent (sometimes violent), compromise scarce, and tension permanent. There would be mounting antagonism between "the West and the rest," as rising cultures of the world sought to acquire and assert commensurate shares of power.

6. **Continuing Globalization.** A final scenario, by far the most optimistic, envisioned progressive and multilateral movement toward a global regime that could establish and uphold widely accepted rules of the game. At the same time, great powers, including the United States, would devote fewer resources to military arms and more to economic development. There would be a productive (and efficient) reinvestment of the "peace dividend" into social equity, full employment, and human welfare. The world would become a gentler, kinder, more livable place.

As of 2012, there were traces of evidence in support of each of these forecasts. It was at that time unclear which scenario—or combination of scenarios—would come to prevail.

Whatever the case, the eventual shape of these scenarios will depend upon two principal axes of power, the geoeconomic and the geopolitical. In this context international actors will continue to abide by the rules of the "two-level games" that are currently in evidence. The continuing juxtaposition of these two codes will therefore perpetuate the complexity, uncertainty, and volatility of conduct in the world arena. Issues will vary in content, alignments will shift, and the relative salience of geoeconomic and geopolitical concerns will change over time. For the foreseeable future, however, the rules of games are likely to remain intact.

In such ways the global structure of power will shape the conduct and tone of inter-American relations for generations to come. A key determinant of U.S. policy toward Latin America will be the relative importance of the region within the overall global arena. This value will depend largely on U.S. relationships with major extrahemispheric powers and its own position in the world system. The more important Latin America is for purposes of U.S. policy, the more attention the area will receive; the less important the region, the less the attention.

A central challenge for Latin America concerns collective solidarity. The more unified the countries of the region, the greater their overall bargaining power with the United States (and other world powers); the less the unification, the less the bargaining power. One might have imagined that the current international climate would encourage regional collaboration. Quite the opposite has taken place. Rival leaders have come forth with differing strategic options: close collaboration with the United States (Vicente Fox), strident opposition to the United States (Hugo Chávez), and an intermediate ground (Lula). All have done so in the name of continental unity—and, as a result, they have sharply divided the region. The war on terror unleashed centrifugal political forces throughout Latin America. Notwithstanding recent efforts to forge a regional consensus, the Bolivarian ideal of solidarity seems more elusive than ever.

The outbreak of the war on terror exerted decisive impacts on U.S.–Latin American relations. It has altered the content of the inter-American agenda, shifted the locus of policymaking in the United States, and rearranged the menu of strategic options available to Latin America. As in all historical eras, the United States devotes primary effort to strengthening its place in the global arena, Latin America copes with the fact of U.S. power, and the structure of the international system shapes the terms of U.S. interactions with Latin America. As the twenty-first century speeds onward, paradox and continuity abound.

# A Guide to Further Reading

This bibliography offers a selected guide to recent English-language publications on U.S.–Latin American relations. It lists key sources for the writing of this opus and loosely follows the thematic organization of the study. Its more important goal is to encourage independent reading and research in an area of enormous complexity. It offers a way to begin, not end, searches for precious information.

## PERIODICAL LITERATURE

Scholarly journals provide up-to-date access to current research and debates on inter-American affairs. Leading publications in the general area of international relations (IR) include *Foreign Affairs*, *Foreign Policy*, and *International Organization*. Also important are the *American Historical Review* and *Diplomatic History*.

Major journals on Latin America include, in alphabetical order, the *Bulletin of Latin American Research*, the *Hispanic American Historical Review*, the *Journal of Latin American Studies*, *Latin American Politics and Society* (formerly known as the *Journal of Inter-American Studies and World Affairs*), the *Latin American Research Review*, and the *NACLA Report on the Americas*.

The monthly *Current History* devotes one issue every year (usually February) to in-depth analysis of contemporary developments throughout Latin America. And though traditional scholars might hate to admit it, search engines like Google and Yahoo! can provide near-instant access to useful information. Respectable websites for up-to-date news include www.latinnnews.com and www.lanic.utexas.edu. Still, surfing the Internet does not qualify as genuine research. There can be no substitute for the serendipitous cruising of library collections.

## CONCEPTUAL APPROACHES AND HISTORICAL BACKGROUND

The study of IR has generated a vast and burgeoning industry. Central canons in the field include Kenneth Waltz, *Man, the State, and War: A Theoretical Analysis*

(New York: Columbia University Press, [1959] 1969); Robert O. Keohane (ed.), *Neorealism and Its Critics* (New York: Columbia University Press, 1986); Robert O. Keohane and Joseph S. Nye, Jr., *Power and Interdependence*, 2nd ed. (Glenview, IL: Scott, Foresman, 1989). Especially important for my book have been Stephen Krasner (ed.), *International Regimes* (Ithaca, NY: Cornell University Press, 1983), and Joseph S. Nye, Jr., *Soft Power: The Means to Success in World Politics* (New York: Public Affairs, 2004). A long-term historical perspective can be found in Paul Kennedy, *The Rise and Fall of the Great Powers: Economic Change and Military Conflict from 1500 to 2000* (New York: Random House, 1987), which presents the provocative concept of "imperial overstretch." Thoughtful interpretations of the post-9/11 international arena include Leslie H. Gelb, *Power Rules: How Common Sense Can Rescue American Foreign Policy* (New York: HarperCollins, 2009); Zbigniew Brzezinski, *Strategic Vision: America and the Crisis of Global Power* (New York: Basic Books, 2012); Robert Kagan, *The World America Made* (New York: Alfred A. Knopf, 2012); and Fareed Zakaria, *The Post-American World* (New York: W.W. Norton, 2008).

Fascination with hemispheric affairs has led to numerous interpretive syntheses. Among them are Michael J. Kryzanek, *U.S.–Latin American Relations*, 3rd ed. (Westport, CT: Praeger, 1996); Don M. Coerver and Linda B. Hall, *Tangled Destinies: Latin America and the United States* (Albuquerque: University of New Mexico Press, 1999); G. Pope Atkins, *Latin America and the Caribbean in the International System* (Boulder, CO: Westview, 2001); Robert A. Pastor, *Exiting the Whirlpool: U.S. Foreign Policy toward Latin America and the Caribbean* (Boulder, CO: Westview, 2001); and Mark Eric Williams, *Understanding U.S.–Latin American Relations: Theory and History* (New York: Routledge, 2012). Essays on the subject also appear in Peter Kingstone and Deborah Yashar (eds.), *Handbook of Latin American Politics* (New York: Routledge, 2013).

Prominent historical studies include Mark T. Gilderhus, *The Second Century: U.S.–Latin American Relations since 1889* (Wilmington, DE: Scholarly Resources, 2000); and Thomas F. O'Brien, *The Century of U.S. Capitalism in Latin America* (Albuquerque: University of New Mexico Press, 1999), which explores the changing roles of American business interests. Greg Grandin offers an original and devastating critique of U.S. policy in *Empire's Workshop: Latin America and the Roots of U.S. Imperialism* (New York: Henry Holt, 2006). A similar outlook appears in Brian Loveman, *No Higher Law: American Foreign Policy and the Western Hemisphere Since 1776* (Chapel Hill: University of North Carolina Press, 2010). An excellent collection of original materials is Robert H. Holden and Eric Zolov (eds.), *Latin America and the United States: A Documentary History,* 2nd ed. (New York: Oxford University Press, 2011), excerpts from which are dispersed throughout this book.

The attitudinal underpinnings of U.S. policy toward Latin America have captured particular interest. By far the most outstanding example of this genre is Lars Schoultz, *Beneath the United States: A History of U.S. Policy toward Latin America* (Cambridge, MA: Harvard University Press, 1998). Others include Eldon Kenworthy, *America/Américas: Myth in the Making of U.S. Policy toward Latin America* (University Park: Pennsylvania State University Press, 1995); and James

Williams Park, *Latin American Underdevelopment: A History of Perspectives in the United States, 1870–1965* (Baton Rouge: Louisiana State University Press, 1995). A graphic record of U.S. popular disdain for Latin America emerges from John J. Johnson, *Latin America in Caricature* (Austin: University of Texas Press, 1980).

## I  THE IMPERIAL ERA

The formative era of U.S.–Latin American relations has inspired classic works of historical scholarship. An invaluable starting point is Samuel Flagg Bemis, *The Latin American Policy of the United States: A Historical Interpretation* (New York: Harcourt, Brace and Company, 1943), which presents an unabashedly pro-American account. Conceptualization of U.S. hemispheric strategy as a form of "imperialism" emerged through such subsequent studies as Walter LaFeber, *The New Empire: An Interpretation of American Expansionism, 1860–1898* (Ithaca, NY: Cornell University Press, 1963); David Healy, *U.S. Expansionism: The Imperialist Urge in the 1890s* (Madison: University of Wisconsin Press, 1970); and Ruben Francis Weston, *Racism in U.S. Imperialism* (Columbia: University of South Carolina Press, 1972). A thoughtful reanalysis appears in John J. Johnson, *A Hemisphere Apart: The Foundations of United States Policy toward Latin America* (Baltimore: Johns Hopkins University Press, 1990), emphasizing America's rivalry with Great Britain in the 1815–1830 period. Also insightful is the little gem by Arthur P. Whitaker, *The Western Hemisphere Idea: Its Rise and Decline* (Ithaca, NY: Cornell University Press, 1954). A creative (but not easily accessible) approach to processes of cultural interpenetration appears in Gilbert M. Joseph, Catherine C. LeGrand, and Ricardo D. Salvatore (eds.), *Close Encounters of Empire: Writing the Cultural History of U.S.–Latin American Relations* (Durham, NC: Duke University Press, 1998).

The notion of "manifest destiny" has sparked continuing scholarly interest. An early and remarkable book, still relevant today, is Albert K. Weinberg, *Manifest Destiny: A Study of Nationalist Expansion in American History* (Baltimore: Johns Hopkins University Press, 1935). Later studies include Frederick Merk, *Manifest Destiny and Mission in American History: A Reinterpretation* (New York: Alfred A. Knopf, 1963, republished by Harvard University Press in 1995); Anders Stephanson, *Manifest Destiny: American Expansion and the Empire of Right* (New York: Hill and Wang, 1995); and Sam W. Haynes and Christopher Morris (eds.), *Manifest Destiny and Empire: American Antebellum Expansion* (College Station, TX: Texas A & M Press, 1997).

American interests and adventures in the Caribbean have spawned numerous interpretations. Leading examples are two books by Dana G. Munro, *Intervention and Dollar Diplomacy in the Caribbean, 1900–1921* (Princeton, NJ: Princeton University Press, 1964) and *The United States and the Caribbean Republics, 1921–1933* (Princeton, NJ: Princeton University Press, 1974); and works by Lester D. Langley, *Struggle for the American Mediterranean: United States–European Rivalry in the Gulf-Caribbean* (Athens: University of Georgia Press, 1976) and *The United States and the Caribbean in the Twentieth Century* (Athens: University of Georgia Press, 1982). The building of the Panama Canal has received magisterial treatment from David McCullough, *The Path Between the Seas: The Creation of the Panama Canal, 1870–1914* (New York: Simon & Schuster, 1977), while political legacies and complications are explored in Walter LaFeber, *The Panama Canal: The Crisis in Historical Perspective*, rev. ed. (New York: Oxford University Press, 1989). A masterful recent study is Lars Schoultz, *That Infernal Little Cuban Republic: The United States and the Cuban Revolution* (Chapel Hill: University of North Carolina Press, 2009).

The U.S. role in promoting (or obstructing) political change in the Americas has been a subject of intense controversy. A path-breaking study is Cole Blasier, *The Hovering Giant: U.S. Responses to Revolutionary Change in Latin America* (Pittsburgh, PA: University of Pittsburgh Press, 1976). An important case study of unsuccessful democracy promotion is Mark T. Gilderhus, *Pan American Visions: Woodrow Wilson in the Western Hemisphere, 1913–1921* (Tucson: University of Arizona Press, 1986). A highly influential (and mildly skeptical) collection of essays is Abraham F. Lowenthal (ed.), *Exporting Democracy: The United States and Latin America* (Baltimore: Johns Hopkins University Press, 1991). Resolutely critical interpretations come from David F. Schmitz, *Thank God They're on Our Side: The United States and Right-Wing Dictatorships, 1921–1965* (Chapel Hill: University of North Carolina Press, 1999) and *The United States and Right-Wing Dictatorships, 1965–1989* (New York: Cambridge University Press, 2006).

On a more positive note, FDR's Good Neighbor policy has attracted considerable attention. The classic studies are Bryce Wood's two volumes—*The Making of the Good Neighbor Policy* (New York: Columbia University Press, 1961) and *The Dismantling of the Good Neighbor Policy* (Austin: University of Texas Press, 1985). A sweeping interpretation is Fredrick B. Pike, *FDR's Good Neighbor Policy: Sixty Years of Gently Chaotic Chaos* (Austin: University of Texas Press, 1995), which attributes a long-lasting legacy to Good Neighbor diplomacy.

## II   THE COLD WAR

The priorities and processes of U.S. policymaking during the Cold War have offered numerous topics for continuing research. An especially influential interpretation of "bureaucratic politics" has been Graham T. Allison and Philip Zelikow, *Essence of Decision: Explaining the Cuban Missile Crisis*, 2nd ed. (New York: Longman, 1999), first published in 1971. Broader in focus is Lars Schoultz, *Human Rights and United States Policy toward Latin America* (Princeton, NJ: Princeton University Press, 1981), which illustrates the roles of Congress and public opinion, and his subsequent study, *National Security and United States Policy toward Latin America* (Princeton, NJ: Princeton University Press, 1987), which concedes that national security doctrines were, in the long run, more influential than preoccupations with democracy or human rights. A historical overview of the Cold War period emerges from Gaddis Smith, *The Last Years of the Monroe Doctrine, 1945–1993* (New York: Hill and Wang, 1994). Recent interpretations include Gilbert M. Joseph

380 A GUIDE TO FURTHER READING

and Daniela Spenser (eds.), *In from the Cold: Latin America's New Encounter with the Cold War* (Durham, NC: Duke University Press, 2008), and Hal Brands, *Latin America's Cold War* (Cambridge, MA: Harvard University Press, 2010).

Probing treatment of the Eisenhower years (1953–1961) appears in Stephen G. Rabe, *Eisenhower and Latin America: The Foreign Policy of Anticommunism* (Chapel Hill: University of North Carolina Press, 1988). Critical analyses of the Guatemalan intervention (1954) appear in Piero Gleijeses, *Shattered Hope: The Guatemalan Revolution and the United States, 1944–1954* (Princeton, NJ: Princeton University Press, 1991); and in Stephen Schlesinger and Stephen Kinzer, *Bitter Fruit: The Story of the American Coup in Guatemala* (Cambridge, MA: David Rockefeller Center for Latin American Studies, Harvard University, [1982] 1999).

JFK's brief but promising presidency is the subject of Stephen G. Rabe, *The Most Dangerous Area in the World: John F. Kennedy Confronts Communist Revolution in Latin America* (Chapel Hill: University of North Carolina Press, 1999). A useful compendium is L. Ronald Scheman (ed.), *The Alliance for Progress: A Retrospective* (New York: Praeger, 1988). And not surprisingly, Cuba has been a subject of continuing research and interpretation. Key works include Thomas G. Paterson, *Contesting Castro: The United States and the Triumph of the Cuban Revolution* (New York: Oxford University Press, 1994); and Peter Kornbluh (ed.), *The Bay of Pigs Declassified: The Secret CIA Report on the Invasion of Cuba* (New York: New Press, 1998).

Aside from the already-cited Allison–Zelikow book, the Cuban missile crisis of October 1962 continues to prompt scholarly curiosity. A helpful overview is Don Munton and David A. Welch, *The Cuban Missile Crisis: A Concise History* (New York: Oxford University Press, 2006). More specialized analyses can be found in Sheldon Stern, *Averting "The Final Failure": John F. Kennedy and the Secret Cuban Missile Crisis Meetings* (Stanford, CA: Stanford University Press, 2003); and Alice L. George, *Awaiting Armageddon: How Americans Faced the Cuban Missile Crisis* (Chapel Hill: University of North Carolina Press, 2003).

As described in chapter 7, anticommunist concerns led to repeated U.S. interventions in Latin America. On the Dominican Republic (1965), the most prominent study is Abraham F. Lowenthal, *The Dominican Intervention* (Cambridge, MA: Harvard University Press, 1972). On Chile (1973), solid treatments appear in Paul E. Sigmund, *The Overthrow of Allende and the Politics of Chile, 1964–1976* (Pittsburgh, PA: University of Pittsburgh Press, 1977); and in Pamela Constable and Arturo Valenzuela, *A Nation of Enemies: Chile under Pinochet* (New York: W. W. Norton, 1991).

Ronald Reagan's policies toward Central America throughout the 1980s produced a raft of scholarly analyses. Prominent among them are Thomas Carothers, *In the Name of Democracy: U.S. Policy toward Latin America in the Reagan Years* (Berkeley and Los Angeles: University of California Press, 1991); Walter LaFeber, *Inevitable Revolutions: The United States in Central America*, 2nd ed. (New York: W. W. Norton, 1993); John H. Coatsworth, *Central America and the United States: The Clients and the Colossus* (New York: Twayne, 1994); William M. LeoGrande,

*Our Own Backyard: The United States and Central America, 1977–1992* (Chapel Hill: University of North Carolina Press, 1998); and Greg Grandin, *The Last Colonial Massacre: Latin America in the Cold War* (Chicago: University of Chicago Press, 2004). Also pertinent is Peter M. Sanchez, *Panama Lost? U.S. Hegemony, Democracy, and the Canal* (Gainesville: University Press of Florida, 2007).

English-language literature on Latin American reactions to the Cold War is spotty and diverse (with much written in Spanish or Portuguese). Starting points include Roger D. Hansen, *Beyond the North–South Stalemate* (New York: McGraw-Hill, 1979); Richard E. Feinberg, *The Intemperate Zone: The Third World Challenge to U.S. Foreign Policy* (New York: W. W. Norton, 1983); Paul E. Sigmund, *Liberation Theology at the Crossroads: Democracy or Revolution?* (New York: Oxford University Press, 1990); and Timothy Wickham-Crowley's superb *Guerrilla Movements and Revolution in Latin America* (Princeton, NJ: Princeton University Press, 1992).

A handful of testimonials by Latin American political actors has appeared in English translation. An influential anthology is Rolando E. Bonachea and Nelson P. Valdés (eds.), *Che: Selected Writings of Che Guevara* (Cambridge, MA: MIT Press, 1969); see also Jorge Castañeda's controversial *Compañero: The Life and Death of Che Guevara* (New York: Alfred A. Knopf, 1997). Memoirs from Central America include Rigoberta Menchú, *I, Rigoberta Menchú: An Indian Woman in Guatemala* (London: Verso, 1984); and Omar Cabezas, *Fire from the Mountain: The Making of a Sandinista* (New York: Crown, 1985). Ugly memories from Argentina appear in Jacobo Timerman, *Prisoner Without a Name, Cell Without a Number* (New York: Random House, 1981); and Horacio Verbitsky, *The Flight: Confessions of an Argentine Dirty Warrior* (New York: New Press, 1996).

## III  GLOBALIZATION AND WAR

The ending of the Cold War ushered in a hopeful period of change. In varying degrees, this optimism is apparent in Abraham F. Lowenthal, *Partners in Conflict: The United States and Latin America in the 1990s* (Baltimore: Johns Hopkins University Press, 1990); Richard E. Feinberg, *Summitry in the Americas: A Progress Report* (Washington, DC: Institute for International Economics, 1997); John D. Martz, *United States Policy in Latin America: A Decade of Crisis and Challenge* (Lincoln: University of Nebraska Press, 1995); and Jorge I. Dominguez (ed.), *International Security and Democracy: Latin America and the Caribbean in the Post-Cold War Era* (Pittsburgh, PA: University of Pittsburgh Press, 1998). An insightful analysis of political prospects for the Americas appears in Jorge G. Castañeda, *Utopia Unarmed: The Latin American Left after the Cold War* (New York: Alfred A. Knopf, 1993). Recent trends are placed in global and historical context in Peter H. Smith, *Democracy in Latin America: Political Change in Comparative Perspective*, 2nd ed. (New York: Oxford University Press, 2012).

The only book-length treatment to date of Bill Clinton's presidency is David Scott Palmer, *U.S. Relations with Latin America during the Clinton Years:*

*Opportunities Lost or Opportunities Squandered?* (Gainesville: University Press of Florida, 2006). A critical interpretation of one key development appears in Joaquín Roy, *Cuba, the United States, and the Helms-Burton Doctrine: International Reactions* (Gainesville: University Press of Florida, 2000). Also revealing is Orlando J. Pérez (ed.), *Post-Invasion Panama: The Challenges of Democratization in the New World Order* (Lanham, MD: Lexington, 2000).

The 1990s witnessed successful efforts to promote peace and democracy in Latin America. Important studies include Tom Farer (ed.), *Beyond Sovereignty: Collectively Defending Democracy in the Americas* (Baltimore: Johns Hopkins University Press, 1996); and Tommy Sue Montgomery (ed.), *Peacemaking and Democratization in the Western Hemisphere: Multilateral Missions* (Coral Gables, FL: North-South Center Press, 2000). Equally significant is the measured assessment in Kathryn Sikkink, *Mixed Signals: U.S. Human Rights Policy and Latin America* (Ithaca, NY: Cornell University Press, 2004), which focuses on U.S. policy over the previous fifty years.

Predictably, the turn of the twenty-first century ushered in a spate of prognostications by experts. Among them were Victor Bulmer-Thomas and James Dunkerley (eds.), *The United States and Latin America: The New Agenda* (New York: Oxford University Press, 1999); Albert Fishlow and James Jones (eds.), *The United States and the Americas: A Twenty-First Century View* (New York: W. W. Norton, 2000); and Jorge I. Dominguez (ed.), *The Future of Inter-American Relations* (New York: Routledge, 2000). Unfortunately, the attacks and aftermath of 9/11 rendered these outlooks largely obsolete.

Understanding of Latin America's debt crisis and neoliberal reforms must begin with Pedro Pablo Kuczynski, *Latin American Debt* (Baltimore: Johns Hopkins University Press, 1988); Robert Devlin, *Debt and Crisis in Latin America: The Supply Side of the Story* (Princeton, NJ: Princeton University Press, 1989); and, perhaps most important, John Williamson (ed.), *Latin American Economic Adjustment: How Much Has Happened?* (Washington, DC: Institute for International Economics, 1990). Benefits of hindsight appear in Dani Rodrik, *Has Globalization Gone Too Far?* (Washington, DC: Institute of International Economics, 1997); Pedro-Pablo Kuczynski and John Williamson, *After the Consensus: Restarting Growth and Reform in Latin America* (Washington, DC: Institute for International Economics, 2003); and, more explicitly, in Douglas S. Massey, Magaly Sanchez R., and Jere R. Behrman (eds.), *Chronicle of a Myth Foretold: The Washington Consensus in Latin America*, a special issue of *The Annals of the American Academy of Political and Social Science*, 606 (July 2006).

Migration and U.S. immigration policy receive extended attention in Frank D. Bean, Rodolfo O. de la Garza, Bryan R. Roberts, and Sidney Weintraub (eds.), *At the Crossroads: Mexico and U.S. Immigration Policy* (Lanham, MD, and London: Rowman & Littlefield, 1997); Barry P. Bosworth, Susan M. Collins, and Nora Lustig (eds.), *Coming Together? Mexico–U.S. Relations* (Washington, DC: Brookings Institution, 1997); Wayne A. Cornelius, Philip L. Martin, and James F. Hollifield (eds.), *Controlling Immigration: A Global Perspective*, 2nd ed. (Stanford: Stanford

University Press, 2004); and Jorge Durand, Nolan J. Malone, and Douglas Massey, *Beyond Smoke and Mirrors: Mexican Immigration in an Era of Economic Integration* (New York: Sage Publications, 2002). Peter Andreas explores the symbolic and political dimensions of American policymaking in *Border Games: Policing the U.S.-Mexico Divide* (Ithaca, NY: Cornell University Press, 2000). Cross-border crime is the subject of John Bailey and Roy Godson (eds.), *Organized Crime and Democratic Governability: Mexico and the U.S.-Mexican Borderlands* (Pittsburgh, PA: University of Pittsburgh Press, 2000). A broader regional approach is adopted in Tom Farer (ed.), *Transnational Crime in the Americas* (New York: Routledge, 1999).

Drugs and drug trafficking have produced a recent spate of publications, most of them sharply critical of U.S. policy. In chronological order, they include Peter H. Smith (ed.), *Drug Policy in the Americas* (Boulder, CO: Westview Press, 1992); Bruce M. Bagley and William O. Walker III (eds.), *Drug Trafficking in the Americas* (New Brunswick, NJ: Transaction, 1994); William O. Walker III, *Drugs in the Western Hemisphere: An Odyssey of Cultures in Conflict* (Wilmington, DE: SR Books, 1996); Eva Bertram, Morris Blachman, Kenneth Sharpe, and Peter Andreas, *Drug War Politics: The Price of Denial* (Berkeley and Los Angeles: University of California Press, 1996); Menno Vellinga (ed.), *The Political Economy of the Drug Industry: Latin America and the International System* (Gainesville: University Press of Florida, 2004); Collette A. Youngers and Eileen Rosin (eds.), *Drugs and Democracy in Latin America: The Impact of U.S. Policy* (Boulder, CO: Lynne Rienner, 2005); and Paul Gootenberg, *Andean Cocaine: The Making of a Global Drug* (Chapel Hill: University of North Carolina Press, 2008). The unique plight of Colombia has received special attention in Russell Crandall, *Driven by Drugs: U.S. Policy toward Colombia* (Boulder, CO: Lynne Rienner, 2002), and Robin Kirk, *More Terrible Than Death: Massacres, Drugs, and America's War in Colombia* (New York: Public Affairs, 2003). A broad critique of current U.S. policy appears in Latin American Commission on Drugs and Democracy, *Drugs and Democracy: Toward a Paradigm Shift* (2009).

North American free trade, regional integration, and geoeconomic developments have spawned a burgeoning literature. The economic and political origins of NAFTA are explored in Frederick Mayer, *Interpreting NAFTA: The Science and Art of Political Analysis* (New York: Columbia University Press, 1998), a study distinguished by its theoretical sophistication; Strom Thacker, *Big Business, the State and Free Trade: Constructing Coalitions in Mexico* (Cambridge: Cambridge University Press, 2000); and Maxwell A. Cameron and Brian W. Tomlin, *The Making of NAFTA: How the Deal Was Done* (Ithaca, NY: Cornell University Press, 2002). The consequences of the trade agreement are thoughtfully analyzed in Carol Wise (ed.), *The Post-NAFTA Political Economy: Mexico and the Western Hemisphere* (University Park: Pennsylvania State University Press, 1998); and in Edward W. Chambers and Peter H. Smith (eds.), *NAFTA in the New Millennium* (Alberta and La Jolla: University of Alberta Press and Center for U.S.-Mexican Studies, University of California, San Diego, 2002), which includes a Canadian perspective. Environmental concerns are presented in Carolyn Deere and Daniel Esty (eds.), *Greening the Americas:*

*NAFTA's Lessons for Hemispheric Trade* (Cambridge, MA: MIT Press, 2002); and in Kevin Gallagher, *Free Trade and the Environment: Mexico, NAFTA, and Beyond* (Stanford, CA: Stanford University Press, 2004). Social issues provide the focus for Kathleen Staudt and Irasema Coronado, *Frontera No Más: Toward Social Justice at the U.S.–Mexican Border* (New York: Palgrave Macmillan, 2002). Broad treatment of U.S.-Mexican relations can be found in Robert A. Pastor, *The North American Idea: A Vision of a Continental Future* (New York: Oxford University Press, 2011). Up-to-date scholarly analyses appear in Peter H. Smith and Andrew Selee (eds.), *Mexico and the United States: The Politics of Partnership* (Boulder, CO: Lynne Rienner, 2013).

Beyond NAFTA, questions about regional economic integration have prompted considerable interest. Studies of the "common market of the south" include Riordan Roett (ed.), *MERCOSUR: Regional Integration, World Markets* (Boulder, CO: Lynne Rienner, 1999); Helio Jaguaribe and Álvaro de Vasconcelos (eds.), *The European Union, Mercosul, and the New World Order* (London: Frank Cass, 2003); and Francisco Domínguez and Marcos Guedes de Oliveria (eds.), *Mercosur: Between Integration and Democracy* (Pieterlen, Switzerland: Peter Lang AG, 2004). Concerns about integration in general and FTAA in particular are expressed in Gordon Mace and Louis Bélanger (eds.), *The Americas in Transition: The Contours of Regionalism* (Boulder, CO: Lynne Rienner, 1999); Victor Bulmer-Thomas (ed.), *Regional Integration in Latin America and the Caribbean* (London: Institute of Latin American Studies, 2001); Duncan Green, *Silent Revolution: The Rise and Crisis of Market Economics in Latin America* (New York: Monthly Review Press, 2003); Diana Tussie, *Trade Negotiations in Latin America: Problems and Prospects* (New York: Palgrave Macmillan, 2003); Ana Margheritis (ed.), *Latin American Democracies in the New Global Economy* (Miami, FL: North-South Center Press, 2003); and Antoni Estevadeord et al. (eds.), *Integrating the Americas: FTAA and Beyond* (Cambridge, MA: David Rockefeller Center for Latin American Studies, Harvard University, 2004).

The impacts of 9/11 and geopolitical dimensions of the U.S. war on terror are described in chilling detail in three volumes on "Bush at war" by award-winning *Washington Post* correspondent Bob Woodward: *Bush at War* (New York: Simon & Schuster, 2002); *Plan of Attack* (New York: Simon & Schuster, 2004); and *State of Denial* (New York: Simon & Schuster, 2006). Woodward has followed up this trilogy with *Obama's Wars* (New York: Simon & Schuster, 2010). An informative explanation of neoconservative foreign policies appears in Francis Fukuyama, *America at the Crossroads: Democracy, Power, and the Neoconservative Legacy* (New Haven, CT: Yale University Press, 2006). Important documents for first-hand analysis are the White House, *The National Security Strategy of the United States of America* (September 2002 and subsequent years). Also useful is the compilation in Brian Loveman (ed.), *Strategy for Empire: U.S. Regional Security Policy in the Post–Cold War Era* (Lanham, MD: SR Books, 2004).

International assessments of 9/11 and of the United States appear in Eric Hershberg and Kevin W. Moore (eds.), *Critical Views of September 11: Analyses from around the World* (New York: New Press, 2002); Andrew Kohut and Bruce Stokes, *America against the World: How We Are Different and Why We Are Disliked* (New York: Times Books, 2006); and Julia E. Sweig, *Friendly Fire: Losing Friends and Making Enemies in the Anti-American Century* (New York: Public Affairs, 2006).

Very few studies of Latin America's foreign policies since 9/11 have appeared in English. Exceptions include Frank O. Mora and Jeanne A. K. Hey, *Latin American and Caribbean Foreign Policy* (Lanham, MD: Rowman & Littlefield, 2003); Riordan Roett and Guadalupe Paz (eds.), *Latin America in a Changing Global Environment* (Boulder, CO: Lynne Rienner, 2003); Peter H. Smith, Kotaro Horisaka, and Shoji Nishijima (eds.), *East Asia and Latin America: The Unlikely Alliance* (Lanham, MD, and London: Rowman & Littlefield, 2003); Joseph S. Tulchin and Ralph Espach (eds.), *Latin America in the New International System* (Boulder, CO: Lynne Rienner, 2001); and Ana Margheritis, *Argentina's Foreign Policy: Domestic Politics and Democracy Promotion in the Americas* (Boulder, CO: FirstForum Press, 2010).

Finally, a major collaborative project has produced a multivolume series on bilateral relationships between the United States and individual countries of Latin America. The leadoff volume is Rafael Domínguez and Jorge I. Fernández de Castro, *The United States and Mexico: Between Partnership and Conflict* (New York: Routledge, 2001), now in a second edition (2009), which can be complemented by the revealing memoirs of an outspoken American ambassador, Jeffrey Davidow, *The U.S. and Mexico: The Bear and the Porcupine* (Princeton, NJ: Markus Wiener, 2004). Other studies in the Routledge series are David R. Mares and Francisco Rojas, *The United States and Chile: Coming in Out of the Cold* (New York: Routledge, 2001); Janet Kelly and Carlos A. Romero, *The United States and Venezuela: Rethinking a Relationship* (New York: Routledge, 2001); Deborah L. Norden and Roberto Russell, *The United States and Argentina: Changing Relations in a Changing World* (New York: Routledge, 2002); Cynthia McClintock and Fabian Vallas, *The United States and Peru: Cooperation at a Cost* (New York: Routledge, 2003); Anthony P. Maingot and Wilfredo Lozano, *The United States and the Caribbean: Transforming Hegemony and Sovereignty* (New York: Routledge, 2004); Monica Hirst, *The United States and Brazil: A Long Road of Unmet Expectations* (New York: Routledge, 2005); and Mark Rosenberg, *The United States and Central America: Geopolitical Realities and Regional Fragility* (New York: Routledge, 2007). A capstone volume for the series is Jorge I. Domínguez and Rafael Fernández de Castro, *Contemporary U.S.–Latin American Relations: Cooperation or Conflicts In the 21st Century?* (New York: Routledge, 2010).

# INDEX

*Note: Page numbers in italics indicate tables or figures.*